The lengthy period of the Avignon Papacy in the fourteenth century created circumstances in which the burgeoning bureaucracy of the papal curia could flourish. Papal involvement in the everyday business of the church at the local level reached its fullest extent in the years before the Great Schism.

This book examines the impact of that involvement in Scotland and northern England, and analyses the practical effect of theories of papal sovereignty at a time when there was still widespread acceptance of the role of the Holy See. The nature and importance of political opposition, from both crown and parliament, is investigated from the standpoint of the validity of the complaints as indicated by local evidence, and a new interpretation is offered of the various statutory measures taken in England in Edward III's reign to control alleged abuses of papal power. Points of similarity and difference between Scotland and England are also given due emphasis.

This is the first work to attempt to analyse the full breadth of papal involvement in late medieval Britain by utilising the rich local sources in association with material from the Vatican archives. Thus it has wider implications as a pioneering study of the local impact of papal policies in the Middle Ages.

Cambridge studies in medieval life and thought

THE PAPACY, SCOTLAND AND NORTHERN ENGLAND, 1342–1378

The series Cambridge Studies in Medieval Life and Thought was inaugurated by G. G. Coulton in 1921. Professor D. E. Luscombe now acts as General Editor of the Fourth Series, with Professor R. B. Dobson and Dr Rosamond McKitterick as Advisory Editors. The series brings together outstanding work by medieval scholars over a wide range of human endeavour extending from political economy to the history of ideas.

For a list of titles in the series, see end of book.

THE PAPACY, SCOTLAND AND NORTHERN ENGLAND, 1342–1378

A. D. M. BARRELL
University of Wales, Aberystwyth

CAMBRIDGE
UNIVERSITY PRESS

Published by the Press Syndicate of the University of Cambridge
The Pitt Building, Trumpington Street, Cambridge CB2 1RP
40 West 20th Street, New York, NY 10011-4211, USA
10 Stamford Road, Oakleigh, Melbourne 3166, Australia

First published 1995

Printed in Great Britain, Antony Rowe Ltd

A catalogue record for this book is available from the British Library

Library of Congress cataloguing in publication data

Barrell, A. D. M. (Andrew D. M.)
The Papacy, Scotland and northern England, 1342–1378 / A.D.M. Barrell.
p. cm. – (Cambridge studies in medieval life and thought)
Includes bibliographical references and index.
ISBN 0 521 44182 x
1. Papacy – History – 1309–1378. 2. Great Britain – Church history – 1066–1485. I. Title. II. Series.
BX1302.B37 1995
282'.411'09023–dc20 94-36324 CIP

ISBN 0 521 44182 x hardback

SE

CONTENTS

Preface *page* ix
Note on currencies xi
List of abbreviations xiii

Map 1 xxii
Northern England: dioceses, collegiate churches and major peculiar jurisdictions in the fourteenth century

Map 2 xxiii
Northern England, showing some of the more significant places mentioned in the text

Map 3 xxiv
Scotland: dioceses and archdeaconries in the fourteenth century

Map 4 xxv
Scotland, showing some of the more significant places mentioned in the text

Introduction 1
1 Papal taxation and its collection 13
2 Papal provisions 79
3 Opposition to the Papacy 125
4 Judicial aspects of the Papacy 164
5 The Papacy and the bishops 184
6 The Papacy and the regulars 213
7 Papal licences, dispensations and favours 230
Conclusion 253

Bibliography 258
Index 270

PREFACE

This book has been several years in the making, and it is at last my pleasure to be able to acknowledge the assistance I have received from many people. The volume owes its origin to a doctoral thesis submitted to the University of St Andrews, and my debt to my supervisor, Professor D. E. R. Watt, is deep. His incisive comments saved me from many errors and inconsistencies, and among many kindnesses he generously loaned me his own microfilm copy of the account of the Scottish collector William de Grenlaw. I am most grateful also to Mr J. J. Robertson of the University of Dundee, who helped me with the chapter on papal justice.

Historians are always indebted to the specialist services provided in archives and in academic libraries, and my work was much eased by the courtesy of the staff of St Andrews University Library, especially Miss S. Rowe, the Inter-Library Loans Librarian, and the staff of the Department of Manuscripts and Rare Books, Mr G. D. Hargreaves, Mr R. N. Smart and Mrs Christine Gascoigne. Their willingness to respond to what must sometimes have seemed strange requests and their readiness to grant me immediate access to a number of microfilms and rare books greatly facilitated the research on which this volume is based. I am also most grateful to the staff of the Minster Library in York, especially the Archivist, Mr M. S. Dorrington, for his advice and kindness in providing manuscripts at short notice.

Readers of this book will observe the extensive use I have made of the collection of microfilms of material from the Vatican archives which has been assembled in the Department of Scottish History at the University of Glasgow under the auspices of the Ross Fund. On my visits to Glasgow I was splendidly guided and encouraged by the late Professor Ian Cowan, who generously gave of his time so that mine could be most profitably spent. It is a matter of great regret to me that he was not able to witness the completion of this book.

My debt to other scholars will in part be apparent from the notes and select bibliography. The omission of a particular work should not of course be taken to imply that I consider it of slight value, merely that I did not feel it necessary to refer to it in the context of this book. I am grateful to Dr R. Donaldson, Dr J. R. L. Highfield, Dr P. McDonald, Dr Candace Smith (formerly Carstens) and Dr P. N. R. Zutshi for permission to cite material from their unpublished theses.

My final thanks must be to the staff of Cambridge University Press, and particularly to the editors of this series. Professors David Luscombe and Barrie Dobson have made many constructive comments on the text of this book, and it would have been much the poorer without them. To them and to the many friends and members of my family who have supported and encouraged me in this enterprise I offer my gratitude. Any errors and omissions which remain are of course my own.

NOTE ON CURRENCIES

A large number of currencies were in use in fourteenth-century Europe. The following note gives a very brief explanation of the principal monetary systems referred to in this book.

In England the currency was the pound sterling, made up of twenty shillings each of twelve pence; the mark (two-thirds of a pound or 13s 4d) was also used for purposes of taxation and accounting. The Scottish system was identical, and until the 1360s Scottish money was deemed to have parity with English. The policy in this book is to use the spelling 'merk' in Scottish contexts while retaining 'mark' when referring to England. Although the use of 'merk' is not universal among historians of Scotland, it is the more appropriate rendering when dealing with Scottish material; moreover, by the end of the period covered by this volume English and Scottish currencies were no longer of equal value, and a 'mark' was, therefore, different from a 'merk'.

Papal collectors in the British Isles normally levied taxes on the basis of assessments made in sterling. For accounting purposes the sums collected were then converted, usually into florins but occasionally into other currencies, the normal conversion rate being around 3s to the florin. Fourteenth-century papal sources make reference to several types of florin, but these seem to have been almost equal in value when used in conversions from sterling, and because the subject is extremely complex this book does not normally distinguish between the different types.

Readers requiring further details should consult P. Spufford, *Handbook of Medieval Exchange* (Royal Historical Society, 1986), esp. pp. 198–201 for tables of the exchange rate between sterling and the Florentine florin, and pp. 211–12 for a discussion of Scottish currency.

ABBREVIATIONS

The following abbreviations have been used throughout the notes. Other works cited are accorded a full title on first appearance, and are thereafter referred to by the author's surname and an abbreviated title. Because it is hoped that the short titles are sufficiently distinctive, the abbreviations used in such cases are not listed here. Full details of all works cited in this volume are given in the bibliography.

Aberdeen Registrum	*Registrum Episcopatus Aberdonensis* (Spalding and Maitland Clubs, 1845)
AHP	*Archivum Historiae Pontificiae*
AHR	*American Historical Review*
Annales Monastici	*Annales Monastici* (Rolls Series, 1864–9)
Arbroath Liber	*Liber S. Thome de Aberbrothoc* (Bannatyne Club, 1848–56)
Avesbury, *De Gestis*	Robert of Avesbury, *De Gestis Mirabilibus Regis Edwardi Tertii* (Rolls Series, 1889)
Baildon, *Monastic Notes*	*Notes on the Religious and Secular Houses of Yorkshire*, ed. W. P. Baildon and J. W. Walker (Yorkshire Archaeological Soc. Record Series, 1895–1931)
Bell, 'List of original papal bulls'	'A list of original papal bulls and briefs in the Department of Manuscripts, British Museum', ed. H. I. Bell, *EHR*, 36 (1921), 393–419, 556–83
Beverley Chapter Act Book	*Memorials of Beverley Minster* (Surtees Soc., 1898–1903)
BI	York, Borthwick Institute of Historical Research
BIHR	*Bulletin of the Institute of Historical Research*

Brechin Registrum	*Registrum Episcopatus Brechinensis* (Bannatyne Club, 1856)
Bridlington Cartulary	*Abstracts of the Charters and Other Documents Contained in the Chartulary of the Priory of Bridlington*, ed. W. T. Lancaster (Leeds, 1912)
Burns, 'Sources'	'Sources of British and Irish history in the Instrumenta Miscellanea of the Vatican archives', ed. C. Burns, *AHP*, 9 (1971), 7–141
Cal. IE	GUS, Calendar of Introitus et Exitus
Cal. OS	GUS, Calendar of Obligationes et Solutiones
Cal. Reg. Av.	GUS, Calendar of Registra Avinionensia
Cameron, *Apostolic Camera*	*The Apostolic Camera and Scottish Benefices, 1418–88*, ed. A. I. Cameron (Oxford, 1934)
CCR	*Calendar of Close Rolls*
CCRO	Carlisle, Cumbria County Record Office
CFR	*Calendar of Fine Rolls*
Chron. Angliae	*Chronicon Angliae, 1328–1388* (Rolls Series, 1874)
Chron. Baker	*Chronicon Galfridi le Baker de Swynebroke*, ed. E. M. Thompson (Oxford, 1889)
Chron. Bower (Goodall)	*Joannis de Fordun Scotichronicon, cum Supplementis et Continuatione Walteri Boweri Insulae Sancti Columbae Abbatis*, ed. W. Goodall (Edinburgh, 1759)
Chron. Ed. I and Ed. II	*Chronicles of Edward I and Edward II* (Rolls Series, 1882–3)
Chron. Hemingburgh	*Chronicon Domini Walteri de Hemingburgh* (English Historical Soc., 1848–9)
Chron. Knighton	*Chronicon Henrici Knighton* (Rolls Series, 1889–95)
Chron. Melsa	*Chronica Monasterii de Melsa* (Rolls Series, 1866–8)
Chron. Reading	*Chronica Johannis de Reading et Anonymi*

	Cantuariensis, 1346–1367, ed. J. Tait (Manchester, 1914)
Clément VI: lettres closes (Fr)	*Clément VI: lettres closes, patentes et curiales se rapportant à la France* (Paris, 1901–61)
Clément VI: lettres closes (non-Fr)	*Clément VI: lettres closes, patentes et curiales intéressant les pays autres que la France* (Paris, 1960–1)
Coll.	GUS, Collectorie
Court of York	*Ecclesiastical Cause Papers at York: The Court of York, 1301–1399* (Borthwick Texts and Calendars, 1988)
Cowan, *Parishes*	I. B. Cowan, *The Parishes of Medieval Scotland* (Scottish Record Soc., 1967)
CPL	*Calendar of Entries in the Papal Registers Relating to Great Britain and Ireland: Papal Letters*
CPL Ben. XIII	*Calendar of Papal Letters to Scotland of Benedict XIII of Avignon, 1394–1419* (Scottish History Soc., 1976)
CPL Clem. VII	*Calendar of Papal Letters to Scotland of Clement VII of Avignon, 1378–94* (Scottish History Soc., 1976)
CPP	*Calendar of Entries in the Papal Registers Relating to Great Britain and Ireland: Petitions to the Pope*
CPR	*Calendar of Patent Rolls*
CSSR, I	*Calendar of Scottish Supplications to Rome, 1418–1422* (Scottish History Soc., 1934)
CSSR, II	*Calendar of Scottish Supplications to Rome, 1423–1428* (Scottish History Soc., 1956)
Dubrulle, *Registres d'Urbain V*	*Les registres d'Urbain V (1362–1363)*, ed. M. Dubrulle (Paris, 1926)
Dugdale, *Monasticon*	*Monasticon Anglicanum*, ed. W. Dugdale (London, 1846)
Dunfermline Registrum	*Registrum de Dunfermelyn* (Bannatyne Club, 1842)
EHR	*English Historical Review*
Emden, *BRUO*	A. B. Emden, *A Biographical Register of the University of Oxford to AD 1500* (Oxford, 1957–9)

Eubel, *Hierarchia*	*Hierarchia Catholica Medii et Recentioris Aevi*, ed. C. Eubel and others (Münster, 1913–79)
Exch. Rolls	*The Exchequer Rolls of Scotland* (Edinburgh, 1878–1908)
Fasti Dunelmenses	*Fasti Dunelmenses* (Surtees Soc., 1926)
Fasti Parochiales	*Fasti Parochiales* (Yorkshire Archaeological Soc. Record Series, 1933–85)
Fierens, *Suppliques d'Urbain V*	*Suppliques d'Urbain V (1362–1370)*, ed. A. Fierens (Rome, Brussels and Paris, 1914)
Fierens and Tihon, *Lettres d'Urbain V*	*Lettres d'Urbain V (1362–1370)*, ed. A. Fierens and C. Tihon (Brussels, 1928–32)
Foedera	*Foedera, Conventiones, Literae et Cuiuscunque Generis Acta Publica*, ed. T. Rymer (London, 1816–69)
Furness Coucher	*The Coucher Book of Furness Abbey* (Chetham Soc., 1886–1919)
Glasgow Registrum	*Registrum Episcopatus Glasguensis* (Maitland Club, 1843)
Grégoire XI: lettres secrètes et curiales (Fr)	*Lettres secrètes et curiales du pape Grégoire XI relatives à la France* (Paris, 1935–57)
Grégoire XI: lettres secrètes et curiales (non-Fr)	*Lettres secrètes et curiales du pape Grégoire XI (1370–1378) intéressant les pays autres que la France* (Paris, 1962–5)
GUS	Glasgow University, Department of Scottish History, Ross Fund collection of microfilms of material in the Vatican archives relating to Scotland
Handbook of British Chronology	*Handbook of British Chronology* (3rd edn, Royal Historical Soc., 1986)
Highland Papers	*Highland Papers* (Scottish History Soc., 1914–34)
Historians of the Church of York	*The Historians of the Church of York and Its Archbishops* (Rolls Series, 1879–94)
Hoberg, *Taxae*	H. Hoberg, *Taxae pro Communibus Servitiis* (Vatican City, 1949)
IE	GUS, Introitus et Exitus

Innocent VI: lettres secrètes et curiales	*Innocent VI: lettres secrètes et curiales* (Paris and Rome, 1959–)
Instr. Misc.	GUS, Instrumenta Miscellanea
JEH	*Journal of Ecclesiastical History*
Kelso Liber	*Liber S. Marie de Calchou* (Bannatyne Club, 1846)
Kirkstall Coucher	*The Coucher Book of the Cistercian Abbey of Kirkstall* (Thoresby Soc., 1904)
LAO	Lincoln, Lincolnshire Archives Office
Liber censuum	*Le Liber censuum de l'Eglise romaine* (Paris, 1889–1952)
Lunt, *Accounts*	*Accounts Rendered by Papal Collectors in England, 1317–1378*, ed. W. E. Lunt (Philadelphia, 1968)
McNulty, *Thomas Sotheron*	*Thomas Sotheron v. Cockersand Abbey: A Suit as to the Advowson of Mitton Church, 1369–70*, ed. J. McNulty (Chetham Soc., 1939)
Melrose Liber	*Liber Sancte Marie de Melros* (Bannatyne Club, 1837)
Memorials of Ripon	*Memorials of Ripon* (Surtees Soc., 1882–1908)
Mirot and Déprez, 'Les ambassades anglaises'	'Les ambassades anglaises pendant la guerre de cent ans', ed. L. Mirot and E. Déprez, *Bibliothèque de l'Ecole des Chartes*, 59 (1898), 550–77; 60 (1899), 177–214; 61 (1900), 20–58
Moray Registrum	*Registrum Episcopatus Moraviensis* (Bannatyne Club, 1837)
Murimuth, *Continuatio Chronicarum*	Adam Murimuth, *Continuatio Chronicarum* (Rolls Series, 1889)
Newbattle Registrum	*Registrum S. Marie de Neubotle* (Bannatyne Club, 1849)
Northern Convocation	*The Records of the Northern Convocation* (Surtees Soc., 1907)
Northern Registers	*Historical Papers and Letters from the Northern Registers* (Rolls Series, 1873)
Ord. Reg. Zouche	BI, Reg. 10A: Ordination Register of Archbishop Zouche
Paisley Registrum	*Registrum Monasterii de Passelet, 1163–1529* (Maitland Club, 1832)

Polychronicon	*Polychronicon Ranulphi Higden Monachi Cestrensis* (Rolls Series, 1865–86)
Priory of Hexham	*The Priory of Hexham, Its Chroniclers, Endowments and Annals* (Surtees Soc., 1864–5)
PRO	London, Public Record Office
PRO List	*List of Diplomatic Documents, Scottish Documents and Papal Bulls Preserved in the Public Record Office* (PRO Lists and Indexes, 1923)
Reg. 5A	BI, Reg. 5A: Register *sede vacante*
Reg. Appleby	CCRO, DRC/1/2, pp. 141–367: Register of Bishop Appleby
Reg. Av.	GUS, Registra Avinionensia
Reg. Bury	*Richard d'Aungerville of Bury: Fragments of His Register and Other Documents* (Surtees Soc., 1910)
Reg. Hatfield	Durham, Prior's Kitchen: Register of Bishop Hatfield
Reg. Kirkby	CCRO, DRC/1/1, fols. 122–256v: Register of Bishop Kirkby
Reg. Langham	*Registrum Simonis Langham Cantuariensis Archiepiscopi* (Canterbury and York Soc., 1956)
Reg. Melton	BI, Reg. 9: Register of Archbishop Melton (the new foliation is used)
Reg. Melton	*The Register of William Melton, Archbishop of York, 1317–1340* (Canterbury and York Soc., 1977–88)
Reg. A. Neville, I	BI, Reg. 12: Register of Archbishop Neville
Reg. Sudbury	*Registrum Simonis de Sudbiria Diocesis Londoniensis AD 1362–1375* (Canterbury and York Soc., 1927–38)
Reg. Supp.	GUS, Registra Supplicationum
Reg. Thoresby	BI, Reg. 11: Register of Archbishop Thoresby
Reg. Vat.	GUS, Registra Vaticana
Reg. Welton	CCRO, DRC/1/2, pp. 1–128: Register of Bishop Welton
Reg. Zouche	BI, Reg. 10: Register of Archbishop

	Zouche
Roth, *English Austin Friars*	F. Roth, *The English Austin Friars, 1249–1538* (New York, 1961–6)
Rot. Parl.	*Rotuli Parliamentorum* (London, 1783–1832)
Rot. Scot.	*Rotuli Scotiae* (London, 1814–19)
RPD	*Registrum Palatinum Dunelmense* (Rolls Series, 1873–8)
RSCHS	*Records of the Scottish Church History Society*
St Andrews Liber	*Liber Cartarum Prioratus Sancti Andree in Scotia* (Bannatyne Club, 1841)
Salley Cartulary	*The Chartulary of the Cistercian Abbey of St Mary of Sallay in Craven* (Yorkshire Archaeological Soc. Record Series, 1933–4)
Scone Liber	*Liber Ecclesie de Scon* (Bannatyne Club, 1843)
Scriptores Tres	*Historiae Dunelmensis Scriptores Tres* (Surtees Soc., 1839)
SHR	*Scottish Historical Review*
Smith, 'Vicars-general register'	'A reconstruction of the lost register of the vicars-general of Archbishop Thoresby of York', ed. D. M. Smith, *Borthwick Institute Bulletin*, 3 (1983–4), 29–61, 102–13
Statutes of the Realm	*Statutes of the Realm* (London, 1810–28)
Stubbs, *Registrum Sacrum Anglicanum*	W. Stubbs, *Registrum Sacrum Anglicanum* (Oxford, 1858)
Taxatio	*Taxatio Ecclesiastica Angliae et Walliae Auctoritate P. Nicholai IV circa AD 1291* (London, 1802)
Test. Ebor.	*Testamenta Eboracensia* (Surtees Soc., 1836–1902)
Thompson, 'Pluralism'	A. H. Thompson, 'Pluralism in the mediaeval church, with notes on pluralists in the diocese of Lincoln, 1366', *Associated Architectural Societies Reports and Papers*, 33 (1915), 35–73; 34 (1917), 1–26; 35 (1919–20), 87–108, 199–242; 36 (1921), 1–41

Thompson, 'Richmond registers'	'The registers of the archdeaconry of Richmond', ed. A. H. Thompson, *YAJ*, 25 (1920), 129–268
Tihon, *Lettres de Grégoire XI*	*Lettres de Grégoire XI (1371–1378)*, ed. C. Tihon (Brussels and Rome, 1958–75)
TRHS	*Transactions of the Royal Historical Society*
Urbain V: lettres communes	*Urbain V: lettres communes* (Paris and Rome, 1954–86)
Urbain V: lettres secrètes et curiales	*Lettres secrètes et curiales du pape Urbain V se rapportant à la France* (Paris, 1902–55)
Vat. Quel., I	*Die Einnahmen der Apostolischen Kammer unter Johann XXII*, ed. E. Göller (*Vatikanische Quellen*, I, Paderborn, 1910)
Vat. Quel., IV	*Die Einnahmen der Apostolischen Kammer unter Benedikt XII*, ed. E. Göller (*Vatikanische Quellen*, IV, Paderborn, 1920)
Vat. Quel., V	*Die Einnahmen der Apostolischen Kammer unter Klemens VI*, ed. L. Mohler (*Vatikanische Quellen*, V, Paderborn, 1931)
Vat. Quel., VI	*Die Ausgaben der Apostolischen Kammer unter den Päpsten Urban V und Gregor XI (1362–78)*, ed. K. H. Schäfer (*Vatikanische Quellen*, VI, Paderborn, 1937)
Vat. Quel., VII, VIII	*Die Einnahmen der Apostolischen Kammer unter Innozenz VI*, ed. H. Hoberg (*Vatikanische Quellen*, VII, VIII, Paderborn, 1955–72)
VCH	Victoria County History
Vet. Mon.	*Vetera Monumenta Hibernorum et Scotorum Historiam Illustrantia*, ed. A. Theiner (Rome, 1864)
Walsingham, *Hist. Angl.*	Thomas Walsingham, *Historia Anglicana* (Rolls Series, 1863–4)
YAJ	*Yorkshire Archaeological Journal*
YML	York, Minster Library
Ypodigma Neustriae	Thomas Walsingham, *Ypodigma Neustriae* (Rolls Series, 1876)

Zutshi, 'Original papal letters'	P. N. R. Zutshi, 'Original papal letters in England, 1305–1417: a study and a calendar', Ph.D thesis, University of Cambridge (1981)

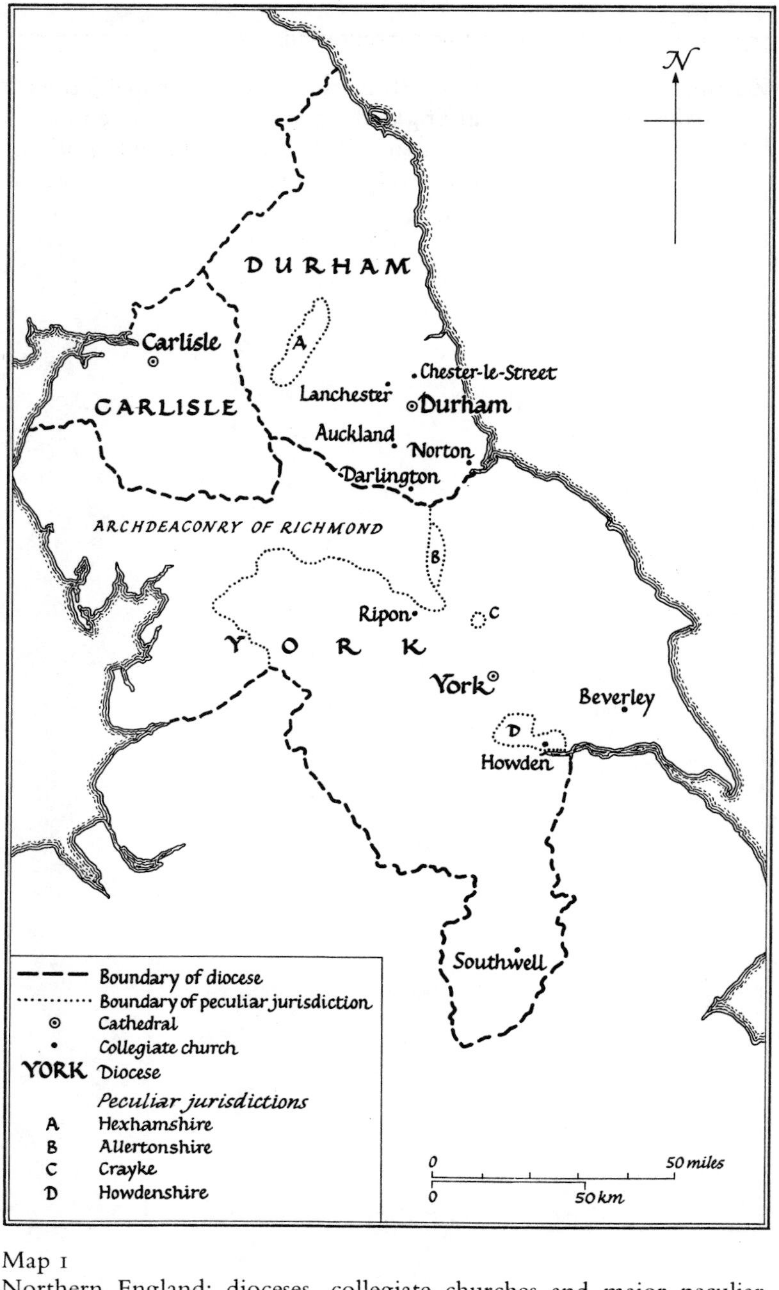

Map 1
Northern England: dioceses, collegiate churches and major peculiar jurisdictions in the fourteenth century

Map 2
Northern England, showing some of the more significant places mentioned in the text

Map 3
Scotland: dioceses and archdeaconries in the fourteenth century

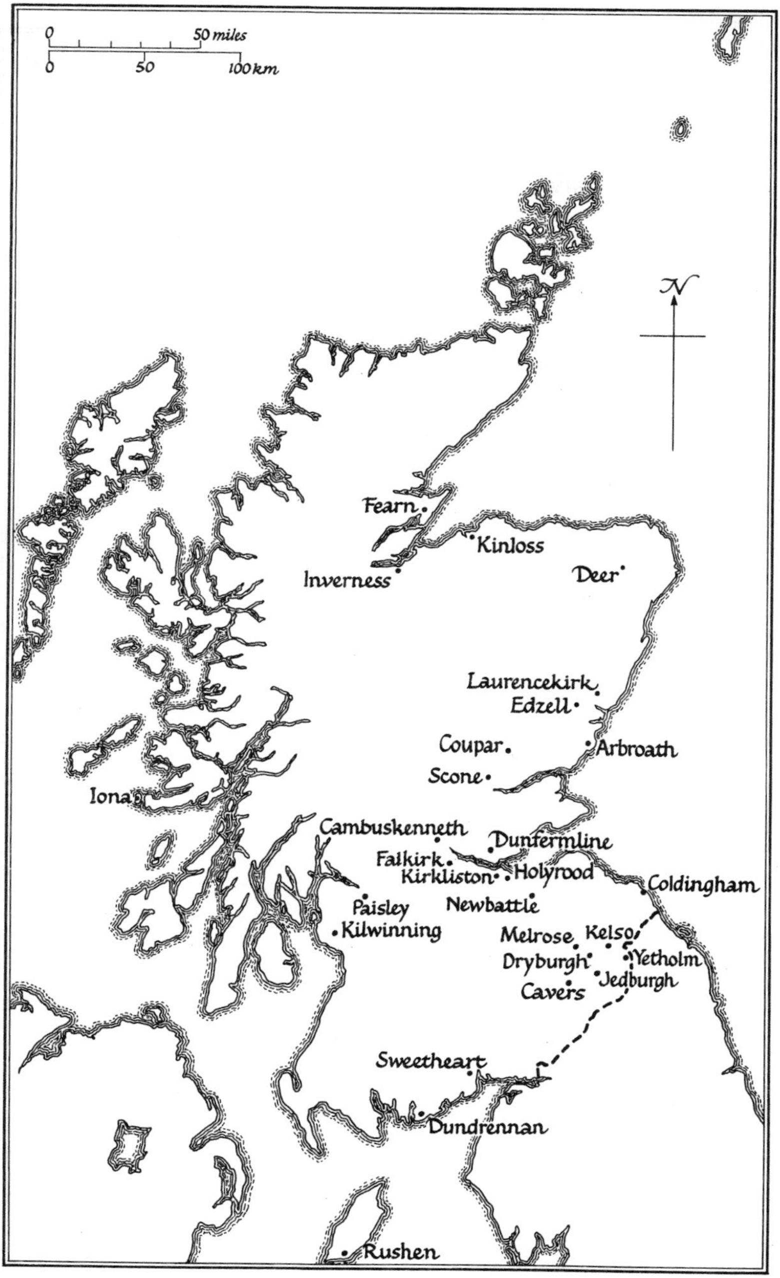

Map 4
Scotland, showing some of the more significant places mentioned in the text

INTRODUCTION

The period in the fourteenth century during which the Papacy was based north of the Alps is one which has long invited comment and controversy. From contemporaries such as the scholar and author Petrarch and the Roman revolutionary Cola di Rienzo down to our own day, the lengthy absence of the Holy See from its traditional home in the Eternal City has often been regarded as an aberration, an episode in papal history which was neither constructive nor justifiable. But the exile of the bishop of Rome in distant Avignon was not undertaken lightly; it was a consequence of the endemic political and inter-familial strife in much of Italy and of the threat to the pope's personal security which this occasioned. At the turn of the century the lordly and antagonistic Boniface VIII had played his part both in the factional struggles of the Italian cities and in arousing controversies in which the respective powers of church and state had been debated anew; he was ultimately to be assaulted in his own residence at Anagni by a force which included agents of the king of France as well as representatives of Italian families who had suffered at the hands of the pope. As Dante said, Christ was made captive in the person of his Vicar.

While some of Boniface VIII's problems were of his own making, there were nonetheless considerable attractions for the popes in living north of the Alps. For all their professions of desire to return to Rome – a journey actually undertaken by both Urban V and Gregory XI – the pontiffs from 1305 to 1378 are almost invariably called the popes of Avignon. For it was in that city on the Rhône that the papal curia was based for much of that period. A new papal palace was constructed and beautified; and the institutions of papal government found a secure and semi-permanent home far from the turmoil of Rome and free from the constraints imposed by the peripatetic nature of the late thirteenth-century Papacy. This stability was a fertile breeding-ground for much of the centralisation and bureaucratisation of church life which was such a feature of the period. Avignon was also much closer than was Rome to the major secular powers of the Latin West, France and England; as a capital of the western church it was more convenient than Rome because it was more central to the world in which papal authority was recognised.

Avignon was not then part of the kingdom of France, but the court which grew up there was predominantly French both in personnel and in taste. All the popes between 1305 and 1378 hailed from French territory, and many of the cardinals they created were also French. The Roger family from the Limousin provided two popes, Clement VI and Gregory XI, and Clement's brother Hugh was also elected in 1362, only to decline the honour; other members of the family too became cardinals. The Frenchness of the curia had, however, its disadvantages. Many of the cardinals and curial officials were unenthusiastic about the Papacy returning to Italy, whatever historical justification there might be for it; to some extent this reluctance occasioned the split in the Sacred College after the election of the Neapolitan Bartholomew Prignano as Urban VI in 1378 and provoked the Great Schism which followed. The division of western Christendom for nearly forty years, and the need for the rival popes to grant concessions widely in order to maintain the support of secular powers, irretrievably weakened the authority and the mystique of the medieval Papacy. In institutional terms, therefore, the Papacy can be said to have reached its zenith in the middle of the fourteenth century, which makes study of the period particularly instructive.

Many scholars have directed their attention towards the Avignon Papacy, but most have concentrated on affairs at the centre. Some have studied the outlook and philosophy of individual popes,[1] or the organisation and structure of the papal curia itself.[2] Others have examined the major political or military issues of the time from the standpoint of the Papacy: its role in the interminable negotiations aiming to settle the territorial, juridical and dynastic conflicts between Plantagenet and Valois;[3] its wars in Italy;[4] or its sponsorship and direction of the crusade in its various manifes-

[1] E.g. D. Wood, *Clement VI: The Pontificate and Ideas of an Avignon Pope* (Cambridge, 1989); P. R. Thibault, *Pope Gregory XI: The Failure of Tradition* (Lanham, 1986).

[2] B. Guillemain, *La cour pontificale d'Avignon (1309–1376): étude d'une société* (Paris, 1962).

[3] E.g. E. Déprez, *Les préliminaires de la Guerre de Cent Ans: la Papauté, la France et l'Angleterre* (Paris, 1902). See also below, n. 20.

[4] E.g. G. Mollat, *The Popes at Avignon, 1305–1378*, trans. J. Love (London, 1963), 67–189.

tations.[5] Readable and reliable general histories[6] have made use of this research to draw attention to the wide range of matters which came to the attention of the Avignon popes, and how they dealt with the political, fiscal and spiritual problems which they faced.

Rather less work has been done on how the policies of the Avignon popes, enshrined within the elaborate framework of canon law and illuminated by the regulations for the Chancery which each pontiff laid down,[7] actually affected the lives of clerks and lay people in particular localities. It is neither original nor profound to point out that the enforcement of a law or the execution of a measure is not necessarily as straightforward as the formulation of a policy. But it is frequently well worth while to consider that essential feature of all governmental activity. Medieval popes claimed sovereign power, at least over those affairs which fell within the ecclesiastical sphere, and the definition of that area of authority was often extremely broad. They claimed a fullness, a plenitude, of power; they had a right to intervene in virtually all aspects of church business and even in areas which temporal monarchs claimed for themselves. But they could exercise that power only as far as it was accepted by others, whether in theory or, more importantly, in practice.

It would be idle to speculate as to the extent to which the inhabitants of Roman Christendom understood the theoretical basis which underpinned papal plenitude of power. The legal and philosophical arguments are extremely complicated, and the academic controversies which raged in the universities and at the curia must surely have passed by the great majority of contemporaries, including many of those high in the ecclesiastical hierarchy. True, the arguments of Ockham and others were put at the disposal of the pope's opponents such as Lewis IV, claimant to the imperial throne, but this was largely for purposes which were nakedly political; the ideas of those who opposed what they saw as papal arrogance had to be formulated in the same legal, philosophical and theological terms as those of the pope's defenders. But none of this can have influenced – except perhaps very tangentially – the

[5] N. Housley, *The Avignon Papacy and the Crusades, 1305–1378* (Oxford, 1986). See also A. Luttrell, 'The crusade in the fourteenth century', in *Europe in the Late Middle Ages*, ed. J. R. Hale, J. R. L. Highfield and B. Smalley (London, 1965), 122–54.

[6] Two works in English translation are Mollat, *Popes*; and Y. Renouard, *The Avignon Papacy, 1305–1403*, trans. D. Bethell (London, 1970).

[7] For these see *Die päpstlichen Kanzleiregeln von Johannes XXII bis Nicolaus V*, ed. E. von Ottenthal (Innsbruck, 1888).

attitude of the vast majority of fourteenth-century Christians towards the Holy See.

There was, however, a deep-rooted acceptance of papal authority, especially in the spiritual sphere. The popes were approached for indulgences, dispensations and favours, which implies both a recognition that the Holy See could legitimately offer a means of release from the demands of canon law or from the pains of purgatory, and a belief in the ultimate efficacy of papal favour. The same attitude also underpinned the use of excommunication and other canonical sanctions, whereby the Papacy imposed its authority on those who were inclined to disobey it. The Papacy was also a fount of justice; it could help to resolve arguments. But this acceptance of papal authority was not blind or unquestioning; self-interest saw to that. Kings and other laymen objected to what they saw as papal encroachments on their jurisdiction and to attempts to tax the clergy for purposes to which they were unsympathetic; even the clergy, part of the pyramid of which the pope was the pinnacle, sometimes grumbled and prevaricated. But the objections were more to the exercise of papal power than to papal power as such; the authority of the Holy See was largely accepted as part of the system of government in a hierarchical society.

But it is the grumbling and the complaints which manifested themselves at the local level, and which determined how far the policies of the Papacy could be translated into reality in particular locations. And it is this issue, the extent to which the measures of the Avignon popes were put into practice and what local effect this had, which lies at the heart of this book. Concentrating on the period between the accession of Clement VI in 1342 and the death of Gregory XI in 1378, it examines in detail the various areas of papal involvement in the kingdom of Scotland and the ecclesiastical province of York in northern England. It aims to offer a comparison between two adjoining, but politically distinct and often mutually hostile, geographical areas, and to analyse the impact in them of the manifestation of papal power.

Medieval Scotland was a small, poor country, geographically at the edge of the Christian world, and in political terms relatively unimportant compared with the great powers of England and France. But its people had resisted the attempts of Edward I and Edward II to reduce it to a feudal satellite of its larger southern neighbour; and Scotland became a significant player in the events of the Hundred Years War, when its alliance with the French kings meant that England frequently had to fight on two fronts. Its king ruled over a political entity which, by the fourteenth century, was essentially consolidated and held together by more than a mere hostility to England. However, in a mountainous country with a very long seaboard, local interests were strong and royal power correspondingly weak, especially in comparison with England. This had the consequence that the Scottish crown was in a less powerful position than its English counterpart to intervene in ecclesiastical affairs and oppose papal exactions; this was especially so after the king, David II, was captured at the Battle of Neville's Cross near Durham in 1346 and imprisoned for eleven years in England. The Scottish church was also less highly organised than that in England. It was only in the twelfth century that Anglo-Norman influence brought to Scotland the full flowering of a diocesan and parochial structure familiar rather earlier in England, along with a relatively small number of monastic establishments, mostly of the reformed orders such as the Cistercians. The same century, however, also saw the Scottish sees – except that of Whithorn or Galloway in the south-west – receive papal support to sever their ties, always theoretical but nonetheless potentially threatening, with the metropolitan see of York; in the bull *Cum universi* they each became 'special daughters' of the Papacy, a relationship which brought Scotland more securely into the orbit of Roman Christendom. But the reforms were most effective in lowland Scotland, and even there, there remained the vestiges of an earlier ecclesiastical structure, with semi-laicised colleges of Culdees and a rather casual attitude towards the canon law on such matters as the need for ordination, a fact which was to be exploited in the fourteenth century. Scotland, like north Wales, was still not quite assimilated into the mainstream of the western church.[8]

Politically, the province of York is not directly comparable with Scotland, for it was merely a part of the kingdom of England. But it was of similar size to Scotland in the number of its parishes, both having over a thousand, and this makes the joint study of the two units valuable. To have examined the whole of England in conjunction with Scotland would have been to subsume the northern kingdom in the much greater volume of evidence from

[8] For an excellent general account of the late medieval Scottish church see A. Grant, *Independence and Nationhood: Scotland 1306–1469* (London, 1984), chap. 4.

its larger neighbour. The province of York, moreover, provides a more instructive comparison than England as a whole. It was distant from the centre of affairs, especially when the government's attentions were turned towards France; and like Scotland it suffered from the warfare which was provoked by Edward I's claims to sovereignty north of the border. It also contained its share of mountain and moor, and in economic terms it was much poorer than the south. But essential differences remain. It was still part of the English state, and the extensive authority of the English crown was very much exercised there. What happened nationally – in terms of royal policy towards the French kings, of taxation, and of attempts to limit some aspects of the papal plenitude of power – also affected the northern province. In addition, it contained the sees of two of the wealthiest prelates in Christendom, the archbishop of York and the bishop of Durham; no Scottish churchmen could rival them in worldly riches or potential influence on European affairs. However, the province of York constitutes as valid a point of comparison with Scotland as can be obtained, and one of the purposes of this study is to show how the same papal theories and the same papal policies sometimes (though by no means always) had a different effect on the two sides of the political border.

The period between 1342 and 1378 is of great historical interest. We are able to examine the working of an extensive foreign jurisdiction in northern Britain at a time when it was both wide-ranging and generally tolerated, and to analyse the impact upon it of both war and plague. It is also a period for which the surviving sources, both in Britain and in the Vatican archives, are especially valuable for the sort of study with which this book is concerned. On the papal side, there are extant registers of supplications from 1342 to 1366, two extensive and informative series of registered bulls, including some of political and diplomatic interest, and a range of sources dealing with the financial aspects of the Holy See, most notably a series of accounts from the English collectorate and a unique Scottish collector's account, rendered in 1362. On the local level, episcopal registers survive from all three dioceses of northern England, providing a wealth of information on the local administration of the church, while the central records of the English state – especially the Close and Patent Rolls and the Rolls of Parliament – offer an insight into the nature of any opposition to the Papacy and what, if any, executive measures were taken to support that opposition. Scotland has in general been much less fortunate than England in avoiding the ravages of time with regard to its records; a few cartularies have often had to suffice for information on local conditions, although knowledge of English diocesan administration can sometimes be used profitably to illuminate otherwise tantalising references in Scottish sources. It would be misleading not to concede that the local evidence is much more copious in England; but equally it would be negative to dismiss studying the question of papal relations with Scotland on such grounds. The papal records themselves offer plentiful opportunities for useful comparisons with northern England.

Considering the excellent combination of sources and the availability of many of them in print, remarkably little work has been done on papal relations with the British Isles in the fourteenth century, although the papal registers have been used extensively for works of reference such as biographical dictionaries[9] and lists of benefice-holders.[10] Few historians have specialised in the interpretation of the evidence, W. E. Lunt being an outstanding exception. His magisterial work on the papal finances, with particular reference to England, made use both of material in the Vatican archives and of local sources, and my debt to his careful scholarship is deep; he often illuminates areas outside the strict sphere of taxation, for the imposition and implementation of fiscal policy affected also the level of opposition to papal exactions and was – or became – inextricably linked with the practice of the appointment, or provision, of clerics.[11] But in many areas this book is intended to break new ground[12] and to act as a stimulus to similar studies of other localities and other periods.

9 D. E. R. Watt, *A Biographical Dictionary of Scottish Graduates to AD 1410* (Oxford, 1977); A. B. Emden, *A Biographical Register of the University of Oxford to AD 1500* (3 vols., Oxford, 1957–9).

10 Examples include J. Le Neve, *Fasti Ecclesiae Anglicanae, 1300–1541* (new edn, 12 vols., London, 1962–5); D. E. R. Watt, ed., *Fasti Ecclesiae Scoticanae Medii Aevi ad Annum 1638* (Scottish Record Soc., 1969); and the volumes of *Fasti Parochiales* published by the Yorkshire Archaeological Society.

11 See especially his *Financial Relations of the Papacy with England to 1327* (Cambridge, Mass., 1939); and *Financial Relations of the Papacy with England, 1327–1534* (Cambridge, Mass., 1962); cf. also his *Papal Revenues in the Middle Ages* (2 vols., New York, 1934). For a similar study in France see C. Samaran and G. Mollat, *La fiscalité pontificale en France au xiv*e *siècle* (Paris, 1905).

12 For other examples of work similar in nature to this see C. Carstens, 'The enforcement of the Statute of Provisors', Ph.D thesis, Harvard University (1937); P. McDonald, 'The relations between the Papacy and the religious orders in England, 1305–1352', DPhil. thesis, University of Oxford (1984).

In the past, much historical writing on the fourteenth-century church has been coloured – often subconsciously and rarely deliberately – either by a desire to detect the roots of the sixteenth-century Reformation,[13] or by a faithfulness to a religious tradition which has often been antagonistic to the Papacy and has condemned most features of medieval ecclesiastical practice.[14] Both show the continued importance of the Reformation in the history of both Scotland and England and its influence on society. It would be presumptuous for me to claim not to have been affected by these historiographical trends; moreover, the great upheaval in the western church in the sixteenth century is an event of such importance that no historian of the late Middle Ages can or should ignore it altogether. But this volume endeavours to examine what contacts there were between the Papacy and northern Britain at a time when papal power, although extensive and (at least within the church) all-pervasive, was fundamentally accepted; there was no inevitability about the Reformation in the middle of the fourteenth century. Papal policies had a bearing on national wealth, for the popes raised taxes and used the proceeds overseas; they in large part determined the personnel of the upper echelons of the ecclesiastical hierarchy and thereby of the government and civil service; they affected the spiritual life of the faithful; and at times they aroused opposition which both demonstrated the limits beyond which papal exactions were deemed unacceptable and provided new opportunities for the age-old clash of authority which is simplistically referred to as the clash between church and state. The issues discussed in this book concern not only the life and administration of the church, but also that of the political entities of which the medieval church was so important a part.

The period under review covers the pontificates of four popes of different characters. Peter Roger, who became Clement VI in 1342, was munificent and magnificent. His extravagance, a reaction to the parsimony of his predecessor Benedict XII, plunged the Papacy into deficit and thereby created severe difficulties for his successors. His generosity in bestowing benefices and other favours led to a

[13] This is perhaps most notable in the attitude often taken in the past to the 1351 Statute of Provisors: e.g. J. H. Ramsay, *Genesis of Lancaster* (2 vols., Oxford, 1913), I, 375, who wrote, 'It marks the beginning of the breach with Rome.' See below, pp. 141–4.

[14] E.g. J. H. Cockburn, 'Papal collections and collectors in Scotland in the Middle Ages', *RSCHS*, I (1926), 173–99.

large number of disputes, especially where papal authority conflicted with the rights of the English king. He was widely suspected in England of favouring the interests of the French crown, probably rightly in view of his earlier connections with the French court;[15] and his nepotism did not go unnoticed by contemporaries. His successor, Stephen Aubert, who took the name Innocent VI on his election in 1352, was rather more restrained, although he in no way reduced the Papacy's powers of involvement. He was much less ostentatious than Clement, and was regarded as having an impressionable personality, but he swiftly rejected the proposal agreed to in the conclave to give future popes much less control over the creation and removal of cardinals. He was harsh against those who dwelt at the papal court rather than on their benefices, as was his successor William Grimaud, who was elected as Urban V in 1362. But while it was the penury of the Holy See which had forced Innocent VI into economies, Urban seems genuinely to have hated luxury. He took steps to curb the avaricious elements at the curia; and he sponsored education and tried to link preferment to academic attainment. But he continued the Papacy's policy of making large numbers of appointments to benefices, and his measures to curb pluralism ran up against too many entrenched vested interests to be brought to a successful conclusion. Gregory XI, nephew and namesake of Clement VI, succeeded Urban on 30 December 1370. He did not share the more lordly qualities of his uncle, and tried to continue the reforms of Innocent and Urban. Among a number of diplomatic successes, he came to a compromise with the English king over several controversial issues.[16] But the costs of the papal court continued to necessitate heavy taxation throughout Christendom, and Gregory's pontificate coincided with bitter anti-papal sentiments among the laity represented in the English parliament.

An immediate question to be posed is the extent to which individual popes, however noble their reforming tendencies, could in reality influence events, especially in areas where traditional practices and procedures held sway. The bureaucratic machine could function largely without papal involvement, and it was the increasing power of this machine which marked the Avignon Papacy. Popes could and did involve themselves in matters of

[15] It is unlikely that Clement VI was chancellor of France, but he did preside over the Chambre des Comptes: Wood, *Clement VI*, 10–11.

[16] See below, pp. 155–8.

international politics: D. Wood has shown how Clement VI's partiality towards the French government influenced his handling of negotiations between the warring powers of England and France;[17] Urban V's difficult relationship with Edward III was at least partly caused by a similar pro-French tendency which became intermingled with the question of whether a particular dispensation to marry should be granted or not.[18] But in the everyday business with which this book is primarily concerned, individual pontiffs were usually both disinclined to intervene and powerless to influence particular decisions for good or ill. Urban's attempt to limit the abuse of pluralism foundered partly because it aroused too much opposition, but partly also because the complexity and legalism of the system did not permit swift and lasting change. The Avignon popes were certainly not puppets of their bureaucracy, but in routine matters the influence of that bureaucracy should not be overlooked.

During the Avignon Papacy, the central administration of the Roman church was divided between four chief institutions: the Chancery; the Apostolic Camera; the Penitentiary; and the organs of papal justice. The system was complex, with many built-in safeguards to try to prevent injustice or fraud, and only the briefest of descriptions is offered here.[19] The Chancery consisted of several departments involved with the despatch of papal letters and with bringing to the pope's attention the petitions which preceded them. It also contained the office for examining non-graduate clerks who had supplicated for benefices. If the beneficiary so desired, the Chancery would register his bull; the registers thus created are a priceless source of information on the grants made. The Camera (or chamber) dealt with the financial affairs of the Holy See; it was presided over by the *camerarius*, who among other duties appointed and supervised the collectors who were responsible for the levy locally of many papal taxes. The collectors' accounts and other cameral sources record not only receipts but often also give reasons for non-payment, thereby frequently casting light on whether particular papal provisions had borne fruit or not. The administration of justice was by 1342 divided into four: the pope and his cardinals in consistory; cardinals' tribunals; the

[17] Wood, *Clement VI*, chap. 6. [18] See below, pp. 146–52.

[19] See generally Mollat, *Popes*, 285–305. Cf. also C. R. Cheney, 'The study of the medieval papal chancery', in his *The Papacy and England, 12th–14th Centuries* (London, 1982), no. I; Lunt, *Papal Revenues*, I, 15–25.

audientia litterarum contradictarum (where legal challenges and objections were made to the plaintiff or magistrate); and the Court of the Apostolic Palace or Rota. Collectively they dealt with lawsuits, including those over benefices, which were brought to the Holy See in the first instance or on appeal, and represented the pope in his capacity as judge. The Penitentiary had a similar function in lifting canonical sentences and granting dispensations to those who had acted – or intended to act – in breach of requirements of canon law; the office also heard confessions and granted absolution. The records of the Penitentiary and the judicial organs of the curia do not survive from the fourteenth century, and information on the pope's use of his judicial and dispensing powers has to be gleaned largely from the Chancery records or from local sources.

The principal features of papal relations with the British Isles in the period before the Great Schism were taxation, provisions, judicial matters and the use of the Holy See's authority to dispense. There was also a considerable volume of correspondence of a diplomatic nature, a result of the Hundred Years War. This last area is not discussed in this study, because the book is concerned with the impact of papal practices locally, in Scotland and northern England, rather than with the role of the Papacy as a mediator in a major international conflict.[20] Of the issues which are examined, taxation and papal provisions are the most weighty; they were the areas which contemporaries found most controversial and which therefore aroused the strongest feelings among those who felt themselves adversely affected by them.

Provision was the practice whereby the pope appointed a clerk to a particular benefice or reserved for a clerk a benefice which was not vacant but would in due course become so. As will be seen, the system had strict rules, and the scale of its use was largely determined by the number of individual churchmen who elected to avail themselves of it. But it severely limited local patronage and inevitably aroused opposition, although this was more noticeable among the laity than the clergy. Most provisions affected prebends in cathedrals or collegiate churches; these were benefices which did

[20] For some works on this see E. Déprez, 'La conférence d'Avignon (1344): l'arbitrage pontifical entre la France et l'Angleterre', in *Essays in Medieval History Presented to Thomas Frederick Tout*, ed. A. G. Little and F. M. Powicke (Manchester, 1925), 301–20; G. Mollat, 'Innocent VI et les tentatives de paix entre la France et l'Angleterre', *Revue d'histoire ecclésiastique*, 10 (1909), 729–43; E. Perroy, *L'Angleterre et le Grand Schisme d'Occident* (Paris, 1933), chap. 1.

not involve the pastoral care of parishioners, for, although most of them drew their revenues from a parish, a substitute was almost always permanently resident locally to exercise the cure of souls. Prebends were also frequently held by royal servants, and the reader should bear in mind that most provisors were no less attentive to the needs of the faithful than the majority of royal clerks. But provisions had their price; from 1342 the heavy tax called annates had to be paid on all successful provisions to benefices which were already vacant at the time of the grant. Papal taxation and the practice of provision therefore became closely linked, which was one of the reasons why the English parliament opposed both so vehemently. The way in which the various forces at work battled and compromised is one of the chief themes of the following chapters.

Chapter 1

PAPAL TAXATION AND ITS COLLECTION

In the centralisation of the papal administration at Avignon, the question of finance naturally loomed large. An elaborate bureaucracy was expensive; so too were the ambitious and ill-starred schemes for a fresh crusade and the confused warfare in the Papal States which was one of the chief causes of the Papacy's long absence from Italy. By being beyond the Alps, the Papacy was deprived of most of its traditional sources of income from its Italian lands; and this, coupled with the ever-increasing cost of the papal court and its governmental machinery, forced the Avignon popes to extend and refine the taxes imposed by their predecessors.

By the middle of the fourteenth century the western church had come to be divided into collectorates, each presided over by a papal collector appointed by the pope or his chamberlain (*camerarius*) and responsible to the curia's financial arm, the Camera. Until the 1340s the British Isles, including Ireland, usually constituted a single collectorate,[1] but from 1345 Scotland had a collector of its own, and in 1368 Ireland was accorded similar status.[2] These changes represent no more than an admission of political reality. It could no longer be claimed that Scotland was subject to England, and the Scots were more likely to oppose the work of a principal collector established in London than one based locally, while Ireland's political chaos made the work of collection unusually difficult there. Subcollectors with wide powers had in the past been required in both Scotland and Ireland, and it was a pragmatic step on the part of the Holy See to assign both countries in due course to independent general collectors.

1 Scotland was removed from the collectorate of Itier de Concoreto in 1329; Bernard de Sistre, collector from 1335 to 1343, recorded no receipts from Scotland even though he was collector there: Lunt, *Accounts*, xxiii, xxviii. Raymond Pelegrini was described as nuncio in Scotland as well as England and Ireland as late as 7 April 1348 (*CPR 1348–50*, 46), although there was an independent Scottish collector by this date. The income tax of 1274–80 was collected separately in Scotland without English involvement.

2 Lunt, *Accounts*, xxxix.

The careers of the English collectors are detailed elsewhere,[3] and a few salient points will serve to establish the chronology of their activities. At the beginning of Clement VI's pontificate the collector in the whole of Britain and Ireland was Bernard de Sistre, who had been appointed in 1335. Although no renewal of his commission is extant, he continued in office until his death on 18 June 1343. His successor, Raymond Pelegrini, remained as collector in England and Ireland until July 1350, although his brother Hugh acted on his behalf from the summer of 1349, when Raymond left England for a time. Hugh was reappointed by Innocent VI and continued to act as collector until 1 September 1363, even though his successor had been appointed in the previous June. During his tenure of the office Hugh was absent from England several times, mainly on Edward III's behalf, and it was Raymond Pelegrini who functioned as his deputy on these occasions. Raymond's involvement was not insignificant, because after his death without rendering a final account his property was sequestrated at the pope's order until his affairs were settled and debts to the Camera paid.[4]

The Pelegrini brothers thus co-operated in controlling the English collectorate for some twenty years. Hugh was succeeded in 1363 by John de Cabrespino, who spent little time in England after an initial and very productive visit in the autumn and winter of 1363–4. Indeed, in 1368 he was given duties in the collectorate of Rheims,[5] even though he continued to take responsibility for English revenues until 1371, when he was appointed collector in Germany, Hungary, Bohemia and Poland.[6] He appears to have been a curialist at heart, and left much of the work of collection to his deputy John de Caroloco, prior of Bermondsey and later of Lewes. The relative ineffectiveness of Cabrespino's collectorship increased the burden of work on Arnald Garnerii, who was appointed general collector by Gregory XI in October 1371. Garnerii was in England much more than his predecessor, until his

[3] Ibid., esp. pp. xxviii–xli. Readers are referred to Lunt's work for full details of the collectors' commissions. [4] *CPL*, IV, 18–19.

[5] Ibid., 28; *Urbain V: lettres secrètes et curiales*, nos. 2863–4; Fierens and Tihon, *Lettres d'Urbain V*, nos. 2273–4. Cabrespino was given a faculty to examine the accounts of John Maubert, collector in Rheims, whose commission was renewed in January 1371: Samaran and Mollat, *La fiscalité pontificale*, 181.

[6] *CPL*, IV, 148; *Grégoire XI: lettres secrètes et curiales (non-Fr)*, nos. 240–2, 245, 275.

final departure in March 1378, but his lack of tact antagonised both taxpayers and parliament.

William de Deyn, bishop of Aberdeen, was appointed collector in Scotland on 27 May 1345[7] and died in 1350.[8] He certainly collected some annates because his successor's account refers to receipts by him, and two merchants of Asti were told to give acquittances for sums received from Bishop Deyn,[9] but little else is known about his collectorship. After a break of more than two years, William de Grenlaw was appointed by Innocent VI on 30 December 1352. He continued in office until his death in 1374, although, like John de Cabrespino, he resided mainly at the curia and carried on the work of collection through deputies.[10] His successor was John de Peblis, who was appointed in October 1374 to collect papal taxes in Scotland, including Sodor and Orkney, although Sodor was soon removed from his collectorate and responsibility for levying taxes there entrusted to the local bishop.[11] Like his predecessors, Peblis was a prominent Scottish churchman, but unlike Grenlaw he was destined to be promoted to a bishopric.

A significant difference between England and Scotland is that while the Scottish collectors were local men of some importance, the English collectors of the period were invariably foreigners by birth with benefices in France. The Pelegrini brothers and Arnald Garnerii were from Aquitaine, whose duke was king of England, but their French origin on occasion led to prejudice against them: parliament petitioned in 1346 that Raymond Pelegrini be forced to leave the country; and there was bitter opposition to Arnald Garnerii in the Good Parliament of 1376.[12] Paradoxically, the reason for the appointment of Frenchmen may have been the very strength of the royal government in England; the Papacy may have feared that a native churchman might temper his zeal for the work of the Camera by paying too much heed to the interests of the English clergy and his own position with regard to the king. In Scotland, governmental activity was less highly developed and opposition to the Holy See in parliament less marked, and it may have been felt that locally born collectors would be more effective.

[7] *CPL*, III, 18; *Clément VI: lettres closes (non-Fr)*, no. 673. The latter source specifies annates only. [8] Possibly on 20 August: Watt, *Dictionary*, 150. [9] *CPL*, III, 36.

[10] See generally A. D. M. Barrell, 'William de Grenlaw, papal collector in Scotland, and his account', *Innes Review*, 42 (1991), 3–18. [11] *CPL*, IV, 152, 109.

[12] Lunt, *Accounts*, xxxi, xli.

The collectors periodically had to render accounts to the Camera. Although these vary considerably in form and quality, they are invaluable for any study of the collectors' activities and of the taxes which they levied. The survival rate for this source is unusually good for the period of the Avignon Papacy, for as well as a long series of accounts from the English collectorate there is also a unique Scottish account, rendered by William de Grenlaw in 1362.[13]

These accounts, however, deal only with those revenues which the papal nuncio-collectors were commissioned to levy. Several important sources of papal income, most notably the service taxes demanded of bishops who owed their promotion to the pope, were paid directly to the Camera.[14] Some of these revenues were shared between the pope and the College of cardinals, which may partly explain why they continued to be collected centrally rather than through the agency of the collectors, since the College had no financial representatives outside the papal court. Evidence for these taxes must be found in sources other than the accounts, but again the information is reasonably complete for the fourteenth century. The period is, therefore, especially suitable for the study of the impact of papal taxation in Scotland and northern England and of its effect on diplomatic relations between the Holy See and the respective royal governments during a time of war.

Students of papal finance in the Middle Ages must acknowledge their debt to the work of W. E. Lunt, whose research on the various taxes in general and their levy in England in particular provides an essential basis for the current study. Although the analysis which follows draws extensively on Lunt's scholarship, a close investigation of an area of England which was much affected by economic dislocation in the wars of the fourteenth century, and of a remote kingdom which Lunt did not study in detail casts fresh light on how an elaborate system worked on the ground, in places refines and questions Lunt's more general impressions, and reveals substantial differences in practice and procedure between Scotland on the one hand and the northern province of England on the other.

[13] The English material is printed in Lunt, *Accounts*. Grenlaw's account is in Coll. 14, fols. 158–193; see Barrell, 'William de Grenlaw'.

[14] In the fifteenth century service taxes in Scotland and Ireland were often paid to the local collector because of the areas' remoteness: Lunt, *Papal Revenues*, I, 88.

PAPAL REVENUES

PETER'S PENCE

The oldest papal revenue in England was Peter's Pence. This was instituted by the Anglo-Saxon kings and continued until the Reformation. Originally it may have been levied on the basis of a penny from each inhabited house, but its collection was subject to local variations, and by the fourteenth century it had come to be regulated by custom.[15] Each level of the ecclesiastical hierarchy made a certain profit from the tax,[16] and the amount paid to the papal collectors, a little under £200 per annum, was much less than the total collected from parishioners. Attempts were made by, among others, Innocent III and John XXII to exact the full amount, but these foundered on the rocks of ancient custom and royal prohibitions,[17] with the result that in our period only the traditional amount was sent on to the Camera.

In the northern province, the archbishop of York paid £11 10s each year, although in fact he received far more than this from his subordinates.[18] The bishop of Durham collected the pennies due from his peculiars of Allertonshire and Howdenshire, which were geographically within the diocese of York, and delivered the proceeds to the archbishop, but there is no evidence that Peter's Pence was ever collected in the diocese of Durham itself; nor was it levied in Carlisle diocese, nor in the deanery of Coupland, which was in Cumberland but lay within the diocese of York. Lunt suggests that the exemption of parts of the north, along with Wales, came about because when Peter's Pence was undergoing its territorial expansion under the Anglo-Saxon kings, these districts were outside royal control; in addition, the bishop of Durham enjoyed an extensive immunity in the late Anglo-Saxon period.[19]

[15] Lunt, *Financial Relations ... to 1327*, 81–2; Lunt, *Financial Relations ... 1327–1534*, 38–48.

[16] E.g. the archdeacon of Richmond kept all the Peter's Pence he collected and paid the archbishop only £1 for this and *sinodalia*; the archdeacon of York received an undisclosed amount from the collection of Peter's Pence; in some of the deaneries of York diocese the rural dean kept the pennies paid by his own parishioners: Lunt, *Financial Relations ... 1327–1534*, 33.

[17] Lunt, *Papal Revenues*, II, 62–4, 66–8; Lunt, *Financial Relations ... 1327–1534*, 3.

[18] Lunt, *Financial Relations ... to 1327*, 78–9; Lunt, *Financial Relations ... 1327–1534*, 32.

[19] Lunt, *Financial Relations ... to 1327*, 19–22. For Coupland cf. *The Register of the Priory of St Bees*, ed. J. Wilson (Surtees Soc., 1915), 594.

Peter's Pence had never been established in mainland Scotland, although periodically attempts were made to levy it there. In 1316 John XXII ordered an enquiry into Peter's Pence in Scotland, but the legates Gaucelin and Luca Fieschi were not allowed to enter the country, and lawlessness on the border rendered the papal mission abortive. In 1329 the papal nuncios Bertrand Cariti and Raymond de Quercu were granted a faculty to exact Peter's Pence in Scotland, albeit perhaps only from the clergy, but even though this was a time when the Scottish crown desired an agreement with the Holy See there is no evidence that the tax was ever paid.[20] An earlier attempt to levy Peter's Pence in Caithness at the instance of Harald Maddadson, earl of Orkney and Caithness, was snuffed out by the bishop and the king of Scots by the early thirteenth century and does not appear to have been revived thereafter.[21] In 1321 one of the arguments used to prove that Scotland was not subject to England was that, when King Alfred granted a penny from every house from which smoke was emitted, this due was not imposed in Scotland.[22] It is, however, noteworthy that Peter's Pence had never been levied in mainland Scotland, as it was commonly paid by smaller countries in return for papal support in the secular sphere, and it was still being paid in the fourteenth century in Orkney, part of the province of Trondheim or Nidaros.[23] During his suit with the archbishop of Canterbury before Innocent III, Gerald of Wales offered Peter's Pence in return for exemption of the Welsh church from the jurisdiction of Canterbury,[24] but no comparable offer is known to have been made by the Scots in return for the bull *Cum universi*, which had been issued just a few years before and was alluded to by Gerald of Wales.

In northern England and mainland Scotland, therefore, this ancient tax was paid only by the archbishop of York. He did not pay the collector the sum due every year, but was rarely more than one or two payments in arrears. Lunt has suggested that in 1365 and the first half of 1366 the collector may deliberately have left sums owed in the hands of debtors to prevent their being impounded by the government, and conjectures that this may have led to some

[20] B. E. Crawford, 'Peter's Pence in Scotland', in *The Scottish Tradition*, ed. G. W. S. Barrow (Edinburgh, 1974), 15–17; *CPL*, II, 490.

[21] Crawford, 'Peter's Pence', 17–22.

[22] P. A. Linehan, 'A fourteenth-century history of Anglo-Scottish relations in a Spanish manuscript', *BIHR*, 48 (1975), 118.

[23] Lunt, *Papal Revenues*, II, 74.

[24] Giraldus Cambrensis, *Opera*, ed. J. S. Brewer, J. F. Dimock and G. F. Warner (8 vols., Rolls Series, 1861–91), III, 55, 78, 175.

delay in the receipt of Peter's Pence for the years from 1365.[25] This was indeed a period of crisis in Anglo-Papal relations, although there is no evidence that the proposal in the 1365 parliament to stop the payment of Peter's Pence[26] was ever seriously considered. Moreover, Archbishop Thoresby did not accumulate unusually great arrears of Peter's Pence during this time, even though he had paid the tax for 1359–62 inclusive only on 5 February 1364.[27] The archbishops appear to have considered Peter's Pence to be a regular liability, not to be withheld indefinitely but not necessarily to be offered voluntarily as soon as it was due or even to be paid annually.

CENSUS

Similar to Peter's Pence, though even less significant financially as far as the British Isles were concerned, was the census paid by protected or exempt ecclesiastical foundations and some laymen. Not all exempt monasteries paid census and some houses which did, such as Carlisle Priory, were not exempt and paid merely for papal protection. Carlisle paid one mark each year; the only other payer in the province of York was the church of Scarborough, which belonged to Cîteaux but for which census of 15d per annum was paid to the English collectors. In Scotland several religious houses as well as Glasgow Cathedral, the church of Monymusk and the earl of Mar should have been paying census in our period, although in most cases evidence is lacking. The liability was incurred only by certain individuals and corporations, usually in particular historical circumstances, and it was often expressed in obsolete currencies. During the Wars of Independence, if not before, many Scottish payers probably ceased to hand over census to papal agents and were able to use the long period of desuetude to their advantage in the event of later demands. But census was not merely an archaic protection payment with no relevance to the late medieval world. In 1379 the abbot of Holyrood promised one merk every two years in return for the papal grant of pontifical insignia, and as late as 1470 the college of St Giles in Edinburgh became liable for census in return for exemption from episcopal control.[28]

[25] Lunt, *Financial Relations . . . 1327–1534*, 10–12.

[26] *Chron. Reading*, 163–4. In the first parliament of Richard II's reign (1377) the payment of Peter's Pence was again questioned, but the government decreed that it should be paid in the customary manner: *Rot. Parl.*, III, 21.

[27] Lunt, *Accounts*, 141, 172.

[28] *Liber censuum*, I, 230–2.

In November 1376 Bishop Wardlaw of Glasgow made an agreement with the papal treasurer about resuming the payment of census from his cathedral; he paid eighty florins at the rate of three merks per annum for the pontificate of Gregory XI and was to come to an arrangement concerning an unspecified sum of arrears which had accumulated before 1371.[29] The liability had been imposed on the church of Glasgow by Honorius III in 1216,[30] and its high rate and Wardlaw's close links with the Holy See perhaps influenced the Camera in its decision to attempt to recover it. The situation as regards the other potential payers is less clear. The English collector Bernard de Sistre, whose commission covered Scotland as well, reported that no census had been received from north of the border during the period 1335–43 on account of the continuing warfare,[31] and although Grenlaw mentions census in his account no receipts are detailed and it is possible that Glasgow Cathedral alone is referred to.[32] Most of the amounts due from other ancient obligations were small, and the Camera may have decided that it would be uneconomic to establish the Papacy's right to them and then endeavour to collect them.

For England, Lunt found that most payers were reasonably prompt in handing over census, except in the difficult period from 1365 to 1368; only a few fell behind for more than a year or two.[33] In the case of the church of Scarborough the accounts bear out this generalisation, but Carlisle Priory, which had paid census promptly to the Pelegrini brothers in the 1340s and 1350s, gave nothing to the next collector John de Cabrespino. His successor, Arnald Garnerii, wrote to Bishop Appleby of Carlisle in February 1372, saying that the priory was in arrears for the years 1362–71, to the sum of £6 13s 4d in all.[34] Why the priory was in debt for a decade is unclear. This was not a period of unusually high Anglo-Scottish tension or royal taxation, and although there was undoubtedly some parliamentary opposition to papal exactions in the mid-1360s, this was not a new phenomenon and its effect on other payers of census was much less marked. The prior, John de Horncastle, had been ousted by a papal provisor from the see of Carlisle to which he had been elected in 1353, and this may have rankled, but it had not prevented the payment of census in the

29 IE 347, fol. 12v. This implies an exchange rate of 3s to the florin.

30 *Liber censuum*, I, 232.

31 Lunt, *Accounts*, 44.

32 Cf. Barrell, 'William de Grenlaw', 14.

33 Lunt, *Financial Relations ... 1327–1534*, 65.

34 Reg. Appleby, pp. 248–9.

1350s, and it was paid tolerably promptly in the 1370s as well, although Horncastle remained as prior until 1376.[35] Although the plagues of 1361–2 and 1369 probably hit Carlisle diocese disproportionately hard, the delay is more probably the result of John de Cabrespino, never the most energetic of collectors, not exerting himself sufficiently in demanding census from the remote cathedral priory.

TRIBUTE

Akin to census, and often so designated, was the tribute of 1000 marks annually for England and Ireland promised by King John when he submitted to Innocent III in 1213.[36] Henry III, who felt under an obligation to the Papacy because of the support it had shown him, was keen to pay it whenever his shaky financial resources allowed, but his successors used it as a bargaining counter and paid only when it suited their interests to do so. In 1330 John XXII and Edward III came to an agreement whereby the king promised to pay the arrears of the tribute in return for half the proceeds of a new quadrennial tenth and half the revenues from annates; but 1500 marks paid in 1333 proved to be the final gesture.[37] The popes tried in vain to persuade Edward to fulfil his ancestor's obligation. In their mission in early 1345 the archbishop of Ravenna and the bishop of Astorga apparently sought payment of the tribute,[38] and Innocent VI made a further attempt in 1356–7.[39] In June 1365, when Anglo-Papal relations were already in something of a crisis, Urban V sent the abbot of St Bavon's in Ghent as nuncio to deal with Edward III over the tribute.[40] The 1366 parliament responded by declaring, anachronistically but conveniently, that John had had no right to subject the realm to the Holy See without its consent, and that he had acted contrary to his coronation oath.[41] That proved to be the final nail in the coffin of this particular papal tax in England.[42]

35 Le Neve, *Fasti*, VI, 100.
36 Lunt, *Papal Revenues*, II, 45–8.
37 Lunt, *Financial Relations . . . 1327–1534*, 66–7. For the final payment see *Foedera*, II, 864; *Vet. Mon.*, 259.
38 *Chron. Knighton*, II, 31.
39 Ibid., 98; F. Bock, 'Some new documents illustrating the early years of the Hundred Years War (1353–1356)', *Bulletin of the John Rylands Library*, 15 (1931), 99; cf. Lunt, *Financial Relations . . . 1327–1534*, 68–9.
40 *Vet. Mon.*, 329; *Urbain V: lettres secrètes et curiales*, no. 1821; cf. *CPL*, IV, 16.
41 *Rot. Parl.*, II, 290; Lunt, *Papal Revenues*, II, 53–4.
42 It is reported in *Eulogium Historiarum sive Temporis*, ed. F. S. Haydon (3 vols., Rolls Series, 1858–63), III, 337–9 that a Great Council which met at Westminster in 1374 discussed a

INCOME TAXES

Peter's Pence, census and tribute did not need an extensive bureaucracy of collection; the number of payers and the generally small sums due would have made such administration too costly. It was the advent of the era of income taxes to help finance the crusades which made permanent or semi-permanent collectorates desirable, although there was considerable variation in the administrative arrangements decreed, and the general collector was often responsible only for arrears. The taxes also necessitated assessments of clerical income which were used for other taxes as well.

The income taxes dated from 1199, when Innocent III imposed a fortieth for the crusade.[43] The bishops collected it, and the assessments were probably too low. By the later thirteenth century the amount demanded was usually a tenth, and new and more stringent assessments of clerical wealth were made, most notably in 1274 and 1291; the latter valuation was used for both papal and royal taxes in England until the Reformation, with amendments only in special circumstances. The crusade was usually cited as the reason behind the imposition of the tax, but in practice the popes increasingly shared the proceeds with secular rulers, including the king of England, who was in the enviable position of receiving the money without incurring the opprobrium of imposing the tax. In 1330 John XXII started levying a tenth for the defence of the church against heretics, schismatics and rebels, and again shared the proceeds with the English king, whose financial needs were also pressing.[44] This was the last mandatory papal income tax imposed on the English clergy partly for royal use, for a number of reasons. The king was now able to obtain frequent clerical subsidies on his own initiative without soliciting papal help, and in view of this was doubtless unwilling to authorise a tax of which part would pass to a Francophile pope. The popes also may have been reluctant to oblige Edward III out of fear that

bull in which the pope claimed temporal lordship over England on account of John's submission and ordered England to pay a tallage to help him against the Florentines. Even if this council is not wholly fictitious, and it has been argued (by J. I. Catto, 'An alleged Great Council of 1374', *EHR*, 82 (1967), 764–71) that a date in 1373 is plausible, it surely concerns the subsidy demanded in 1372 against the Visconti rather than the tribute: cf. Lunt, *Financial Relations . . . 1327–1534*, 70.

43 Lunt, *Papal Revenues*, II, 82–6.

44 Ibid., 105–11.

he would use his portion of the proceeds to subsidise campaigns against France.

After 1342 very little was raised from the arrears of the mandatory tenths imposed in 1330 and earlier. Raymond Pelegrini, whose accounts are not extant, paid £50 to the royal treasury from the tenths and early levies of annates, which were also shared between pope and king.[45] Raymond's predecessor, Bernard de Sistre, collected £177 13s 6d from the arrears of the quadrennial tenth of 1330–3 in the province of York, but the use of a revised assessment in much of the north meant that the yield was less than a comparable levy would have realised in the thirteenth century. The church of Thornton was £45 in arrears by the old tax but owed nothing according to the new, and as a result nothing further could be received from the abbot of Jervaulx, who was acting as subcollector in the archdeaconry of Richmond.[46] On 15 December 1342 Bishop Kirkby of Carlisle wrote to the official of Lincoln and the officials of all the archdeacons in Lincoln diocese, asking that John de Stokton be released from any sentences he had incurred through slowness to pay £6 5s 8¼d towards John XXII's quadrennial tenth.[47] But by this time any business related to the last of the shared tenths was virtually cleared up.

Income taxes were, however, reasonably straightforward to collect, because the administrative mechanism had had ample opportunity to develop and be perfected. They were also lucrative, because there was a large number of potential payers. The popes were understandably reluctant to abandon them entirely, and both Innocent VI and Gregory XI demanded subsidies. These were theoretically voluntary offerings, although in practice the levy was by papal authority backed by canonical sanctions. In Scotland, Innocent authorised a tenth for three years on 9 August 1359 for the ransom of David II.[48]

The tenth for David's ransom is well documented in the Exchequer Rolls.[49] It was collected in six half-yearly instalments, sometimes by rural deanery and sometimes by diocese. Occasionally the collectors are named, and they seem to have been mainly local clergy, including Alexander de Kylwos, dean of Ross, and William Boyle, precentor of Moray;[50] others named include the

[45] Lunt, *Financial Relations . . . 1327–1534*, 85.
[46] Lunt, *Accounts*, 63.
[47] Reg. Kirkby, fols. 238v–239.
[48] Reg. Av. 141, fols. 578v–580v; cf. *Chron. Bower* (Goodall), II, 362.
[49] *Exch. Rolls*, II, 75–6, 109–11, 163, 171–2.
[50] See Watt, *Fasti*, 222.

rectors of Abernyte and Kinnettles and the vicar of Perth. Excluding an apparently erroneous repeat entry relating to money said to have been received from the diocese of Aberdeen,[51] the total yield of the tenth as recorded in the Exchequer Rolls was £1753 11s 11d, but these payments were all made before 11 December 1364, and it is very possible that further sums were recovered at a later date or that the Exchequer Rolls are incomplete.[52]

Although this tenth was levied by papal authority, the proceeds went to the government rather than to the pope. In practice, the same happened in England in the case of Innocent VI's subsidy of 1362, although the exercise was supposed to fund papal wars in Italy. Innocent first proposed a tax for the defence of papal lands in 1360, and following reiteration of this request the following year the king intervened with the English clergy on the pope's behalf, thereby obtaining a marriage dispensation for his son Edward.[53] The subsidy was set at 100,000 florins, and it was thought that a tenth would produce roughly the desired yield. It was also decided that the king would receive the proceeds from the subsidy and the pope his 100,000 florins from John II of France, the sum being deducted from the ransom he owed to Edward III following his capture at Poitiers and the eventual settlement at Brétigny. This gave Edward a personal interest in the levy of the subsidy, gave the pope the option of showing charity to the French king, and potentially gave John some breathing space with respect to his payments to Edward, although the pope wisely reported that he had actually received the money from the French.[54] It was a manifestation of the new order after the Treaty of Brétigny, but it ensured that the English clergy would be pressed hard for the 100,000 florins.

An immediate difficulty was the revised assessment in the north. This had been made in 1317–19 following destruction of the border counties in Scottish raids after the English disaster at Bannockburn

[51] *Exch. Rolls*, II, 110.

[52] There is also some information relating to this tenth in an unnumbered MS in the possession of the earl of Haddington entitled 'Minute of the rollis of schireffis, Burrowes and Kirklandis anent King Davidis Ranson', pp. 5–6; but it is incomplete, and it is not clear how much, if at all, it duplicates what is in the Exchequer Rolls. Some benefices near the English border yielded nothing on account of destruction or English occupation: ibid., p. 7.

[53] Lunt, *Financial Relations ... 1327–1534*, 95–7; cf. *Foedera*, III, 623–4. For the marriage dispensation see *Foedera*, III, 626.

[54] *Reg. Sudbury*, I, 182–8; *Foedera*, III, 643; Lunt, *Accounts*, xlvii.

in 1314. The reduction in burden had been sweeping, especially in Northumberland and parts of Cumberland, where many benefices were said to be worthless. Further downward adjustments were made in parts of York diocese in 1328 after a further series of raids. The revision extended southwards well into Yorkshire; and although, as we have seen, the tenth of the 1330s was collected in accordance with the new assessment, Benedict XII was insistent that this should not set a precedent for future levies in northern England.[55] Most papal collectors tried to levy the 1291 figure for those taxes which made use of that assessment, but clerical subsidies demanded by the king and granted by convocation were based on the revision, with the result that the northern clergy had good grounds on which to oppose any return to the old taxation, even though it is reasonable to suppose that at least some recovery had taken place since the dark days of the 1320s.

There is little information about the collection of the 1362 subsidy, although it was probably on similar lines to earlier papal tenths and clerical subsidies to the king. As was normal with income taxes, the northern prelates appointed as collectors the heads of prominent religious houses, namely the priors of Durham and Carlisle and the abbot of St Mary's, York.[56] The archbishop of York was, however, ultimately responsible for payment; and acquittances were issued to him by the chief collectors, the archbishop of Canterbury and the bishop of Ely, on 4 November 1362 and 3 May 1363, which show that £3047 14s in two equal instalments had been levied from the province of York, and state that no more was due.[57] Lunt states that only £1523 17s was in fact paid, and that the second acquittance was merely an amendment of the first; he points out that £1523 17s was less than a tenth even by the new valuation. The chief collectors had, however, asked for the old taxation to be used, and the northern clergy had offered the new with a possible supplementary levy to bring their contribution up to a fifth of the national total.[58] Calculating on the basis of a florin being worth about 3s or a little more, the sum of £3047 14s is very close to a fifth of the total required, around 20,000 florins; moreover, a royal letter of October 1365 acknowledges receipt of £15,000 as the subsidy due to the king from the whole of

[55] *RPD*, III, 218–20.

[56] Reg. Hatfield, fol. 43; Reg. Welton, p. 92; Reg. Thoresby, fols. 319, 323v.

[57] Reg. Thoresby, fol. 318, 318v.

[58] Lunt, *Financial Relations . . . 1327–1534*, 101–2.

England.[59] So it would appear that the chief collectors accepted the suggestion put forward by representatives of the northern province and fixed their portion at 20,000 florins. This sum bore no direct relation to either the new or the old taxation, and it was presumably left to the northern prelates to arrange collection of the tax. What method of assessment they used is not known; possibly a fraction other than a tenth was levied, or a tenth collected on the basis of the new valuation with an extra levy of so much in the mark.

Gregory XI first mentioned the levy of a subsidy on 10 March 1372,[60] and on 1 July he ordered the bishops of Scotland and England to pay a tenth for one year, although the English clergy were given the option of paying 100,000 florins in lieu.[61] There was much prevarication. On 8 December 1374 the new Scottish collector, John de Peblis, was told to levy a subsidy in his country,[62] although there is no record of any payments made. In England the tax encountered stiff opposition from both clergy and government until it became one of the elements of an Anglo-Papal concordat negotiated at Bruges in 1375. In return for some concessions over disputed benefices and the grant of a papal court at Bruges to save Englishmen the dangerous journey to Avignon, the government allowed Gregory to levy 60,000 florins, the remainder being due in the event of peace with France.[63] This was seen by some elements in England as a capitulation, and was bitterly attacked by the Good Parliament of 1376, which claimed that the pope wanted the money for his wars in Italy and to ransom French nobles taken by the English,[64] but the clergy had little option but to pay in view of the crown's accommodation with Gregory. The subsidy was paid to Arnald Garnerii and appears in his account. The archbishop of York paid a total of £1780 in six stages from 14 May 1376 to 28 October 1377, including £460 paid in Bruges to the archbishop of Rouen.[65] As in 1362 this represents approxi-

59 *Foedera*, III, 776; *CPR 1364–67*, 164. For an earlier, partial acquittance see *CPR 1361–64*, 268.

60 *Grégoire XI: lettres secrètes et curiales (Fr)*, no. 2462; *Grégoire XI: lettres secrètes et curiales (non-Fr)*, no. 575.

61 *CPL*, IV, 101, 150; *Grégoire XI: lettres secrètes et curiales (non-Fr)*, nos. 843–6.

62 *CPL*, IV, 153, 160.

63 Ibid., 111; cf. 154, 160, 218; *Grégoire XI: lettres secrètes et curiales (non-Fr)*, no. 3378. On the negotiations at Bruges see below, pp. 156–7.

64 *Rot. Parl.*, II, 339.

65 Lunt, *Accounts*, 532. The archbishop of Rouen, who was involved in the peace negotiations, was granted a faculty on 1 July 1376 to receive sums collected in England and transmit them to the Camera: *CPL*, IV, 155, 161.

mately a fifth of the total required at an exchange rate of roughly 3s to the florin.

These income taxes were paid with considerable rapidity, testimony to the efficiency of the collection procedure, even though the amount demanded did not constitute a tenth by either of the valuations current in the north. Such taxes were, in fact, relatively easy to levy: they fell on the same benefices each time, irrespective of the identity or status of the incumbents. But their very success had encouraged the king to adopt the tenth as his preferred method of taxing the English clergy, and after the 1330s the Papacy could levy income taxes in England only in certain circumstances and after an agreement had been made with the secular power. The Holy See was, therefore, forced to rely increasingly heavily on taxes connected with papal provisions to individual clerks, namely service taxes and annates.

SERVICE TAXES

Service taxes were owed by bishops and some abbots who were provided or confirmed by the pope in consistory, and comprised a number of elements. Common services were assessed at around a third of the estimated gross annual income of the prelacy, although by the middle of the fourteenth century the amount due had come to be fixed and was only altered in exceptional circumstances or as the result of error.[66] The revenue was divided equally between the pope and the College of cardinals. Each of the five petty services was equivalent to the amount received by one cardinal from common services, and so the sum levied varied along with the size of the College. The petty services were used to pay the salaries of certain members of the households of the pope and cardinals.[67] If the prelate was consecrated or blessed at the curia, he had in addition to pay the *sacra*, which was a twentieth of the total amount of common services, and a due called the subdeacon, which was equal to a third of the *sacra*. Archbishops had to pay a fee for receipt of the pallium, and fees for the issue of bulls and certain gratuities had to be paid by all prelates.[68] The expenditure incurred at the curia in connection with a provision meant that many prelates had to contract loans, on which interest was paid.

[66] Lunt, *Financial Relations . . . to 1327*, 467, App. IX; Lunt, *Financial Relations . . . 1327–1534*, App. II.
[67] Lunt, *Papal Revenues*, II, 245–9.
[68] Lunt, *Financial Relations . . . to 1327*, 474–5.

On his provision, a bishop obliged himself, his successors and his see to pay the service taxes for which he was liable, and also any arrears left by his predecessors,[69] and terms were set for payment. After 1348 these became more liberal than they had been formerly, perhaps because of economic dislocation caused by plague.[70] Even so, many prelates in the third quarter of the fourteenth century found it difficult to meet their obligations on time; it is noteworthy that papal licences to contract loans are much less common after 1349, and if this means that no loans were in fact made, then this might explain the slowness of prelates to pay services at this period.[71]

During the vacancy of an English see, the king administered the temporalities and the cathedral chapter the spiritualities, with the result that a newly consecrated bishop had no supply of ready money on which to draw. Subsidies often had to be imposed on the clergy of the diocese, as in the case of Bishop Hatfield of Durham in 1345[72] and Bishop Welton of Carlisle in 1353–4,[73] to allow the new bishop to meet his various obligations. William Rae of Glasgow also received papal authority to levy a subsidy which was probably connected with his provision; a little under £250 had been raised by 26 November 1342.[74] The local clergy were, therefore, financially involved in the provision of their bishop.

Evidence of payment is most complete for the pope's share of common services, although it is clear that the cardinals' half and instalments of petty services were usually handed over at the same time. Bishops normally employed a proctor to make the payments, usually a curial official, a cameral merchant, or a servant employed by the prelate at home. On 18 November 1345 Robert de Den handed over money from the bishops of Aberdeen, St Andrews and Caithness,[75] and in view of the distances involved it was sensible to employ as proctor someone who was already going to Avignon. The unavailability of suitable agents to convey the money may well sometimes have been alleged as an excuse for dilatory payment.

The prelates of northern England were able to make at least a

[69] Lunt, *Financial Relations . . . 1327–1534*, 217. Bishop William Rae of Glasgow was excused payment of the services of his predecessor: *Vat. Quel.*, v, 55.

[70] Lunt, *Financial Relations . . . 1327–1534*, 185.

[71] Ibid., 199–200, 214. Cf. below, pp. 201–2.

[72] *CPP*, I, 100; *CPL*, III, 216; Lunt, *Financial Relations . . . 1327–1534*, 283–4.

[73] Reg. Welton, pp. 1, 5, 13–14.

[74] *Glasgow Registrum*, I, 251–2.

[75] *Vat. Quel.*, v, 114.

creditable attempt to pay their services on time, despite the fact that some of their revenues came from areas damaged by the Anglo-Scottish conflict. It was not always possible to do so, but bishops do not seem to have been prepared to procrastinate and risk ecclesiastical censures in the way that many of their lesser brethren did in regard to annates.[76]

Some bishops in Scotland in the period under review escaped paying service taxes. A few, such as Michael de Malconhalgh of Galloway, did not owe their position to the pope; and Alan de Moray of Caithness, Philip Wilde of Brechin and Thomas of Galloway died before any payments could be made. There is no record of any services being paid by Malcolm de Drumbreck, who promised 700 or 750 florins for Caithness on 15 March 1369.[77] The great majority of Scottish bishops, however, paid the tax, and the usual period over which payments were spread was from two to five years; this often necessitated an extension of the original terms set. John de Rate, who promised 1250 florins for Aberdeen on 26 January 1351, was given terms of 1 November 1351 and 15 August 1352,[78] and made his final payment on 3 January 1353.[79] Alexander Stewart, bishop of Ross, was given the same terms as Rate,[80] although he did not complete payment until 28 November 1355, handing over the money in three instalments.[81] Walter de Wardlaw paid the 2500 florins he owed for Glasgow also in three instalments, from December 1368 to July 1370,[82] having made his obligation on 30 April 1367.[83] Some bishops, however, paid rather more quickly and others more slowly. Martin, bishop of Argyll, obliged himself on 6 April 1345 to pay 200 florins, the terms being set at 2 February and 29 September 1346;[84] and he paid the full amount of common services due to the pope on 16 May 1346, although on this occasion no petty services are recorded.[85] Michael de Monymusk, whose obligation for 450 florins for Dunkeld was taken on 9 December 1370,[86] paid the pope's half in full along with

[76] For the figures see Lunt, *Financial Relations . . . 1327–1534*, App. II.

[77] Cal. OS 35, fol. 126v; Cal. OS 36, fol. 219v; Hoberg, *Taxae*, 33. Robert Stretton, bishop of Coventry and Lichfield from 1360, similarly seems to have escaped services: Lunt, *Financial Relations . . . 1327–1534*, 171, 738.

[78] Coll. 385, fol. 89v; cf. Cal. OS 23, fol. 121; Hoberg, *Taxae*, 3.

[79] *Vat. Quel.*, VIII, 33.

[80] Coll. 385, fol. 89v; cf. Hoberg, *Taxae*, 103.

[81] *Vat. Quel.*, VIII, 34.

[82] Burns, 'Sources', no. 232; IE 327, fol. 128; IE 331, fol. 41v.

[83] Cal. OS 36, fol. 180v; Hoberg, *Taxae*, 59.

[84] Cal. OS 22, fol. 257v; cf. Hoberg, *Taxae*, 52.

[85] *Vat. Quel.*, V, 123.

[86] Cal. OS 35, fol. 145; Hoberg, *Taxae*, 48.

47 florins 10s 4d in petty services on 16 July 1372.[87] Towards the other end of the scale, William, bishop of Dunblane, was given generous terms for payment on 5 December 1347: a quarter of the 800 florins due was to be paid on 30 November 1348, a further quarter on the same date the following year, and the remainder on 30 November 1350.[88] He met the first two terms, but it was 27 September 1352 before he made a further payment of 150 florins, and 28 November 1354 before he completed handing over the services due.[89] William Russell of Sodor obliged himself for 600 florins on 25 May 1349, with terms set at 16 May 1350 and 17 April 1351.[90] He did not make his first payment until 28 November 1354, and needed further extensions before completing delivery of the services he owed on 13 March 1357.[91] Occasionally prelates were very late in handing over a final instalment. Thomas de Rossy paid most of his services for Sodor by 2 March 1333,[92] but delivery of the petty services and six florins in common services was then delayed until 18 April 1341.[93] Alexander Bur of Moray, who obliged himself for 1200 florins on 19 January 1363,[94] paid most of the services due to both pope and cardinals on 7 September 1364,[95] but the remaining 46 florins 6s 4d of common services and 10 florins 19s 6d of petty services were not handed over to the pope until 30 July 1372.[96] Bishops who were bound to pay for their short-lived predecessor as well as for themselves had mixed records. Thomas de Fingask paid two sets of services for Caithness within six years,[97] while Adam de Lanark paid two sets for Galloway within four years.[98] Patrick de Locrys, bishop of Brechin, however, took over twenty years to pay the services of himself and his predecessor Philip Wilde. Obliged from 1351,[99] he made payments in 1355, 1359, 1361, 1367, 1369, 1371 and 1372.[100]

87 Coll. 465, fol. 48; Cal. OS 39, fol. 320v; cf. Burns, 'Sources', no. 253.

88 Cal. OS 22, fol. 31; cf. Hoberg, *Taxae*, 47.

89 *Vat. Quel.*, v, 167, 190, 306; VIII, 33.

90 Cal. OS 27, fol. 10v; Cal. OS 23, fol. 84; cf. Hoberg, *Taxae*, 112.

91 *Vat. Quel.*, VIII, 34.

92 Ibid., I, 261, 270.

93 Ibid., IV, 89.

94 Hoberg, *Taxae*, 82; Cal. OS 36, fol. 44.

95 *Moray Registrum*, 161–4.

96 Cal. OS 39, fol. 324; cf. Coll. 465, fol. 49v; Burns, 'Sources', no. 253.

97 For the obligation see Cal. OS 6, fol. 196; PRO, Roman Transcripts, 31/9/59, pp. 293, 334–5. For the payments see *Vat. Quel.*, v, 90, 114, 321; Coll. 462, fol. 19.

98 He made his obligation on 16 December 1363 (Hoberg, *Taxae*, 28; Cal. OS 36, fol. 92v); his four payments were concluded by 17 November or 16 December 1367 (Cal. OS 37, fols. 56v, 131v; Cal. OS 38A, fol. 75v; Cal. OS 38, fol. 49v; cf. IE 306, fol. 70v; IE 317, fol. 20v; IE 319, fol. 24; IE 325, fol. 5).

99 Cal. OS 23, fol. 135v; Cal. OS 27, fol. 60; Hoberg, *Taxae*, 23.

100 *Vat. Quel.*, VIII, 33; Cal. OS 38A, fol. 75v; Cal. OS 38, fol. 190v; Cal. OS 39, fols. 209, 298v.

But he is a somewhat exceptional case.[101] If few bishops met their obligations punctually, it was rare to be more than a year or two in arrears, although the Scottish bishops were probably rather slower in handing over their service taxes than their counterparts in northern England. It seems that there was a general readiness in Scotland to pay as soon as was practicable, although on occasions extensions of the term were sought and granted, and even Locrys appears to have faced no serious trouble on account of his dilatoriness.

No abbots or priors in the province of York paid services at this period; those who received papal provision were held liable for annates.[102] However, some Scottish abbots were liable for services following a provision, and obliged themselves for payment in the same way as bishops. Those involved were the abbots of Kilwinning in 1346,[103] Dunfermline in 1351,[104] Kelso in 1351 or 1352,[105] and Rushen on the Isle of Man in 1365.[106] Several other Scottish abbots obliged themselves for services in the fifteenth century, but the practice of providing regulars in Scotland was less widespread in the fourteenth, and some paid annates after confirmation of their election by the pope.

VISITATION TAX

All bishops who received consecration and abbots who received benediction at the hands of the pope were deemed to be obliged to visit Rome periodically, in person or by proctor. Only a few were bound to pay a designated sum on the occasion of each visit,[107] and the only English prelates who were regularly liable were the two archbishops and the abbot of St Augustine's, Canterbury. Like

[101] But cf. Canterbury, where Islip was the third archbishop to be provided in just over a year in 1348–9; his debt for services was still not fully paid when he died in 1366: Lunt, *Financial Relations . . . 1327–1534*, 218, 724–7.

[102] However, Durham Priory had promised 3000 florins in 1307 and 1325: Lunt, *Financial Relations . . . to 1327*, 679, 681. The abbot of Kirkstall obliged himself to pay $33\frac{1}{3}$ florins in 1419: Hoberg, *Taxae*, 154.

[103] Hoberg, *Taxae*, 154; Cal. OS 22, fol. 15. For the provision see Reg. Vat. 216, fols. 77v–78.

[104] Hoberg, *Taxae*, 216; but cf. Coll. 456, fol. 169 for a different date. For the provision see *CPL*, III, 423. He paid on 5 January 1353: *Vat. Quel.*, VIII, 34.

[105] Cal. OS 22, fol. 129v; Hoberg, *Taxae*, 226. A successor paid on 24 December 1353: *Vat. Quel.*, VIII, 34.

[106] Hoberg, *Taxae*, 162. For the provision in January 1364 see *Urbain V: lettres communes*, III, no. 12609.

[107] Lunt, *Financial Relations . . . to 1327*, 482–3.

common services, the revenue was divided equally between the pope and the College of cardinals.

The archbishop of York owed 300 marks at the rate of four florins to the mark every three years. He was often seriously in arrears, and efficiency of collection was not aided by the fact that the visitation tax was sometimes paid direct to the Camera and on other occasions was intended to be levied locally by the papal collector. Bernard de Sistre, collector from 1335 to 1343, reported that he had received nothing from the archbishop's visitation tax because payment was made at the papal court;[108] and Melton had in fact made payments direct to the Camera in respect of the years 1335 and 1338.[109] On 20 May 1343 Clement VI ordered Bernard to collect the tax from the archbishops of Canterbury, York and Armagh, but the collector died soon afterwards.[110] For York the years in arrears were stated to be 1317 and 1341, and in due course Zouche paid the 300 marks outstanding from 1317, for which he was discharged by Raymond Pelegrini on 6 June 1349.[111] It is not clear, however, whether Zouche made any other payments.[112] Certainly his successor Thoresby obliged himself to pay off Zouche's arrears as well as his own visitation tax, and terms were laid down in 1356.[113] His own payments thereafter were punctual, and he cleared Zouche's debts at least for 1341 and 1344.[114] There is no specific evidence relating to the sums due in 1347, 1350 and 1353, but it is likely that the arrears were paid. In 1359, when Thoresby's proctors paid the tax due in that year, they also paid 300 florins to the Camera as part of the sum due from the archbishop's predecessors;[115] and when proctors were appointed for the visitation of 1362 they were ordered to pay 600 florins for Zouche's arrears in addition to the sum owed in that year.[116] Further arrears were paid off in 1365 and 1368.[117] Thoresby was clearly more

108 Lunt, *Accounts*, 44.

109 *Vat. Quel.*, IV, 14–15, 38.

110 *CPL*, III, 1; Lunt, *Accounts*, xxix.

111 Reg. Zouche, fol. 269. This was probably the sum paid over to the Camera by Raymond Pelegrini on 11 January 1350: *Vat. Quel.*, V, 36.

112 Zouche apparently paid for 1344 on 19 December 1345, but Thoresby certainly paid for that year too (*Vat. Quel.*, V, 19; VII, 126). Proctors were appointed on 16 September 1348 to make a visitation (Reg. Zouche, fol. 269), but this may be connected with the payment for which Raymond Pelegrini gave an acquittance.

113 Reg. Thoresby, fol. 30v.

114 Ibid., fols. 308 (1341, 1344), 319v–320 (1356), 319v (1359), 320 (1362), 323 (1365), 325–325v (1368), 320v (1371).

115 *Vat. Quel.*, VII, 258.

116 Reg. Thoresby, fol. 303; cf. Burns, 'Sources', no. 177.

117 Burns, 'Sources', nos. 209, 230.

diligent than some of his predecessors in paying the triennial visitation tax, and was responsible for settling a number of ancient debts in addition to what he himself was bound to pay.

ANNATES

By far the most important single revenue collected locally in the later Avignon period, and the one which occupies the most space in the collectors' accounts, was annates. This was a tax on the revenues of the first year during which an incumbent held a benefice, and it was an extension of the practice in some areas whereby certain churchmen were entitled to receive such a payment. Earlier in the fourteenth century annates had been levied on several occasions on all benefices falling vacant within a specified period, but after 1342, when Clement VI issued a fresh bull reserving annates,[118] the only benefices affected were those filled by papal provision, those confirmed to their possessors by papal authority, and those appropriated to a religious house or corporation with papal blessing.[119] Provisions and annates were, therefore, two sides of the same coin. The extensive use of provisions meant that there were many liabilities for annates, and the levy of the tax made the practice of provision potentially very profitable. At a time of war and financial stringency such a link did not go unnoticed or unchallenged by the royal government or the English parliament. Although few provisions slipped through the net in the sense that the collectors did not learn about them, the actual collection of annates was difficult, and excuses and procrastinations were legion. It was easy to impose the tax, and reasonably easy to make the provisions which incurred obligations for it, but the task of collection stretched the machinery of the Camera and its agents to the limit.

At a basic level, the collector depended on information furnished by the officers of the Camera. There appear to have been two stages in the registration of provisions from which annates were due. Firstly, details were extracted from the records of the papal chancery and entered on to lists which were not organised geographically; secondly, this material was sorted and relevant

[118] YML, L2/1, pt. III, fol. 100v – pt. IV, fol. 2.

[119] On 19 May 1373 Gregory XI reserved the first fruits of all benefices vacant or falling vacant (*Grégoire XI: lettres secrètes et curiales (Fr)*, no. 2954), but this seems not to have been extended to England.

information despatched to the collectors at irregular intervals, usually of a few months' duration.[120] At least sometimes the collector or his staff further sorted the lists and arranged the obligations by diocese. Errors of transcription inevitably occurred and often caused the collectors much trouble, but checks of the cameral records were sometimes made and the collectors notified of any previously unknown obligations within their jurisdiction. The fact that annates were so lucrative made such enquiries worth while.

When the collector had received the register of obligations, he summoned the provisor through the agency of the bishops and had the fruits of his benefice sequestrated. When the debtor appeared, the amount due was established and he obliged himself to pay the agreed sum, usually in instalments at specified times. If the provisor had not yet received his benefice, his obligation was normally postponed. It was theoretically possible for the holder to hand over the income of his benefice to the collector and leave the latter to pay burdens incumbent on it and keep the remainder for annates, and although this was probably uncommon in England it may explain some apparent discrepancies in the amounts levied. If payments fell into arrears, the collector could order the bishop to sequestrate the delinquent's benefice until annates were paid, and could summon the debtor before him. If the debtor died, annates could be collected from his goods if they sufficed or from the benefice and his successors in it if they did not.[121]

It was never the intention to take all the revenues of the first year. Where a benefice had been assessed for the tenth, this was usually the amount taken, although it was open to the collector to leave the possessor with the assessed amount and take the remainder.[122] The assessed value was by now sufficiently nominal to leave enough for services to be maintained and for the possessor to support himself, even after the deduction of annates. If the benefice was not assessed, half the value by common estimation was usually exacted; and very poor benefices were, in theory at least, exempt.

In England, annates were usually levied on the basis of the last

[120] In total sixteen volumes of Collectorie contain lists of provisions: D. E. R. Watt, 'Sources for Scottish history of the fourteenth century in the archives of the Vatican', *SHR*, 32 (1953), 120. For the original lists see e.g. Coll. 281, 282, 286, 288, 290, 291, 294, all of which contain Scottish material. For the extracts sent to the collectors see e.g. *CPP*, I, 305–26; Coll. 287, fol. 77–77v.

[121] Lunt, *Financial Relations . . . 1327–1534*, 358–75.

[122] This was rarely even considered in England: ibid., 359.

valuation for the tenth, made in 1291–2, but, as with income taxes, problems arose from the existence of the later revision in the north. Lunt considers that the revised figure was taken for annates until the 1370s, when Arnald Garnerii began in some instances to levy the higher sum of the 1291 assessment,[123] but the reality is less clear-cut. Hugh Pelegrini and John de Cabrespino sometimes accepted the new taxation and sometimes demanded the old, although as time passed the higher figure came to be sought more frequently. There is, however, no pattern regulating the use of the old as opposed to the new taxation: Hugh Pelegrini accepted the new assessment of £6 13s 4d for a provision to the church of Slingsby in 1362 but had received £13 6s 8d for a provision in 1357.[124] Many benefices in Northumberland and parts of Cumberland had been assessed at nil in 1317–19, but the collectors usually asked for a specific sum from provisors to churches in these areas. Sometimes the old rate was demanded, as by Hugh Pelegrini from the vicars of Whittingham and Kirknewton;[125] on other occasions a wholly different rate appears to have been in operation. The church of Rothbury was taxed at £133 6s 8d by the old tax and at nil by the new, but John de Cabrespino reported a figure of £66 13s 4d and this was the figure accepted by Arnald Garnerii.[126] Hugh Pelegrini collected £42 13s 4d from a provisor to the vicarage of Bedlington, a benefice assessed at nil in 1317–19 and at only £12 14s 6d in 1291.[127] Even some benefices which were not reassessed paid a sum which differed from the 1291 figure. The collector received £26 13s 4d from the provision of John de Chestrefeld to the prebend of Grindale in York, even though the assessed value of this benefice was only £10.[128]

Some explanations for these inconsistencies can be suggested. The collectors kept a register of assessments, and in some cases may well have had only one figure for a particular benefice; this may have been especially so when the revised figure was nil. On other occasions they were unaware of any assessment, for they reported some benefices as untaxed which almost certainly had an assessed value. Sometimes they had a figure which did not tally with either the old or the new taxation or which referred to a benefice which

123 Ibid., 360. 124 Lunt, *Accounts*, 139, 138; *Taxatio*, 302, 324, 335.
125 Lunt, *Accounts*, 157; *Taxatio*, 316, 317.
126 *Taxatio*, 317, 331; Lunt, *Accounts*, 314, 373. It was said to be worth thirty marks in 1351: *CPL*, III, 364. 127 Lunt, *Accounts*, 90; *Taxatio*, 316, 331.
128 Lunt, *Accounts*, 89; *Taxatio*, 297, 322, 334.

had not in fact been assessed in 1291. Since the Camera's machinery of collection was not integrated with the king's, especially after the demise of taxes shared between king and pope, some discrepancies were inevitable. However, it is clear that sometimes the collectors were aware of both valuations, and they then had to make a decision whether to follow the relatively unexceptionable course of collecting the lower figure, or to risk opprobrium by seeking the 1291 amount. There were various factors at play: the economic condition of the benefice; the shadowy question of the estate and friends of the provisor; the likelihood or otherwise of objections being raised if the collector seemed to be too exacting; the feeling that any levy was better than none at all. The collectors were on the horns of a dilemma, desirous of raising as much as possible for the papal Camera, but also keen not to antagonise the king or some powerful magnate or to alienate the clergy by appearing grasping and inflexible.

However, it is clear that the general basis for the liability for annates in England was the 1291 assessment, with some account being taken of the later revisions in the north. For Scotland, evidence is much less copious, but it is clear that a different system of assessment for annates was in operation.

There is nothing surviving from Scotland which even approaches the comprehensiveness of the various copies of all or part of the 1291 valuation which were made in England. The corresponding assessment in Scotland, made by Bishop Halton of Carlisle, survives only for the archdeaconry of Lothian.[129] A rather wider geographical picture is provided by records of the sexennial crusading tenth imposed in 1274 and collected by Baiamundus de Vicia,[130] but some at least of the surviving evidence records merely what was received and does not in itself constitute evidence of the level of assessment. A few assessments dating from the middle of the thirteenth century survive for the dioceses of St Andrews, Brechin and Aberdeen,[131] and there is a

[129] *The Correspondence, Inventories, Account Rolls and Law Proceedings of the Priory of Coldingham*, ed. J. Raine (Surtees Soc., 1841), pp. cviii–cxvii.

[130] 'Bagimond's Roll for the archdeaconry of Teviotdale, from a thirteenth-century transcript in the Vatican archives', ed. A. I. Cameron, *Scottish History Soc. Miscellany*, 5 (1933), 79–106; 'Bagimond's Roll: statement of the tenths of the kingdom of Scotland', ed. A. I. Dunlop, ibid., 6 (1939), 3–77; 'Bagimond's Roll for the diocese of Moray', ed. C. Burns, ibid., 10 (1965), 3–9.

[131] *St Andrews Liber*, 28–39, 355–61; *Arbroath Liber*, I, 231–47; *Dunfermline Registrum*, 203–12; *Aberdeen Registrum*, II, 52–4.

similar valuation for Moray which may owe its origin to the thirteenth century or the fourteenth.[132] Few benefices appear in all these sources, although it is certain that the assessments of Baiamundus and Halton were substantially higher than the rates of the middle of the thirteenth century.[133]

Evidence from the account rendered by the collector William de Grenlaw in 1362, taken in conjunction with values expressed in papal bulls and in supplications to the pope, indicates that annates were collected in accordance with a fresh assessment. It resembled the rates of the middle of the thirteenth century more closely than it did the more recent taxations, and for some benefices was the same, but overall it was clearly no slavish return to the position before 1274. It perhaps originated from a bull of 1308, in which Clement V pointed out that the wars of Edward I had caused a great diminution in the revenues of Scottish ecclesiastics, and ordered that the collection of a contemporary tenth was to be carried out on the basis of the current value of benefices rather than of the figures in Halton's assessment.[134] A similar concession had been granted to the clergy of Carlisle diocese in 1302,[135] although this was soon superseded by the full reassessment of 1317–19.

It is unlikely that the reassessment in Scotland was made during the turbulent days of the Wars of Independence, but approval had been given by the Holy See for some reduction in the now excessive burden on the Scottish church. Who conducted the new valuation, and with what specific purpose in mind, is not known; nor is it clear whether every benefice was reassessed at the same time or at all. However, the assessment used by Grenlaw appears to have been considerably higher than might have been expected from the figure reported to the Scots parliament in 1366 as the 'true value' of the Scottish church.[136] The revised taxation was not, moreover, of long currency, for values expressed for benefices in late fourteenth-century and fifteenth-century sources are very variable.[137] For some benefices at least there appears to have been

132 *Moray Registrum*, 362–3.

133 I am grateful to Professor D. E. R. Watt for allowing me to consult his unpublished work on the dates and nature of these assessments.

134 *Vet. Mon.*, 178.

135 *Northern Registers*, 161–3; cf. 145.

136 *The Acts of the Parliaments of Scotland*, ed. T. Thomson and C. Innes (12 vols., Edinburgh, 1814–75), I, 499–500.

137 E.g. the vicarage of Montrose, said to be taxed at 10 merks in 1369 (*Urbain V: lettres communes*, VIII, no. 24024; *CPL*, IV, 76), was worth 20 merks according to a petition of 1423 (*CSSR*, II, 32), but as much as £40 in a supplication of 1419 (*CSSR*, I, 132); the

no fixed rate at all, or at least no widely recognised rate, in sharp contrast to the steady use of the 1291 Taxation of Pope Nicholas in England.

As has been stated, liability for annates after 1342 fell on those who received benefices by direct papal provision or were confirmed in possession by papal authority. Those who were surrogated into another's right to a disputed benefice were also liable, as were religious houses or corporations in respect of churches appropriated to them with papal involvement. Most regulars who were provided owed annates rather than services, and in 1365 Urban V decreed that this should always be so in the case of priors.[138]

Accepting a benefice as a result of an expectative grace did not incur any liability for annates until 1371, when Gregory XI declared that the tax should be paid when the provisor gained possession of a benefice; this reservation of annates was for three years only and did not extend to graces to poor clerks.[139] As a result a large number of expectancies appear in Arnald Garnerii's accounts pending the success which would incur a liability for annates. Graces of this type rarely feature in the accounts before this. An early example is the grant of a canonry, with expectation of a prebend or dignity, in Moray, made to William de Pilmor in August 1343. This was said to be ineffective,[140] and was probably noted by the Camera originally in error. A few expectancies appear, however, in the accounts with dates in 1369 or 1370. Although there is no documentary evidence for it, it is posssible that Urban V contemplated collecting annates from benefices received as the result of an expectative grace, thereby anticipating Gregory XI's move in 1371. The death of Urban probably invalidated these expectancies shortly after their issue, and no annates were paid on them.

Other entries appear in the lists sent by the Camera to the collectors which were not provisions of the normal type, and it seems that annates were demanded – or were envisaged – from these favours. Most were rehabilitations or dispensations, or the result of decisions which had resolved litigation over benefices, and

deanery of Dunkeld, which Grenlaw said was taxed at 120 merks (Coll. 14, fols. 182, 191v), was valued in the fifteenth century at £40 (Cameron, *Apostolic Camera*, 127), £50 (ibid., 191), £60 (ibid., 32, 132, 180) and £140 (*CSSR*, I, 185).

138 Lunt, *Papal Revenues*, II, 265.

139 Lunt, *Accounts*, 478–9; cf. xlix.

140 Coll. 14, fol. 158v.

so very similar to confirmations, for which annates were indubitably due. A more unusual example, although akin to an appropriation, was the confirmation by Urban V in 1363 of royal grants to the bishop, dean and chapter of Aberdeen of the second tenth of royal revenues between Dee and Spey;[141] it is not known whether annates were in fact paid in this instance.

Establishing liability is one thing; collecting a tax is quite another. A very few taxpayers bypassed the collector and paid direct to the Camera. Some cardinals adopted this course,[142] as did Richard de Derby, who was at Avignon prosecuting a lawsuit over the archdeaconry of Nottingham. He undertook on 12 March 1356 to pay £18 for the benefice, half at Christmas and half on 24 June 1357, and duly paid £17 on various dates in 1356.[143] Adam de Tyningham, dean of Aberdeen, paid 100 florins for his prebend there in 1374,[144] and the collector Grenlaw was used as proctor by Walter de Rol for the payment of 30 francs in annates for Tarbolton on 26 October 1372.[145] In addition, Guy de la Roche promised 60 florins for the Glasgow prebend of Stobo on 31 October 1358 or 1359,[146] and the collector was forbidden to levy annates in connection with his provision.[147]

Overwhelmingly, however, annates were paid to the collectors. It is extremely difficult to assess how quickly payment was made because of the long period covered by some of the accounts, but some certainly paid swiftly: Thomas de Roselay had handed over the £6 13s 4d due from his provision to the church of Slingsby on 7 March 1362 by 1 September 1363 at the latest, since Hugh Pelegrini closed his second account on that date;[148] John de Campeden, provided to the prebend of Dunham in Southwell on 20 January 1368, had paid £36 13s 4d in full by 1 November 1370.[149] Most, however, appear to have delayed for several years. The full amount of annates due from Henry de Walton's provision to the archdeaconry of Richmond in April 1349 was not received until 1366 at the earliest,[150] and many others were left in arrears in successive

[141] Ibid., fol. 169.

[142] Lunt, *Financial Relations ... 1327–1534*, 379–80 and note; cf. Lunt, *Accounts*, 511–12; Burns, 'Sources', nos. 174, 274; *Vat. Quel.*, VII, 418.

[143] Lunt, *Financial Relations ... 1327–1534*, 363, 380n; *Vat. Quel.*, VII, 138–9.

[144] IE 341, fol. 49v.

[145] Coll. 391, fol. 110v.

[146] Coll. 385, fol. 174; Coll. 387, fol. 81v; Cal. OS 23A, fol. 65.

[147] Coll. 14, fol. 182v.

[148] Lunt, *Accounts*, 139.

[149] Ibid., 320; for the provision see *Urbain V: lettres communes*, VII, no. 20966.

[150] *CPP*, I, 152; *CPL*, III, 290; Lunt, *Accounts*, 263.

accounts even though their provisions had been successful. The cardinals who held prebends of York were notoriously slow to pay, and the collectors found it difficult to proceed against such high-ranking debtors during their lifetime. It is probably true to say that most provisors were induced to pay eventually, but it required much effort and persistence on the collector's part. The tax was heavy, but service taxes were also, and they were paid with much greater despatch.

There is insufficient evidence in the province of York to evaluate the success of Arnald Garnerii in levying annates from successful expectative graces, although clearly some fruitful attempts were made to do so. On 28 January 1371 John Caldwell was granted a canonry of Southwell, with expectation of a prebend.[151] In due course he accepted the prebend of Rampton, taxed at £20, and was given terms by Garnerii to pay annates; he handed over £10 on 31 October 1377.[152] But in general it must have been far from easy to collect annates from expectancies without diligent investigation. Quite apart from the large number of graces which were never put into effect, the clerk with an expectancy could in theory receive any one of several benefices within the terms of his grant. Monitoring the situation was more complicated than in the case of a direct provision to a single named benefice.

Where the benefice in question was not assessed, or if the taxation rate could not be found, half the estimated annual income was taken for annates: for example, Peter Fercythe paid twelve merks for the vicarage of Ayr,[153] and William de Cammon £5 for the vicarage of Cliffe.[154] Many of these amounts were decided upon in a composition between the collector and the taxpayer, but the sum owed was sometimes established by local investigation, as when Grenlaw learnt from the bishop that the precentorship of Dunkeld was worth twenty merks.[155] The revenues of the archdeacons, which were liable for annates only in part, caused the collectors some problems; and on other occasions the collector came to arrangements which were probably rather generous. The prior of St Andrews and the abbot of Paisley agreed with Grenlaw to pay 100 merks each, yet in the fifteenth century St Andrews Priory was valued for annates at £1000, £1080 and £1200, and in 1419 Paisley Abbey was said to be worth 1000 merks.[156]

[151] Lunt, *Accounts*, 428. [152] Ibid., 515, 531. [153] Coll. 14, fols. 178v, 187v.

[154] Lunt, *Accounts*, 264. [155] Coll. 14, fols. 182v, 192.

[156] Ibid., fols. 179v, 180v, 186, 187v; Cameron, *Apostolic Camera*, 131, 159, 206, 308; *CSSR*, I, 61.

Details of taxpayers' formal obligations to pay, and the terms laid down, rarely survive. At the end of a lawsuit at the curia arrangements might be made for a binding acknowledgement of annates due. In the late 1350s John Marshall promised to pay 200 marks for the church of Rothbury,[157] and in August 1366 Michael de Monymusk bound himself to satisfy the collector for 55 merks in arrears from his provision to the deanery of Aberdeen; he had now lost possession, but it was decided that the grace had at one point borne fruit.[158] Similar obligations were presumably made in other cases, though normally to the collector, who entered them in a book.[159] Terms for payment were no doubt fixed at the same time, although details are rarely given in the accounts, and then normally in cases where the provisor had shown himself unwilling to pay promptly. John de Hayton, provided to the vicarage of Northallerton in 1371, swore on 29 November 1372 to pay £10 on the following 1 August and a further £10 a year later, pledging his vicarage and all his goods and benefices to the Camera, and placing himself under pain of excommunication in the event of default.[160] The prior of Cartmel, provided by Urban V on 7 March 1369, was given terms of the quinzaine of Easter and Michaelmas in 1377 and the following year by equal portions.[161] Some, such as William Bonde, prebendary of Monkton in Ripon, were ordered to pay the whole amount due in one lump sum.[162] The collectors may have included in their accounts details of arrangements made with debtors only when they deemed it necessary to emphasise to the Camera that action was indeed being taken; it is significant that most of the evidence is to be found in the reports of Arnald Garnerii, who seems to have been particularly eager to draw attention to his own diligence.

If it was easy to delay payment of annates even when they were due, it was even easier for the provisor to refuse if he had not yet received corporal possession of his benefice. Some men promised to pay in the event of the provision bearing fruit at a later date, but usually the collectors did not expect to levy annates from ineffective provisions and frequently gave failure of the grace as their excuse for inability to levy annates in a particular case. This was not the universal practice, however. On 20 January 1353 Edward III

[157] Coll. 387, fol. 81v. [158] Instr. Misc. 2453; cf. below, pp. 176–7.
[159] Lunt, *Accounts*, 201. [160] Ibid., 453.
[161] Ibid., 512; cf. 320, 358, 399 for the date.
[162] Ibid., 203. The year in question is probably 1365.

forbade Hugh Pelegrini to levy annates from benefices where the provision had not been effective,[163] so it looks as though the collector sometimes demanded – or was believed to demand – annates before possession, to the detriment of incumbents who had been presented by the local patron. A possible example is that of the cardinal Anibaldus Gaetani, who paid £30 to Raymond Pelegrini and £22 9s to his brother for the prebend of Wetwang in York which he may never have obtained; certainly the collector declared as much,[164] but the history of this benefice in the 1340s is extremely complicated and it is not impossible that Anibaldus was in possession for a time. A more worrying instance from the king's point of view also involved a stall in York Minster. On 7 December 1349 William de Savinhaco was provided to the prebend of Holme, and Hugh reported that annates amounting to £16 13s 4d were paid. However, commenting on an ineffective later provision to Ralph Daventre, the collector pointed out that Savinhaco never had possession and that John de Ferriby, who occupied the prebend at the same vacancy, 'voluntarily made satisfaction for that vacancy ... because of the reservation, even though he possessed it by another right'.[165] Thus it appears that Hugh Pelegrini considered that annates were a liability on the benefice if provision had been made to it, and it was this practice that the king was eager to stop, because if it were to be pushed to its logical conclusions, its implications would be serious indeed.[166]

After the royal prohibition it appears to have been accepted that annates were paid only when the provision bore fruit. When William Gunfort lost a lawsuit at the curia over one of the Norwell prebends in Southwell, he asked that the annates he had paid be credited towards his payment for another benefice,[167] but when he made his payment he had presumably thought that he had secure possession.

Liability for annates after a provisor's death was, in England at least and probably in Scotland too, usually attached to the benefice, which meant that a successor was sometimes held responsible. Matthew de Abborthkoc paid eighteen merks in respect of Walter Hundbit's confirmation in the church of Kinnettles,[168] and Henry,

163 *Foedera*, III, 250; *CCR 1349–54*, 457.
164 Lunt, *Accounts*, 80; cf. 101.
165 *CPL*, III, 343; Lunt, *Accounts*, 89, 117 (the quotation is from p. 117).
166 Cf. *CCR 1349–54*, 186 (Haughton-le-Skerne), 407–8 (Greatham), 560 (South Cave), where royal presentees were threatened by a levy of annates.
167 Lunt, *Accounts*, 527.
168 Coll. 14, fols. 178, 186.

vicar of Ellon, paid ten merks for the annates due from a provision to Alexander de Abyrcromby.[169] Both clerks were presumably successors of the respective provisors. Henry de Barton, prebendary of Osbaldwick in York, paid some of the annates left in arrears by one of his predecessors;[170] and after John Henry's provision to the vicarage of Crosthwaite a successor, Thomas de Eskiheved, paid £4 in annates, producing a royal letter testifying that this was the assessed value of the vicarage.[171] The collectors erroneously believed that Henry had been provided to the rectory and continued to press for more, although without success; Arnald Garnerii eventually acknowledged that the rectory was appropriated to Fountains Abbey.[172]

Occasionally the executors of the deceased were called upon to pay, although this usually applied only to the benefices of cardinals. Arnald Garnerii recommended proceedings against the executors of Talleyrand de Périgord for the annates of the prebend of Strensall and those of Stephen Albert for the archdeaconry of York and prebend of Wistow, but was unable to do anything himself. He also suggested that the Camera should proceed against the executors of William de Aigrefeuille for the annates due from his provision to the prebend of Masham, since the farmer John de Stoke claimed to have handed over all monies collected in his time.[173]

Garnerii took action against the farmers of some benefices held by cardinals, although he appears to have had little success. William Snokere, farmer of the prebend of Strensall for the current prebendary, was warned in connection with the annates left unpaid by Talleyrand. The collector proceeded against the executors of the farmer of Wistow and the archdeaconry of York, but one of them swore that the fruits had been received by others. The farmer of the prebend of Driffield was warned about annates due from a provision to Hugh de St Martial, but some of the tax had been paid directly to the Camera. He made a fresh attempt against the farmers of Masham in connection with Aigrefeuille's provision.[174] All these arrears were still outstanding when Garnerii left England in 1378, and since the provisions had all been made by 1363 it is unlikely that the Camera ever received much in annates from them. Cardinals were powerful enough to ignore collectors, and because in many benefices one member of the College was

[169] Ibid., fols. 179v, 190. [170] Lunt, *Accounts*, 138–9. [171] Ibid., 182.
[172] Ibid., 373. [173] Ibid., 371, 377. [174] Ibid., 511–12.

succeeded by another it was difficult to proceed against the next incumbent. The farmers were often shadowy figures who moved on after their cardinal died, and even if the full truth about them could be ascertained they could be proceeded against by sequestration only if they themselves held a benefice which could be seized.

Very occasionally someone other than the provisor's successor or executors was held liable for annates. William Strode was provided to the church of Brantingham on 17 August 1361 and was given terms of 24 February 1364, Easter and Michaelmas, to which he bound himself under pain of excommunication. John de Cabrespino added the comment that a Florentine merchant living in London was obliged for the first two terms.[175] The same William Strode was obliged to pay 40s when Richard de Wylyngton obtained peaceful possession of the church of Stanhope, over which he was litigating.[176] It is not clear whether these arrangements are connected, or why Strode was responsible for Wylyngton's annates, but it does show that it was possible for the payment of annates to become entangled in other financial deals.

Many reasons besides ineffectiveness of the provision were alleged to justify non-payment of annates. The tax was due only once if two provisions were made to the same benefice within a year. This rule was often cited in the 1360s in cases where provisors were apparently given more than one bull within a short period of time; and it was also used when more than one provision was made at the same vacancy, such as at Hutton Bushel in 1363.[177] In such instances, however, at least one of the grants would inevitably fail in any event. There are very few examples where provisions were made at two separate vacancies within a twelve-month period. The precentorship of Moray was given to John de Fieschi on 18 July 1348 and to John de Rate on 3 March 1349.[178] John Parker's provision to the vicarage of Gilling on 23 April 1361 was less than a year after a provision to John de Beck on 24 August 1360,[179] although in the latter instance possession of the vicarage was apparently disputed.[180] In these cases the collectors accepted that only one set of annates was due.

A very common reason for non-payment of annates was that the king intervened to prevent any levy. Evidence for this in Scotland

175 Ibid., 203.
176 Ibid., 205.
177 Ibid., 204, 221.
178 Coll. 14, fols. 161, 181v, 189.
179 Lunt, *Accounts*, 203, 238, 371.
180 *CPP*, I, 368

is exiguous; although it is known that a royal letter forbade collection of annates from the church of Turriff, to which John de Cromdole had been provided in 1345 on the grounds that the lay patron had given the church to a minor,[181] it is unclear whether this was an exceptional case. In England, where the crown was stronger and the government not impaired by the long-term absence of the king, there are numerous instances where royal intervention interrupted attempts to collect annates from a particular benefice. Some prohibitions were intended to stop proceedings in connection with provisions which had in fact failed; most seem to have been issued to protect royal presentees who had either ousted or succeeded a provisor. The king would not allow annates to be levied as a result of Richard de Wylyngton's confirmation in the church of Stanhope because this would have harmed an incumbent who held the church by royal authority.[182] A similar prohibition was issued in favour of a royal nominee in the chapel of Jesmond.[183] Henry de Ingelby, who held his prebend in Southwell by both royal grant and papal confirmation, formally renounced the papal grace before a public notary, and so avoided paying annates.[184] The levy of annates from John Marshall, rector of Rothbury, was prohibited on the grounds that Marshall was indebted to the king, but a sentence of excommunication ultimately induced him to pay £36 13s 4d on 6 June 1374, over ten years after his provision.[185] This, however, is a very unusual case. Collectors like Arnald Garnerii could complain all they liked, but most provisors would take shelter beneath a royal prohibition; and a successor who had the good fortune to be the king's man seems to have been immune, in practice at least, from proceedings to recover arrears of annates from his benefice.

In prohibiting the levy of annates in certain cases, the king was upholding his rights and those of his clerks; but there was never any attempt on the part of the government to interfere with collection where no royal rights were infringed. Nor was there ever a concerted attempt to prevent the levy of annates from churches in lay patronage in the few cases where they were subject to provision. Arnald Garnerii accepted that lay patronage prevented the levy of annates after John de Thresk's confirmation in the priory of Newbrough,[186] but the tax was collected from Ald-

181 Coll. 14, fol. 160. 182 Lunt, *Accounts*, 277, 332. 183 Ibid., 333.
184 Ibid., 117. 185 Ibid., 373. 186 Ibid., 514.

ingham in Furness,[187] Catton,[188] Ilkley,[189] Romaldkirk[190] and Bowness.[191] Before the Great Schism annates were clearly due from provisions to English benefices in lay patronage,[192] because once a provision had borne fruit annates were due irrespective of who was the local patron, and the pope's right to make a grant in the first place was based on the manner in which the benefice had fallen vacant rather than on its patronage. It may have been dangerous for the collector if the church was in the gift of a layman, but the Camera was insistent that a levy must be made, and told Arnald Garnerii that he could not use lay patronage as an excuse for failure to collect annates.[193] In papal eyes, if the benefice was in one of the reserved categories at a particular vacancy, its patronage was irrelevant.[194]

Taxpayers sometimes attempted to escape payment by alleging that their benefice was worthless. This was always the excuse given for non-payment of annates from the prebend of Byers Green in Auckland.[195] The Galloway churches of Rerrick and Kirkmabreck, appropriated to the abbey of Dundrennan, yielded no annates because of destruction.[196] Even the collector Grenlaw himself claimed that his prebend in Moray was destroyed and largely worthless.[197] Not all stories of hardship due to war, plague or other calamities need be taken at face value, but the provisor who could plausibly allege poverty bought himself a delay; the facts would have to be checked, which might be a long and cumbersome process, and at the end his liability would be no greater than it had been before.

In England, archdeacons claimed certain exemptions from annates. Arnald Garnerii, whose desire for conformity caused him to dislike their privileges, complained to the Camera about the archdeacons' failure to pay annates on procurations or the profits of

187 Ibid., 415. For the patronage see *CPR 1367–70*, 285; Thompson, 'Richmond registers', 155.

188 Lunt, *Accounts*, 131. For the patronage see VCH, *A History of Yorkshire East Riding*, ed. K. J. Allison (6 vols. to date, London, 1969–), III, 155; Smith, 'Vicars-general register', no. 163; Reg. Zouche, fol. 183v; Reg. Thoresby, fol. 219v; *CPP*, I, 293.

189 Lunt, *Accounts*, 318; Reg. Thoresby, fol. 122. The advowson was disputed at this time.

190 Lunt, *Accounts*, 138. For the patronage see Thompson, 'Richmond registers', 150–1, 173.

191 Lunt, *Accounts*, 139. For the patronage see Reg. Kirkby, fol. 236v; Reg. Welton, p. 6.

192 Cf. Samaran and Mollat, *La fiscalité pontificale*, 33.

193 Lunt, *Accounts*, 477, 484.

194 However, in the 1390s it was stated, in an annotation, that benefices in lay patronage were not to pay annates: Lunt, *Papal Revenues*, II, 369.

195 Lunt, *Accounts*, 282, 335, 340, 375, 380, 516.

196 Coll. 14, fols. 182, 192v.

197 Ibid., fols. 182, 189.

jurisdiction, revenues which constituted a major part of their overall income. The Camera took the side of the archdeacons and told Garnerii to levy annates only on other sources of revenue.[198] In practice this meant churches annexed to the archdeaconries, but even this interpretation was open to challenge, with the result that archdeacons, like royal clerks and those alleging poverty, had a convenient excuse to delay payment.

For all these delays and difficulties in collection, the yield from annates was substantial. In the period 1349–78 over half the total income received by the collectors in England came from annates, and at times three-quarters or more.[199] The great majority of Grenlaw's recorded receipts came from annates. The pattern of yield in Scotland and the province of York is as follows.

In the period before he rendered his extant acccount in 1362, Grenlaw received around 600 merks from annates, and probably more because there is reason to suppose that details of some receipts have perished.[200] Grenlaw was appointed collector on 30 December 1352,[201] and so his average annual receipt from annates can be put at something over £40. There are some notes in his account concerning annates paid to his predecessor and a few later stray references to Scottish annates, but no totals can be estimated for annates in isolation from other revenues.

The English collectorate was much bigger and much wealthier. Evidence is more abundant than for Scotland, but even if allowances are made for the shortcomings of the Scottish material it is clear that the average annual yield from annates in the relatively impoverished province of York alone was well in excess of that from the whole of Scotland.

In his first account, covering the period from 1 August 1349 and finishing on 1 June 1358, Hugh Pelegrini received a total of £330 2s 4d from seven benefices in the diocese of York left in arrears by his brother Raymond; all were wealthy benefices, especially the church of Hemingbrough (£106 13s 4d) and the prebend of Driffield (£100). From provisions made during his own period as collector he received a further £452 12s 4d from twenty-four provisions. In Durham diocese he obtained £53 from two benefices left in arrears by Raymond and £57 from three benefices to which provisions were made in his own time. He also received £5 from the church of Caldbeck in the diocese of Carlisle. Hugh's total

198 Lunt, *Accounts*, 477, 483.

199 Lunt, *Financial Relations ... 1327–1534*, 379.

200 Barrell, 'William de Grenlaw', 4–5.

201 *Vet. Mon.*, 300; *CPL*, III, 611.

yield from annates in the province of York during the period of his first account was thus £897 14s 8d, an annual average of a little over £100.

In his second account, from 1 June 1358 to 1 September 1363, the exact yield is uncertain because the archdeacon of Richmond, who paid in part, did so in conjunction with other benefices held in plurality, and how much he paid for Richmond in isolation is unclear. Omitting this uncertain figure, Hugh collected £261 3s 4d from twelve benefices in the diocese of York and £17 13s 4d from three in the diocese of Durham left in arrears in his first account, and a further £431 from thirty provisions in York, £6 from a prebend of Norton in Durham diocese, and £4 from the church of Bowness in the diocese of Carlisle from provisions made since 1358. His total of £719 16s 8d gives an annual average of around £137, but the yield from Durham had declined sharply and he left eighteen benefices in that diocese totally in arrears.

John de Cabrespino's first account covers the short period from 1 September 1363 to probably 31 March 1364, a very lucrative few months for the collector. Excluding a part-payment for the subdeanery of York and the prebend of Rampton in Southwell, held by the pluralist William de Retford, he received £224 from twenty-four benefices in York diocese, £23 from two benefices in Durham diocese, and £4 from Crosthwaite in Carlisle, all left in arrears by Hugh Pelegrini. His receipts of £251 give an extrapolated annual rate of £430 from the province of York alone. In his analysis of the whole of England, Lunt similarly found that much was collected in the period of Cabrespino's first account.

Cabrespino's success did not last. His second account, rendered on 20 May 1366, is again affected by uncertainty regarding the archdeaconry of Richmond, the subdeanery of York and the prebend of Rampton. Omitting these uncertain figures, he received £80 6s 8d from eleven provisions in York diocese and £39 13s 4d from four in Durham diocese which he had left in arrears in his first account, and £36 from grants to five benefices in the diocese of York made since 6 March 1364. He received nothing from Carlisle, and his average annual yield from the northern province was under £70.

The low yield continued into the period of Cabrespino's third account, which was closed on 18 February 1368. He left no fewer than eighty-seven provisors in the province of York totally in arrears, and received £121 6s 8d from eight benefices in York diocese and £17 13s 4d from three in Durham diocese, an annual average yield of under £80.

The receipts show a marked improvement in the period from 18 February 1368 to 1 November 1370, when Cabrespino closed his final account. However, this was partly because the benefices from which annates were levied were rather wealthier than normal. Well over a hundred benefices were left in arrears. The sum of £405 13s 4d was received from the diocese of York, but only fifteen provisors were involved: the prebendary of Wistow paid £78 3s 4d, the prebendary of Laughton £73 6s 8d, and the prior of Lancaster £70. Cabrespino additionally received £44 16s 8d from five benefices in Durham diocese but yet again nothing from Carlisle. His annual average for annates in the province of York was about £166.

The reports of Arnald Garnerii show him to be the most exacting collector of the period; he was able to pursue arrears of annates from many of the provisions of the 1360s which had not proved ineffective. In his first account he received a total of £742 19s 6d, excluding a prebend of Beverley held in plurality, from annates in the province of York, and much of this revenue derived from provisions made before his appointment. For the period to 27 July 1374 Garnerii thus received nearly £200 per annum from annates in the north. Less was received in the period of his second account, but only around fifty benefices were left totally in arrears, a reflection on his success in levying annates.

Comparison of average annual yields has limited value because of variations in the number of provisions made and in the value of the benefices affected. But it is clear that John de Cabrespino's collectorship was less productive in northern England than those of his predecessor and successor, and Lunt finds much the same trend for England as a whole.[202] After 1364 most of the work of collection was carried out by a deputy, John de Caroloco, and this may have had some effect on the receipts. Certainly there was an unusually high degree of inefficiency, particularly in regard to not removing from the lists of obligations provisions which had borne no fruit, and this may have extended to a rather casual attitude towards the actual task of collection. While it is true that there was some parliamentary and governmental opposition to papal exactions in the mid-1360s and that papal funds in the hands of the

[202] Lunt, *Financial Relations . . . 1327–1534*, 379.

collector were impounded by the crown,[203] this anti-papal activity was not of long duration and it had little effect on the success of provisions. There was no war with France between 1360 and 1369, nor was border warfare more prevalent than usual. One is forced to conclude that John de Cabrespino and his deputy were not as diligent in demanding annates as they might have been.

Arnald Garnerii was undoubtedly the most officious collector of the period; his tactless enthusiasm for upholding the Camera's rights created antagonisms and on occasion was counter-productive. More than any of his predecessors, he wanted to justify himself to his masters in Avignon. His first account, rendered in 1374, contains a list of excuses for the paucity of his receipts from England, along with the Camera's responses.[204] He blamed royal interference, reluctance to pay by cardinals and their proctors, the exemptions of archdeacons, ineffective provisions, and the use of the new taxation in northern England; in short, he summarised the difficulties of collection. The Camera counselled diligence and discretion, but a path so hedged around by custom and actual or supposed privileges was very difficult for the collector to follow.

Annates were undoubtedly difficult to collect, especially if taxpayers were inclined to be recalcitrant or had powerful backers. But how efficient was the administrative machinery, and how much was the method of collection to blame for the success of provisors' delaying tactics?

Considering the size and geographical scope of the papal bureaucracy, surprisingly few provisions fell through the net. A provisor was certainly very fortunate if he escaped the attentions of collectors indefinitely. However, the lists sent to collectors by the Camera were often liberally sprinkled with errors which inevitably took time to come to light and be corrected. Some entries were incomplete. Others referred to dioceses outside the collectorate of the recipient: Grenlaw received one relating to the provostship of Linköping in Sweden,[205] and some provisions to churches in continental Europe appear also in the English accounts. There was considerable confusion between Ross in Scotland, Ross in Ireland, and Rochester, and details of several provisions were sent to the wrong collector as a result. Sometimes an incorrect diocese was given; on other occasions the place-name had become hope-

[203] Ibid., 349; cf. 10–11; Lunt, *Accounts*, 225. See below, pp. 146–52 for discussion of opposition to the Papacy during the pontificate of Urban V.

[204] Lunt, *Accounts*, 477, 483–4.

[205] Coll. 14, fol. 172v.

lessly corrupted. Some names of provisors were omitted;[206] sometimes a man was left in arrears when he had in fact paid, such as Richard de Welles, who had paid Raymond Pelegrini for his provision to the church of Slingsby but appeared in Hugh Pelegrini's lists of obligations too.[207] A certain degree of error was inevitable, but it was compounded when collectors refused to take bishops' comments seriously and continued to pester them in connection with provisions which did not involve the diocese in question or which had irrevocably failed.

The mechanism for collecting annates is difficult to reconstruct in detail from surviving evidence. It is, however, clear that sequestration was used at two stages of the procedure. Firstly, the fruits of a benefice reserved to the Holy See which had fallen vacant were seized until the provisor obliged himself to pay annates. Secondly, sequestration was used to impose pressure on a debtor who had fallen behind with his payments or shown himself to be disinclined to obey the collector's mandates.

Considering the number of provisions and the very high level of arrears, the volume of surviving information about sequestration is disappointingly small. The collectors seem normally to have acted through the agency of the bishops, although the chapter of York dealt with business relating to its cathedral prebends. Clearly, sequestration of benefices reserved to the pope was normal practice, or at least sufficiently likely for the chapter of York to write to Raymond Pelegrini in January 1349 to inform him of the vacancy of the prebend of Driffield and ask if its fruits fell under a papal reservation.[208] In July 1370 John de Caroloco, deputy of John de Cabrespino, told the rector of Settrington to sequestrate the recently vacant prebend of Ampleforth and deliver the revenues to him by 18 October; sixty marks was said to be owed for annates.[209] It is not clear in what capacity the rector, John de Stoke, acted, although the collector seems to have dealt with him directly rather than via the chapter or archbishop. Nor is it apparent whether he was expected to levy annates independently of the new prebendary Roger de Freton, who had been provided on 1 May 1370,[210] or, as is more likely, merely to seize the fruits and have them delivered to Caroloco pending terms being set for Freton to meet his obligations. This prebend was clearly recently vacant, but in some

[206] E.g. ibid., fol. 161 (deanery of Aberdeen); Lunt, *Accounts*, 204 (prebend of Norwell in Southwell). [207] Lunt, *Accounts*, 115–16. [208] YML, H1/1, fol. 59v.
[209] YML, H1/3, fols. 94–95. [210] *Urbain V: lettres communes*, IX, no. 27533.

other instances it is uncertain at exactly what stage the collector ordered sequestration. In early 1345 Raymond Pelegrini ordered the seizure of the fruits of the York prebend of South Cave, and on 3 November 1346 the vicar of South Cave and Otley was ordered to sequestrate the benefice on Raymond's authority and respond about annates.[211] The length of time between these events strongly suggests that the matter was not entirely straightforward, and indeed after the death of Napoleon Orsini in March 1342[212] a dispute had arisen between Robert de Kildesby and Paul de Monte Florum.[213] Both originally had royal title, and it was not until 5 June 1345 that Monte Florum received provision.[214] However, the fact that Orsini was a cardinal should have rendered the benefice liable for provision, and Raymond may have imposed sequestration with this in mind. Raymond also ordered the seizure of the much-disputed prebend of Wetwang so that annates could be levied, and in December 1346 the York chapter commissioned the vicars of Wetwang and Fridaythorpe to execute this mandate.[215] Initial sequestration was probably lifted when the provisor made his obligation, and annates do not seem to have been levied during the seizure. It was only if he fell into arrears that his benefice was taken back into the hands of the Holy See.

There are many references to sequestrations in cases of slow payment, although very little detail is available and few mandates survive. The collector wrote to the bishop (or, in the case of peculiars, presumably the chapter or other administering body) to order him to enforce payment of annates, imposing sequestration if necessary provided that divine services were not damaged. A copy of one of the collector's letters is written in the register of Bishop Hatfield of Durham. It is sufficiently similar to the relevant part of John de Cabrespino's first account to indicate that it was based on information extracted from the collector's records. The mandate is dated 13 October 1363, and on 25 October the vicar-general and sequestrator-general were told to collect the sums due, use sequestration and keep the bishop informed. According to Hatfield, the benefices in question were all sequestrated.[216]

A series of such mandates is to be found in the register of Bishop

211 YML, H1/1, fols. 1v, 28v.

212 Le Neve, *Fasti*, VI, 42.

213 Reg. Zouche, fol. 242.

214 *CPL*, III, 199; cf. *CPR 1340–43*, 395–6, 410, 428, 503, 531. Although his royal grants were revoked, Kildesby was admitted locally in April 1342 (Reg. 5A, fol. 97), and he ultimately won the case at the curia (Lunt, *Accounts*, 116).

215 YML, H1/1, fol. 30v.

216 Reg. Hatfield, fol. 44–44v; cf. Lunt, *Accounts*, 204–6.

Appleby of Carlisle. On 12 October 1363 Cabrespino told the bishop that the fruits of all benefices in debt to the Holy See could be seized and taxes collected on the basis of the assessed value or, in the case of untaxed benefices, of half the true value.[217] On 20 February 1364 the collector wrote to Appleby asking for information about the provision of Robert Kerrot to the church of Musgrave in 1357, which Richard Upton had claimed was ineffective; he had already sequestrated the fruits of the church.[218] A few days later he sent another mandate, this time on the vexed question of Crosthwaite.[219] No further mandates from Cabrespino to the bishop of Carlisle are recorded; and although this does not necessarily mean that none were sent, their absence from a register which otherwise has an unusually high number of them is suggestive, especially in the light of Cabrespino's general ineffectiveness. After Cabrespino's replacement by Arnald Garnerii, John de Caroloco continued to act on the Camera's behalf. On 14 June 1371 he ordered Appleby to sequestrate the church and vicarage of Crosthwaite and the churches of Wigton, Bowness and Kirkland. The bishop replied by stating that the rectories of Crosthwaite and Wigton were appropriated to Fountains and Holm Cultram respectively; he named the vicar of Crosthwaite and the rectors of Kirkland and Bowness, although the rector of Bowness was not resident in his diocese and could not be apprehended.[220] Garnerii again ordered the sequestration of Kirkland in February and April 1372, calling upon the bishop to investigate the claim by John de Langholme that he had held the church for twenty years without provision. In his reply, Appleby said that he had assembled a jury which had reported that Langholme had been instituted by ordinary authority and inducted by the archdeacon on 14 September 1350.[221]

The effectiveness of sequestration can be doubted. Despite apparent instructions to that effect in some mandates, there is no

217 Reg. Appleby, p. 159. In his first account, John de Cabrespino claimed 12s for the expenses of a messenger sent to the bishops of Coventry and Lichfield and Carlisle with processes against debtors: Lunt, *Accounts*, 184, dated 31 October.

218 Reg. Appleby, pp. 158–9.

219 See above, p. 43. The bishop replied that John Henry's supposed provision to the rectory had borne no fruit: Reg. Appleby, p. 161.

220 Reg. Appleby, pp. 229–30.

221 Ibid., pp. 248–9, 250, 251. The demand for annates from Kirkland was affected by an error in the name of the provisor in the collectors' records: see A. D. M. Barrell, 'Papal relations with Scotland and northern England, 1342–70', Ph.D thesis, University of St Andrews (1989), 69.

evidence that the amount due for annates was ever collected either during the initial seizure of the fruits or when the benefice was sequestrated on account of dilatoriness in payment; presumably the revenues were simply held by the bishop's agent or by the collector or one of his representatives, pending the swearing of an obligation or evidence of willingness on the part of the provisor to pay annates. Sometimes a sequestration had to be lifted because the provision had failed. When the archbishop of York tried to seize the fruits of the prebend in Howden granted to Richard de Drax, he discovered that the provisor had never obtained possession, and the order was withdrawn.[222] Also lifted was the sequestration placed on the church of Keyingham, imposed after the provision to Robert de Brompton. The church was in fact appropriated to Meaux Abbey, which procured the removal of the sequestration.[223] Even where the seizure was justified, it could be violated, as several Scottish examples demonstrate. John de Stallys, canon of Holyrood, occupied the vicarage of Falkirk by force and took the sequestrated fruits.[224] David de Mar ignored the sequestration of the prebend of Oyne in Aberdeen despite being excommunicated,[225] and both excommunication and interdict were used against Henry de Smalham, archdeacon of Teviotdale, in an attempt to induce him to pay.[226] The large number of sequestrations that it was necessary to impose is testimony to the slowness with which annates were paid, and the failure of the sanction to prevail upon the defaulter to pay swiftly hints at its ineffectiveness.

From a mass of material on annates it is obvious that this was the most difficult papal tax to collect in the middle of the fourteenth century. Quite apart from the natural reluctance of clerks to pay this tax, there were several factors which made collecting annates a slow process. Basically, the problem was to establish whether the provision was effective, and this was often surprisingly difficult. The bishop seems to have borne the brunt of the work of enquiry,

222 Lunt, *Accounts*, 204.

223 *Chron. Melsa*, III, 124–6. Cf. a mandate from Arnald Garnerii to the bishop of Coventry and Lichfield asking him to investigate whether the chapel of Clitheroe, to which a number of provisions had been made, was indeed appropriated to Whalley Abbey as the monastery claimed: *The Coucher Book or Chartulary of Whalley Abbey*, ed. W. A. Hulton (4 vols., Chetham Soc., 1847–9), IV, 1172.

224 Coll. 14, fols. 181v, 186v–187. The collector had apparently imposed this sequestration himself.

225 Ibid., fol. 182–182v; cf. fol. 190. Grenlaw was authorised to use excommunication to enforce payment in a bull dated 30 April 1358: Reg. Vat. 243, fol. 119v.

226 Coll. 14, fols.. 182v, 188.

and he must have been irritated by repeated demands to investigate provisions which he had reported as ineffective or which affected benefices outside his diocese. Although definite errors were fairly uncommon, many ineffective provisions could have been deleted from the registers of obligations much sooner than they were, and the time and effort expended in pursuing such graces could have been spent in actively seeking annates from those who were in fact liable to pay. Payment was often made years after the provision, and presumably long after the original terms had elapsed, and could be delayed still further if royal writs of prohibition could be obtained, if the provisor was powerful, or if he could allege that the benefice was worthless; in the north of England, the existence of two assessments, and efforts by Arnald Garnerii in particular to collect annates at the 1291 rate even when the lower sum had already been paid, offered a particular excuse to procrastinate. Sanctions such as sequestration and excommunication had little immediate effect. Annates constituted the most important source of locally collected papal revenue after 1342, but the tax was hard to levy because, unlike Peter's Pence or census, it affected a relatively large number of taxpayers, and, unlike a tenth, it did not fall on virtually every benefice. Rather, it fell on a large number of often obscure clerks in connection with a provision to a particular benefice; even if both the clerk and the benefice could be traced, problems arose if the provisor had moved on, because annates fell on his successor only if the provision had borne fruit, which was sometimes unclear and could certainly often be denied. The amount of investigation necessary to establish whether annates were in reality due took long enough to encourage those who were liable to raise difficulties in the hope of delaying payment almost indefinitely or avoiding it altogether.

INTERCALARY FRUITS

John XXII and Benedict XII reserved for the Camera the intercalary fruits of certain benefices, these being the revenues during a vacancy. In the first half of the fourteenth century this tax was usually collected by special commissioners, often those collecting the spoils of the late incumbent. Later, intercalary fruits were levied by the general collectors, but they in turn usually appointed special administrators who collected revenues, paid the expenses of the benefice and the debts of the deceased incumbent, and delivered the surplus to the collector or the Camera.[227] Clement VI did not levy intercalary fruits,[228] and although the tax was reimposed by Innocent VI and used by Urban V and Gregory XI it was extended to England only in a few special cases.[229] The tax was always liable to provoke allegations that the Papacy was deliberately leaving benefices vacant for long periods, and the degree of anti-papal activity in the English parliament from 1343 onwards perhaps partly explains the sparing application of this tax in England.

In the northern province, the only benefices which were affected by the levy of intercalary fruits in the period under review were the deanery of York and the prebends of Strensall and Masham. In his first account, rendered in early 1364, John de Cabrespino acknowledged receipt of £45 11s 6d for the reserved fruits of the prebend of Masham, which had been held by the cardinal Audoin Aubert.[230] The other two benefices were both vacant through the death of Talleyrand de Périgord on 17 January 1364, although the years of the vacancy were reckoned from 23 February 1364 and it was apparently not until March 1365 that Cabrespino was told to levy intercalary fruits from Talleyrand's benefices.[231] The York chapter came to an agreement with John de Caroloco and paid a total of £460 in the second half of 1365 for the fruits during the vacancy of these two benefices.[232] By the time that Cabrespino rendered his second account on 20 May 1366 a further £200 had been collected in part-payment for the second year of the deanery's vacancy.[233] On 5 October 1366 Caroloco issued an acquittance to the chapter for a further £200, which completed payment for the second year.[234] In his third account, rendered on 18 February 1368, Cabrespino acknowledged receipt of £75 10s for the second year of the vacancy of the prebend of Strensall and £33 6s 8d in part-payment for the farm of the third year, despite a provision to Elias de St Irieux on 3 January 1365. It seems that the Camera gave the cardinal 600 florins in return for the right to levy the revenues of this prebend, and a further £66 13s 4d was received from the farmers for two terms in 1366 and 1367. The collector also received £100 for the prebends of Masham and Strensall, which included £40 received by the chapter from Talleyrand's farmers. The

227 Lunt, *Papal Revenues*, I, 99–101.
228 Cf. YML, L2/1, pt. IV, fol. 1v.
229 Lunt, *Accounts*, l.
230 Ibid., 183.
231 *Urbain V: lettres secrètes et curiales*, no. 1645.
232 YML, H1/3, fols. 77v–78; cf. Lunt, *Accounts*, 224.
233 Lunt, *Accounts*, 224.
234 YML, H1/3, fol. 81v.

chapter also paid £105 for the third and final year of the vacancy of the deanery; £420 was owed in all, but the remainder was adjudged to be the responsibility of the new dean Angelicus Grimaud.[235]

The total income from this source was thus £1286 1s 6d. This can be compared with the £996 10s which John de Cabrespino received in annates from the province of York in the whole of his collectorship. Intercalary fruits may have been levied in England only rarely, but they could be a lucrative source of revenue for the Camera. The three benefices were wealthy, especially the deanery and Masham, and relatively little investigation was required; moreover, these intercalary fruits were gathered much more promptly than most annates were.

The Scottish collector's accounts for the pontificate of Urban V do not survive, and so it is impossible to say whether there were any levies in Scotland to compare with those in York. On 9 January 1366 William de Grenlaw promised to pay 60 florins in respect of the vacancy of the prebend of Stobo in Glasgow, to which he had been provided; the sum was to be paid at All Saints in two successive years,[236] and on 31 July 1366 it was declared that he was not to be molested in this connection.[237] In the event, he did not pay until 1 October 1372.[238] This payment has come to light only because it was made directly at the curia; the tax may possibly on other occasions have been collected locally, but the yield from the poorer Scottish church would not have been on the scale received from York, and it is unlikely that intercalary fruits were levied in Scotland after 1342 on more than an occasional basis.

FRUITS WRONGFULLY RECEIVED

In certain cases the Holy See demanded payment of fruits wrongfully received, namely the revenues received by clerks during a period when they had a less than canonical title to a benefice. Monies levied were usually earmarked for crusading purposes. Many men who were granted confirmation in their livings by the pope on the grounds that they had obtained them in an irregular fashion should have been liable to hand over the fruits illicitly

[235] Lunt, *Accounts*, 264; cf. Burns, 'Sources', no. 203. In his third account John de Cabrespino claimed expenses of 6s 6d for a messenger taking a letter to the York chapter in respect of the arrears from Masham and Strensall: Lunt, *Accounts*, 266.

[236] Cal. OS 23A, fol. 91v. [237] Coll. 353, fol. 74. [238] Coll. 465, fol. 65.

received, but there are few records of payment, and it must be assumed that the tax was usually either remitted or tacitly ignored.

Only a few instances survive where fruits are specifically remitted. Usually these involve clerks who had received a church in good faith and then found that irregularities among past incumbents had caused the benefice technically to be subject to papal reservation. On 7 December 1345 Clement VI granted William de Coventre's request for provision anew to the church of Inverarity and remission of the modest fruits received over four years; he had been ordained on the title of the church, but feared that his predecessors had not been ordained, in which case the right to collate would have devolved to the pope.[239] In July 1346 John de Bothevil was allowed to keep the revenues he had obtained from the church of Kinkell, to which he had been presented by David II, even though a predecessor had been a pluralist.[240] Such remissions were probably more common than the sources suggest, at least in practice.

In England, payment of fruits wrongfully received was made sometimes to the collector, sometimes direct to the Camera. Guy de Luco held for a time the incompatible benefices of Aston-en-le-Morthen in York diocese and Wootton in that of Winchester; he agreed to pay 100 florins and satisfied the Camera on 10 December 1358.[241] Richard de Meaux and Richard de Landoy obliged themselves to pay 300 florins in connection with the former's tenure of the prebend of St Katherine's Altar in Beverley. Of that sum, 100 florins was paid on 22 March 1352 and the same amount in 1355, with a further 50 florins being handed over on 29 November 1361, but Meaux was excommunicated on 12 July 1359, allegedly owing 200 florins.[242] Both these examples involved payment at Avignon. John Wellesbourne, prebendary of Husthwaite in York, preferred to pay locally in the same way as he paid the annates due from one of his two confirmations in the benefice.[243] The probable reason for his uncanonical title, and thereby his liability to pay 200 florins as a subsidy to the Holy Land, was that when he accepted the prebend on the death of Edmund Arundel and was admitted by the chapter on 24 March 1348, by virtue of an expectative grace dated 9 June 1343,[244] he ousted

[239] PRO, Roman Transcripts, 31/9/44, pp. 59–60. [240] *CPL*, III, 230.

[241] *Vat. Quel.*, VII, 234. [242] Ibid., V, 453; VII, 105, 373; Burns, 'Sources', no. 169.

[243] *CPP*, I, 166, 213; Lunt, *Accounts*, 89, 120.

[244] YML, H1/1, fol. 44; for the expectancy see *CPP*, I, 56; *CPL*, III, 130; YML, H1/1, fol. 27.

Stephen Maleon of Flanders, who had been admitted the day before and had an earlier expectancy dated 14 January 1343.[245] Wellesbourne paid £30 by 1363 at the latest,[246] but the sum was entered among legacies to the Holy Land and the obligation was not deleted from the collector's registers, with the result that the sum due continued to be sought until 1366.[247]

Grenlaw's account records a number of Scots paying fruits wrongfully received, including the abbot of Deer[248] and the archdeacon of Dunblane.[249] The entries are uninformative, and the only Scottish example for which details of the irregularity survive is that of Thomas de Wedale. On 25 October 1344 he was rehabilitated so as to be allowed to hold the church of 'Kritome' or 'Kircome', which he had obtained six and a half years before, when aged only twenty. He was to pay a quarter of the fruits which he had illicitly received to the subsidy against the Turks, and discharged this obligation to William de Deyn, Grenlaw's predecessor as collector.[250] The identification of the church is uncertain,[251] but the tax was paid reasonably swiftly compared with most annates, even though the revenues had allegedly been affected by warfare.[252]

Why Wedale was singled out to pay tax on fruits wrongfully received is not known. Potentially such levies were lucrative, but actual receipts were not very large. The canonical impediment usually came to light when a concerned clerk sought papal confirmation, an act which made him liable for annates. In most cases the Papacy apparently decided that annates alone would be exacted, perhaps because levies of fruits wrongfully received would have posed difficulties of both assessment and collection. Moreover, demands for even a proportion of past revenues might have served to deter clerks from seeking rehabilitation, or at least

245 YML, H1/1, fols. 44v, 27. 246 Lunt, *Accounts*, 120. 247 Ibid., 237.

248 Coll. 14, fol. 190. 249 Ibid., fol. 191; cf. fol. 180v.

250 Ibid., fol. 158v; Reg. Supp. 7, fol. 45v. The form 'Kirconnia', given in *CPP*, I, 80, is incorrect.

251 In the account the benefice is said to be in the diocese of St Andrews, in which case Crichton is the obvious identification, even though another parson is attested as late as 27 May 1338 (*Newbattle Registrum*, 165–6). However, the supplication for rehabilitation states that the church was in the collation of the bishop of Whithorn by full right (*pleno iure*), which implies that the benefice was probably in Galloway. Possible identifications in Galloway are: Kirkcolm, although this was in the patronage of Sweetheart Abbey (Cowan, *Parishes*, 119); Kirkcowan or Kirkennan, now Parton (Watt, *Dictionary*, 579); Kirkchrist, which in the fifteenth century was in the patronage of the bishop of Whithorn (Cowan, *Parishes*, 119) but earlier was probably a mere chapel; or Kirkinner. See also below, pp. 192–3. 252 Reg. Supp. 7, fol. 45v.

delayed payment of annates. The Papacy possibly took a different view in cases of blatant and deliberate irregularity, but normally made little use of its right to collect fruits wrongfully received.

LEGACIES TO THE HOLY LAND

During the period of crusading fervour some legacies were made to funds for the recovery of the Holy Land. However, by the middle of the fourteenth century the Hundred Years War was under way, Benedict XII's proposed crusade had had to be cancelled, and it looked unlikely that any expedition to the Holy Land would set out in the foreseeable future. Receipts from legacies and from sums paid for the redemption of vows fell markedly after the collectorship of Bernard de Sistre. Bernard reported several substantial amounts,[253] but by the time of Hugh Pelegrini much less was forthcoming. Hugh received £10 from the will of John de Bordon, rector of Rothbury, and at least a further 60s from laymen in the northern province; some other entries under this head do not specify the diocese of the testator, but the total amount received from the whole of England during Hugh's period as collector was only £136 3s 3d, including the £30 from John Wellesbourne for revenues illicitly taken from the prebend of Husthwaite.[254] John de Cabrespino received £20 from the executors of Thomas de Bucton, prebendary of Weighton in York, for the goods of one William de Braydeley bequeathed in Thomas's will,[255] but by 1370 receipts from legacies to the Holy Land had all but dried up.[256]

SPOILS

As well as collecting legacies made to the Holy Land, the Papacy claimed a right to collect the goods of deceased clerics, especially those dying intestate or making what were termed indistinct

253 Lunt, *Accounts*, 48–9.

254 Ibid., 84, 120. The position is not substantially affected by occasional payments made direct to the Camera, such as that of 20 *floreni fortes* from John de Eboraco, alias Gizerbortz, of York diocese, in 1361 to the Holy Land subsidy in commutation of his vow to visit the Holy Sepulchre: *Vat. Quel.*, VII, 362. A small payment for commutation of a vow was also made by a London woman in 1338: ibid., IV, 132.

255 Lunt, *Accounts*, 321. For Bucton's will see *Test. Ebor.*, I, 77–9; he died at Lyons on 2 December 1366: Mirot and Déprez, 'Les ambassades anglaises', no. cclxvii.

256 Cf. Lunt, *Financial Relations . . . 1327–1534*, 534.

bequests. Urban V, Gregory XI and Clement VII claimed that the Papacy had a right to receive some goods even from ecclesiastics who had made a will, or at least make some deductions from their legacies. Cattle and church ornaments were exempt from the reservation if they had belonged to the church before the time of the late incumbent, and arrangements had to be made to pay debts and deal with the burial of the deceased.[257]

The Papacy never established a general claim to spoils in England, even when the clerk died intestate, although on occasion the pope reserved the goods of a particular ecclesiastic. In the thirteenth century the chronicler Matthew Paris, whose antipathy to the Papacy is very marked, commented that the reservation of the goods of an intestate cleric was a sign of manifest cupidity on the part of the Holy See, but the king forbade the levy anyway, saying that it was damaging to the realm.[258] Local fears about the Papacy's intentions, however, continued. In the 1307 parliament an attack was made on several papal exactions, including the levy of legacies indistinctly bequeathed and of the chattels of intestates.[259] Urban V conceded that his claim to the goods of churchmen who had made a will should not be extended to England or France;[260] and, in response to a question to the Camera, Arnald Garnerii was informed that spoils were not levied in England.[261]

There is little evidence for the collection of spoils in Scotland, although Gregory XI in particular envisaged their levy there. In October 1374 John de Peblis, the new Scottish collector, was told to bring to effect the recent reservation made of the movables and other personal property of deceased bishops and abbots, of the rents and rights pertaining to the mensal income of prelates during vacancies, and of the intercalary fruits of all benefices held by bishops and abbots at the time of their death;[262] and in August 1373 Grenlaw too had been ordered to levy spoils.[263] In the absence of accounts for this period, it cannot be proved that these mandates were acted upon, although it is clear that in the 1370s and earlier the Camera received, as was traditional practice, the goods of Scottish clerks who died at or near the papal court. John de

257 Lunt, *Papal Revenues*, II, 403–4; Samaran and Mollat, *La fiscalité pontificale*, 233–5.

258 Lunt, *Papal Revenues*, II, 388–9.

259 *Rot. Parl.*, I, 207, 219–20. Testa received nothing from indistinct legacies: W. E. Lunt, 'William Testa and the parliament of Carlisle', *EHR*, 41 (1926), 345.

260 Lunt, *Papal Revenues*, II, 404.

261 Lunt, *Accounts*, 484.

262 *CPL*, IV, 152.

263 Ibid., 108.

Muskilburgh undertook to pay 32 francs for the spoils of John de Ketenis, who had died while following the curia.[264] The pope also received a small amount in 1348 from the property of Gilbert Fleming, dean of Aberdeen and auditor of the papal palace,[265] and 106 florins in September 1377 from the goods of Andrew, bishop-elect of Dunkeld, following his death at the papal court.[266]

PROCURATIONS

A due which fell widely across the ecclesiastical spectrum was the obligation to pay procurations to papal legates and nuncios. Usually the sums collected went directly to the envoys, although occasionally a pope reserved a portion of them for himself.[267] Innocent VI appropriated a portion of the procurations customarily paid to bishops on their visitations, although originally this was only if bishops visited by deputy.[268] While levies which benefited the Camera directly were rare, procurations were indirectly very valuable to the Papacy, since no salaries from central funds had to be paid to papal collectors or nuncios.

Lunt has studied the levy of procurations in England in great detail,[269] and only a few points need be made here. The papal collectors received 7s per day from prelates and some conventual or capitular communities, but envoys levied procurations as income taxes on all clergy at rates proportionate to their rank; deputy collectors of procurations sometimes raised small additional sums to cover their expenses.[270] Despite complaints in the parliament of 1346,[271] levies for the collectors' benefit encountered little opposition, but resistance sometimes arose to demands for procurations on behalf of cardinals and other high-ranking nuncios whose embassies for peace between England and France did not always involve their crossing the Channel. The bishops investigated those not paying and imposed ecclesiastical sanctions,[272] but the impression is that procurations were paid much more quickly than were annates. This is partly because of the smaller amounts involved, but

264 Coll. 391, fol. 180v; IE 345, fol. 39v. The amount paid was 25 florins.

265 Cal. IE 248, fol. 25. 266 IE 345, fol. 44v.

267 E.g. Boniface VIII: Lunt, *Papal Revenues*, II, 407–8.

268 Lunt, *Financial Relations ... 1327–1534*, 713–16; *Chron. Knighton*, II, 98.

269 Lunt, *Financial Relations ... 1327–1534*, chaps. 13, 14.

270 Lunt, *Financial Relations ... to 1327*, 569–70; Lunt, *Financial Relations ... 1327–1534*, 621, 642, 693. 271 *Rot. Parl.*, II, 163.

272 E.g. Reg. Kirkby, fol. 227. No year is given in this entry.

partly also because the levies fell on all beneficed clergy in accordance with the fixed assessment used for income taxes; as has been seen, it was administratively much easier to collect monies due from benefices than from individuals.

Lunt has little to say about another type of levy of procurations. On 23 August 1355 the collectors, including Grenlaw and Hugh Pelegrini, were told to visit all exempt clergy and receive from them procurations at the rate exacted by a bishop visiting non-exempt bodies.[273] Hugh appears not to have exerted himself in this duty, although on 25 April 1357 he instructed Bishop Welton of Carlisle to send him details of exempt clergy in his diocese; Welton told him on 3 June that he had discovered only the Cistercian monastery of Holm Cultram and the Premonstratensian abbey of Shap.[274] Grenlaw, however, was more active. He collected six merks from Paisley, three merks from Soulseat and two merks from Tongland; Whithorn Priory paid two merks and owed four; Fearn, which paid three merks and ten shillings, and Dryburgh, which paid three merks, were said to be destroyed and incapable of rendering any more. Kelso, which owed six merks, could not be reached by the collector, although he was confident that the amount would in due course be forthcoming.[275] These visitations, which raised for the Camera the very modest sum of 19 merks 10s, were presumably made while Grenlaw was in Scotland between the summer of 1358 and the first half of 1362,[276] and it is probable that a renewed commission to visit exempt clergy, issued on 2 February 1358,[277] is connected with his impending journey to Scotland. Grenlaw reported that he had also visited a number of Cistercian houses and levied procurations, but had had to restore them following the intervention on behalf of the whole order by William, cardinal-bishop of Tusculum.[278]

By the middle of the fourteenth century the system of papal taxation was complex and wide-ranging. It had evolved over a

[273] *Innocent VI: lettres secrètes et curiales*, no. 1699; cf. *CPL*, III, 617.

[274] Reg. Welton, p. 33. [275] Coll. 14, fol. 181. [276] Watt, *Dictionary*, 245.

[277] Reg. Vat. 243, fols. 94–95.

[278] Coll. 14, fol. 181v; *CPL*, III, 633; Reg. Vat. 244L, fol. 88. Cf. *Chron. Melsa*, III, 153: the Cistercian order as a whole is said to have paid 6000 florins for exemption from visitation by collectors. Any arrears incurred by the Cistercians for procurations or spoils were remitted on 21 November 1372: Tihon, *Lettres de Grégoire XI*, nos. 1892, 4041. The collectors were also told, on 19 October 1356, to cease visiting houses of Austin hermits: *Innocent VI: lettres secrètes et curiales*, no. 2453.

long period, and this partly explains why some revenues were collected centrally and others locally, and some on a different basis from others. John XXII, a most capable administrator, had been driven to perfect the system in view of the increasing cost of the papal bureaucracy and the drastic reduction in revenue from traditional sources in Italy; and his successors sought new opportunities to increase the yield from taxes. But the popes could not escape from political realities. The strength of the English crown was sufficient to enable Edward III to suspend payment of the tribute; and potentially lucrative taxes such as spoils and intercalary fruits could be levied in England only rarely. The English king's success in raising his own subsidies from the clergy was one of the factors which influenced the switch from tenths to annates as the most important papal tax collected locally. Moreover, in both England and Scotland the Camera and its agents struggled against intrinsic difficulties in levying certain taxes. Those easiest to administer, such as Peter's Pence and census, were fiscally relatively unimportant, while annates proved to be very hard to collect quickly or easily. Even though the collectors usually knew the names of potential taxpayers and their benefices, they had to establish whether the provision of the churchman to the benefice for which annates were due had in fact been effective. Unlike the other revenues, where exemptions were rare and usually clear-cut, annates were paid by only a proportion of those men potentially liable for them, and this allowed clerks to resist the levy by using excuses which were legitimate so long as they were true, and the truth could be difficult to establish. Between 1342 and 1378 the levy of annates dominated the working lives of the Camera's local agents, the collectors, and it is to their activities that we must now turn.

THE COLLECTORS

The collector's job was no sinecure; his work was arduous and potentially dangerous, since he was in a position between the Camera, keen to exact as much money as possible, on the one hand, and the local clergy and the government, worried about their own and the country's wealth, on the other. But the position attracted able administrators, for it was a stepping-stone to higher office, particularly in the first half of the fourteenth century, and it carried with it extensive power and influence. Within his field of activity, the collector was superior even to bishops; and he sometimes had large supplies of ready money for considerable periods, which he could use to accommodate the king or others with loans. In addition, he was well paid by procurations and could claim expenses.[279]

The collector's primary duty was to levy those papal taxes detailed in his commissions. It was normal for individuals to remain in office even after the death of a pope, although their commissions were often renewed by the succeeding pontiff, lest doubts be cast on the validity of their work. Surviving letters of appointment and subsequent mandates do not, however, always make it clear exactly what taxes are involved; they must, where possible, be studied in the light of accounts detailing the sources of revenue actually collected. But basically the tasks undertaken by the collectors in connection with papal finance, in both Scotland and England, were essentially similar; where there are significant differences between individuals are in the number of mandates they received which were not strictly connected with finance, and in the accumulation of benefices.

As trusted agents of the Holy See, the collectors were sometimes asked to intercede with the king on political matters. In September 1350 Clement VI sent Raymond Pelegrini, recently collector, to encourage Edward III to make peace with the new French king, John II, and he was given letters of safe-conduct and credence and the right to levy procurations.[280] In September 1360 Hugh Pelegrini was sent with the abbot of Cluny to persuade the king to help the pope against the Visconti,[281] and he was also involved in 1352 in the delicate task of negotiating with Edward III on the matter of the royal seizure of benefices held by aliens.[282] In 1367 John de Cabrespino was commissioned to urge the king to dissuade John of Gaunt from invading Provence.[283] Arnald Garnerii was briefly involved in the peace negotiations at Bruges in 1375.[284]

The collectors were also asked to deal with business of an ecclesiastical nature. Grenlaw was commissioned in 1358 with the bishop of Aberdeen to look into benefices unlawfully held and confirm their holders where appropriate.[285] Hugh Pelegrini had to

279 Lunt, *Financial Relations ... to 1327*, 587.
280 *Foedera*, III, 202; *Clément VI: lettres closes (Fr)*, nos. 4697–4704, 4707
281 *Foedera*, III, 509.
282 *Clément VI: lettres closes (Fr)*, no. 5448; ct. no. 5446.
283 *Foedera*, III, 830.
284 Lunt, *Accounts*, xl–xli, 537.
285 *CPL*, III, 634; Coll. 14, fol. 180–180v.

examine several candidates for expectative graces and for the office of notary public, and he acted as proctor for several foreigners, including the cardinals Talleyrand de Périgord and Peter Roger.[286] As the century wore on, however, such mandates became less frequent. This trend is strikingly illustrated by the number of occasions on which the English collector received a mandate to execute a papal provision, either alone or, as was more usual, in partnership with two others. Raymond Pelegrini dealt with seven such mandates before his appointment as collector and well over fifty during his term of office. Hugh Pelegrini received around thirty-five such commissions from Clement VI and Innocent VI, either as treasurer of Lichfield or in a personal capacity. John de Cabrespino was given extensive powers to grant dispensations,[287] but only twice is he named in provision mandates in any of the registers of Urban V (which cover the whole of Roman Christendom). One related to the prebend of Strensall in York, the other to a chaplaincy in Avignon.[288] No such mandates involving Arnald Garnerii have come to light.

Involvement in the execution of provisions was normally confined to senior ecclesiastics, usually prelates and prominent members of cathedral chapters, and the increasing rarity with which collectors are named may be connected with a comparable decline in the size of their portfolio of benefices. In the early fourteenth century the material rewards for a conscientious collector were great: Rigaud d'Assier, collector in England from 1317 to 1323, had even become bishop of Winchester.[289] The Pelegrini brothers did not reach such heights, but before, during and after their periods as collector, they were well endowed with benefices, usually as a result of papal provision. Raymond held prebends in Lincoln, Salisbury, London, Wells, Shaftesbury and Dublin at some point in his career, as well as the churches of Arreton, East Grinstead, Withington, Crondall and Harrow.[290] Hugh was provided to a string of prebends in Lanchester, Lincoln, London and Salisbury, and to the treasurership of Lichfield and the rectories of Boxley, Horncastle and Maidstone; in 1366 his benefices were

286 Lunt, *Accounts*, xxxiv.

287 E.g. *CPL*, IV, 87; *Urbain V: lettres secrètes et curiales*, nos. 530–3.

288 *Urbain V: lettres communes*, I, no. 2143; IV, no. 15272.

289 Lunt, *Accounts*, xxii–xxiii.

290 *CPL*, II, 230, 326, 328; III, 316, 414, 416; *CPP*, I, 45, 507, 510, 511, 517; *CCR 1339–41*, 271; Lunt, *Accounts*, xxxi–xxxii. At the time of his death he also held benefices overseas: Fierens, *Suppliques d'Urbain V*, nos. 1561, 1588.

taxed at £360.[291] By contrast, John de Cabrespino and Arnald Garnerii received no English benefices and not many elsewhere: Cabrespino was a canon of Narbonne, and in 1375 was provided to the archdeaconry of Murviedro in the diocese of Valencia; while Garnerii held canonries of Châlons and Narbonne.[292] The contrast between the Pelegrini brothers and their successors as collectors in England, none of them natives, is very marked; and this must be viewed in the context of a considerably diminished number of provisions to foreigners, other than cardinals, after the pontificate of Clement VI.

The Scottish collectors benefited greatly from papal favour. Early in his life, Grenlaw had held some benefices in France, but it was natural that he should look for major benefices in his native Scotland when the opportunity arose, even though he spent most of his life abroad. His main dignity was the deanery of Glasgow, but he also held the archdeaconry of St Andrews, the church of Edzell, the prebends of Stobo in Glasgow and Botary in Moray, and a claim to the archdeaconry of Brechin.[293] He was also a papal chaplain under Urban V,[294] and in 1373 was the recipient of letters conservatory.[295] The next collector, John de Peblis, also received letters conservatory,[296] and in September 1374 he succeeded Grenlaw as archdeacon of St Andrews.[297] He already held prebends in Glasgow and Aberdeen and the church of Douglas, and in 1378–9 was promoted to the see of Dunkeld.[298] However, he seems to have been locally elected before receiving papal confirmation, and it would be rash to speculate that his services to the Holy See alone were responsible for his elevation to a bishopric.

To enjoy success, the collectors needed the co-operation or at least the acquiescence of the king. For Scotland there is little evidence of relations between the collector and the monarch, although the collector is known to have been recommended to the

[291] *CPL*, II, 373; III, 82, 277, 293, 348, 415, 419; *CPP*, I, 195; *Reg. Sudbury*, II, 150.

[292] Lunt, *Accounts*, xxxv, xxxix, xli.

[293] Watt, *Dictionary*, 244. It should be noted that Grenlaw had a contemporary namesake, who succeeded him in Edzell (PRO, Roman Transcripts, 31/9/53, p. 98) and was twice granted an English safe-conduct to study (*Rot. Scot.*, I, 822, 877; cf. *Foedera*, III, 717). On the namesake see Watt, *Dictionary*, 246.

[294] PRO, Roman Transcripts, 31/9/59, p. 360; *CPL*, IV, 85; *Urbain V: lettres communes*, IX, no. 26637.

[295] Reg. Av. 188, fol. 247.

[296] Reg. Av. 193, fol. 250.

[297] Reg. Av. 194, fols. 333v–334v; cf. Reg. Av. 197, fol. 364–364v.

[298] *Handbook of British Chronology*, 308. Benefices held earlier in Peblis's career included the treasurership of Glasgow and the church of Glencairn: *CPP*, I, 417, 506; *CPL*, III, 546.

king and leading bishops and nobles.[299] In England it is clear that the collector had to take certain precautions, such as presenting his credentials to the king and not violating royal prohibitions, especially those imposed on the levy of annates from particular benefices. On 13 February 1372 Arnald Garnerii had to swear an oath of fealty, by which he promised to take no action prejudicial to the king, the realm, its laws or any of the king's subjects; to give faithful counsel to the king and not reveal royal secrets; to execute no papal mandates displeasing to the king or his subjects and receive no such bulls without delivering them to the royal council for inspection; to send no money out of the country, even by letters of exchange, without permission; to maintain the king's honour, estate, laws and rights; and to leave the realm only with royal licence.[300] This oath, which seems to have been an innovation in 1372, but became a permanent obligation on all future collectors, reflects contemporary suspicion of the Papacy and its agents, especially in wartime, suspicion vividly expressed in the rolls of parliament. The king usually gave an evasive answer to parliamentary petitions aimed at reducing papal powers in England, but the oath of fealty hints at much of the contemporary xenophobia.

Three decades earlier, Bernard de Sistre had been on good terms with Edward III. He was a royal clerk, and represented the king in negotiations with the pope; he made loans to the king between 1339 and 1342, probably from the papal revenues he had in his possession.[301] Raymond Pelegrini was also a royal clerk and a member of the king's council; on 20 June 1349 he was declared to be a denizen rather than an alien.[302] His brother Hugh was also a king's clerk and a royal envoy; although there was some friction over the levy of annates, relations between the king and the collector were generally smooth, and it was only in the 1370s that Edward III deprived Hugh of his benefices on the grounds that he adhered to his enemies in Aquitaine and elsewhere.[303] After 1363, however, the relationship between crown and collector became much more formal. John de Cabrespino had fewer commitments in England than the Pelegrini brothers and was rarely in the country; he does not appear to have been given the customary title of king's clerk.[304] Edward granted him protection in December

299 *Vet. Mon.*, 304–5, 314; *Grégoire XI: lettres secrètes et curiales (non-Fr)*, no. 1779.

300 *Foedera*, III, 933–4; *CCR 1369–74*, 424.

301 Lunt, *Accounts*, xxx.

302 *CPR 1343–45*, 111, 376; *CPR 1345–48*, 429; *CPR 1348–50*, 346.

303 Lunt, *Accounts*, xxxiv–xxxv.

304 Ibid., xxxix.

1366 and March 1367, and allowed him in February 1368 to cross from Dover with a retinue and a merchant's letter of exchange for £1600,[305] but it was made clear that protection was given only on the understanding that he did not act in a manner prejudicial to the king or his people. Arnald Garnerii's collectorship coincided with a period of strong antipathy to the Papacy in parliament, including demands for his expulsion.[306] Even though many of the parliamentary claims were greatly exaggerated, Garnerii's attempts to collect annates in the north on the basis of the old taxation, his attack on the archdeacons' exemptions, and his general lack of tact clearly provoked opposition and made co-operation with the government difficult. His approach is exemplified by a list of complaints he presented to the royal council about alleged interference with his work,[307] but this had predictably little effect in persuading the king's officials to change what he saw as a hostile attitude towards the papal fiscal system.

The previously warm relationship between the English king and the papal collector had, therefore, cooled noticeably. While individual personalities undoubtedly had an effect, it was probably inevitable that friction would increase. The tenths of the late thirteenth and early fourteenth centuries, and the early levies of annates, were shared between pope and king, and the king thus used papal authority to levy the clerical taxes he needed. In such circumstances it was advisable for the king to cultivate cordial relations with papal financial agents in England, and sometimes he could even secure loans from the collectors. The Pelegrini brothers were useful to the king because both he and the pope trusted them, making them useful royal representatives at the papal court. But even during their period as collectors, the crown and the Papacy were becoming rivals rather than assistants in creaming off clerical wealth. The arrival of John de Cabrespino and Arnald Garnerii, with their limited English interests, coupled with the increasingly frequent reports and assignments of money to the Camera in the 1360s and the prohibition of unauthorised loans from cameral funds in 1373,[308] caused the collectors to become competitors rather than allies of the English king.

The collector also needed some co-operation from bishops and their clergy, not the easiest part of a papal tax-gatherer's job. There must have been many hundreds of letters to taxpayers, especially

[305] *Foedera*, III, 813; *CPR 1364–67*, 338, 386; *CPR 1367–70*, 129.
[306] Lunt, *Accounts*, xli. [307] Ibid., 477–8. [308] *CPL*, IV, 151.

those who owed annates, and to bishops ordering the sequestration of benefices of delinquents, but very little of this voluminous correspondence has survived. This dearth of information leaves us in the dark about much of the administration of levying taxes, and almost totally uninformed as to how local clergy viewed papal exactions. It is likely that only a deep-seated recognition of papal authority and a belief in the ultimate efficacy of canonical sanctions enabled the collector to bring his labours to a fruitful conclusion.

SUBCOLLECTORS

The levy of tenths had been on such a scale as to render necessary the appointment of subcollectors in each diocese. After 1291 the subcollectors were usually the heads of religious houses, such as the prior of Coldingham, who acted in the archdeaconry of Lothian in the 1290s;[309] and this practice continued into the early fourteenth century. The first general levy of annates, which fell on all vacant benefices, was similarly levied partly by local subcollectors.[310] In the period under review subcollectors were still employed by the bishops to collect the procurations of papal nuncios, likewise a tax on income which affected the majority of beneficed clergy, and for other income taxes such as the tenth for David II's ransom and presumably the subsidies of the 1360s and 1370s, as well as subsidies for the bishop's own needs. None of these taxes was the concern of the papal collectors, so what use did they make of deputies after the abandonment of papal tenths?

There was in northern England a local receiver of the collector's procurations, which were levied from certain monasteries and collegiate communities;[311] but the extensive accounts of Hugh Pelegrini, John de Cabrespino and Arnald Garnerii do not record the names or activities of any local subcollectors of annates in the province of York. It seems that the usual procedure was for the taxpayer or his proctor to make a personal appearance before the collector to establish the amount due and when it was to be paid, with actions against defaulters being pursued through the bishops;

309 He was appointed by Bishop Halton of Carlisle: Lunt, *Papal Revenues*, I, 293–4. For a list of the subcollectors of Clement V's tenth in Scotland, all of whom were heads of religious houses, see *The Register of John de Halton, Bishop of Carlisle, AD 1292–1324*, ed. W. N. Thompson, with intro. by T. F. Tout (2 vols., Canterbury and York Soc., 1913), I, 267–8.

310 W. E. Lunt, 'The first levy of papal annates', *AHR*, 18 (1912), 56–7.

311 Lunt, *Financial Relations ... 1327–1534*, 700–1.

sequestration was used both before the taxpayer made his obligation and again later in cases of default. Bishops and their appointees were certainly involved in investigating the success or otherwise of provisions, and sometimes it is implied that they should actually collect the amount due. But there is no certain evidence that bishops did in fact receive payments of annates from debtors, and in the context of such a large number of obligations in arrears this suggests that they were not regularly employed as tax-gatherers. If, however, the bishops were not involved and there were no local subcollectors in the north, how and where was payment of annates made?

There are a few references to subcollectors elsewhere in England, although it is not apparent even what revenues they were responsible for, still less how their activities can shed light on the situation in the north. In April 1363 Geoffrey Salyng was described as a papal collector in the archdeaconry of Essex,[312] and in January 1366 Adam Robelyn, archdeacon of St David's, was said to be subcollector in England.[313] If these men and others like them were involved with the levy of annates, it could be assumed that they would have their counterparts in northern England, a region further from the principal collector's base, but if so their work has not been recorded for posterity.

Larger collectorates usually had a general subcollector with authority over other subcollectors,[314] and the deputies who acted on behalf of the collectors during the latter's absence fall into this category. From 1343 to 1363 the Pelegrini brothers appear to have acted in concert, although sometimes Hugh also employed as deputy his registrar and kinsman Pontius de Vereriis.[315] After 1363 there was usually at least one formal deputy. John de Caroloco, who was based at Southwark, acted as collector without the title during John de Cabrespino's absences, and after Cabrespino's replacement until Arnald Garnerii arrived in England, when Caroloco accounted to the new collector. Caroloco is known to have sent letters ordering sequestrations and the payment of annates;[316] he issued receipts for Peter's Pence[317] and intercalary

312 *CPP*, I, 417.

313 *Urbain V: lettres communes*, V, no. 16937. Subcollectors are also found on the continent: e.g. Tihon, *Lettres de Grégoire XI*, nos. 193–5, 197, 200; *Grégoire XI: lettres secrètes et curiales (Fr)*, no. 158.

314 Samaran and Mollat, *La fiscalité pontificale*, 82.

315 Lunt, *Accounts*, xxxiii–xxxiv; *CPP*, I, 327, 329, 359.

316 YML, H1/3, fols. 94–95; Reg. Appleby, pp. 229–30.

317 Reg. Thoresby, fols. 321v, 324, 326.

fruits;[318] and he continued to levy the arrears of procurations for Cabrespino until at least May 1375.[319] After his replacement, in November 1371, Cabrespino appointed John de Wendlyngburgh as his deputy, and in that capacity he delivered a sum of money to an Italian firm for transfer to the Camera,[320] but this was possibly no more than an *ad hoc* commission. Arnald Garnerii's deputy was Laurence de Nigris, and when Garnerii left England for the last time he was given full authority and put in possession of the accounts, bulls and registers necessary for the conduct of his office; he swore an oath, backed up by sureties, that he would exercise his duty faithfully and render accounts.[321] At an earlier point he had had to find security that he would not go abroad without royal licence or do anything prejudicial to the king.[322] He seems to have acted as subcollector even when Garnerii was in England, and was probably a general deputy of the type well known in larger collectorates on the continent.

The English collector had a household of servants and minor officials, but these persons enter the records only tangentially. Hugh Pelegrini's sequestrator, John de Empryngham, was given royal letters of protection in December 1352 and June 1354 while he was engaged in papal business and collecting debts due to the Camera.[323] His role in the task of collection is not defined. On 28 March 1371 Edward III licensed the papal collector's registrar, John de Strensall, to cross to the curia on cameral business,[324] and Garnerii's registrar went to Rome in April 1378 with the collector's account book of receipts, assignments and arrears to 6 March 1378, spending six months on this mission.[325]

Surprisingly in view of the relative paucity of evidence, the situation as regards subcollectors in Scotland in Grenlaw's time is more straightforward than, and probably somewhat different from, the practice in England. Grenlaw was largely an absentee, and his second-in-command was Adam de Tyningham, later bishop of Aberdeen. He made a payment to the Camera on Grenlaw's behalf on 12 November 1359,[326] and in September 1364 was present with the collector at the payment of the bishop of Moray's service taxes.[327] He is attested as subcollector on 28

318 YML, H1/3, fols. 77v–78, 81v. 319 Lunt, *Accounts*, xxxviii.
320 Ibid., xxxvii. 321 Ibid., 479. 322 *CCR 1369–74*, 481.
323 Lunt, *Accounts*, xxxv; *CPR 1350–54*, 378; *CPR 1354–58*, 76.
324 *CPR 1370–74*, 64. 325 Lunt, *Accounts*, 538.
326 Coll. 14, fol. 183v; *Vat. Quel.*, VII, 281. 327 *Moray Registrum*, 163.

January 1360,[328] 9 November 1361,[329] 4 February 1364[330] and 29 February 1368,[331] and in 1370 there seems to have been a plan to make him principal collector, although the appointment was cancelled and he is not named as collector or subcollector thereafter.[332] Tyningham perhaps succeeded Robert de Den, who was William de Deyn's deputy in April 1348 and was said in April 1358 not to have paid Grenlaw all the sums he had collected.[333] These men were probably general deputies. They did not function only when the collector was absent, as may at times have been the case in England, for Tyningham was active during Grenlaw's visit to Scotland in 1358–62; and they did not have to remain in the locality while the principal collector was away, for both Grenlaw and Tyningham were in Avignon simultaneously in 1364, and the latter was involved in litigation there in the 1360s over the deanery of Aberdeen.

Grenlaw's account contains a section detailing money received from local subcollectors, much of it relating to annates and other benefice taxes,[334] and there are other references to subcollectors in Scotland. Urban V decreed that in general there should be one in each diocese,[335] and a papal bull of 1373 implies that such was the case in Scotland.[336] However, those named specifically appear mainly to be connected with the remoter areas of the north and west, especially Moray and Ross. It is possible that they had their counterparts in the Lowlands, with whom Grenlaw had fully accounted and whose names he therefore did not report, but it is more likely that he had few, if any, subcollectors in the less inaccessible parts of Scotland.[337]

The clerks involved as subcollectors were all of high ecclesiastical rank, men with cathedral benefices and the bishop of Argyll, collector in his diocese.[338] Alexander de Kininmund, bishop of

[328] *CPP*, I, 350; Cal. Reg. Av. 143, fol. 352–352v.

[329] Coll. 14, fol. 167v; *CPP*, I, 326, 379.

[330] Coll. 14, fol. 170; *CPP*, I, 480; *Urbain V: lettres communes*, III, no. 12172.

[331] Coll. 14, fol. 174v. [332] Watt, *Dictionary*, 553.

[333] *CPL*, III, 234, 634–5; Reg. Vat. 243, fol. 118. He was dead by 5 September 1358: *CPL*, III, 593. [334] Coll. 14, fol. 183.

[335] Lunt, *Papal Revenues*, II, 230; Samaran and Mollat, *La fiscalité pontificale*, 80.

[336] *CPL*, IV, 108. [337] Cf. Barrell, 'William de Grenlaw', 10–11.

[338] As well as the men listed in Grenlaw's account, the following are named as subcollectors: Walter de Moffet, archdeacon of Lothian, who died in 1358 and had in the past been a collector of benefice taxes (*CPP*, I, 339; cf. 565); Alexander de Kylwos, dean of Ross (who had also been involved with the collection of the tenth for David II's ransom)

Aberdeen, received ten merks from the vicar of Ellon which he handed on to the collector; this may imply that he was involved with the levy of annates or at least was acting in a similar capacity to those English bishops who were told to proceed against debtors, although his involvement in 1358–62 with Grenlaw in confirming incumbents who held benefices uncanonically[339] makes him something of a special case. A subcollector in the city and diocese of Aberdeen is attested on 9 March 1377,[340] when Kininmund was still alive, and it cannot be proved that the bishop was ever a regular agent for the payment of annates. The bishop of Argyll certainly was, although this may have been because of the very small number of provisions to benefices in Argyll or, more likely, an indication of the absence of suitable senior clergy in a diocese with a very small cathedral chapter.

The Scottish subcollectors were all prominent local churchmen, and although they understandably stressed their services to the Camera when supplicating for benefices it would be too bold to assert that they owed their promotion solely to their work as tax-gatherers. Some of the clerks who worked for the English collectorate, however, may well have owed their material gains directly to their record of service. Laurence de Nigris obtained the prebend of Welton Beckhall in Lincoln even though he was of Roman origin; he exchanged it for the church of Barking in March 1380.[341] It was unusual by this time for a foreigner other than a cardinal to receive an English benefice, and it is likely that the prebend was a reward for his work and a convenient means of paying his salary. Pontius de Vereriis held a prebend in Wells from 1358 to 1361, and also entertained a claim to a prebend in London; he also held the church of Walpole in Norwich diocese.[342] The prebends were obtained by provision, in the supplications for which his relationship with Hugh Pelegrini was stressed;[343] and it is probable that these grants too were made in recognition of good service. For these men, probably permanent employees of the

in 1368 (Watt, *Dictionary*, 316); and Simon de Ketenis, canon of Aberdeen, in 1377 (Reg. Av. 201, fol. 506v). Bertrand Cariti, parson of Fettercairn, had been a subcollector before his death in February 1358, but his work had been on the continent: *CPL*, IV, 64; Samaran and Mollat, *La fiscalité pontificale*, 175, 179. A statement that Hamo Johannis of Quimper diocese was collector in Scotland (*CPP*, I, 497) is incorrect; he was in fact a familiar of Grenlaw (Reg. Supp. 42, fol. 163).

339 Coll. 14, fols. 179v, 180–180v; *CPL*, III, 634.

340 Reg. Av. 201, fol. 506v.

341 Lunt, *Accounts*, xl, 484; Le Neve, *Fasti*, I, 121.

342 Le Neve, *Fasti*, V, 68; VIII, 37; *CPP*, I, 327.

343 *CPP*, I, 327, 329, 359.

Camera in England and foreigners as well, provision was the only means of reward; many of the Scots probably worked for the collector only on a part-time basis and pursued their careers independently of the everyday work of the collector's office.

THE ACCOUNTS

The fruits and frustrations of the collectors' work are, of course, best illustrated in the reports they periodically submitted to the Camera for accounting purposes. These are not all identical in format, and they cover periods from a few months to nearly a decade. The English accounts often start with receipts from debtors left in arrears in the previous account, and then move on to payments which had fallen due since the last report had been rendered, usually finishing with details of arrears and in some cases also lists of ineffective provisions. All the accounts include details of assignments to the Camera, either directly or through merchants, and of expenses claimed, and most also contain a brief summary. In the 1360s, when receipts were low and accounts were rendered frequently, there is considerable repetition between successive reports, especially with regard to annates. The surviving copy of Grenlaw's business is in three parts. The first section comprises a list of provisions and confirmations from which annates were due, covering the years from 1342 to 1369. It is followed by an official and presumably audited account, rendered in 1362. The final section details payments of annates and fruits wrongfully received, arranged by diocese; it is a rough summary, probably for the collector's own use, and apparently dating from slightly later than the account proper. The information which survives is, therefore, diverse; it is likely that what we have is a copy made of Grenlaw's papers after his death in 1374.[344]

The totals collected for the Camera were carefully noted and checked. Some errors can be detected, but they are few and far between. Total receipts can be calculated, but are of limited interest in an examination of how the fiscal system actually operated; and annual averages can also be computed, though these are largely meaningless in view of the fact that the potential total of receipts from annates varied depending on how many provisions there had been, what benefices they had affected, and whether they had been

[344] See Barrell, 'William de Grenlaw', 4–5.

successful. But it is clear that the Scottish collectorate was very much less lucrative than even northern England, and that by far the bulk of the revenue levied came from annates. Indeed, the only large sum in the accounts from a source other than annates relates to the 1375 subsidy, which Arnald Garnerii accounted for but did not collect.

Collectors could pay over money to the Camera in person, but it was more usual for the business to be conducted through merchants who had been appointed to transact it. This was a much safer and more convenient way of transferring revenues than carrying cash through war-ridden France. The firms of merchants, who were usually Italians, were normally required to pledge all their assets to the Camera in case of default,[345] and even if a company failed steps were taken to recover the Papacy's money.[346] Details of in-payments usually appear both in the collectors' accounts and in other sources detailing the Camera's income and expenditure; the English funds were usually converted to florins at a rate of around 3s or a little more to the florin. Underpayments or overpayments were subsequently adjusted: for instance, in his first report in 1358 Hugh Pelegrini was found to have paid £762 13s 4d more than he had collected, a discrepancy corrected in his second account.[347] The accounts also refer to payments by the collector, on the order or at least with the permission of the Camera, to individuals ranging from the king of France to papal servants, and to expenditure on the pope's behalf, for example in the purchase of orphreys. In the 1360s and 1370s fruits were assigned to the Camera more frequently than before, especially by Arnald Garnerii. In his second account Arnald recorded a large number of payments on behalf of the pope's brother Roger de Beaufort while the latter was a prisoner in England, and he kept notes of assignments from the usual revenues separate from those from the proceeds of the subsidy. The large number of in-payments necessitated a simplified list in the account's summary, and an even briefer one was made also.[348] It seems that the Camera was keen to ensure that the collectors did not retain the pope's money for longer than was

[345] Lunt, *Financial Relations ... to 1327*, 601.

[346] E.g. in 1355 the bishop of Rimini was told to recover from representatives of the Acciaiuoli of Florence 4000 florins which they had been bound to pay in exchange for £550 deposited by Bernard de Sistre in April 1342, when the company was still solvent: *CPL*, III, 617; *Innocent VI: lettres secrètes et curiales*, no. 1768.

[347] Lunt, *Accounts*, 140; cf. 96.

[348] Ibid., 540–1, 481.

necessary, and the prohibition on lending money without special licence confirms that the Holy See had become concerned about leaving the collector with too much opportunity to use his private initiative.

Receipts from Scotland were smaller than from England, and assignments were rather less frequent. Grenlaw's career at the curia meant that he personally had little need of bankers, although the services of firms of merchants may well have been used to transfer funds from Scotland to the curia in the first place. His account records seven payments to the Camera, in a wide variety of currencies, each with a different conversion rate, and he continued to assign money to the Camera at intervals throughout the 1360s and early 1370s.[349] The account as it has survived poses many problems of addition and interpretation, but it was decided by the Camera that he owed 75 merks 9s 7d, a sum which he paid on 11 July 1362.[350]

There are no details of the expenses claimed by Grenlaw,[351] but all the extant English accounts list them.[352] Legitimate items included the cost of messengers to and from the curia, within England and Ireland, and on other missions; the cost of parchment, paper, ink and wax at a fixed rate of 20s per annum; the cost of writing copies of accounts and other records; and the rent and upkeep of the collectors' dwelling in London, fixed at £6 13s 4d a year. Arnald Garnerii characteristically quibbled over the customary allowances for writing materials and for the upkeep of his London base, alleging a need to guard the latter more closely than normal because the proceeds of the subsidy were stored there and on account of 'wars', but his moaning was ignored. Sometimes, though not always, a collector was granted travel expenses. Garnerii claimed £30 for his journey from Avignon to England in March and April 1375, which included over ten days at Bruges involved with the Anglo-French peace talks and the cost of two lost horses.

349 For details see Coll. 14, fols. 183v–185; Barrell, 'Papal relations', 127n.

350 The sum of 336 *floreni fortes* 12s 8d at the rate of 3s per florin is just about right: *Vat. Quel.*, VII, 414.

351 When Grenlaw's account to 12 January 1365 was audited, he was allowed the sum of 123 florins 6s 8d which he had not paid and also a further 100 merks for expenses (Coll. 353, fols. 35v–36).

352 Lunt, *Accounts*, 92, 141, 183–4, 225–7, 265–6, 321, 414, 476, 537–8; cf. Burns, 'Sources', no. 199.

The personalities of the collectors emerge only obliquely from the impersonal, formal records which they have left behind. Even efficiency is hard to gauge, because success largely depended on the level of receipts from annates, and external factors such as royal intervention could have a bearing on the sums collected, despite (or even because of) the collector's best efforts. John de Cabrespino seems to have been the least enthusiastic upholder of the Camera's rights: Carlisle Priory paid no census for a decade; and a large number of provisors fell into arrears without being much harmed by canonical sanctions. His frequent approaches to bishops about benefices which the latter could not find or about provisions which they had consistently stated to be ineffective must have annoyed the prelates and given an impression of inefficiency. Yet Cabrespino was given another commission after his withdrawal from England, and so even he cannot have been regarded as totally useless as a tax-gatherer. There seems to have been little corruption; when acquittances were issued to taxpayers, as was customary for a small fee, there was a real risk of the misappropriation of funds being detected, and this may have been a risk not worth taking. In the main the collectors were able men, active administrators of a fiscal system which cannot have been popular and which sometimes aroused vehement opposition in the English parliament, but which nonetheless was effective in meeting at least some of the Papacy's needs. It was from the collectors that the Holy See received much of its revenue during the Avignon period, and it was on the collectors that was laid the responsibility for treading the delicate line between executing the demands of the Camera and not antagonising those political forces which could seriously hinder their work. Their ability normally to find this line is testimony to their pragmatism.

Chapter 2

PAPAL PROVISIONS

The practice of providing clerks to benefices with and without cure was one of the most controversial features of papal relations with Scotland and England. It was, of course, no new phenomenon under the Avignon popes, nor was the controversy which it engendered. In the thirteenth century even Bishop Grosseteste, who had accepted the pope's right to dispose of all benefices, had lamented the unsuitability of some of the clerks who received provision.[1] But the system had been more highly organised by John XXII and codified by Benedict XII, so that by the period here studied papal provisions were numerous, some clerical patrons saw their right to present severely restricted, and the English parliament frequently petitioned the king for redress.

Provisions were of several types. Some were direct grants of a particular benefice at a specific vacancy; others were confirmations of a clerk's position in a benefice he already held where there was reason for doubt about the canonical legality of his institution, or surrogations of an ecclesiastic into the right of another to a disputed benefice. Many, however, were what were termed expectative graces, promising a prebend in a named cathedral or collegiate church when one next fell vacant, or a living in the gift of a particular patron. Expectative graces were sometimes issued and registered in the same way as direct provisions, in which case they were said to be *in forma speciali*; but many were given *in forma communi pauperum*, in other words to poor clerks without a benefice, and were normally not registered by the papal chancery. The large number of provisions, in particular the extensive use of expectative graces, has often been bewailed as a serious abuse of papal power, but very little work has been done to analyse how the system worked in practice. Who were the provisors? Who backed

[1] W. A. Pantin, 'Grosseteste's relations with the Papacy and the crown', in *Robert Grosseteste, Scholar and Bishop*, ed. D. A. Callus (Oxford, 1955), 193.

them? What type of benefice did they seek? Why were some benefices reserved to papal collation and others not? How successful were the provisions? What happened when the system broke down? This chapter will examine these issues in the context of Scotland and northern England in order to assess the impact of provisions at the local level. Provisions to episcopal sees and religious houses will be discussed in subsequent chapters.

A distinction will be made throughout between 'direct provisions', that is, grants of a particular benefice deemed to be actually or theoretically vacant, including confirmations and surrogations, on the one hand, and the various forms of expectative grace on the other.[2] While not all grants can be neatly categorised for statistical purposes, it is important to bear in mind that expectancies were merely promises of an unspecified benefice at some future date; direct provisions could in theory be brought to immediate effect.

To aid understanding of the nature of the papal records it is necessary to describe briefly the mechanics of obtaining a provision.[3] The hopeful clerk or someone acting on his behalf had to make a petition to the pope, which, if accepted, was endorsed by the pope, sometimes with conditions, and copied into the Registers of Supplications. The clerk was then examined, normally at the curia, and if he passed, a bull was drafted, checked, sealed and commonly registered[4] in order to ensure that it would be considered genuine; at this period it was written first in the paper Avignon registers (*Registra Avinionensia*) and later in the parch-

2 In his book *The Church and the English Crown, 1305–1334* (Toronto, 1980), J. R. Wright makes a rather different distinction; in particular he includes among 'direct provisions' the very frequent grants of a canonry with reservation of a prebend, on the grounds that this form combined both provision and expectation. But he himself admits that a canonry without a prebend 'was in practice not much more than an honorary title' (p. 32); and by the style of the papal chancery a clerk granted a canonry of a named cathedral or collegiate church became a titular canon of that place regardless of whether the provision was to a specified vacant prebend or merely reserved one for the future, until such time as it was clear that the provision or expectancy was not going to bear fruit (A. B. Emden, Review of Le Neve, *Fasti*, I and II, *Medium Aevum*, 32 (1963), 97). From the standpoint of assessing the effectiveness of provisions it is, therefore, preferable to treat grants of canonries with reservations of a prebend as expectative graces.

3 G. Mollat, 'La collation des bénéfices ecclésiastiques à l'époque des papes d'Avignon', intro. to *Jean XXII: lettres communes* (Paris, 1921), 39–57; cf. Mollat, *Popes*, 289–94.

4 In the thirteenth century perhaps only a tenth of papal letters were registered; the proportion probably increased during and after the pontificate of John XXII on account of changes in the practice of registration: Cheney, 'Study of the medieval papal chancery', in *The Papacy and England*, additional note.

ment Vatican registers (*Registra Vaticana*). The Apostolic Camera kept notes of provisions for the purpose of collecting annates, but these only summarised the grants which had been made. Executors were appointed to ensure that, as far as was possible within a legal process, the bull was effective and the provisor obtained possession of his benefice.

Little evidence survives of the actions of the executors, but in many cases details of the provision appear in the surviving registers of supplications, bulls and liabilities for annates. However, the absence of a grant from any of these sources should not necessarily be seen as implying that it was not effective. This is so even if the provision is found only in the Registers of Supplications. While some provisions were abandoned at this early stage, it is too simplistic to assert that all grants found only among the supplications were not pursued.[5] Some registers of bulls are lost, and some provisors seem to have failed to take the precaution of having their graces registered; certain petitions were undoubtedly rejected by the pope, but these were normally not copied into the Registers of Supplications in the first place.

The chances of survival of sources and the policy behind the selection of material for printed calendars have had an effect on the interpretation of the evidence relating to provisions in the British Isles. The effect has sometimes been adverse, and historians have been led into serious misconceptions about the number of provisions, particularly in the two decades before the Great Schism. Firstly, the Registers of Supplications cover only the period between 1342 and 1366, after which there is a long hiatus, although petitions certainly continued to be made in large numbers. Secondly, the compilers of the published *Calendar of Papal Letters* used the neat Vatican registers rather than the less legible Avignon series, which is unfortunate because after around 1350 the routine copying of letters from the latter into the former began to break down,[6] so that by the 1360s and 1370s most provisions do not appear in the Vatican series. Examination of the Avignon registers for this period makes it abundantly clear that the practice of provision continued unabated; and the conclusions of those who noted the almost total absence of provisions in the *Calendar of Papal*

[5] As argued by G. Barraclough, *Papal Provisions* (Oxford, 1935), 33–4.
[6] Cf. Watt, 'Sources for Scottish history', 111–12.

Letters for the pontificates of Urban V and Gregory XI, and assumed that none had been made, are seen to be flawed.[7]

A further peculiarity of the sources – again potentially misleading – is that the episcopal registers of northern England contain very little information about provisions or, except indirectly, about the people who received them. Very few provisors are recorded in bishops' registers as being instituted or collated to a benefice, even though many graces can be proved to have been successful. This is because the induction of provisors was in the hands of the executors appointed by the pope or subexecutors named by them, and was carried out without regard for the ordinary diocesan administration. As a result, the effectiveness of provisions can be traced from episcopal registers only incidentally, and this makes it unexpectedly difficult to use diocesan sources to trace the historical effect of papal intervention in a particular locality.[8] Only in the case of resignation or deprivation was a bishop commonly involved before he received a letter of presentation from the patron,[9] and so a benefice void by death could be filled by a provisor without any involvement at all by the diocesan authorities. There is, however, a major exception to this general rule. In the case of dignities, prebends and archdeaconries in York Minster the collation, mandate to induct and admission are usually recorded both in the archbishop's register and in the Chapter Act Books, even if the clerk concerned was a provisor; indeed, the provision, whether direct or an expectancy, is often mentioned. A similar, if less regular, pattern can be discerned for Ripon, but provisors to benefices in other collegiate churches and to parochial livings had their collation or institution recorded in the episcopal sources only exceptionally. The bishops' registers cannot, there-

7 Brief summaries of all the material in the Avignon registers for the pontificate of Urban V are printed in *Urbain V: lettres communes*. Further material relating to Scotland from the pontificates of Innocent VI and Gregory XI is available on microfilm in Glasgow. Financial records too contain information about provisions, including some not otherwise attested. It has not been possible to search the Avignon registers of Gregory XI for provisions to benefices in the province of York, and so any attempts below at numerical analysis are based only on the period 1342–70. The evidence in these sources casts doubt on the findings of J. T. Driver, 'The Papacy and the diocese of Hereford, 1307–1377', *Church Quarterly Review*, 145 (1947), 31–47; and of W. Greenway, 'The Papacy and the diocese of St David's, 1305–1417', ibid., 161 (1960), 436–48; 162 (1961), 33–49. The present author is not qualified to judge the conclusions of U. Flanagan, 'Papal provisions in Ireland, 1305–78', *Historical Studies*, 3 (Cork, 1961), 92–103; or of Barraclough, *Papal Provisions*, 31–2, where the situation in the Rhineland is discussed.

8 R. M. Haines, *The Administration of the Diocese of Worcester in the First Half of the Fourteenth Century* (London, 1965), 215.

9 Ibid., 192.

fore, be used as a check on the effectiveness of provisions, except incidentally. Some provisors appear as recipients of licences to be absent or other favours or in commissions, and the provisor's role in the history of a particular benefice can frequently be established from evidence relating to other incumbents; but a certain amount of caution must always be exercised.

NUMBERS OF PROVISIONS

It is impossible to make an accurate count of the number of provisions because of the incompleteness of the evidence and the problems caused by a variety of dates being assigned to papal graces, which may sometimes mask several provisions to the same clerk in quick succession. Omitting the graces *in forma pauperum*, bulls appropriating benefices to corporations, and confirmations by lesser ecclesiastics working under a papal commission, around 875 provisions are recorded to benefices in the province of York in the period 1342–70, slightly under 400 being direct grants and the rest expectancies. For Scotland the corresponding figure is just 364, around 60 per cent of these grants being direct provisions. Innocent VI seems to have been slightly less generous in both countries than his predecessor and successor.

In Scotland, over half the total number of provisions affected cathedral benefices, bestowed either directly or in expectation; there were also twenty-four provisions to archdeaconries. In percentage terms provisions to parsonages became steadily more frequent as the period goes on, while the number of grants to vicarages dwindled; there was also a provision of the hospital of Rathven in 1344.[10] Direct provisions to parochial benefices outweighed expectative graces to benefices in the gift of a particular patron, which would usually issue in a parsonage or vicarage, and these direct grants were most frequent to parishes in the coastal plain between the Tay and the Moray Firth; there were also some affecting benefices in the diocese of Glasgow, Fife and Lothian, but very few indeed concerned churches in the Highlands.

In England, the situation was somewhat different. Only around 20 per cent of the provisions in the northern province went to clerks seeking cathedral benefices, but since only one cathedral in the region was secular as opposed to nine in Scotland (excluding

[10] Coll. 281, fol. 106.

Orkney and the Isles), it is clear that York Minster was much more troubled by papal graces than an average Scottish cathedral. There were over 300 direct provisions or expectancies of benefices in collegiate churches such as Beverley, Ripon, Southwell, Howden, Auckland, Chester-le-Street, Lanchester, Darlington and Norton, and stalls in these churches were often bitterly disputed. The number of direct provisions to parochial benefices, both rectories and vicarages, rose steadily during the period, and 30 per cent of Urban V's grants were expectancies in the gift of a named patron. There were also seven provisions to hospitals and three to chapels.

Although it is very hard to establish accurate figures for the number of benefices available at this time, it is clear that provisions were relatively more numerous in the province of York than in Scotland, especially where sinecure prebends were concerned. Provisions to parishes were less useful to the clerk who sought to hold benefices in plurality, since rectories and vicarages involved the cure of souls and absence from them had to be licensed. Most parochial benefices received only one or two provisors during this period, if any at all, whereas prebends could be filled continually by papal authority of one kind or another. The imbalance between Scotland and England is much less marked where parishes are concerned than as regards prebends, probably because there were fewer Scottish prebends, particularly in collegiate churches, which were sufficiently valuable to attract much attention from provisors. Although we do not know the incidence of expectative graces *in forma pauperum* north of the border, it would on the face of it appear that Scottish patrons witnessed less interference with their right to present than did their English counterparts.

The wealth of benefices affected by papal provisions varied widely, and it is certainly inaccurate to view the system of papal favour as operating exclusively to the detriment of wealthy benefices. Although such benefices were undoubtedly more attractive to clerks whose main concern was the accumulation of worldly goods, direct provisions could be made only if a benefice fell vacant in certain specified circumstances: for example, the wealthy prebend of Langtoft in York, taxed at £100,[11] escaped the attention of provisors during our period because it never fell vacant in a way which rendered it liable to papal collation.

[11] *Taxatio*, 297, 321.

PROVISIONS TO GRADUATES

Critics of papal provisions sometimes concede that many graduates, cut off from local patronage through long years at university, needed the support of the pope in order to secure suitable advancement. But how far in reality was the process of provision used to help graduates during our period?

In Scotland, some 77 per cent of recorded provisions, including both direct grants and expectative graces, went to graduates or at least to men who had spent some time in a university; under Urban V the figure was nearly 90 per cent.[12] For the province of York, the corresponding proportion was around a third, and even under Urban V non-graduates outnumbered graduates by a considerable extent. Only in the restricted case of York Minster in the 1360s did the rate of provisions to graduates approach the overall Scottish figure, while as the number of grants to parishes in York diocese rose during the period, so the proportion of graduates fell. The graces *in forma pauperum* have been excluded from the present analysis, but it is unlikely that many of the obscure poor clerks who received them were in fact graduates. Some were, such as Nicholas de Wartre, who accepted the church of Roos by virtue of such a grant,[13] but he was probably in a minority in view of the fact that most English clerks who received graces even *in forma speciali* promising a benefice in the gift of a named patron were not graduates.

The reason for the difference between Scotland and England is probably connected with the fact that there were fewer requests for provisions on the part of Scottish clerks. Most who did not go abroad to study seem to have relied on local patronage; only the graduates of French universities had been severed for so long from their homes as to need papal support on a regular basis. We must assume that for non-graduate clerks in Scotland local presentation rather than papal provision was the normal means of access to a benefice in the middle of the fourteenth century; in England all classes of clerk could and did seek provision, although graduates doubtless used the system more than did those with strong personal ties in the locality.

[12] On graduates in Scotland over a longer period see D. E. R. Watt, 'University graduates in Scottish benefices before 1410', *RSCHS*, 15 (1966), 77–88.

[13] Reg. Zouche, fol. 187.

The Scottish non-graduate provisors are sufficiently few in number to enable us to investigate the level of success of their grants. Including expectative graces, eighty-two provisions are recorded in the period from 1342 to 1370 and the outcome of forty-nine of these is unknown. Of the remainder, five failed and three probably did so, although there is no reason to suppose that the clerks in question were unsuccessful solely or mainly because they were not graduates. Of the nineteen successful grants, eighteen were confirmations of a clerk in a benefice he already held, including six by the papal commissaries William de Grenlaw and Alexander de Kininmund, and one was an expectative grace; in addition, three expectancies, two confirmations and one direct provision, that of the church of Kinnettles to Walter Hundbit, chaplain of the bishop of St Andrews,[14] were probably successful.

Many of the non-graduates were backed by powerful patrons: the queen petitioned on behalf of the royal chaplain and almoner Thomas Bur, who was granted reservation of a benefice in the gift of the bishop of St Andrews in September 1350,[15] while the bishop of Dunblane was behind a petition on behalf of William Emery in 1361, the provisor being his chaplain.[16] This raises the more general question of the nature of the supplications.

SUPPLICATIONS FOR PROVISIONS

Apart from a few grants, mainly to cardinals, said to have been made by the pope on his own initiative (*motu proprio*), all provisions were initiated by a supplication outlining the request and the hopeful clerk's academic or other qualifications. Even the *motu proprio* grants were essentially of this type, although they were immune from challenge on the grounds that they contained an inaccuracy.[17] A clerk could petition the pope on his own account and many did, although it was considered beneficial to be included on a roll or in a set of petitions sent for consideration by some powerful patron.

Graduates were often included on university rolls, sent on the accession of a new pope or other great event, but also at other times for no special reason.[18] The large Paris rolls included a few Scots

[14] *CPP*, I, 82; *CPL*, III, 153; Coll. 281, fol. 148v.
[15] *CPP*, I, 205; *CPL*, III, 389.
[16] *CPP*, I, 375; Reg. Av. 147, fol. 378.
[17] Zutshi, 'Original papal letters', p. 137.
[18] D. E. R. Watt, 'University clerks and rolls of petitions for benefices', *Speculum*, 34 (1959), 216–17.

studying there,[19] while the Oxford and Cambridge rolls concerned mainly English clerks.[20] Usually the rolls were accepted or rejected in their entirety, but Urban V started the practice of adding amendments to individual petitions:[21] the Oxford academic John Wyclif, still happy in 1363 to use the system of papal provision, was granted only a canonry of Westbury instead of a grace in York.[22] The vast majority of clerks with university sponsorship received only expectancies, and they sometimes found competitors among their colleagues. Graduates who were not backed by their university also naturally stressed their academic attainments.

Some graduates as well as non-graduates were sponsored by the king or members of the royal family and nobility. Edward III had extensive patronage from regalian right and the seizure of advowsons held by alien priories, but he nonetheless saw provisions as a useful adjunct to his largesse. As far as the northern province was concerned, 1361 and 1368 were years of many royal supplications, perhaps because the alien priories had been released and the king was confident of papal support following the Treaty of Brétigny, although generally attempts to correlate the incidence of royal petitions with events in the Hundred Years War are inconclusive. Edward was not as frequent a supplicant as some of his family, notably the prince of Wales, or his leading subjects such as Henry of Lancaster,[23] doubtless because of his already wide powers of patronage. David II was a regular petitioner,[24] and those who could claim kinship with him did so; when he was a prisoner in England he obtained a canonry of York, with expectation of a prebend, for the German Conrad Scoenweder,[25] although the expectation appears to have been unfulfilled. The French kings John II and Charles V backed some Scottish clerks, and Englishmen

19 E.g. *CPP*, I, 175, 505; Reg. Supp. 28, fol. 193; see fol. 192v for note that this was a Paris roll.

20 The petitions made by universities in 1371 on the accession of Gregory XI are largely lost because the Registers of Supplications do not survive. A draft roll, however, exists from Cambridge; it names seventy-five clerks, only fifteen of whom have no corresponding provision in the Avignon registers. Ten of those nominated had been on the 1363 Cambridge roll. See E. F. Jacob, 'Petitions for benefices from English universities during the Great Schism', *TRHS* 4th series, 27 (1945), 47, 51–5.

21 Watt, 'University clerks', 222.

22 *CPP*, I, 390.

23 During his lifetime Henry requested 66 prebends and dignities and 32 lesser benefices, 80 of which were for his clerks: K. Fowler, *The King's Lieutenant* (London, 1969), 179.

24 All David's petitions are conveniently summarised in *The Acts of David II, King of Scots, 1329–1371*, ed. B. Webster (*Regesta Regum Scottorum*, 6, Edinburgh, 1982), 44–8.

25 *CPP*, I, 203.

who served John during his captivity after Poitiers also received his support.

A connection with a bishop could be useful for a petitioner, especially if the prelate's normal patronage had been restricted by provisions and his ability to support his family and connections had been reduced. Archbishop Thoresby regularly asked for papal favour, as he had done as bishop of St David's and Worcester, and Bishop John de Pilmor of Moray's earlier connection with Clement VI[26] was put to good use during that pope's pontificate.

The number of petitions which were backed by the royal family and leading nobles and prelates is, however, sufficiently large as to raise the question of whether the clerks who benefited were personally well known to their sponsor. This is statistically unanswerable, but it is unlikely that such personages as the king or the duke of Lancaster were directly responsible for the placing on a roll of petitions of all the names which appear there. Clerks may well have been recommended by leading officials of the sponsor with whom he was in contact, and perhaps some payment was sometimes required in order to obtain a place on a roll and thereby avoid the prospect of what could have been a fruitless journey to Avignon. But this is not to say that the royal family, bishops and secular lords did not personally know and recommend *some* of the clerks whose names are to be found on rolls of supplications.

It has been claimed that the share which officials at the papal curia had in provisions was out of all proportion to their place in the church,[27] and while this is undoubtedly true in a numerical sense it must be remembered that those who resided at the curia had no other obvious avenues of advancement. Cardinals had expensive establishments, and despite the fulminations of the English parliament they appear to have experienced relatively little difficulty, except in the 1340s, in obtaining rich benefices in York Minster. Papal collectors, auditors of the papal palace, agents and attendants of cardinals, and other servants of the Holy See naturally looked to the pope as the source of patronage.

In short, a clerk hoping for papal favour would, if possible, seek the help of someone in an influential position in church or state. In any case, such matters as academic standing, relationship to the king or a powerful lord, services to the Papacy or a cardinal, would be stressed, very much in the manner of a *curriculum vitae*, aiming to

[26] He had been Clement's vicar in spirituals when the latter was archbishop of Rouen (1330–8): ibid., 76.

[27] Barraclough, *Papal Provisions*, 73.

make the best possible impression on the pope. But it was also necessary to draft the petition correctly and to mention any impediment caused by defect of birth or irregularity, as well as detailing benefices or expectancies already held. These *non obstante* clauses are often very informative, and show that many clerks were already well endowed with benefices when they sought direct provisions or even expectative graces, and were looking not so much for a foothold on the lowest rung of the ecclesiastical ladder as for promotion to an even more exalted position.

These clauses were important, and if the clerk did not correctly express his wishes and the benefices he already held the petition could be rendered invalid. Petitions could be granted in principle but at the same time amended; this was especially so if the pope wanted the supplicant to resign any or all of his benefices on the fulfilment of the papal grace, or to reduce the permitted maximum value of a church to be accepted by means of an expectancy. Other amendments are also found. When Robert de Stratton was given the York prebend of Masham on 14 November 1369 he was told not only to resign a prebend in Wells but also to cease taking the payments and emoluments at the curia due to him as a commensal papal chaplain.[28] When William de Calabre was provided to the church of Ellon in 1366 he was told that he must reside on the benefice.[29] Angus de Ergadia's grant of the church of Liston on 15 January 1343 was not to prejudice his claim to the see of Argyll.[30]

During the Schism it became common practice to backdate the provision or otherwise manipulate it in order to give a clerk an advantage over actual or potential rivals. It was particularly significant in the case of expectancies, when position on the list of hopeful clerics determined the length of the wait for preferment.[31] It is unclear how widespread this practice was in the years before 1378, but the very large number of provisions supposedly made on the first day of a pontificate suggests that it was used to some extent. The possibility of a false date, and the appearance of different dates in different sources must be borne in mind when endeavouring to establish a precise chronology of events; the procedure of obtaining a provision inevitably took some time, irrespective of any manipulation of the date of the grace.

Some petitions by or on behalf of Scots mentioned the poverty of benefices already held. On 22 July 1343 Clement VI granted a

[28] *Urbain V: lettres communes*, IX, no. 27491. [29] Ibid., VI, no. 18832.
[30] *CPL*, III, 82. [31] See Watt, 'Sources for Scottish history', 104.

supplication on behalf of Alexander Bur for a canonry of Moray, with reservation of a prebend, even though he had a prebend in Dunkeld which was almost worthless because of the wars.[32] War had also damaged David de Mar's canonry of Aberdeen and treasurership of Moray, which led to his needing provision to a canonry of Glasgow, with expectation of a prebend, in December 1354.[33] When the bishop of Glasgow petitioned Urban V for a canonry of Glasgow for John Leche, he pointed out that the church of Hawick was valueless on account of war and plague.[34] The damage appears to have been nationwide, and not confined to the border areas: Andrew de Bosco's prebend in Ross was said in 1353 to be reduced in value by war and epidemics.[35] How accurate these assertions were may be doubted, but it is interesting that, as far as individual churchmen were concerned, complaints about poverty seem to have been much commoner in Scotland than in the border regions of England.

Geographical factors also came into play. When Brice Ker was provided to the church of Glencairn on 18 January 1363, he offered to resign the distant vicarage of Gamrie on the grounds that it was so far from his birthplace.[36] In December 1369 Alexander de Neville was provided to the archdeaconry of Durham and freely resigned that of Cornwall, eight days' journey from his home and the other benefices he had.[37] When Richard de Wymondeswold recommended his brother Hugh for the church of Leake in place of Slingsby, the proximity of the Nottinghamshire church to the family home was stressed.[38] On his abortive provision to the church of Acaster Malbis, John Harold had to resign a church in St David's diocese because he was ignorant of the Welsh language.[39] In 1366 John Wasil offered to resign the chancellorship of Caithness in return for a canonry and prebend of Moray, especially as he found the local language hard to follow;[40] and in the same year John Dugaldi was given a benefice in Dunkeld, but only if it was true that the church of Argyll, of which he was archdeacon, was a day's journey from Dunkeld, that the dioceses were coterminous and that he spoke the language of both well.[41] Urban V at least seems to have been concerned that provisors could speak the

[32] *CPP*, I, 66; cf. *CPL*, III, 98. [33] *CPL*, III, 520. [34] *CPP*, I, 400.
[35] Ibid., 250. [36] Ibid., 398; cf. *Urbain V: lettres communes*, I, no. 1915.
[37] *Urbain V: lettres communes*, IX, no. 26283. [38] *CPP*, I, 108.
[39] *Urbain V: lettres communes*, VII, no. 21059.
[40] *CPP*, I, 528; cf. *Urbain V: lettres communes*, V, no. 16641.
[41] *CPP*, I, 530; *Urbain V: lettres communes*, V, no. 16650.

language of the common people in the area in which their benefice was situated, and this may explain why he moderated the number of provisions to aliens.[42]

PAPAL RESERVATIONS

Provisions were based on a right of reservation which the popes used to extend their patronage. Reservations could affect either a single benefice or all benefices in a particular category in a diocese, province, realm or all Christendom. The classes of reserved benefices had increased steadily since 1179.[43] In that year archbishops were given the duty of filling benefices if the local patron and bishop let them be vacant for too long, and by the fourteenth century there was a custom whereby it lapsed to the pope to appoint a suitable clerk if the benefice continued to be vacant. In 1265 Clement IV issued a decree, said to be based on ancient custom, reserving to the Papacy any benefice void by the death of its incumbent at the Holy See, and this was extended by Boniface VIII to cover the benefices of those dying within two days' journey of the papal curia and of *curiales* who were left behind through illness when the court travelled. The term *curialis* was deemed to include not only papal servants and cardinals, but also those in residence to transact business on behalf of themselves or others. Clement V added benefices void by resignation or exchange at the Holy See or by consecration of bishops at the curia. John XXII defined and extended the reservations to include benefices vacated by papal deprivation, the quashing by the pope of an election, and the consecration or promotion of an incumbent by papal authority; benefices vacated under the anti-pluralism constitution *Execrabilis* of 1317 were also reserved to the pope. In 1335 Benedict XII further defined the classes of reservation, and it was his decree *Ad Regimen* which was the basis upon which later popes made additions of their own. These were on a limited scale: Clement VI reserved benefices held by members of his household before their death and those held by clerks who married or became soldiers or died on the Jubilee pilgrimage in 1350; Urban V widened the reservation of benefices held by papal officials to include those vacated by the death anywhere of papal collectors or deputy

[42] See below, p. 146. Foreigners were even less numerous in Scotland.

[43] In what follows I rely on the useful summary in Lunt, *Financial Relations . . . 1327–1534*, 320–3. See also Mollat, 'La collation', 10–16; see 28–9 for a list of reasons for provision being used.

collectors or scribes of the penitentiary; Gregory XI applied a reservation to benefices vacated by entrance into a religious order, although in practice this right had been exercised by earlier popes.

This is a somewhat simplified account of the general reservations, and the existence of special reservations of particular benefices must also be borne in mind in any examination of how the system affected particular geographical areas. The exercise of the papal right to provide depended very largely on whether the vacancy was brought to the pope's attention by someone who wished the benefice to be conferred on himself or a connection; not all opportunities for papal involvement were necessarily utilised. In analysing the reasons offered by petitioners for papal involvement, it is important to realise that not all the claims made in supplications were based on truth, and that by no means all provisions were successful. What is clear, however, is that while there was a variety of pretexts for papal intervention, there was little or no attempt to overstep the limits of the established classes of reserved benefices.

Many benefices were said to be vacated by the death of the previous incumbent at the curia; although there is reason to suppose that on occasion the form of words was applied to reservations which did not necessarily imply the physical presence of the late clerk at the Holy See, most of the vacancies at the curia were brought about by the actual demise there of the previous holder of the benefice. The prebend of Sharow in Ripon was sought by two clerks in 1361 on the death of William de Driffeld at Villeneuve by Avignon;[44] and Adam de Peblis received the Glasgow prebend of Durisdeer on 3 May 1370 on the death at the curia of Thomas Harkars, a member of the household of the cardinal-bishop of Tusculum.[45] Resignation at the curia for the purpose of exchange or for other reasons also rendered the benefice liable for provision, although this was infrequent compared with the very large number of resignations made to the local bishop.

The consecration of a bishop after provision by the Holy See was a very common reason for papal provision, as bishops often had several desirable benefices before their promotion.[46] The prebend of Laughton in York was provided to John de Bokingham on 20

[44] *CPP*, I, 375, 383. One of the petitions is cancelled.

[45] *Urbain V: lettres communes*, IX, no. 27536.

[46] Occasionally the papal right to provide to benefices vacated by a new bishop was waived. On 10 April 1363 the bishops of Winchester and Worcester were granted a faculty to confer the benefices of the new bishop of Lincoln on persons chosen by the king: ibid., II, no. 6184.

January 1368 on the consecration of William de Wykeham as bishop of Winchester, on which date his prebend in Beverley went to Philip de Weston and his stall in Southwell to John de Campeden.[47] Most of the benefices vacated by the promotion of bishops were prebends in cathedral or collegiate churches, but on 2 April 1346 the church of Idvies was belatedly provided to Thomas le Graunt on the consecration of Thomas de Rossy as bishop of Sodor, which had taken place in 1331,[48] and the church of Inverarity was granted to Andrew Ox in August 1361 on the consecration of Walter, bishop of Dunblane.[49] A slightly different situation prevailed on the death of Archbishop Zouche, who had been allowed to hold benefices *in commendam*: the church of Brompton was provided in 1352 to John de Provane[50] and probably also to John de Appleby.[51]

Promotion of any ecclesiastic by the pope in fact led to provision if any benefices were resigned as a result, but sometimes this was not immediately realised locally. On 9 September 1350 the chancellorship of Ross was granted in confirmation to John de Abbroyot, who had accepted it on the promotion of Alexander de Kylwos to the deanery of that church.[52] Promotion by means of an expectative grace also led to resigned benefices being reserved to the pope; when William de Spyny used an expectancy to obtain the precentorship of Aberdeen, James de Rosse was provided in 1370 to his former church of Dunnottar.[53]

A provision was often made because a benefice was reserved to the pope or the petitioner feared that it was.[54] This was often the result of special reservations made in the lifetime of the previous incumbent. In October 1349 the prebend of Grindale in York was given to John de Chestrefeld, it having been reserved in the lifetime of the late John Giffart.[55] Sometimes the date of the reservation is given: the prebend of Glasgow granted to Adam de Tyningham in February 1364 had been reserved on the previous 1 July during the lifetime of William de Curry.[56]

47 Ibid., VII, nos. 20965, 20966, 20973.

48 Coll. 282, fol. 193.

49 *CPP*, I, 375; Reg. Av. 145, fol. 161v.

50 *CPL*, III, 470.

51 Lunt, *Accounts*, 118; but cf. *CPP*, I, 236.

52 *CPP*, I, 204.

53 *Urbain V: lettres communes*, IX, no. 25965.

54 On 23 June 1346 Clement VI declared that where a reserved benefice had been filled in ignorance of the reservation and the holder of it was confirmed, the reservation continued and the benefice could be filled only by the pope: *Clément VI: lettres closes (Fr)*, no. 2607.

55 *CPP*, I, 179; *CPL*, III, 318; Lunt, *Accounts*, 89.

56 *CPP*, I, 480; *Urbain V: lettres communes*, III, no. 12172; Coll. 14, fol. 170.

The benefices of those dying while making the 1350 Jubilee pilgrimage were reserved to papal provision. The prebend of South Cave in York was granted to Nicholas de Hethe in January 1351 on the death of Robert de Kildesby during his return from the Jubilee,[57] while the vicarage of Kirknewton was still being filled by provision in the 1360s on account of the death of Robert de Jarum on the pilgrimage: it was given in September 1359 to Robert de Heppe[58] and on 3 March 1363 to John of Barnard Castle, although this was also after an exchange of benefices.[59]

The death of cardinals released to papal provision benefices which were normally rich, and often another cardinal was the man favoured. The archdeaconry of York provides a good example of unopposed provisions to cardinals. Peter de Prés was provided on 1 June 1321 and admitted on 14 September.[60] The benefice was presumably seized into the king's hands in 1346 because it was held by an alien, and it was still controlled by the king in June 1352,[61] but there do not appear to have been any attempts to oust Peter, who was succeeded on his death in 1361 by Stephen Albert.[62] He held the archdeaconry until 1369, when his demise vacated it for Philip de Cabasolle, who was admitted on 16 March 1370[63] and received a papal indult to visit by deputy in October 1371.[64] Following Philip's death Gregory XI provided Peter Gomez de Albornoz on 2 October 1372, and he in turn was collated to the archdeaconry by Archbishop Thoresby.[65] The English cardinal Simon Langham followed him in 1374,[66] and he too was allowed to conduct the duty of visitation by deputy.[67] Langham was succeeded in 1376 by another cardinal, Guy de Maillesec, who was admitted on 27 November 1376;[68] he is attested in 1377 and 1378,[69] before probably being deprived during the Schism for being an adherent of Clement VII.[70] There is no evidence of any opposition to these provisions to cardinals, despite the parliamen-

57 *CPL*, III, 415; cf. *CPP*, I, 206.

58 *CPP*, I, 347.

59 Ibid., 414; cf. *CPL*, IV, 33; *Urbain V: lettres communes*, II, no. 5290.

60 *CPL*, II, 213; Reg. Melton, fol. 94v.

61 *CCR 1349–54*, 431; but at least some of its revenues were allowed to the cardinal.

62 *CPP*, I, 376; Reg. Thoresby, fol. 49.

63 YML, L1/7, p. 683; for the provision see *Urbain V: lettres communes*, VIII, no. 24868.

64 *CPL*, IV, 168.

65 Lunt, *Accounts*, 473; Reg. Thoresby, fol. 76v.

66 Lunt, *Accounts*, 513; Reg. A. Neville, I, fol. IV.

67 *CPL*, IV, 197.

68 YML, L1/7, p. 683; cf. Lunt, *Accounts*, 515.

69 J. R. L. Highfield, 'The relations between the church and the English crown from the death of Archbishop Stratford to the opening of the Great Schism (1349–78)', DPhil. thesis, University of Oxford (1950–1), 356.

70 Le Neve, *Fasti*, VI, 18.

tary agitation against aliens and anti-papal ordinances and statutes. A benefice held by cardinals would always fall vacant at the Holy See; in this case the chapter perhaps approved of having an archdeacon who was in so influential a position at the curia.

Few cardinals were interested in Scottish benefices, but papal chaplains had benefices there, and on their death or resignation these were filled by provision. The chancellorship of Glasgow was provided in March 1343 to Reginald de Ogston on the death of William Comyn,[71] while on the death of Thomas de Kininmund, another papal chaplain, provisions were made to the church of Conveth, now Laurencekirk,[72] and a prebend in Aberdeen.[73] The benefices of other papal officials were also liable to provision. The deanery of Aberdeen was given in December 1348 to Walter de Coventre on the death of the papal auditor Gilbert Fleming,[74] and in the same year the treasurership of York was provided to Anibaldus Gaetani on the death of a papal notary.[75]

Other benefices fell liable for a provision or confirmation because the incumbent or one of his predecessors had held a church uncanonically. David de Wollore was provided to the disputed church of Bishop Wearmouth in April 1369 after he had shown that Thomas Clervaus had used an expectative grace to obtain a benefice which was too valuable to be covered by its terms.[76] The church of Marton-in-Craven was confirmed to John de Newham in 1365 because he had used a grace of Clement VI after its revocation by the succeeding pope.[77] William de Irton needed confirmation in the vicarage of Sutton-on-the-Forest in 1363 because he was a canon-regular holding a living usually filled by secular clergy.[78]

Especially in the 1360s, many provisions were made because the incumbent was a pluralist. In 1368 Walter Lenevaunt was granted the church of Ratcliffe-on-Soar on the grounds that Henry de Blakeborn held another parish church and a prebend.[79] The

[71] *CPP*, I, 14–15; *CPL*, III, 54. Comyn died outside the curia (Reg. Supp. 3, fol. 70v), and so was probably a chaplain of honour rather than a commensal papal chaplain based in Avignon.

[72] *CPP*, I, 215, 328; *CPL*, III, 425; Coll. 14, fol. 166; Reg. Av. 145, fols. 388v–390. The provision to Conveth in 1358 was also on the grounds of devolution to the pope: Reg. Supp. 31, fol. 84v.

[73] Coll. 14, fol. 175v. He too died outside the curia.

[74] *CPP*, I, 145; cf. *CPL*, III, 290.

[75] *CPP*, I, 141.

[76] Lunt, *Accounts*, 358.

[77] *CPP*, I, 504–5; *Urbain V: lettres communes*, IV, no. 13481.

[78] *CPP*, I, 424; *Urbain V: lettres communes*, I, no. 6321.

[79] *Urbain V: lettres communes*, VII, no. 21137.

church of Fetteresso was provided to Robert Monypeny in 1368 and Thomas Lang in 1370 because Gilbert Armstrong held it along with the provostship of St Mary on the Rock in St Andrews.[80] The question of pluralism had long concerned the Papacy, but it is no coincidence that many attempts to dispossess clerks with several benefices were made during the pontificate of Urban V, who made strenuous efforts to control pluralism. His endeavours were ultimately unsuccessful because of obstruction from powerful vested interests, and most of the provisions made in accordance with Urban's decrees failed to dispossess incumbents.[81]

If a benefice was left unfilled for too long, collation to it lapsed to the pope. This excuse was often used in the 1360s after churches had been appropriated, the supplicant wishing to cast doubt on the legality of the union. The churches were usually vacant only in theory, and it is quite rare to find an instance of a church which was truly devoid of an incumbent.

Benefices also devolved to the pope if the incumbent had failed to be ordained within a year and had not obtained the requisite dispensation. This reason for voidance was uncommon in England but quite common in Scotland, especially in the 1340s. The vicarage of Ellon was given to Martin Stephani in 1344 because Adam de Elon had held it for seven years without ordination,[82] while in the same year the hospital of Rathven was given to Angus de Ergadia because of the failure of John de Wemes to be promoted to orders.[83] The church of Lethnot was provided to Ingram de Ardelors in February 1366 because David de Mar and Friskin de Strivelin had not been ordained,[84] while Alexander de Caron needed confirmation in the church of Kilmany on 5 February 1367 because his unordained predecessor had held it for over a year.[85] Sometimes a confirmation could secure the position of a clerk who had himself been slow to seek ordination: the church of Kinnell was provided anew to the illegitimate David de Cunerys on 2 October 1345 after he had failed to receive priest's orders in time;[86] while Adam de Carrothurs was granted the church of Mouswald on 1 April 1370 after he had held the benefice unordained for over a year.[87] The large preponderance of Scottish examples perhaps indicates that the system of ordination was working less well than

[80] Ibid., no. 21094; IX, no. 25851. [81] See also below, p. 152.
[82] *CPL*, III, 152. [83] Coll. 281, fol. 106. [84] *CPP*, I, 518.
[85] Coll. 14, fol. 174. [86] *CPL*, III, 205; PRO, Roman Transcripts, 31/9/44, pp. 32–3.
[87] *CPL*, IV, 84; cf. XX; *Urbain V: lettres communes*, IX, nos. 25784, 26573.

in England, or that some clerks ignored the requirements of canon law and held benefices for long periods without being ordained to the priesthood. In the absence of details of ordinations carried out by Scottish bishops, it is impossible to check on the frequency of episcopal ordinations, but the problem of unordained clerks was not new: statutes had been needed in the thirteenth century to attempt to stop the abuse.[88]

A benefice held by someone under the canonical age of twenty-four could also be filled by provision. John de Cromdole received the church of Turriff in August 1345 because Michael Ramsay had been admitted to the parsonage while under age.[89] A clerk who had himself been under twenty-four required papal confirmation, which was granted to Thomas Mercer on 25 February 1370 to enable him to continue to hold the church of Methven.[90] Benefices held by illegitimates were also fair game: the church of Washington was provided to Thomas de Penreth in April 1363 because Robert de Warchopp had held it for two years without a suitable dispensation from illegitimacy;[91] and in 1345 the prebend of Rattray in Dunkeld was given to Thomas de Pilmor because William de Angus had held it without the requisite dispensation.[92] An illegitimate provisor could receive confirmation, as did Thomas de Balcaska in the church of Culter in 1366 after he had received it by exchange without the necessary grace to transfer from one benefice to another.[93] Some clerks needed papal confirmation for other reasons: Roger de Skutebury was confirmed in the vicarage of Kildwick in March 1363 after accepting it when excommunicated by a papal auditor;[94] John de Akum needed papal help to obtain a prebend in the chapel of St Mary and the Angels in York, because in lay life he had been responsible for condemning someone to death.[95] If an incumbent married, his successor needed papal provision, as did Gilbert de Welton, who was confirmed in the York prebend of Osbaldwick because Aymeric de Cusornio had married before obtaining possession.[96]

There were thus many reasons for a benefice being filled by provision. An alert clerk who was able to spot a vacancy where

[88] J. Dowden, *The Medieval Church in Scotland* (Glasgow, 1910), 127; *Statutes of the Scottish Church, 1225–1559*, ed. D. Patrick (Scottish History Soc., 1907), 43, 56, 66, 67.

[89] *CPP*, I, 104. [90] *Urbain V: lettres communes*, IX, no. 25739.

[91] *CPP*, I, 419; *Urbain V: lettres communes*, I, no. 2264. [92] *CPL*, III, 149.

[93] *CPP*, I, 519; Coll. 14, fol. 171v; *Urbain V: lettres communes*. V, nos. 16216, 17640.

[94] *CPP*, I, 413–14. [95] Ibid., 237; *CPL*, III, 471; Lunt, *Accounts*, 138.

[96] Lunt, *Accounts*, 117.

collation was reserved to the Holy See was in a good position to supplicate for a grace, and if he was first in the queue he had a good chance of obtaining provision. But the Papacy could not check the accuracy of the supplicant's claims, especially in cases where irregularity was alleged; that was left to the executors of the provision and the local authorities. The grant of a provision did not necessarily mean that the benefice was in reality vacant in the manner described, merely that it was alleged to be so and that the type of vacancy fell into one of the categories of reservation. Obtaining corporal possession of the benefice was frequently much more difficult than obtaining the bull of provision.

EXPECTATIVE GRACES

It is very difficult to measure the success rate of expectative graces, even in England, where the abundance of local evidence would seem at first sight promising. Of around eighty grants of canonries of York, with expectations of prebends, about half were successful, at least in giving a claim to a stall if not actual possession; and very many of the thirty-six prebends were affected during our period. John de Gynewell, who had been granted reservation of a prebend in April 1344,[97] was admitted to the prebend of Givendale on 3 May 1346 on the death of Richard de Chester.[98] William de Kirkby, who had an earlier grace,[99] appeared before the chapter on 21 August 1346 and showed his bulls, only to discover that Gynewell had already been inducted;[100] however, he was admitted on 17 October 1346,[101] and appears securely to have succeeded Gynewell on the latter's promotion in 1347 to the see of Lincoln, holding the stall until 1366.[102] William Woderoue, whose expectative grace was dated 5 May 1353,[103] had to wait for seven years before gaining admission as prebendary of Ulleskelf.[104]

The money prebend of Botevant was filled in this period by three men in succession who had expectative graces. Henry de Walton was granted a canonry of York, with expectation of a prebend, on 29 May 1348[105] and was admitted as a canon by the archbishop on 9 December 1350.[106] However, the grant probably lapsed when he acquired the archdeaconry of Richmond in 1349,

[97] *CPP*, I, 49; *CPL*, III, 127; YML, H1/1, fol. 27. [98] YML, H1/1, fol. 19.
[99] *CPL*, III, 134; YML, H1/1, fol. 27. [100] YML, H1/1, fol. 26.
[101] Ibid., fol. 28. [102] Reg. Thoresby, fol. 61v. [103] *CPP*, I, 244; *CPL*, III, 498.
[104] YML, L1/7, p. 1156. [105] *CPP*, I, 132; *CPL*, III, 294.
[106] Reg. Zouche, fol. 235v.

and the death of Clement VI would certainly have called it into question, necessitating a renewal on 25 January 1353.[107] Doubtless as the result of this expectancy, Walton was admitted to Botevant on 1 July 1355 on the death of John de Wodehouse,[108] and was succeeded on his death in 1359 by Walter de Campeden, who was admitted on 24 December.[109] His expectative grace, given on 10 January 1359 on the petition of John, earl of Richmond, was thus speedily fulfilled.[110] His successor, William de Forde, had rather longer to wait. He received a canonry, with reservation of a prebend, in the gift of the archbishop of York in July 1363,[111] and was collated to Botevant only on 2 September 1370;[112] however, he then held the benefice until his death in the first decade of the fifteenth century.[113]

When a prebend fell vacant there were often a number of hopeful claimants in the fray. An example is the prebend of North Newbald in the 1360s.[114] But most of the clerks who received a reservation of a prebend in York were in fact well endowed with benefices elsewhere, and probably saw the chance of a York prebend as merely one possibility among several for promotion. Many who were unlucky in York found preferment elsewhere within a few years.

The number of expectations of benefices in York Minster, however, severely limited the archbishop's freedom to collate, since there were usually several provisors with unfulfilled reservations at every vacancy; in the context also of a large number of royal presentees it was very difficult for the archbishop to offer his clerks preferment in the cathedral. Both Zouche and Thoresby received papal indults to reserve a number of benefices for their nominees: Zouche probably used his to give the prebend of South Newbald to Ralph Tervill in April 1346;[115] and Thoresby favoured his namesake in Grindale in 1367 and John de Waltham in South Newbald in 1368.[116] It was the use of expectancies, which could be applied to any vacant benefice, not merely those vacant in

[107] *CPP*, I, 238; *CPL*, III, 478.
[108] YML, H1/3, fol. 17. He continued to hold the archdeaconry: Le Neve, *Fasti*, VI, 25.
[109] YML, L1/7, p. 1101.
[110] *CPP*, I, 337.
[111] Ibid., 439; *Urbain V: lettres communes*, II, no. 7789.
[112] Reg. Thoresby, fol. 70–70v.
[113] Le Neve, *Fasti*, VI, 37.
[114] See Barrell, 'Papal relations', 178–80.
[115] Reg. Zouche, fol. 222v. For the indult see *CPL*, III, 142.
[116] Reg. Thoresby, fols. 66, 67. For the faculty to reserve benefices see *CPP*, I, 387; *Urbain V: lettres communes*, I, nos. 1179, 4644.

a particular manner, which seriously interrupted the flow of episcopal patronage; direct provisions had much less impact in this connection.

Grants of canonries of collegiate churches, with reservations of prebends, were very numerous, and the archbishop's right to collate again suffered, although it was perhaps never totally removed. In January 1349 Zouche collated Simon de Bekingham to the prebend of North Leverton in Southwell on the death of William de Leverton,[117] while in 1373 Thoresby gave the provostship of Beverley to his nephew and namesake.[118] The prior and convent of Durham presented William de Kildesby in 1341,[119] Ralph Tervill in 1346,[120] and Alexander de Neville in 1362[121] to prebends in Howden, although Tervill obtained his stall by exchange, and Neville had a long fight to oust a provisor whom he had believed to be dead. Zouche's collation of Henry de Ingelby to the prebend of Oxton in Southwell was made only by using his faculty to nominate some prebendaries in spite of papal reservations.[122] The complexities caused by the system of provision sometimes caused confusion when the archbishop tried to collate. On 16 November 1361 Thoresby gave Thomas de Middelton a prebend in the chapel of St Mary and the Angels near York Minster, said to be fully in his patronage.[123] On 28 August 1362 Middelton received the stall again, this time under the archbishop's right as an ordinary to confer benefices worth under twenty pounds of Tours with cure and fifteen without even if they were void at the curia.[124] In 1363 a third collation was made,[125] and Middelton also received a number of papal confirmations.[126] His predecessor may have died at the Holy See,[127] but only the prevailing sense of uncertainty can explain why three collations and several papal grants were apparently needed.

It is difficult to give an accurate indication of the success rate of expectative graces to collegiate churches because of the deficiencies of the sources; this is particularly so in the case of the Durham churches. Some clerks, however, certainly used expectancies to obtain benefices in collegiate churches. Reginald de Buggewille,

[117] Reg. Zouche, fol. 226v. He was confirmed by Clement VI on 5 May 1351: *CPL*, III, 386–7. [118] Reg. Thoresby, fol. 78. [119] Reg. 5A, fol. 104.
[120] Reg. Zouche, fol. 223v. [121] Reg. Thoresby, fol. 282. [122] *CPP*, I, 224.
[123] Reg. Thoresby, fol. 51; cf. fol. 52v.
[124] Ibid., fol. 57; see *CPP*, I, 420–1 for the faculty. [125] Reg. Thoresby, fol. 54v.
[126] *CPP*, I, 417, 420–1, 442. [127] Lunt, *Accounts*, 303.

given expectation of a prebend in Southwell on 22 July 1342,[128] had vacated the prebend of North Leverton by 28 August 1355.[129] Thomas de Salkeld used an expectative grace dated 11 January 1371 to obtain the prebend of Shildon in Auckland.[130] Two men who had been granted a canonry of Ripon, with expectation of a prebend, succeeded in obtaining the prebend of Nunwick: Richard atte Lane de Walton, on whom papal favour was bestowed in February 1355,[131] was succeeded on 24 September 1368 by John Turk,[132] whose expectancy was dated 24 November 1362.[133]

Prebends in collegiate churches and theoretically even in cathedrals could be accepted by men with papal reservations of benefices in the gift of the appropriate patron. Richard Bydik, who claimed the stall of Pelton in Chester-le-Street in April 1371,[134] may have used a grace promising a benefice in the gift of the bishop, prior and chapter of Durham dated 12 January 1363;[135] John Godewyk was granted an expectancy in the gift of the archbishop of York on 28 November 1362,[136] and resigned the prebend of Woodborough in Southwell on 29 March 1365;[137] Ralph Scull de Setrington was promised a benefice in the patronage of the bishop, prior and chapter of Durham in 1363,[138] and as a result claimed the deanery of Chester-le-Street.[139] But most clerks with this type of expectative grace accepted parochial benefices. William de Beverley was granted expectation of a benefice in the gift of St Mary's Abbey in York in November 1362,[140] and is attested as rector of Garforth, a church in that monastery's patronage, from September 1363 to July 1368.[141] Robert de Bulmer had an expectancy promising a benefice in the gift of the bishop of Durham dated 2 August 1354,[142] and resigned the Durham church of St Nicholas in 1362.[143] Matthew de Bolton was granted a benefice in the gift of the bishop of Carlisle in August 1348,[144] and from March 1353 is

[128] *CPP*, I, 2; *CPL*, III, 93.

[129] Reg. Thoresby, fols. 92, 94v. But he had probably been litigating with Simon de Bekingham: Reg Zouche, fol. 226v; cf. *CPL*, III, 334.

[130] Lunt, *Accounts*, 425, 517.

[131] *CPP*, I, 284; *CPL*, III, 545.

[132] Reg. Thoresby, fol. 66v.

[133] *CPP*, I, 392; *Urbain V: lettres communes*, I, no. 4632; II, no. 7226. It must be assumed that a royal grant in 1364 (*CPR 1361–64*, 440) was ineffective.

[134] *CPL*, IV, 162.

[135] *CPP*, I, 411; *Urbain V: lettres communes*, I, no. 1216; II, no. 3225.

[136] *Urbain V: lettres communes*, I, no. 3121.

[137] Reg. Thoresby, fol. 58v.

[138] *CPP*, I, 400; *Urbain V: lettres communes*, I, no. 3283.

[139] *Urbain V: lettres communes*, IX, no. 27071.

[140] Ibid., I, no. 3081.

[141] Reg. Thoresby, fols. 353v, 150v.

[142] *CPP*, I, 261; *CPL*, III, 531.

[143] Reg. Hatfield, fol. 56v.

[144] *CPP*, I, 136; *CPL*, III, 280.

attested as vicar of St Nicholas, Newcastle, a benefice in the patronage of the bishop of Carlisle.[145]

There is little evidence of the mechanism employed to place these clerks in benefices. Presumably the bull was shown to the patron, who then allowed the induction to be performed by the papal executors when a suitable benefice fell vacant.[146] In the case of some disputed churches more information is available, and it is noteworthy that the point at issue was often whether the benefice was too valuable to be accepted under the terms of an expectative grace, where a maximum taxable value was usually expressed for benefices with and without cure of souls. In most cases the admission was probably unopposed.

The success rate of graces registered at the curia (*in forma speciali*) reserving a benefice in the patronage of a named patron does not appear to have been particularly high. It is true that the virtual absence of information in the episcopal registers relating to the induction of provisors makes it problematic accurately to assess the impact of these provisions, but very few of the men who were given graces of this sort are ever attested in likely benefices, and it must be concluded that a considerable number failed or were rendered superfluous by the clerk receiving better preferment from some other source.

Very many clerks, however, received what were termed graces *in forma communi pauperum*.[147] These were usually not registered at the curia, and record of some of them has not survived. Most were made at the beginning of a pontificate, and this came to be the only time when they could normally be granted. To qualify, a clerk had to have no benefice or one worth less than fifteen pounds of Tours; livings over this value had to be resigned in advance of the grace, and all benefices had to be demitted when the grace became effective. As with other provisions, a clerk had to be of legitimate birth or dispensed from any defect. He had to supplicate in person, and if the petition was approved he was examined by men specially deputed by the pope, who confined themselves to testing ability, leaving the question of the moral worth of the clerk in the hands of

[145] Reg. Hatfield, fol. 29.

[146] Cf. a notarial instrument of 1387 certifying that the proctor of a provisor had appeared at the abbey of St Mary's, York with a bull reserving a benefice in the gift of that monastery: YML, M2/1f, fol. 24.

[147] On what follows see C. Tihon, 'Les expectatives *in forma pauperum*, particulièrement au xive siècle', *Bulletin de l'Institut historique belge de Rome*, 5 (1925), 51–118.

the executors; from 1373 the candidate was also examined in the language of the place to which he wanted to go. Those who achieved the best results in the examination had priority over others examined at the same time, and in practice at least the date of the grace was determined by the standard of the performance in the test. The clerk took the bull to the executors who had been appointed, and they then endeavoured to bring the provision to fulfilment. The benefice was usually conferred in the clerk's native diocese and was limited in England to a taxable value of twenty marks with cure of souls and fifteen without; cathedral prebends were not available to clerks with these graces, although stalls in collegiate churches were. The grace did not supplant general or special papal reservations, although on 19 October 1344 Clement VI allowed men with expectations to accept prebends and other benefices up to a value of sixty pounds of Tours with cure and forty without for a period of two years despite special reservations,[148] and on 5 October 1347 the same pope suspended for one year reservations of benefices to the same value so as to offer an opportunity for poor clerks with expectative graces to obtain preferment.[149] Normally a clerk who took a benefice liable for direct provision required and would receive papal confirmation of his tenure. If the provisor obtained another benefice or expectancy before the grace *in forma pauperum* was fulfilled, the latter was usually declared void, and from the time of Benedict XII onwards a new pope revoked the ineffective grants of his predecessor, if only to allow the new pontiff to be more generous.

Graduates were allowed to have slightly richer benefices than non-graduates,[150] and sometimes letters of poor graduates were registered at Avignon. It should also be noted that some grants to poor clerks who appear not to have been graduates are found in the Registers of Supplications. Some 104 Englishmen are noted there under Urban V,[151] and at an earlier stage the poor clerks John de Prestenwyc, William de Spyny and John de Karale are listed in the papal sources as having received expectations of benefices in the patronage of Dunfermline Abbey, the bishop of St Andrews and Haddington Priory respectively, Karale being told to renounce an

[148] *Clément VI: lettres closes (Fr)*, no. 1172.

[149] Ibid., no. 3497. [150] Tihon, 'Les expectatives', 60.

[151] Lunt, *Financial Relations . . . 1327–1534*, 348 n. 322; *CPP*, I, 427–34. For earlier grants to poor clerks see *CPP*, I, 2, 7, 54–6, 136.

expectancy promising a benefice in the gift of Arbroath.[152] It is, however, not clear that these grants were technically *in forma communi pauperum*.[153]

The number of graces *in forma pauperum* is very difficult to determine. It is believed that around 100,000 hopefuls congregated at Avignon around the time of the accession of Clement VI.[154] The new pope granted these provisions from the day of his coronation (19 May 1342) to the following 24 June, and by 11 June 80,000 clerks had arrived in search of expectancies *in forma pauperum*, including over forty asking for graces in the church of Hamburg.[155] What the comparable numbers for England and Scotland were is not known, but it must be assumed that, despite the difficulties of travel, a large number of clerks from the British Isles sought this sort of provision in 1342.

Apart from stray references, the only evidence we have of clerks with expectancies *in forma pauperum* is found in the English episcopal registers, where the ordinary, the normal executor of graces not affecting his own patronage, subdelegated the papal mandate to others, usually dignitaries and the heads of religious houses, but sometimes a wider body of clergy.[156] Grants *in forma pauperum* reserving benefices in the gift of the bishop were entrusted by the pope to three local executors,[157] and most of these have disappeared without trace. Even in the case of provisions of which the ordinary was the executor, there is no means of telling how full the episcopal registers are. Certainly some clerics are attested in other sources with otherwise unrecorded graces *in forma pauperum*, such as John Pole de Clifford, who was told in 1363 to resign his provision to a benefice in the gift of Whitby Abbey,[158] or Simon Spark, who in 1352 had a grant *in forma pauperum* promising a benefice in Bridlington Priory's patronage;[159] but how numerous omissions from the episcopal registers were it is

152 For Prestenwyc see *CPP*, I, 34. For Spyny see Reg. Supp. 23, fol. 180v; cf. fol. 177 showing that this was a poor clerks' roll. For Karale see *CPP*, I, 268; cf. *CPL*, III, 531–2. Of these, only Spyny was a graduate.

153 However, there is a section in one of Urban V's registers entitled 'De beneficiis sub expectatione in forma communi': *Urbain V: lettres communes*, I, nos. 1422–95, from Reg. Av. 154, fols. 327–344.

154 Barraclough, *Papal Provisions*, 31 n. 2, 106.

155 *Das Formelbuch des Heinrich Bucglant*, ed. J. Schwalm (Hamburg, 1910), xlii.

156 Tihon, 'Les expectatives', 83, says that the executor usually subdelegated the mandate to all the clergy of the diocese, but this was the exception rather than the rule as far as York was concerned. In Worcester the bishop commonly named a single subexecutor: Haines, *Administration of the Diocese of Worcester*, 213.

157 Tihon, 'Les expectatives', 81.

158 *CPP*, I, 398; *Urbain V: lettres communes*, I, no. 1908.

159 *CPP*, I, 224; *CPL*, III, 425–6.

impossible to tell. Very occasionally a provisor was from further afield: a clerk from Utrecht diocese was promised a benefice in the patronage of the bishop of Durham,[160] despite the fact that normally supplicants had to confine their ambitions to benefices in their own locality.[161]

Relatively few expectative graces *in forma pauperum* are found in the episcopal registers of Durham and Carlisle; perhaps the fact that a large proportion of the spiritual patronage in those dioceses was vested in the bishop goes some way towards explaining this, although the gaps in the records must also be borne in mind. The York evidence is much fuller, and some idea of relative numbers of this type of grace can be derived from it.

Archbishop Zouche's register records 133 graces of which the archbishop was the executor; these all relate to grants made by Clement VI, and several affected the patronage of ecclesiastics based outside the diocese, including the bishop of Durham.[162] The majority were subdelegated in the period between 5 November 1342 and the end of 1343, although there is a trickle of them until 13 October 1349,[163] which indicates either that some clerks were unaccountably slow in bringing their bulls to Zouche's attention, or that grants *in forma pauperum* continued to be made throughout the pontificate, even if not on the scale of 1342. Provided that the evidence is consistent, Clement VI was much more liberal with this type of grace than were his immediate successors. Thoresby's register records only six such grants from Innocent VI, all subdelegated in the spring and summer of 1353, twenty-eight from Urban V, including three subdelegated in 1365, and only five from Gregory XI. A cautionary note must, however, be sounded. The poor priest Ralph de Allerton was said to have had an expectation of a benefice in the gift of the Hospitallers when he received the vicarage of Marnham on 27 March 1367;[164] and John Aligod, poor clerk, obtained the vicarage of Atwick on 18 May 1373 by means of a grace promising a benefice in the patronage of Bridlington Priory.[165] In both these cases there is no record of the original subdelegation of the executorial bull.

The survival of this information is fortuitous, for in common with other types of provision the institutions of clerks with

[160] In August 1363 he offered to resign this grace in return for another provision: Fierens, *Suppliques d'Urbain V*, no. 1011.

[161] Tihon, 'Les expectatives', 84.

[162] Reg. Zouche, fols. 217v, 222v, 223.

[163] Ibid., fol. 231v.

[164] Reg. Thoresby, fols. 264v–265.

[165] Ibid., fol. 277v.

expectancies *in forma pauperum* are rarely recorded in the episcopal registers. Indeed, the only other instances where the entry to a benefice of a clerk with such a grace is recorded are John Tankard's admission in 1343 to the disputed church of Fewston,[166] and Robert Boner de Synelington's induction to the church of Heslerton in 1363,[167] although in 1348 Zouche's registrar reported the profession of obedience of three others who had used an expectancy *in forma pauperum* to obtain a benefice: Nicholas de Wartre, rector of Roos;[168] Hugh Bellers de Middelton, vicar of Sherburn;[169] and Adam de Blida, vicar of Muston.[170] Why these particular examples appear in the episcopal sources is not clear: the registrar may have been inconsistent, or there may have been difficulties in these cases in obtaining the benefice. What is clear is that it is impossible, except very occasionally, to fill gaps in the survival of subdelegation mandates with references to grants *in forma pauperum* elsewhere in the episcopal registers.

Evidence for the success of these graces thus rests on finding men who had received such grants in possession of appropriate benefices. In some respects this is more difficult than for provisions *in forma speciali*, since most of the casual references to provisors in episcopal sources are in licences to be absent or in commissions, and these generally involved more prominent clerks than the theoretically impoverished recipients of grants *in forma pauperum*. The death or resignation of an incumbent is usually noted in the institution of his successor, but if the latter also had a papal grace the institution would not be recorded at all and the information about the previous holder of the living is not available. Moreover, during the Black Death pressure of business meant that the name of the deceased incumbent was often not written in full; this is particularly unfortunate because some of Clement VI's provisors will have perished in the plague. So any figures must be qualified by stressing that they represent an underestimate of the success of grants *in forma pauperum*, and that those graces which we know about themselves constitute a mere part – an indeterminable part – of the total granted; in addition, firm evidence that an expectancy was actually used to obtain a particular benefice is usually lacking.

In view of these problems, it is somewhat surprising that over a

166 Reg. Zouche, fol. 218v; see fols. 214v–215 for the expectancy.

167 Reg. Thoresby, fol. 208v; see fol. 54 for the expectancy.

168 Reg. Zouche, fol. 187; see fol. 221 for the expectancy.

169 Ibid., fol. 192v. The expectancy was subdelegated by the archbishop only on 11 April 1347: ibid., fol. 224v.

170 Ibid., fol. 192; see fol. 214v for the expectancy.

quarter and possibly as many as a third of the recorded graces *in forma pauperum* can be shown to have borne fruit. Richard de Percy, on whom Clement VI bestowed an expectancy of a benefice in the gift of the Hospitallers,[171] died as vicar of Whitkirk, which was in the patronage of the knights, before 11 August 1349.[172] Another Black Death victim was William de Wolferton, rector of the York church of St Saviour's,[173] who had been promised a benefice in the gift of St Mary's Abbey.[174] On 3 October 1349 Roger del Dale resigned the vicarage of East Retford, which was in the gift of the sacristan of the chapel of St Mary and the Holy Angels,[175] to a benefice in whose patronage he had been provided.[176] John de Hemyngburgh is attested as rector of a moiety of Treswell on 30 September 1347,[177] and his tenure of the benefice was probably the result of an expectative grace affecting the patronage of the chapter of York.[178] On 18 April 1370 Richard de Hemyngburgh resigned the vicarage of Hunsingore,[179] a cure which he had probably accepted by means of an expectative grace to a benefice in the gift of the Hospitallers.[180] Examples could be multiplied. It is clear that even in the days of great pressure after the generous policy of Clement VI's early months a good proportion of men with expectancies *in forma pauperum* obtained a suitable benefice, some of them very speedily.[181]

Only a few provisors encountered difficulties in the sense that their tenure of the benefice was challenged. John Tankard, who had had to wait only until 2 August 1343 before receiving the church of Fewston,[182] found the benefice claimed by both Edmund de Theddemersh[183] and William de Waynflet.[184] William Vavasour was inducted to the vicarage of Aldburgh in Holderness by the prior of Haltemprice, who had been appointed as subexecutor of his papal grace, but the benefice was in the king's gift on account of his holding the temporalities of the alien priory of Burstall, and he had presented William de Pulhowe. In 1353 the prior was forced to submit under a fine of five marks.[185] Perhaps

[171] Ibid., fol. 219. [172] Ibid., fol. 34. [173] Ibid., fol. 35v.

[174] Ibid., fol. 214v. [175] Ibid., fol. 134v. [176] Ibid., fol. 219.

[177] Ibid., fol. 122v. [178] Ibid., fol. 215v.

[179] Thompson, 'Richmond registers', 176, no. 73. [180] Reg. Thoresby, fol. 54v.

[181] In a study of the effect of these graces on monastic patronage, evidence was found for their routine implementation, especially in the dioceses of Bath and Wells and Exeter: McDonald, 'Relations', 336–9. [182] Reg. Zouche, fol. 218v; cf. fols. 214v–215.

[183] Ibid., fol. 242v. [184] *CPR 1343–45*, 235; Reg. Zouche, fols. 6v, 11.

[185] *Court of York*, 23; *CFR 1347–56*, 358. For Vavasour's expectancy see Reg. Zouche, fol. 227.

more successful was Roger de Gysburn, who claimed the vicarage of Long Preston by virtue of a provision *in forma pauperum* reserving a benefice in the patronage of Bolton Priory;[186] he was opposed by Robert Lacer, who was instituted on 14 December 1367,[187] but Gysburn probably obtained possession because he was given a licence to be absent in 1375.[188]

Why the grants *in forma pauperum* were more successful than the apparently more elaborate and more secure expectancies *in forma speciali*, at least where parochial benefices were concerned, can only be guessed at. The answer perhaps lies in the type of men involved. Poor clerks by definition had no benefice or at least one of very low value; they were likely to press as far as was within their power for the grace to be effected, and would almost certainly accept any suitable benefice which might be offered. Some perhaps received patronage from elsewhere, but for most the papal grace would be their sole hope of advancement. By contrast, many of the recipients of expectancies *in forma speciali* were already well endowed with benefices or had powerful backers who could use their influence in other directions if the papal provision failed. Many of them probably saw the grant as another iron in the fire, rather as an application for a better job by one already in employment than as their only hope of promotion. Because in practice benefices already held were resigned only when a grace *in forma speciali* bore fruit, beneficed clerks could view expectancies in the manner of an investment, and could give them up if they received a fresh papal provision or advancement from some other quarter to a better incumbency than that offered by the expectative grace.[189]

In the absence of episcopal registers, the success rate of Scottish expectancies is almost impossible to ascertain; all that can be done is to give instances of the success or probable success of expectative graces. On 19 June 1342 Walter de Wardlaw received a canonry of

[186] *Fasti Parochiales*, IV, 106. [187] Reg. Thoresby, fol. 145v.

[188] Reg. A. Neville, I, fol. 18v.

[189] T. N. Cooper, 'The Papacy and the diocese of Coventry and Lichfield, 1360–1385', *AHP*, 25 (1987), 87–92, found little evidence that expectative graces were fulfilled: under a tenth of reservations of prebends in Lichfield succeeded in the period from 1360 to 1385, and no expectancies *in forma pauperum* are thought to have been realised. From the York evidence this seems unlikely, and it is possible that the author has found no institutions of men with these graces and has not recognised that they were rarely registered in episcopal sources. The expectancies listed in the collectors' accounts were surely not *in forma pauperum* as is conjectured, but rather graces from which annates were due for a period in the early 1370s; the fact that nothing was paid does not necessarily imply failure of the grace.

Glasgow, with expectation of a prebend;[190] he occurs as prebendary in 1349,[191] and on his consecration as bishop in 1367 his prebend was Renfrew.[192] John de Cromdole, given expectation of a prebend of Ross on 6 August 1345,[193] held the stalls of Cullicudden and later Nonakiln and Roskeen.[194] By 27 January 1371 Thomas de Duns was prebendary of Cardross in Glasgow,[195] having been given a reservation of a prebend in that cathedral on 10 April 1366.[196] In contrast with England, it is impossible to say how quickly these graces came to fruition, although it can be assumed that the time between provision and effect varied as it did south of the border. It is even more difficult to estimate the effect of grants to benefices in the gift of a particular patron, although some were fruitful within a very few years. William de Lytthon, for whom was reserved a benefice in the gift of the bishop of St Andrews in June 1350,[197] was rector of Dysart by 14 September 1353;[198] Adam Pullur, granted a benefice in the gift of the bishop of Dunkeld on 24 June 1345,[199] was vicar of Strathmiglo by 8 October 1347.[200] Thomas de Torreth, who became vicar of Musselburgh,[201] perhaps used an expectative grace affecting the patronage of Dunfermline Abbey.[202] John Rede, who in 1350 was granted reservation of a benefice in the gift of the bishop and chapter of Dunkeld,[203] may have used it to become a canon of the cathedral and prebendary of Forgandenny.[204]

One Scottish expectative grace is known to have run into trouble. John de Stallys, canon of Holyrood, was on 19 June 1348 granted reservation of a benefice in the gift of the bishop of St Andrews.[205] This proved ineffective for the simple reason that the bishop had no benefices in his patronage which could be conferred on canons-regular, so on 9 August 1350 Stallys received a fresh grace entitling him to a benefice to the value of 70 merks in the gift of any patron in St Andrews diocese, despite his litigation over the vicarage of Falkirk.[206]

Such wide-ranging grants as this were rare, and usually the beneficiaries were cardinals. In 1342 Aymar Robert was granted

190 *CPL*, III, 58. 191 *CPP*, I, 175, 176.
192 Watt, *Dictionary*, 571; *CPL Clem. VII*, 196. 193 *CPP*, I, 104; *CPL*, III, 200.
194 Watt, *Dictionary*, 129. 195 Ibid., 169. 196 *CPP*, I, 525.
197 Ibid., 200; *CPL*, III, 365–6. 198 Watt, *Dictionary*, 364.
199 *CPP*, I, 95; *CPL*, III, 207. 200 *CPP*, I, 130; *CPL*, III, 258.
201 Watt, *Dictionary*, 536.
202 *Urbain V: lettres communes*, III, no. 8980. He was a poor clerk: Reg. Supp. 42, fol. 163.
203 *CPP*, I, 201; *CPL*, III, 389. 204 Cf. Watt, *Dictionary*, 467. 205 *CPP*, I, 131.
206 Ibid., 202; *CPL*, III, 420.

expectation of benefices up to an assessed value of 1000 marks in the province of York.[207] This grant provoked considerable opposition in parliament, especially in 1343,[208] and it is instructive to examine how Aymar fared in seeking northern benefices.

The cardinal had accepted the archdeaconry of the East Riding by 1 August 1343, and is named as archdeacon in royal sources in February 1345 and April 1349,[209] although in 1347 Clement VI complained that persons had been intruded into the benefice, his proctors had been cited to parliament, and his letters of provision had been taken away.[210] Aymar also claimed the York prebend of Warthill. In September 1344 he was said to be unable to obtain the fruits of the annexed church of Axminster,[211] and in 1348 the benefice was in the king's hands because it was held by an absentee foreigner.[212] Aymar had been admitted to Warthill on 29 June 1343,[213] and probably held both the prebend and the archdeaconry until his death in 1352, even though the revenues were diverted to the royal coffers following Edward III's seizure of the fruits of benefices held by aliens in 1346. The cardinal also pursued for a time a claim to the church of Manfield, although this was apparently disputed, and in March 1347 Peter de Langeton was surrogated into his right.[214] Aymar Robert also claimed the prebend of St Mary's Altar in Beverley until his resignation in 1346.[215]

On their accession, popes frequently annulled the unfulfilled expectancies of their predecessor. On 29 January 1353 Innocent VI revoked the grants of Clement VI,[216] and as a result Richard de Fogow needed renewal of his reservation of a prebend of Glasgow,[217] as rather later did Gilbert Armstrong.[218] It is uncertain whether Urban V similarly revoked the graces bestowed by his predecessor, but in January 1364 Thomas Harkars received confirmation of his expectation of a prebend of Moray,[219] first granted by Innocent VI on 14 December 1353.[220]

Those who ignorantly accepted benefices after the revocation were sometimes pardoned and allowed to hold the benefice which

207 *CPL*, III, 74.

208 *Rot. Parl.*, II, 141.

209 *CPL*, III, 112; *CCR 1343–46*, 501; *CPR 1348–50*, 279.

210 *CPL*, III, 34.

211 Ibid., 10. The revenues of Axminster were divided between the prebendaries of Warthill and Grindale: YML, L2/2a, fols. 25v–26.

212 *CPR 1348–50*, 51.

213 YML, L1/7, p. 1065.

214 *CPL*, III, 239–40.

215 Ibid., 199.

216 *Innocent VI: lettres secrètes et curiales*, nos. 101–2.

217 *CPP*, I, 259–60; cf. *CPL*, III, 519.

218 *CPP*, I, 346; cf. Reg. Av. 141, fols. 347v–348.

219 *CPP*, I, 476.

220 Ibid., 255.

they had obtained. Thomas Bur used a grace dated 9 August 1350[221] to receive the prebend of Rhynie in Moray, in which he was confirmed on 18 January 1354 with the proviso that the confirmation was valid only if he had indeed been ignorant of Innocent VI's revocation of Clement's grants.[222] John Pray needed a similar confirmation in the vicarage of St Laurence, Appleby in December 1355; he had accepted the benefice by means of a grace *in forma pauperum* even though this had been annulled.[223] Sometimes also it was necessary for an acceptance under an expectative grace to be ratified because the right to provide to the benefice in question had been reserved to the pope: in December 1354 Brice Ker was confirmed in the vicarage of Gamrie, having accepted it on the promotion of William Boyle to the precentorship of Moray in ignorance that the circumstances of the vacancy had rendered the living liable to direct provision.[224]

Papal favour in the shape of an expectative grace was certainly a useful means of promotion for some, although if there were several rivals also in the field problems were very likely to arise. The length of time during which it was necessary to await a benefice depended largely on the individual's place in the queue and the availability of benefices in the patronage of the appropriate person or corporation or in the named cathedral or collegiate church. English patrons were probably more seriously affected by expectancies than their Scottish counterparts, but that does not necessarily imply that Scots with such graces fared better than those in England. In any event, a man who obtained a better benefice from some other source or through a later provision would probably be quite happy to abandon his unfulfilled promise of an unnamed benefice. Direct provisions, though often disputed and by no means always successful, seemed at least on the surface more secure, and it is to these that we must now turn.

DIRECT PROVISIONS

It is in fact far from straightforward to estimate the success rate even of direct provisions. Sometimes several grants relating to the

[221] Ibid., 204; *CPL*, III, 365.

[222] *CPL*, III, 523; Reg. Supp. 27, fol. 10v; cf. Coll. 14, fol. 164v; Coll. 287, fol. 77v.

[223] *CPP*, I, 290. However, Innocent VI also appears to have a granted him an expectancy *in forma pauperum*: Reg. Welton, p. 19.

[224] *CPP*, I, 265; *CPL*, III, 530.

same benefice were made to the same clerk, but on other occasions this is only apparent and is due to different dates being given in different sources or to obvious repetitions. In the case of some provisions, especially in Scotland, insufficient information is available even to guess at the success or otherwise of a provision, while some which were ultimately successful were certainly disputed either immediately or later on. But, if the provisions whose effect is uncertain are discounted, the success rate of direct grants (including those where the recipient triumphed over rival claimants) is around 56 per cent in the province of York in the period 1342–70, with provisions to benefices in York diocese being more successful than those in Durham and Carlisle, and as much as 73 per cent in Scotland.

Most benefices, especially parish churches, were filled by provisors only occasionally, and in many cases the provisions were unopposed and incumbents with papal title took their place among clerks instituted by the ordinary.[225] Cases where provisions failed or were disputed are often encountered in the sources, but this was often because a lawsuit ensued or the disappointed clerk sought preferment through a further petition to the pope; unfulfilled graces were often mentioned in supplications because of the necessity to bring to the pope's attention any factor which might be deemed relevant to his considering the new request. But by no means all provisions ran into difficulty.

Some provisions failed because another clerk had received provision as well. Thomas Arundel's provision to the York prebend of Ampleforth on 1 May 1370[226] duplicated a grant to Roger de Freton,[227] and was, therefore, to be annulled.[228] The provisor might find the benefice he sought already detained by someone else who could not be ousted. Duncan de Strathern, given the prebend of Cruden in Aberdeen in July 1344, was unable to remove John de Carrick,[229] and his successor Alexander Stewart was no more successful.[230] Sometimes a provisor withstood a whole series of papal provisions to his benefice, as in the case of the York church of All Saints, Pavement after the death of Simon

225 For an example (Slingsby) see A. D. M. Barrell, 'The effect of papal provisions on Yorkshire parishes, 1342–1370', *Northern History*, 28 (1992), 97–8.

226 Lunt, *Accounts*, 407.

227 *Urbain V: lettres communes*, IX, no. 27533; Lunt, *Accounts*, 413.

228 *Urbain V: lettres communes*, IX, no. 27535.

229 *CPL*, III, 150, 243; Coll. 14, fol. 159.

230 *CPL*, III, 243; Coll. 14, fol. 160v.

Ward in 1361.[231] Three provisors entertained a claim to the vacant church, but were unsuccessful because Ward had been defeated in a lawsuit by an unnamed possessor.[232] Only in 1372 did the last of the provisors, John de Lund, achieve admission to the church after winning a suit against two other claimants.[233] The failure of Ward to maintain possession was the reason why several papal grants did not come to fruition; the ensuing lawsuits must have involved the litigants in considerable expense.

A provision could fail because the wrong reason was advanced for the vacancy of the benefice, or because the benefice was not in fact vacant. After John de Asshebourn had been provided to the hospital of Bolton in Durham diocese it was discovered that the benefice was not vacant at the Holy See and was held by ordinary authority by Alexander de Neville.[234] Walter Morin was provided to the church of Sedgefield in October 1349 on the death of John de Whitechirch,[235] but the latter was still alive at that time.[236] In June 1347 Clement VI granted to Robert de Askeby the church of Sturton-le-Steeple on the death of Adam de Haselbeche,[237] but he required a further provision in February 1348 because Adam had not then been dead;[238] the new grant also failed since Haselbeche had in fact resigned the benefice in September 1346.[239] Angelicus Grimaud was so eager to obtain the rich prebend of South Cave in York that he was twice provided to it on the falsely reported death of Henry de Ingelby,[240] before accepting it by means of an expectative grace, after which he received papal ratification on 28 November 1375.[241] Although provisions to benefices which were not vacant usually failed, the claims which resulted could involve both parties in considerable trouble and expense.

When royal nominees also entertained claims to a benefice, a dispute could ensue which was prolonged and bitter. The most celebrated instance during our period concerned the rich deanery of York, vacated when Zouche became archbishop of York.

231 Ward was granted letters dimissory on 14 February 1361 (Reg. Thoresby, fol. 106v), but was allegedly dead by 4 July (*CPP*, I, 370).

232 See e.g. Lunt, *Accounts*, 301, 336, 376. For further details see Barrell, 'Papal relations', 218–19.

233 Reg. Thoresby, fol. 164v. For Lund's original provision in 1366 see *CPP*, I, 525; *Urbain V: lettres communes*, v, no. 16245. He was confirmed by Urban V in 1369: Lunt, *Accounts*, 359. He probably held the church until 1406: YML, L1/8, fol. 71.

234 Lunt, *Accounts*, 118.

235 *CPP*, I, 178.

236 Lunt, *Accounts*, 118.

237 *CPP*, I, 125; *CPL*, III, 240.

238 *CPL*, III, 259.

239 Reg. Zouche, fol. 116.

240 Lunt, *Accounts*, 404, 513.

241 *CPL*, IV, 212–13.

Within about a year, three rival jurisdictions had each put forward a candidate. The chapter elected one of its members, Thomas Sampson; the pope provided Cardinal Talleyrand de Périgord; and, rather later, the king presented John de Offord.[242] The king had sanctioned the election,[243] and it was only after it was opposed by the pope[244] that he made a presentation of his own. Clement VI based his right on the fact that Zouche had been provided to the see and so his benefices were reserved to the Holy See; Edward III asserted that Zouche had vacated the deanery before the temporalities of the see had been restored to him, and so it could be filled under regalian right, and that the archbishop had alienated the advowson without royal licence.[245] Sampson withdrew, and the royal grant to Offord was not pursued, but a later presentation by the king in 1347, in favour of Philip de Weston, proved to be a more serious threat to Talleyrand.[246] The king ordered Weston's admission, and the pope prohibited it. The hapless archbishop decided to obey the secular power, and by the end of November 1347 Weston had been admitted.[247] Clement excommunicated Weston on 1 March 1348 for his contumacy in not obeying his citation to the curia;[248] and in June 1349, despite having made a proposal to Edward III that Weston would be shown other favour if the king let Talleyrand act as dean,[249] he cited the archbishop and chapter before him and deprived the royal nominee of all his benefices.[250] Talleyrand's position had been undermined in 1346 by the seizure of revenues from benefices held by foreigners, but references to the deanery being in the king's hands imply that the cardinal had had some success in pursuing his provision.[251] Indeed, he is named as dean in a royal record in February 1345,[252] and by 1 February 1350 he had come to an agreement with Weston.[253] Thereafter Talleyrand seems to have enjoyed secure possession until his death in 1364.

242 Ibid., III, 71, 74; *CPR 1343–45*, 52.

243 *CCR 1341–43*, 603.

244 *CPL*, III, 71; cf. *Clément VI: lettres closes (non-Fr)*, no. 106; Reg. Zouche, fols. 216v–217.

245 *CPR 1343–45*, 52.

246 For Weston's presentation see *CPR 1345–48*, 263; cf. 412. Sampson continued to be canon of York and prebendary of Holme until his death in 1349.

247 *CPR 1345–48*, 376, 412; *CPL*, III, 255; Reg. Zouche, fols. 225v, 227–227v. According to the seventeenth-century antiquary Torre, Weston was admitted on 24 August: YML, L1/7, p. 557.

248 *CPL*, III, 253.

249 Ibid., 40; *Clément VI: lettres closes (non-Fr)*, no. 2009.

250 *CPL*, III, 337.

251 *CFR 1347–56*, 231, 284.

252 *CCR 1343–46*, 501; *Foedera*, III, 29–30.

253 YML, H1/1, fol. 68. This is hinted at in June 1349: *CPL*, III, 40; *Clément VI: lettres closes (non-Fr)*, no. 2009.

This bitter dispute provoked a large number of royal mandates and papal citations and even led to the excommunication of Archbishop Zouche.[254] As well as the principles at stake, there was the personality of Cardinal Talleyrand, who was said to be a great enemy of Edward III at the papal court.[255] Despite that, the provisor prevailed over the royal nominee, even though Weston continued to be prebendary of Langtoft and so a member of the York chapter until his resignation in 1362.[256]

There are several other instances around this time where papal provisors clashed with royal nominees. Each example is different, and all that can be said by way of generalisation is that there was no certainty that a royal presentation would prevail over a provision or vice versa. Edward II's success in enforcing appointments which were opposed by provisors was likewise mixed.[257] There may be something in the argument advanced by C. Davies that royal claims were tempered after 1347 on account of Edward III's shortage of money and desire for papal help after the Crécy campaign and the capture of Calais, and the arrival soon afterwards of the Black Death;[258] but the general impression of a fall in the number of royal presentations in the years which followed is more likely to have been the result of the king exhausting the regalian right he claimed in respect of earlier vacancies than of his needing to be accommodating towards the pope, with whom relations remained generally poor until the death of Clement VI.[259] It has been argued that even if a provisor won a case against a royal presentee the latter could resign and the king present someone else, thereby initiating a new lawsuit and potentially continuing the process almost indefinitely.[260] Although sometimes there was a string of royal nominees to a benefice, a provisor sometimes prevailed, which implies royal consent or at least acquiescence and a willingness on the king's part to compromise; this may have been most likely if he needed papal aid or goodwill, but such a correlation is almost impossible to prove. What the disputes do show is how both royal and papal grants interrupted local patronage and

254 *CPL*, III, 434. 255 Murimuth, *Continuatio Chronicarum*, 230.

256 Le Neve, *Fasti*, VI, 62.

257 W. E. L. Smith, *Episcopal Appointments and Patronage in the Reign of Edward II. A Study in the Relations of Church and State* (Chicago, 1938), chap. 4.

258 C. Davies, 'The Statute of Provisors of 1351', *History*, 38 (1953), 122.

259 See below, pp. 133–44.

260 A. Deeley, 'Papal provision and royal rights of patronage in the early 14th century', *EHR*, 43 (1928), 518–19.

made it difficult for chapters to elect and bishops to collate; however the clashes between king and pope were resolved in individual cases, the weakness of local jurisdictions is noteworthy.

Evidence of royal presentation in Scotland is exiguous, although David II's grant is said to have impeded Robert de Den's provision to the church of Liston,[261] and a royal presentation to the church of Kinkell required papal confirmation in 1346.[262] Ironically, royal presentations in Scotland are best attested where they involved the area controlled, at least nominally, by Edward III. The border prebend of Old Roxburgh in Glasgow was provided in February 1348 to Thomas Todd in exchange with Hugh de Douglas for the church of Skirling.[263] Todd's rivals were presented by the king of England. On the day of the provision the position of Richard de Swynhope in the benefice was ratified by Edward III,[264] this following three royal grants in December 1346 and January 1347;[265] although these were unsuccessful in themselves, Edward allowed Swynhope to take the fruits of the benefice, which was under English occupation.[266] Edward proceeded to present William de Emeldon in February 1352,[267] Roger de Bromley in November 1360,[268] John de Baumburgh in October 1361,[269] Richard de Swynhope again in October 1362,[270] and finally Richard de Middelton in November 1369,[271] but there is no reason to suppose that these English clerks were recognised outside the area of occupation. Canonically, Todd doubtless continued to hold the benefice, as he is described as canon of Glasgow regularly to 15 November 1372,[272] including several times in English sources,[273] and on his death he was succeeded in 1379 by Henry de Wardlaw;[274] but whether he ever enjoyed the fruits of his prebendal church is very doubtful. The papal collector stated that Todd had paid no annates because of the English occupation, and indeed the assessment of the benefice was in doubt;[275] there is no reason to suppose that these difficulties were short-term, and the benefice was probably useful to Todd only insofar as it gave him the right to

261 Coll. 14, fol. 159v.

262 *CPP*, I, 113; cf. *CPL*, III, 230, 238–9. For a presentation, using regalian right, to a Glasgow prebend by Robert I in 1325 see *Glasgow Registrum*, I, 230–1.

263 *CPL*, III, 243; Coll. 282, fol. 103v.

264 *CPR 1348–50*, 10.

265 *CPR 1345–48*, 213, 222, 225; cf. *Rot. Scot.*, I, 709.

266 *CPR 1350–54*, 137.

267 *Rot. Scot.*, I, 749.

268 *Foedera*, III, 553; *Rot. Scot.*, I, 852.

269 *CPR 1361–64*, 90; *Rot. Scot.*, I, 857.

270 *Rot. Scot.*, I, 865.

271 Ibid., 935.

272 Reg. Av. 187, fol. 61v.

273 *Rot. Scot.*, I, 891, 901, 921; *CPR 1367–70*, 133.

274 Watt, *Dictionary*, 535.

275 Coll. 14, fols. 181v, 188.

a stall in the cathedral, a voice in chapter, and a share of the revenues of common churches held by that body.

As has been stated, deprivations on the grounds of pluralism rarely succeeded. George Sicilie de Hewden was given the prebend of Thorpe in Ripon on 30 January 1367 on the deprivation of a pluralist, but the grace was not carried through.[276] No more successful was Michael de Monymusk, who was provided in 1366 to the prebend in Aberdeen held by the pluralist John More;[277] the grace led to a lawsuit which was still in progress in 1370 when Monymusk became bishop of Dunkeld, after which Giles, cardinal-bishop of Tusculum, was surrogated into his right to the prebend.[278] The deprivation of unlicensed pluralists was not a new phenomenon in Urban V's pontificate, but it was during this time that the most complex dispute concerning pluralism was at its height.

The rich church of Bishop Wearmouth was a desirable prize, even for cardinals. In October 1325 John XXII granted it to the cardinal John Gaetani de Orsini,[279] but on his death in 1335 it passed to an Englishman, John de Eston,[280] who held it until early March 1359 when he supposedly exchanged it for the church of Spofforth in York diocese.[281] His successor was William Newport, and much of the subsequent trouble was caused by the fact that he apparently continued to hold Spofforth as well as Bishop Wearmouth, even resigning the York benefice again in February 1365 in exchange for the prebend of Ulleskelf.[282] By March 1360 he was claiming possession of Bishop Wearmouth,[283] and he is named as rector up to 13 October 1363.[284] Newport's pluralism soon attracted the attention of provisors. In December 1363 William de Ardene was given the benefice,[285] and this provision was renewed in November 1364[286] and again in January 1367[287] so as to cover the possibility that Newport might have been dispensed to hold two parish churches simultaneously.[288] Ardene

276 Lunt, *Accounts*, 298; cf. 349, 390.

277 *CPP*, I, 527; cf. Reg. Supp. 45, fol. 163v; Coll. 14, fol. 172; *Urbain V: lettres communes*, v, no. 18145.

278 Watt, *Dictionary*, 404; Reg. Av. 176, fols. 171v–172v.

279 *CPL*, II, 247.

280 Ibid., 524.

281 Reg. Thoresby, fol. 103.

282 Ibid., fol. 134.

283 *CPP*, I, 351.

284 Reg. Hatfield, fol. 58v.

285 *CPP*, I, 474–5; *Urbain V: lettres communes*, III, no. 9196.

286 *Urbain V: lettres communes*, IV, no. 14851.

287 Ibid., VI, no. 20032; *CPL*, IV, 65. This was strictly a renewed order to ensure the effectiveness of the provision.

288 Such a dispensation had in fact been granted by Innocent VI on 6 December 1360 and confirmed by Urban V on 8 June 1363: Reg. Hatfield, fol. 43–43v; *Urbain V: lettres communes*, II, no. 6331.

himself held other benefices by 1366,[289] and would have been bound to resign at least one of them had he obtained Bishop Wearmouth. On the death of Newport,[290] David de Wollore was collated locally on 19 October 1366.[291] He too was a pluralist and was challenged not only by Ardene but also by Thomas Clervaus, who tried to accept the church under an expectative grace which did not cover benefices of the value of Bishop Wearmouth.[292] On 19 November 1366 he was provided on the death of Newport and the deprivation of Wollore, with rehabilitation for having improperly used his expectancy;[293] and on 14 July 1368 he was provided anew on his own deprivation, again alleging the death of Newport and the deprivation of Wollore.[294] It was Wollore, however, who won the suit, defeated the intrusion of Clervaus, and on 24 April 1369 was himself granted the church so long as the facts were as stated.[295] He had died by 14 September 1370, when the benefice was collated locally to Simon Langham, the former archbishop of Canterbury and now a cardinal,[296] although shortly afterwards he was provided or at least surrogated into Wollore's claim.[297] Langham had resigned by 23 August 1372, when the bishop ordered the induction of Thomas de Newbi, [298] who perhaps held the church to 1375;[299] Langham's exchange received papal confirmation on 5 December 1372,[300] although some days earlier Robert of Geneva, another cardinal, had been provided on Newbi's supposed death.[301] Robert probably had possession in 1375 or 1376,[302] but the benefice continued to be disputed in the later 1370s and 1380s by a number of royal claimants,[303] and also by Peter Galon, whose position was ratified by Richard II in March 1383,[304] and who had received papal favour from Gregory XI.[305]

289 *Reg. Langham*, 48.
290 Between 1 May and 9 May 1366: *Test. Ebor.*, I, 80–2.
291 Reg. Hatfield, fol. 61v.
292 *CPP*, I, 388; *Urbain V: lettres communes*, I, no. 3197.
293 Lunt, *Accounts*, 297; but cf. *Urbain V: lettres communes*, VI, no. 20131, where he has to resign the church.
294 *Urbain V: lettres communes*, VII, no. 21258.
295 Lunt, *Accounts*, 358.
296 Reg. Hatfield, fol. 67v; cf. Lunt, *Accounts*, 400.
297 Lunt, *Accounts*, 409. The collector stated that another cardinal, Stephen Albert, also held the church (ibid., 380), but this was probably an error.
298 Reg. Hatfield, fol. 77v; LAO, Reg. X, fols. 302–303.
299 *Fasti Dunelmenses*, 93; Thompson, 'Pluralism', no. 77.
300 Lunt, *Accounts*, 474.
301 Ibid., 473.
302 *Fasti Dunelmenses*, 49; Highfield, 'Relations', 353.
303 R. Donaldson, 'Patronage and the church. A study in the social structure of the secular clergy in the diocese of Durham (1311–1540)', Ph.D thesis, University of Edinburgh (1955), II, 40; *CPR 1381–85*, 28, 31, 154.
304 *CPR 1381–85*, 237.
305 T. F. T. Plucknett, 'The case of the miscreant cardinal', *AHR*, 30 (1924), 5.

It was the pluralism – or alleged pluralism – of Newport which caused the difficulty here, and the dispute was exacerbated by the anti-pluralism moves of Urban V, which put Wollore's position in danger, and by Clervaus unwisely accepting the church using an expectative grace which did not cover benefices of this value. The presence in the fray of cardinals was an additional complication, although Langham both accepted and resigned the rectory by ordinary authority.

A very common reason for the failure of provisions made on the basis of devolution to the Holy See was that the church was in fact appropriated to a religious house.[306] Sometimes, however, an appropriation could be delayed by the existence of rivals to the monastery in the shape of provisors or even men with local titles, including those presented by the house concerned. In 1358 the earl of Douglas granted the advowson of the church of Cavers to Melrose Abbey with the intention that the monastery should appropriate the church.[307] The arrangement was confirmed by the king of Scots on 10 January 1360,[308] and on 17 May 1363 the bishop ordered the dean of Teviotdale to induct the house to the benefice on the death or resignation of William de Tostys, then parson.[309] In the event, the annexation was not effective until 1419,[310] and a number of papal and local claims to the church ensued. On 31 October 1364 David de Stravelyn was provided on the resignation of Tostys through the dean of Glasgow to an abbot at the papal court.[311] He was opposed by John Ganon or Govan, who was presented by Melrose[312] but obtained papal confirmation on 1 September 1368 in case the benefice was reserved or had devolved to the Holy See.[313] By this time Edward III had made a presentation too, the nominee being John de Boulton, whom the archbishop of York was ordered to induct.[314] This probably failed, and by the year 1374 Alexander de Caron was parson;[315] he was succeeded by Matthew de Glendonwym,[316] who was confirmed by Gregory XI on 7 February [317] and probably 3 March 1376,[318]

306 A. D. M. Barrell, 'Papal involvement in appropriations in Scotland and northern England, 1342–1378', *Northern History*, 24 (1988), 31–6.

307 *Melrose Liber*, II, 429–31; cf. Cowan, *Parishes*, 30.

308 *Melrose Liber*, II, 432–3.

309 Ibid., 435.

310 Cowan, *Parishes*, 30.

311 *Urbain V: lettres communes*, III, no. 9766; Coll. 14, fol. 170v.

312 Watt, *Dictionary*, 230.

313 Coll. 14, fol. 175.

314 *CPR 1367–70*, 76.

315 *Melrose Liber*, II, 478–80; Watt, *Dictionary*, 86.

316 Cf. Watt, *Dictionary*, 221.

317 *CPL*, IV, 222; Reg. Vat. 289, fols. 554v–555.

318 Reg. Vat. 288, fol. 38–38v.

after being presented by Melrose on the death of Ganon. However, there was also another provisor: Thomas Mercer was granted Cavers on 4 December 1374 on the death of Govan, a papal reservation having been made on 25 September,[319] but he was still not in possession on 23 April 1377.[320] In the absence of bishops' registers to record presentations or institutions it is very hard to trace the history of this benefice accurately, but during the period when it was under dispute the appropriation to Melrose was a dead letter.

Some graces were apparently simply not pursued: the Durham diocesan authorities did not know of Bernard de Lucare of Avignon, who was provided to a prebend in Norton on 25 April 1361.[321] Some provisors died before their grants could be brought to effect, and both Elias Pelegrini and Henry de Ulseby died before the end of their suit over one of the Norwell prebends in Southwell.[322] Sometimes an unusual reason was given by the papal collector for a provision not being pursued: Alan de Crophill, who in June 1349 was provided to the York prebend of South Newbald,[323] became a hermit,[324] although the prebend was probably held by Andrew de Offord,[325] and so the provision might well have failed in any case.

It is difficult to draw firm overall conclusions about either the effectiveness of direct provisions or the considerations which drove individual clerks to seek them; indeed, the mass of information indicates only that there was no such thing as a typical provisor or a typical provision. Even more than in the case of expectancies, direct provisions were, however, usually the preserve of clerks who were already fairly prominent and had both the ambition and the qualifications in terms of ability and support to wish to enhance their position in the church still further. But provision was no certain road to a benefice; as has been seen, many factors could impede a papal grace or threaten its recipient, and disputes over benefices could and did last years. To bring to effect a grant, whether a direct provision or an expectancy, the provisor needed the help of the executors appointed by the pope.

319 Reg. Av. 192, fol. 570v; cf. Reg. Av. 193, fol. 497.

320 Reg. Av. 201, fol. 500.

321 *CPP*, I, 318; Lunt, *Accounts*, 205, 276, 332.

322 *CPL*, III, 424.

323 *CPP*, I, 164.

324 Lunt, *Accounts*, 116.

325 Reg. Zouche, fol. 223v; YML, H1/1, fol. 25v.

EXECUTORS OF PROVISIONS

Most provisions were accompanied by a mandate to named executors, usually three in number, who were responsible for its fulfilment. One was normally resident at the papal curia and was often, though not invariably, a foreigner. The others were usually prominent local ecclesiastics, although they were by no means confined geographically, and many provisions to benefices in the province of York were given executors who were based in the south. Sometimes there was only one mandatory, many of Urban V's provisions to York collegiate churches being in this category.

Scottish provisions were often executed by bishops, but mandates to heads of religious houses, cathedral dignitaries and archdeacons were also common. Many more cathedral canons were used in England, especially under Clement VI. Urban V greatly increased the practice of appointing diocesan officials as executors, naming fifty-four for benefices in northern England and twelve in Scotland. There is little evidence concerning the work of the executors, but subdelegation was clearly practised. When Thomas Sotheron was inducted to the church of Mitton in August 1368 the papal authority was wielded by the abbot of Whalley, whom the abbot of St Mary's, York had appointed as subexecutor.[326] Subexecutors were also used to induct provisors to prebends in Beverley.[327]

The function of the executor was not merely to carry out an order, but also to do justice in accordance with the terms of his commission. He was involved in a legal process whereby the provisor became plaintiff and the patron defendant in a case, albeit often an undisputed one, over a benefice.[328] The executor had to listen to legitimate arguments against the provision,[329] and it is unfortunate that his activities are so poorly documented. As has been seen, some provisions were bitterly opposed, although this did not necessarily, or indeed usually, imply a challenge to the pope's right as such to provide; the system was rooted in law and the executors were merely the agents for the fulfilment of the legal process, although they could impose ecclesiastical sanctions on those obstructing the execution of the bull.[330] But the right to appeal to the pope on the part of those who believed themselves to

[326] McNulty, *Thomas Sotheron*, 3. [327] *Beverley Chapter Act Book*, I, 393–4; II, 120–2.
[328] Barraclough, *Papal Provisions*, 91–4.
[329] Ibid., 95–7. [330] Mollat, 'La collation', 50–2.

have been wronged was safeguarded,[331] and this led to many of the long disputes which are attested in the sources.

It seems that the impact of papal provisions was greater in the province of York than in Scotland, especially where expectative graces were concerned. However, it cannot be stressed enough that the English episcopal registers contain numerous institutions of clerks with no papal title whatsoever. Some benefices were more affected by provisions than others; and while those in collegiate churches and in York Minster itself were particularly popular with provisors, many parish livings never saw a papal nominee, especially if the advowson was in lay hands. Even in the case of benefices in clerical patronage, there seems much reason to question G. Barraclough's statement that 'in the fourteenth century, papal provision was the normal means of access to a benefice',[332] although his statement about the normalisation of the system of provision can be accepted in principle: 'It was safer to go to the supreme authority in the Church – once that authority had shown itself willing to deal with these matters – than to the immediate collator, who might be over-ridden.'[333] However, many clerks who did not go to the Papacy still obtained a benefice peacefully.

It is difficult to see any marked variations in the policy adopted by individual popes in the matter of provisions. Because the system was so highly organised and bureaucratic it was hard for individual pontiffs to stamp their personality on it to any degree. Innocent VI may have made fewer provisions than his predecessor and successor, although the deficiencies in the sources make this impossible to prove. The number of provisions under Clement VI and in the first year of Urban V's pontificate is affected by the serious mortality caused in 1349 and 1361–2 by the Black Death: in the register of Archbishop Zouche the increase in the number of institutions in the summer and autumn of 1349 is striking for all archdeaconries, and it need occasion no surprise that the number of papal provisions also was high in that year and in 1350, this being especially noticeable in Scotland. The plague apart, it is likely that Clement made more provocative grants to anti-English cardinals than his successors did, but Urban's use of expectative graces caused disputes and disillusionment, as the number of petitions for

331 Ibid., 54–7. 332 Barraclough, *Papal Provisions*, 106. 333 Ibid., 151.

benefices of slightly increased value shows. Urban genuinely wished to limit pluralism, and this led to his amending petitions more frequently than his predecessors as well as attempting to impose definite measures against the abuse; but these failed in the face of the entrenched interests of wealthy ecclesiastics and of the king and leading nobles, who needed their servants to have several benefices in lieu of salary.

The system of provision was very much based on law rather than on papal whim. The popes cannot have known personally more than a minute percentage of the hopeful clerics who supplicated for preferment, and although the standing of their sponsors and the nature of their academic qualifications may well have carried weight, it was impossible for the Papacy to dominate appointments to benefices in a way which made it an effective force for either good or ill when it came to the spiritual welfare of the faithful. For provision was but one way to a benefice; others included presentation locally, episcopal collation and royal nomination, and a clerk who sought advancement in the ecclesiastical hierarchy had to choose the avenue which promised the greatest rewards. It is true that, as papal provisions became more numerous, the opportunity for local preferment, especially to sinecure prebends and wealthy dignities in cathedrals, became more limited, but at no time was the older system of local patronage entirely eclipsed. A man with a papal grant had only a claim to a benefice; he did not have the right to occupy one already filled or necessarily even a prior claim to someone presented locally or by the king; he might even be opposed by other provisors. But it is wrong to see provision as being always contentious; it appears by contrast to have been an acceptable form of promotion and as such was approved by the kings of England and Scotland and by their families and leading subjects, who used the system to supplement their own patronage and accepted its validity so long as it did not undermine such privileges as regalian right. A benefice became liable for a direct provision because of the manner of its vacancy, not (except in the case of some benefices specially reserved) because the pope arbitrarily wanted to fill it, perhaps to the advantage of some greedy curialist. Indeed, curial clerks are so relatively prominent in the sources only because the pope was their sole hope of promotion, their work having cut them off from local founts of patronage. Much the same was true of university graduates, especially Scots who had had to travel abroad to study, or poor clerks who were unlucky enough not to be known to a suitable patron at home. That the system survived the problems of war, plague and parliamentary opposition is not because the popes pressed to uphold their right to impose nominees on distant churches, but rather because a large number of men saw in the system a means of advancement potentially more lucrative than local patronage, which they thought had a high enough likelihood of success to make it worthwhile spending the necessary time and money at the curia. It is true that as the system grew more extensive and more complicated it sucked more hopefuls into it, either because expectative graces had restricted the opportunities for local promotion or because confirmation of possession seemed advisable, but this does not explain away its initial attraction, nor the fact that even kings chose the course of supplicating the pope on behalf of their servants rather than enacting and enforcing statutes designed to stop provisions. For the most part, those with political power were unwilling to deny either the usefulness or the propriety of provisions; despite the disputes which papal graces could provoke, they were widely accepted as a valid, ordered, and for some notable churchmen necessary, means of obtaining a suitable benefice.

Chapter 3

OPPOSITION TO THE PAPACY

The reign of Edward III witnessed a number of crises in Anglo-Papal relations. The French origin of the popes, coupled with a long period of intermittent and largely inconclusive warfare between Plantagenet and Valois provided ample opportunities for xenophobic suspicion of the Papacy's intentions. This inevitably became intermingled with opposition to papal taxation and to the use of the system of provision, especially where the beneficiaries were French. Old grievances were exacerbated in an environment of heightened tension; financial stringency and war combined in furnishing ammunition for anti-papal elements in parliament and government.

Parliament and government must, however, be kept distinct. It was unwise for the crown to antagonise the Papacy unnecessarily: the interests of pope and king were usually best served when the two co-operated; and, moreover, Edward III needed papal help, or at least the absence of papal opposition, in the tortuous negotiations to attempt to settle the long-standing problem of sovereignty in Aquitaine and his other continental dominions. The king confronted the pope only as a last resort. Parliament, on the other hand, had no such inhibitions. At least among those vociferous elements whose complaints were recorded for posterity, there were many accusations which could be and were levelled against the Francophile Papacy. At times, parliament forced legislation or other action upon the king; and one of the fascinations of the politics of the period is the manner in which the royal government manoeuvred to placate the Commons without incurring the wrath of the pope, and used the legislation, when appropriate, to pressurise the Holy See.

To earlier generations of historians, the Statutes of Provisors and Praemunire were fundamental in restricting papal power in England and in paving the way for its total repudiation under Henry VIII. More recently, it has been recognised that the statutes did not aim to curb the spiritual authority of the Holy See, but merely to limit the pope's say in advowson matters, which in England, contrary to strict canon law, fell into the cognisance of the royal courts. It has been noted with some surprise that the legislation did not end or even stem the rush of papal provisions to English benefices, still less to bishoprics; and it has been concluded, therefore, that the legislation was ineffective. But the legislation did not constitute a monolithic series of measures, always aiming to prevent provisions from taking effect. Rather, each statute and ordinance must be studied closely and in its own right, with due regard to its political and diplomatic context and to the extent and nature of its enforcement. As will be seen, relations between the Papacy and the English crown were materially affected by military developments, by changes in papal taxation and the number of provisions, and, perhaps more than might have been expected, by the personalities of individual popes.

Whatever the political situation, the crown defended its rights, especially where the juridical competence of the royal courts seemed to be in danger of being undermined. Essentially, the king consistently upheld his own powers of patronage and the cognisance of his courts in cases of advowson; he was particularly insistent that no case cognisable in the royal courts should be taken outside the realm.[1] Legislation was used in pursuit of these aims when necessary, but the measures employed could be taken outside the context of particular fourteenth-century laws.

The king had extensive patronage in his own right, for instance in the royal free chapels, and this was rarely a point of contention between crown and pope. He also controlled the temporalities, and therefore the advowsons, of alien priories during wartime. These houses were dependent on French monasteries, either because they were cells or because they owed allegiance – and more importantly money – to abbeys in France. The Cluniac monasteries fell into this category, and the government was understandably reluctant to see revenues shipped abroad in time of war. There was, however, a potential clash with the Papacy, in that some clerks with expectancies had been promised a benefice in the gift of an alien priory; to accept such a benefice would be to infringe royal rights of patronage. On 2 February 1343 the king ordered the arrest of

[1] See e.g. a letter of July 1342 in which Edward III reminds papal officials of his courts' right to hear cases of patronage: *Foedera*, II, 1208.

anyone acting in derogation of his presentation of William de Cardoill to the vicarage of Paull, made on the grounds that the temporalities of Burstall Priory were in his hands. Adam de Brunnum, who had an expectative grace reserving a benefice in the gift of Burstall, had claimed the vicarage, but this was declared to be invalid, as benefices void while the monastery was in the king's hands could not be filled by provision.[2]

It was, however, the crown's use of regalian right that caused the largest number of clashes between royal and papal authority. The king could present to benefices normally in the patronage of a bishop or religious house of royal foundation during the vacancy of the see or monastery. There was also a theory that no time ran against the king, and that he could exercise the right to present in respect of a vacancy long before if the crown had not used its patronage at the time. Parliament periodically tried to restrict this,[3] but in the early years of Edward III's reign considerable efforts were made on the part of the government to resurrect old claims, some even from Henry III's reign.[4] When the king presented William de Kildesby to the York prebend of Wetwang in 1341, he did so on the basis of a vacancy in the see in 1279,[5] a clear indication that enquiries were being conducted into events beyond living memory. Because the benefices in question were often prebends in cathedrals or collegiate churches, the very benefices to which provisions were most frequently made, disputes between royal and papal nominees were inevitable.

In order to uphold his patronage and to defend decisions made in his courts, the king used writs of prohibition, which had the effect of removing cases from ecclesiastical to royal judges. They were sometimes directed against individual provisors and their agents: when a commission of enquiry was appointed into those opposing a royal grant to the vicarage of Crosthwaite, the provisor Thomas de Salkeld was mentioned by name.[6] It was, however, more usual for the transgressors not to be specifically identified, but for particular presentees to be protected. In October 1370 the king gave the church of Croft to Henry Bowet on the grounds of a vacancy at St Mary's Abbey in York; and on 20 November 1372 this was reinforced by a commission to arrest and imprison all those

2 *CPR 1343–45*, 73.
3 *Statutes of the Realm*, I, 293, 325; *Foedera*, III, 1072.
4 *CPR 1338–40*, 454.
5 Reg. 5A, fols. 93–94, 94v–95v.
6 *CPR 1361–64*, 362; see 281 for the presentation; for Salkeld's provision see *CPP*, I, 397; *Urbain V: lettres communes*, I, no. 1907.

appealing against the judgment whereby the king had recovered the right to present against the abbot of St Mary's and Richard Bell.[7] In the 1340s, protecting William de Kildesby in a number of benefices, the king prohibited proceedings against the immunity from ordinary and papal jurisdiction of the royal free chapel of Tickhill.[8] But in these cases, even if individuals were involved, the king's primary aim was to defend his own rights of presentation and the authority of his courts to determine cases of advowson.

On occasion the king used writs of prohibition in defence of the rights of lay patrons, but this too was usually done independently of any contemporary anti-papal legislation. Again, the main purpose was to uphold the decisions of the royal courts. In May 1341 all churchmen were prohibited from acting contrary to a decision of the Common Bench whereby John de Gemelyng had recovered against the prior of Marton the right to present to the vicarage of Sheriff Hutton. He had nominated William Codelyng, but William Couper de Aslacby was claiming the vicarage by virtue of an expectative grace promising a benefice in the gift of Marton.[9] In November 1374 the king wrote to the archbishop of York, forbidding action on behalf of Henry Westbroke, even though the latter had a royal licence to execute a provision to the church of Normanton; three laymen had recovered the advowson against the prior of the Hospitallers, hence the provision was invalidated.[10] In these and similar instances it was usually declared that the Holy See was not allowed to provide to benefices in lay patronage. While this can be shown not invariably to have been the case, the provisions to Aslacby and Westbroke were clearly in contravention of decisions made in the royal courts, since the advowson had been adjudged not to belong to Marton or the Hospitallers.

The king's protection of ecclesiastics who were threatened by provision was more half-hearted; he acted only where his rights were infringed. The order to arrest Thomas Sotheron and his companions, who had ejected the abbot and convent of Cockersand from the church of Mitton and wasted the parish revenues,[11]

7 *CPR 1370–74*, 11, 243; Baildon, *Monastic Notes*, II, 67.

8 *CPR 1343–45*, 117, 389; see 178, 183 for other benefices.

9 *CPR 1340–43*, 185; cf. Baildon, *Monastic Notes*, I, 200. For the expectative grace see *Reg. Melton*, II, 170, 191.

10 *CCR 1374–77*, 103–4. Westbroke accepted the church by virtue of an expectative grace (*CPP*, I, 392; *Urbain V: lettres communes*, I, no. 2961). For the royal licence see *CPR 1367–70*, 456.

11 *CPR 1367–70*, 190.

was probably made because their actions had contravened a royal licence for Cockersand to appropriate the church. The protection of Meaux Abbey in the churches of Easington, Keyingham and Skipsea was also based on the need to uphold royal rights to license appropriations.[12] Royal intervention to identify the provisor to the vicarage of Kirkham in 1364, on the grounds that the benefice ought to have been held by a monk of Vale Royal, was probably in the king's capacity as patron of the abbey of Vale Royal, since the provision was said to be prejudicial to the crown.[13]

When appeals against judgements of the royal courts were taken abroad, or cases cognisable in the king's courts were heard elsewhere, parliament joined the government in its enthusiasm to uphold the rights of the English crown. This was especially noticeable in wartime and when parliament was complaining generally about papal exactions; and although legislation sometimes resulted, the changes were of procedure rather than of principle.

The most celebrated legislation on the matter of appeals during Edward III's reign is the Statute of Praemunire of 1353.[14] It stated that people were being drawn out of the realm to answer in cases in which the royal courts had cognisance, and that the judgements of those courts were being impugned in the courts of others, to the prejudice of the king and the people and the destruction of the common law; and ordained that anyone who caused another to be cited outside the realm, or who sued in the court of another in derogation of the decision or competence of the royal courts, should be required to appear within two months to answer to the king for his contempt, under pain of being put outside the king's protection, forfeiture and outlawry.

The statute does not mention papal provisions. Although the use of provision was often the decisive element in creating a conflict over a benefice, the statute was not limited to lawsuits which involved provisors. Nor did it in any way restrict the pope's right to provide. What it did aim to control was appeals by disappointed claimants to benefices where the decision of a royal court had gone against them. It does not mention the Holy See specifically, and could be used to block appeals to any courts which presumed to encroach upon royal jurisdiction, including English church courts.

[12] *CPR 1361–64*, 368; *CPR 1374–77*, 55–6.

[13] *CPR 1361–64*, 527–8; Davies, 'Statute of Provisors', 130n.

[14] *Statutes of the Realm*, I, 329.

But in its context, after a decade of anti-papal activity in parliament and years of poor relations between England and the Papacy, its prime concern was surely with interference by the Holy See in the common law of England as rendered in the royal courts.

The statute gave no new grounds for opposing an appeal to Rome. Cognisable cases had long been protected from papal jurisdiction, and in 1351 the king had said as much.[15] Throughout Edward III's reign, the Patent and Close Rolls abound with bans on appeals to the curia and mandates to arrest those making such appeals, but these were issued only when royal rights required protection. Even commoner are licences to go to the papal court despite restrictions on foreign travel during wartime, sometimes specifically permitting a lawsuit to be undertaken there provided that nothing prejudicial to the king or realm was done. The 1353 statute laid down no new penalties for breaking the law, merely a more effective way of dealing with defendants who did not come to court, namely forfeiture on non-appearance after the first summons, with outlawry to follow if they could not then be arrested. 'It was directed primarily against fugitives from justice,' and should be seen as a procedural change and part of a continuing process rather than as a major shift of legislative theory or practice.[16]

Two cases show the procedure at work: these concern one of the Norwell prebends in Southwell and the church of Stanhope. The king recovered the right to present to Norwell and gave the prebend to William de Northwell. Thomas de Ikham was, however, provided and tried to carry the matter to the curia. On 1 May 1360 the sheriff of Nottingham was sent a writ of *praemunire facias* ordering him to warn Ikham and his abettors to be before the Bench on 24 June. None came, and a writ was issued to arrest them. After this, two of the four abettors came, but Ikham and the others did not, so they were placed outside the king's protection and the procedure of exigent and outlawry commenced. It was not until 1366 that Ikham was pardoned and his sureties put up £100 bail that he would do nothing prejudicial to the king or the law in the future. William de Norwich was provided to Stanhope in 1361. After the king had recovered the right to present and had

[15] *Rot. Parl.*, II, 228.

[16] See generally E. B. Graves, 'The legal significance of the Statute of Praemunire of 1353', in *Anniversary Essays in Mediaeval History by Students of Charles Homer Haskins* (Boston and New York, 1929), 57–80. The quotation is from p. 74.

prohibited proceedings in derogation of this judgement, he used the praemunire procedure to have Norwich and others summoned to be before the Bench during the Easter term of 1363. In the event, no one came to prosecute them.[17]

There are many other instances of action being taken against those appealing to the curia against a judgement rendered in the royal courts, although it is rarely clear whether the particular procedure of the 1353 statute was in fact followed. Many ended in a fine and subsequent pardon, before and after 1353. John de Boulton, rector of Lythe, who had failed to appear in a case in which he had been accused of having the prior of Nostell cited to the curia in a matter cognisable in the royal courts, was pardoned on 6 November 1346 after he had made an agreement with the prior and a fine of 100s had been paid.[18] In 1356 Thomas de Bridkirk was excused his offence and his fine was remitted, even though he had prosecuted processes inside and outside England over the hospital of Greatham.[19] Walter de Skirlaw, who resided at the curia, was put outside the king's protection, forfeited and outlawed for his non-appearance to answer a charge of contempt in acting contrary to the judgement whereby the king recovered the right to present to the archdeaconry of the East Riding, but on 2 December 1370 he too was pardoned.[20] The government was, however, clearly concerned about appeals or potential appeals: on 6 November 1355 a commission was ordered to enquire in Yorkshire about the names of all persons who had appealed to foreign parts in derogation of the royal right to present to benefices on the basis of the recent vacancy of the see of York.[21]

The king's authority in benefice matters is seen by the large number of cases in which the position of an individual incumbent was ratified by letters patent. Sometimes a provisor secured his position in this way. Richard de Chester was confirmed in the prebend of Nunwick in Ripon on 20 October 1341,[22] as were John de Bokingham in the York prebend of Laughton on 9 June 1368[23] and John Marshall in the church of Rothbury on 9 May 1373,[24] to

[17] Ibid., 75–6. Cf. below, pp. 177–8.
[18] *CPR 1345–48*, 215.
[19] *CPR 1354–58*, 345; cf. 251; cf. Reg. Hatfield, fol. 23.
[20] *CPR 1370–74*, 25.
[21] *CPR 1354–58*, 329.
[22] *CPR 1340–43*, 331. He had an expectancy from 1317 (*CPL*, II, 166), and was admitted in 1332 (*Memorials of Ripon*, II, 193).
[23] *CPR 1367–70*, 122. For the provision see *Urbain V: lettres communes*, VII, no. 20965.
[24] *CPR 1370–74*, 276. Marshall received papal confirmation in 1363 (*CPP*, I, 414), but there was a long dispute over this church.

name but three. A royal confirmation was not necessarily the end of the story: the provisor Paul de Monte Florum received ratification of his position in the prebend of South Cave in York on 28 June 1346, but he originally had a royal grant, and in due course he fell foul of the government by suing at the curia to the prejudice of the king.[25] But many men who were not provisors had their estate ratified in exactly the same way, such as Nicholas de Burton and John de Sleford in the Ripon prebend of Studley,[26] and Walter de Olby in a prebend of Darlington.[27] No conclusions can be drawn from the occasions on which these ratifications were issued, other than to say that the benefices in question usually were, or had been, the object of at least two conflicting claims, whether through papal provision or as a result of a royal presentation. The existence of the ratifications, however, demonstrates the involvement of the crown both in presenting to benefices and in intervening in disputes over them.

The crown, therefore, acted almost exclusively in defence of its long-established and much-cherished rights. The petitions found in the rolls of parliament sometimes appear to be directed at papal authority in a much wider sense, although even here it can be shown that at stake were the supposed threat to lay rights of patronage and the dire financial consequences of excessive papal taxation. Both issues were of deep concern to the class of lay taxpayers which was represented in the medieval parliament.

Specific grievances were usually subsumed in general expressions of theory and in laments about the financial and spiritual harm wrought by papal taxes and provisions, in particular where English benefices came to be held by absentee aliens. Like many of its successors, the parliament which met at Carlisle in 1307 during Edward I's last Scottish campaign articulated many grievances about papal exactions, but did not suggest specific measures which might be taken against them. The records of the Carlisle parliament nonetheless offer the clearest expression of the ideas behind the theories which were used throughout the fourteenth century that laymen had ultimate control over church appointments.[28]

Basically, the theory was that the church in England in all its

[25] *CPR 1345–48*, 134; *CPR 1340–43*, 410; *CPR 1348–50*, 103.

[26] *CPR 1370–74*, 140, 210. [27] *CPR 1348–50*, 149.

[28] On the Carlisle parliament see *Rot. Parl.*, I, 207–8, 219, 220–1. Cf. a letter sent by the lay lords to the pope after the parliament of 1309: *Chron. Ed. I and Ed. II*, I, 161–5; cf. *Foedera*, II, 84; *CPR 1307–13*, 180.

states of prelacy had been founded by the king and his nobility in order to provide instruction in the faith, services, alms and hospitality. To these pious ends, the founders had donated possessions and rights, but during the vacancy of a see, religious house or other prelacy, the descendants of the founders held the prelacies as though in wardship, and had the right to present to prebends, parish churches and dignities in the gift of the prelates in question. Papal provisions threatened the right of the king and other laymen during vacancies; and it was this, rather than the desirability as such of the exercise of patronage by clerics, which concerned the laity in parliament. The fundamental principle was that the church was founded on the generosity of laymen, for a particular purpose, and on the understanding that in certain circumstances the power vested in the church reverted to the descendants of the original benefactors. It was this argument which was employed to justify opposition to the practices of Clement VI.

Of all the Avignon popes, Clement VI was the one with the closest links to the French court. He was also renowned for the generosity with which he bestowed provisions and other favours, often without sufficient attention to what might be tactful or politically expedient. It was under Clement that the connection between provisions and annates became very close; the increase in the number of provisions, especially noticeable after Benedict XII's restraint, thus had a clear financial corollary. In addition, the war was continuing, and the strain on the royal coffers could be eased only by frequent taxation. The pontificate of Clement VI was a time of crisis in Anglo-Papal relations; and evidence from northern England can shed considerable light both on the reasons for conflict and on the development of royal policy.[29]

The parliament which met at Westminster on 28 April 1343 was the first since Clement's accession. It was scathing in its attack on the new pope's practice of granting provisions to aliens, especially the reservation of benefices up to the value of 1000 marks each for the cardinals Gerald Domar and Aymar Robert, and the favours shown to the king's enemy Talleyrand de Périgord. Parliament suggested that the king should send a letter to the pope; the king,

[29] For a rather different interpretation from that offered here see P. Heath, *Church and Realm, 1272–1461* (London, 1988), 129–32. For relations between Clement VI and the French crown see G. Mollat, 'Le Saint-Siège et la France sous le pontificat de Clément VI (1342–1352)', *Revue d'histoire ecclésiastique*, 55 (1960), 5–24.

for his part, asked the Lords and Commons to ordain a remedy for the abuses.[30] This remedy was the 1343 Ordinance of Provisors.[31]

The ordinance prohibited the import or use of papal bulls and instruments prejudicial to the king or his people. While at first glance it appears to be sweeping in its attack on provisions, it can be shown that it had only two applications. It was directed firstly against provisions to aliens, and secondly against papal graces which interfered with the use of regalian right. It was, therefore, a move to emphasise the unacceptability of granting English benefices to foreigners who would remove the revenues from a financially beleaguered realm, and to reinforce royal rights of presentation on the grounds of a current or earlier vacancy in a see or monastery under royal patronage. Only certain provisions were deemed to be prejudicial to the king and his people.

Unlike much of the later legislation, the 1343 ordinance was used, at least in the short term. Some humble clerks fell foul of it when they, perhaps inadvertently, accepted a benefice which happened to have come into Edward III's gift under regalian right. An order was issued on 16 February 1344 for the arrest of Thomas de Askham, who had accepted the vicarage of Ampleforth by virtue of an expectative grace. The vicarage was in the king's hand for that turn, and Askham was accused of having contravened the 1343 ordinance and the decrees of the Carlisle parliament by bringing into England letters prejudicial to the king and his people.[32] Another poor clerk, Thomas de Morpath, was imprisoned for allegedly having acted against the ordinance, although he claimed to have been properly presented and instituted to his vicarage of Bedlington.[33] Many similar examples can be found, and on occasion royal officials acted with excessive zeal, proceeding against provisors who had been in peaceful possession of their benefices long before 1343. Action was also taken against the agents of the hated cardinals. According to the chronicler Murimuth, the proctors of Aymar Robert and Gerald Domar were summoned before the chancellor and other justices and asked by what authority they had entered England with letters so prejudicial to

[30] *Rot. Parl.*, II, 141, 143–4; cf. Murimuth, *Continuatio Chronicarum*, 138; *Chron. Knighton*, II, 28–9. For the grants to Gerald and Aymar see *CPL*, III, 74.

[31] *Rot. Parl.*, II, 144–5. On what follows see generally A. D. M. Barrell, 'The Ordinance of Provisors of 1343', *Historical Research*, 64 (1991), 264–77.

[32] *CPR 1343–45*, 284; for the provision *in forma pauperum* see Reg. Zouche, fol. 214.

[33] *CCR 1343–46*, 356. He had a grace reserving a benefice in the gift of Durham Priory: *RPD*, III, 517–18.

the king and kingdom. They pleaded papal authority and were imprisoned, although they later received a safe-conduct to leave England.[34]

How widely and for how long the ordinance was enforced is difficult to gauge. The parliament of June 1344 complained that there had been insufficient stringency in bringing provisors to book, and asked that the ordinance be formally converted into a statute.[35] There were allegations that prejudicial bulls had entered the country, and renewed mandates to officials at the ports to keep a close watch for them. But action was certainly taken, both generally in the form of proclamations and in particular cases. Contemporaries were certainly aware of the legislation and its enforcement, as the ordinance is noted in many fourteenth-century chronicles which are silent about later anti-papal activity. There was wide agreement that the king prevented the fulfilment of Clement VI's provisions to cardinals, and some writers quoted sample letters to sheriffs ordering the implementation of the ordinance.[36] But enforcement took place against the backdrop of diplomatic contacts between king and pope, and the period in which the ordinance was cited frequently ended with an accommodation between Edward III and Clement VI brokered by two papal nuncios early in 1345.[37]

It might be expected that, with advowson cases being heard in the royal courts and legislation to limit the success of provisions which prejudiced royal rights, the king's presentee would tend to prevail over the provisor. Sometimes he did: Henry de Ingelby kept Nicholas de Hethe out of the York prebend of South Cave, and withstood the claim of Ralph de Kelleby to the church of Haughton-le-Skerne.[38] Ingelby also renounced a papal confirmation in the prebend of Oxton in Southwell on the grounds that he owed his position to a royal presentation.[39] But this was by no means always the outcome. A wide variety of local and personal factors, as well as the king's relations with the Holy See, doubtless had an effect, but Edward III was unable or unwilling to ride roughshod over papal rights: his grant to Robert de Clipston of the church of Leake in Nottinghamshire was revoked and the rectory confirmed to the provisor Hugh de Wymondeswold in September

34 Murimuth, *Continuatio Chronicarum*, 142–3.
35 *Rot. Parl.*, II, 153.
36 See Barrell. 'Ordinance of Provisors', 276–7 and references there.
37 Ibid., 274–5.
38 Lunt, *Accounts*, 116, 118; cf. Reg. Hatfield, fol. 31v.
39 *CPP*, I, 224; *CPL*, III, 457–8; Lunt, *Accounts*, 117; *CPR 1348–50*, 474.

1347 because the church had not in fact been vacant during the vacancy of the priory of Repton, on the grounds of which the king had made his grant.[40]

Indeed, after the improvement in relations with the pope early in 1345, a number of provisors were allowed to pursue claims which had previously been blocked by royal writs. Thomas de Carleton, who had used an expectative grace to accept the church of Sigston, which was in the gift of Durham priory, found an arrest warrant against him after the king recovered the right to present and gave the church to one of his clerks. Carleton, however, managed to retain the church, and in 1346 the king took him and his advisers into his special protection and allowed him to sue in the ecclesiastical courts for formal restitution of the benefice.[41] When James de Bononia, proctor of the cardinal-bishop of Tusculum, who had been provided to the treasurership of York, promised to do nothing prejudicial to the crown, the king protected James in his capacity as the cardinal's agent for the archdeaconry of Nottingham.[42]

The widespread use of the ordinance to protect royal patronage was, therefore, short-lived. But the desirability of upholding the crown's rights to present did not disappear. The number of potential conflicts declined as regalian right, especially with respect to earlier reigns, was used rather less, and as the large body of poor clerks awaiting benefices with expectancies from Clement VI began to be reduced; but it was still necessary for the government to enforce restrictions on the export and import of prejudicial bulls, especially in periods of Anglo-Papal tension such as the 1360s and when the war broke out again in 1369.[43] The king also took action against clerks residing at the curia, ordering them to appear before him and his council.[44] The spirit of the 1343 ordinance therefore survived long after its letter had been abandoned.

The problem of provisions to aliens is coloured by the vehemence of parliamentary rhetoric, particularly against the favours shown to a small number of cardinals. The main thrust of parliament's anger in 1343, 1344, 1346 and 1348 was against aliens. The matter was certainly important politically, but the

40 *CPR 1345–48*, 262, 409.
41 See Barrell, 'Ordinance of Provisors', 273–4 for this and other examples.
42 *Foedera*, III, 190; *CPR 1348–50*, 408–9; cf. 448, 549.
43 Barrell, 'Ordinance of Provisors', 276.
44 *CFR 1347–56*, 199; *CCR 1349–54*, 339.

number of foreigners in English benefices was never large. In the period before the Statute of Provisors in February 1351, only 8 per cent of Clement VI's provisions to English benefices were granted to aliens, and some of them were Italians rather than Frenchmen.[45] When it is remembered that this figure does not include all expectancies granted to poor clerks, the vast majority of whom were English, and that relatively few benefices were filled by provision in any case, it is clear that – at least in numerical terms – the scale of the problem was exaggerated by contemporaries. It was the high profile of some of the beneficiaries, and their reputedly anti-English attitude, which explain the strength of feeling against them.

Clement's provisions to aliens must be viewed in their context, and comparisons with the pontificate of John XXII are instructive. John made provisions to foreigners throughout his pontificate. Some received only expectative graces, but many were granted direct provisions to a wide variety of benefices, ranging from dignities in York Minster through prebends of collegiate churches to parish churches, including Washington in 1318, Brantingham in 1320, Hornsea in 1321 and 1331, Bishop Wearmouth in 1325, and Kirk Ella and Houghton-le-Spring in 1329.[46] In the province of York, thirteen provisions to cardinals are recorded, seven of them involving parish churches. Parliament would certainly have had grounds for complaint if it had been disposed to criticise the Papacy, but there is little evidence for it. In 1327 the Commons petitioned that aliens should not be permitted to enter the realm to pursue a provision, but the new king, who needed papal help in the dangerous political climate of the time, was less keen to commit himself.[47] Otherwise, parliament concentrated on a small number of specific grievances, including a bitter – but fruitless – petition by a royal nominee to the church of Fishlake, attacking the chancellor for supporting the claim of an alien provisor against him.[48]

Clement VI's policy was broadly similar to John's. He provided aliens to a range of benefices in the northern province, mainly stalls in York Minster, but also prebends in collegiate churches and the rectories of Brantingham and Brompton.[49] In the case of the York prebends and dignities, a remarkable change in practice can be

[45] Carstens, 'Enforcement', 75–6.

[46] *CPL*, II, 178, 198, 211, 247, 287, 314, 326.

[47] *Rot. Parl.*, II, 9, 12.

[48] Ibid., 45–6; cf. *CPL*, II, 264.

[49] *CPL*, III, 75, 95, 470.

detected in 1348. In the first six years of his pontificate, Clement provided no Englishman directly to a Minster benefice; in the next five years he provided over thirty. Conversely, most of the aliens, whether cardinals or not, whom he favoured were provided early in the pontificate. This development is probably connected with negotiations between king and pope in 1348.[50] Clement would not promise to cease to provide aliens to English benefices, but undertook that in future they would be given only sinecures, and that suitable persons would be provided when benefices of aliens fell vacant if the king made nominations. Although this does not exactly explain the change in practice with regard to benefices in York Minster, the new policy reflects the more conciliatory attitude on the part of the pope.

There are three reasons why Clement VI encountered much more opposition than John XXII had done. Firstly, England and France were now locked in conflict, and Clement personally was viewed with considerable suspicion. Secondly, the restraint shown by Benedict XII in providing aliens meant that Clement's liberality was thrown into especially sharp focus. Thirdly, some of his grants were antagonistic and unwise.

The two most provocative grants in the north were Aymar Robert's wide-ranging expectative grace and Talleyrand de Périgord's provision to the deanery of York. The 1344 parliament specifically petitioned that the deanery should be given to someone able to withstand Talleyrand's claim.[51] Despite this, and despite a bitter dispute between the cardinal and the royal nominee Philip de Weston, it was Talleyrand who emerged victorious. Aymar held the York prebend of Warthill until his death and had a serious claim to the archdeaconry of the East Riding.[52] Although the pope was sufficiently concerned about royal actions against Aymar and Gerald Domar to write to exhort the king and his leading subjects to desist from them,[53] and to commission two cardinals to take action against the seizure of their benefices,[54] the government lacked either the means or the will to resist these high-profile provisors indefinitely.

This was partly because in 1346 the king seized the benefices of

[50] Lunt, *Financial Relations . . . 1327–1534*, 334.

[51] *Rot. Parl.*, II, 154.

[52] See above, pp. 109–10, 113–15.

[53] E.g. *CPL*, III, 2, 3, 34; *Clément VI: lettres closes (Fr)*, nos. 275, 375–7, 393–4, 3536–7; Murimuth, *Continuatio Chronicarum*, 149–52; Walsingham, *Hist. Angl.*, I, 259–60.

[54] *Clément VI: lettres closes (Fr)*, nos. 553–4.

aliens. This measure affected secular benefices, and was quite separate from the normal royal seizure of alien priories during wartime on the grounds that they owed allegiance to a French mother-house. The king tried to justify his action in a letter to the pope on 12 February 1346,[55] in which he pointed out that England was torn apart by the exigencies of war and that the royal treasury was exhausted. It was, he argued, justified and reasonable if in times of urgent necessity the goods of the realm, whoever they belonged to, were taken for the defence of the country, provided that they were later returned. In taking the fruits of all benefices held by foreigners, after the deduction of items of necessary expenditure, the king promised to make satisfaction to the incumbents or their proctors at a later date. The chronicler Adam Murimuth said that the benefices of cardinals were seized because most of them favoured the pope and Philip of Valois,[56] which was doubtless a reflection of popular sentiment.

Some light can be shed on the machinery of seizure. A royal letter to Bishop Trillek of Hereford in February 1346 told him to order all beneficed aliens resident in his diocese and the representatives of other foreigners to appear in London on the Monday of the first week in Lent, under pain of forfeiture.[57] Three months later the king wrote to Ralph Tervill, farmer of the deanery of York, reminding him that the fruits of all benefices held by non-resident aliens were to be used to help the war effort, and that it was forbidden to export anything from the benefices in question; Tervill was given terms to pay £500.[58] Similar letters were sent regarding other benefices held by aliens.

Some foreigners were exempted. On the basis of good service to the king rendered by Nicholinus de Fieschi, his son William was permitted to take the fruits of his prebend of Strensall in York, paying clerical tenths along with the native clergy.[59] It was clearly unwise for the king needlessly to make enemies at the papal court; and to have deprived aliens of benefices which they held canonically, as the 1344 and 1346 parliaments advocated,[60] would have been a perilous step, one which would have been regarded as a

55 *Foedera*, III, 68.

56 Murimuth, *Continuatio Chronicarum*, 245.

57 *Registrum Johannis de Trillek, Episcopi Herefordensis, AD MCCCXLIV–MCCCLXI*, ed. J. H. Parry (Canterbury and York Soc., 1912), 260–1.

58 *Foedera*, III, 81–2; *CCR 1346–49*, 18.

59 *Foedera*, III, 79. For Nicholinus' work as a royal diplomat see e.g. ibid., II, 1228; III, 18, 19, 22.

60 *Rot. Parl.*, II, 154, 162.

serious attack on ecclesiastical liberty. However, many benefices held by foreigners were in the king's hand for at least a time between 1346 and the end of Clement VI's pontificate: in the province of York these included the archdeaconry of Richmond, held by John Raymond de Comminges; the treasurership of York, with its annexed prebend of Wilton, held by Anibaldus Gaetani; the church of Hemingbrough, held by Gaucelin Deuza; and the archdeaconry of York and prebend of Wistow, held by Peter de Prés.[61] The church of Hornsea turned out to have been so badly neglected by Cardinal Raymond de Fargiis that the next rector, David de Wollore, petitioned the king to remove his hand from the fruits so that the damage could be repaired.[62] The revenues of the prebend of Wetwang were seized by the king because the benefice was held by the non-resident alien Anibaldus Gaetani, but in July 1348 they were released to John de Melbourne, who claimed to have held this much disputed prebend for about a year.[63]

Relatively few benefices were affected by this seizure, because aliens were not numerous. Only about ten benefices in the province of York are mentioned in royal sources in this connection, but their annual value, as represented by their assessment for the tenth, totalled over £1000. Not all the benefices were in the king's hands for an extended period, but the financial expediency of the seizure is obvious, especially when it is considered that the actual income was probably far in excess of the assessed value. The figure also shows how a relatively small number of foreign churchmen could export a considerable sum each year, and gives credence to the contemporary opinion that vitally important resources were being drained from the realm.

The seizure infuriated the pope. Initially he tried to change royal policy by letters.[64] The cardinals Anibaldus and Stephen, who were sent to England and France primarily to try to arrange peace, were told on 28 April 1347 to present to the king papal letters concerning the seizure, which they had held back out of fear that they might jeopardise the negotiations.[65] In 1349 the pope sent the archdeacon of Perpignan on an abortive mission,[66] and in October

[61] *CPR 1345–48*, 425; *CPR 1348–50*, 51, 202, 582; *CCR 1349–54*, 431.

[62] *CCR 1346–49*, 202–3.

[63] *Foedera*, III, 162–3; *CCR 1346–49*, 553.

[64] *Clément VI: lettres closes (non-Fr)*, nos. 951–3, 1356–7; *CPL*, III, 25–6, 31.

[65] *CPL*, III, 31; *Clément VI: lettres closes (Fr)*, no. 3253.

[66] *CPL*, III, 41; *Clément VI: lettres closes (non-Fr)*, no. 2044; cf. *Clément VI: lettres closes (Fr)*, no. 4225.

1351 he wrote to various notables in England in support of a number of aliens who, he said, had zealously supported Edward III's interests at the curia.[67] By 1352 Clement was taking a tougher line. On 22 June he ordered the king to restore to the cardinals within four months the fruits of their benefices, and to allow them or their proctors to have peaceful possession, under pain of excommunication; the same sentence was pronounced against the king's agents who collected the fruits of the benefices in question;[68] even an interdict was threatened.[69] When the time came, however, Clement did not carry out his threat to excommunicate Edward III, but merely suspended the process to Ascension Day and wrote another letter urging the king to amend his action against cardinals and other members of the papal court.[70] Only the death of Clement VI before the revised term expired was able to end the crisis.

The promulgation of the Statute of Provisors in February 1351 created barely a ripple in the stormy waters aroused by the conflict over the seizure of aliens' benefices. Chroniclers do not mention it, and there is no evidence that it was viewed with other than indifference, still less alarm, in Avignon.[71] Its importance should not be overestimated; but it was a response to a changed situation, it reflected a change of emphasis in parliamentary opposition to the Papacy, and it endeavoured to create a procedure which, if implemented, would markedly have increased the potential for royal intervention in ecclesiastical affairs.

The 1351 parliament[72] was the first to sit after a large increase in the number of provisions in the previous two years, mainly as a result of the mortality caused by the initial outbreak of the Black Death. It accused the pope – almost certainly falsely – of extending the scope of provision out of greed for increased revenues from annates. The outburst was partly the result of fear in the uncertain situation after the plague, the same fear as inspired the labour legislation in an attempt to control peasant wages. But it was true that the increase in the number of provisions would lead to greater demands for annates, and it was the financial aspect which inspired parliament to broaden the scope of its attack on the Papacy away

67 *CPL*, III, 50.

68 Lunt, *Financial Relations ... 1327–1534*, 337; LAO, Reg. VIII, fols. 18–19.

69 *Innocent VI: lettres secrètes et curiales*, no. 260.

70 *CPL*, III, 51, 468; *Clément VI: lettres closes (Fr)*, nos. 5431, 5448.

71 There is no evidence that contemporary popes viewed the 1351 statute 'with particular dismay', as argued by Heath (*Church and Realm*, 130).

72 *Rot. Parl.*, II, 228.

from aliens and towards the system of provision in general. In criticising native churchmen as well as foreigners, parliament claimed that those who procured papal graces caused more money to go to the curia, and so be used by the enemy, than the king obtained from his realm. As well as annates, money was said to be expended in Avignon in order to arrange the provisions in the first place, a charge which was pressed even more vehemently in the 1370s.

The king said that there was already a suitable remedy for the grievance voiced by parliament concerning those who appealed to the Papacy against decisions made by the royal courts, but authorised a statute to deal with the other abuses.[73] While the preamble refers to the Carlisle parliament and recalls the 1343 ordinance in stressing the spiritual and financial consequences of provisions and the loss of patronage which they occasioned, the clauses of substance have very different aims from those of 1343. Because the Statute of Provisors has often been misinterpreted, a few points must be made about it.

The 1351 statute ordained that elections to bishoprics and other dignities should be free, and that clerical patronage should be exercised without interference. The emphasis, however, was on ensuring that the rights of those laymen who originally granted advowsons or faculties to elect were not undermined by provision. If the pope intervened, then the king, or other laymen who were the descendants of the original benefactors, could assume rights of presentation for that turn. This defence of fundamental royal patronage did not represent an advance in theory, but the idea was extended so as to allow the king to intervene in two particular circumstances where he would not normally be involved. Firstly, if a provision was made to a benefice in spiritual patronage and the ecclesiastical patron was unwilling or unable to make a presentation, then the king was to have the right of appointment; the clause harks back to the situation highlighted in the 1344 parliament – where clerical patrons declined to present in face of a provision – so as to authorise the king to step in and thwart the provisor, but it safeguarded the rights of the patron to make a presentation whenever a vacancy occurred, irrespective of whether a provision was made too. Secondly, if a patron did not present to a vacant benefice within six months, and the bishop did not exercise his devolutionary right within a further month, then the right to

[73] *Statutes of the Realm*, I, 316–18; *Rot. Parl.*, II, 232–3.

present was to lapse to the crown. The king was to replace the pope as the ultimate authority in the filling of benefices.

The aim was to ensure that papal pressure on electors or clerical patrons or unwillingness on the part of the clergy to oppose papal wishes could not be used to excuse acquiescence in a provision. The statute did not deal with benefices in lay patronage as such; it merely enshrined the principle that clerical patronage derived ultimately from the free gift of lay benefactors, and in certain circumstances could be recovered by their descendants. Its scope was wider than that of the 1343 ordinance, but it did not specifically ban all provisions. It was concerned with establishing a procedure which could be used to protect the rights of clerics to elect, collate and present, which the 1343 ordinance had ignored, or at least to prevent provisions to benefices in clerical patronage by transferring rights from the pope to the king. It did not repeat the measures against bulls prejudicial to the king or his people, and so was in no sense a replacement for the 1343 ordinance. Rather, it was an addition to existing anti-papal legislation, but its effectiveness was bound to depend on how willing the king and other laymen were to intervene to defend rights of presentation belonging to prelates or clerical institutions rather than to themselves.

The statute laid down a procedure against those who hindered clerks who had been presented in accordance with its terms. Provisors and their agents were to be arrested, and on conviction imprisoned until they had paid a fine to the king, satisfied the aggrieved party, made a formal renunciation of their actions, and promised not to act similarly in future or to sue at Rome or elsewhere about their imprisonment or renunciation. Those who could not be found were to be outlawed, and the king was to take the profits of their benefices except those in collegiate or conventual churches.

But, for all its grand theory and procedural detail, the 1351 statute was used very little. There is no evidence that it was ever employed in connection with any benefice in the province of York, and it was put into operation elsewhere in England only very rarely. Various reasons have been suggested for its insignificance,[74] but the fundamental one was that the king did not have the will to enforce it. The statute protected no long-cherished royal rights, and the clerical patrons whom it was designed to serve were unenthusiastic about being involved in a frontal assault on papal

[74] Davies, 'Statute of Provisors', 118–19.

authority. On 10 May 1352, when Archbishop Zouche commissioned John de Sutton to confer benefices in his collation on suitable persons, he stressed that no prejudice was to be caused to provisors.[75] The king too preferred to avoid confrontation. It is unlikely that he wanted to see bishops elected by chapters, preferring to use his influence with the pope to ensure that vacant sees were filled by suitable persons; Clement VI had made that very point in 1348, when he shrewdly reminded the royal envoys that the present system was better for the king.[76] It was much easier – and diplomatically much safer – for the king and other lay lords to petition for provisions for their clerks and connections than for them to invoke their rights under the 1351 statute; and there is no evidence for any presentations to benefices in clerical patronage in order to prevent the execution of a provision, unless the king had the right to present for some other reason or the provisor disturbed a royal nominee in possession. In view of this, it is ironic that it was this piece of legislation rather than any of the others which was renewed, in a slightly amended form, by Richard II's parliament in 1390;[77] and it was only after that, on 4 February 1391, that the Papacy formally annulled the statute of 1351.[78]

The death of Clement VI provided an opportunity to improve diplomatic relations between England and the Papacy, and it seems that both sides were eager to avail themselves of it. The threat to excommunicate Edward III and his servants was not put into effect; and for his part the king appears at some point to have lifted his sequestration of the revenues of benefices held by aliens. No action was taken to enforce the 1351 statute, while the 1353 measure was concerned only with adjusting the procedure used against those appealing to Rome against decisions of the royal courts. It was not a new policy, and news of it appears to have been received in Avignon with some indifference. Although the rolls of parliament do not survive for most of Innocent VI's pontificate, there is no chronicle or other evidence which might hint at anti-papal activity on the scale of the previous decade. The pope was less closely connected to the French court than his predecessor had been; the war was going well for the English king; and he needed papal help in arriving at an advantageous peace. Papal nuncios were heavily involved in the negotiations which led to the Treaty of Guînes in

[75] Reg. Zouche, fol. 272. [76] Lunt, *Financial Relations ... 1327–1534*, 334.
[77] *Statutes of the Realm*, II, 69–74. [78] *CPL*, IV, 277.

1354, and again after the capture of the French king at Poitiers in 1356. Only in 1356 is there a sign of possible tension. On 8 April Innocent told the nuncios, Talleyrand de Périgord and Nicholas Capocci, to exhort Edward to cease offending against churches and clergy, and to revoke anything he had done in England or any of his other dominions which was contrary to ecclesiastical liberty.[79] In a secret instruction from the king to the prince of Wales in December, the latter was asked to inform Talleyrand of papal encroachments which were again prejudicing the crown and kingdom.[80] This may have been mere posturing, or it may have been a comment on a particular controversy; but the situation was not allowed to develop on the lines of the 1340s.

The change was, however, one of atmosphere rather than of papal practice. Innocent continued to make provisions to English benefices and to collect annates in connection with them. The cardinal-nuncios Talleyrand and Nicholas were given a commission to confirm in their benefices clerks who held them uncanonically, and annates were due from these confirmations. But Innocent showed restraint in two areas where his predecessor had encountered opposition. He granted many fewer expectancies at the start of his pontificate than Clement had done; the number of poor clerks with papal graces was much lower than in 1342. He also restricted the number of provisions to aliens, the chief grievance of the Commons in the 1340s.

Innocent VI not only provided fewer foreigners; a greater proportion of them were cardinals – and so potentially of service to the king in his negotiations with the Holy See – and they received a much narrower range of benefices. Nearly all his provisions to benefices in York Minster were in favour of cardinals, including a sudden rush in 1361 which was perhaps connected with the mortality caused by plague in Avignon in that year. The other provisions in the northern province affected only the collegiate churches and two rectories: Bernard de Turre was confirmed in possession of Brompton, and the German Gerlac de Clave, who held several benefices successively in York diocese, received confirmation in Langton.[81] There was nothing to compare with the grant to Aymar Robert, and none of the provocative gestures which had accompanied Talleyrand's provision to the deanery of York.

[79] *Innocent VI: lettres secrètes et curiales*, nos. 2024, 2073.
[80] Bock, 'Some new documents', 99. [81] *CPL*, III, 516; *CPP*, I, 316, 358.

Innocent's policy with regard to aliens was continued by Urban V. In the province of York, all but one of his grants to foreigners benefited cardinals and involved benefices in York Minster. The one exception was rather a special case. William Raymbaut was provided to the priory of Lancaster in 1366; he had been a monk of St Martin, Séez, but had been in Lancaster as bailiff of the monastery, and spoke the local language.[82] He was not an alien in the same sense of the word as many of the earlier provisors.

With the controversial matter of aliens largely in abeyance, and with England and France at peace for most of Urban's pontificate, it might have been expected that Anglo-Papal relations would have been smooth. Such was not the case. An increase in the number of provisions, especially expectative graces, papal attempts to limit pluralism and to relate preferment to academic achievement, and fresh political differences involving the king personally all conspired to create diplomatic difficulties. Evidence from the north enables us to assess both the causes and the effects of the dispute.

In 1363 royal envoys were sent to Avignon to protest against infringements of Edward's regalian right,[83] and parliament discussed attacks on the franchises of the church.[84] A letter was sent to the pope, complaining about the evil effects of papal reservations, and threatening that existing patrons would consider the disendowment of churches founded by their ancestors if their rights of patronage were not upheld.[85] These complaints are very similar to those of the early 1340s, and for the same reason. Urban probably restricted provisions to poor clerks, but he bestowed an unprecedented number of expectancies *in forma speciali* promising benefices in the gift of a named patron. In the first year of his pontificate he granted seventy of these which affected patrons in the province of York, compared with fourteen from Innocent VI in his first year and five from Clement VI in his. Only a few of these were likely to lead to prebends in York Minster or the collegiate churches; most provisors would hope for parochial benefices, and although they

[82] *Urbain V: lettres communes*, VI, no. 18822; Lunt, *Accounts*, 297.

[83] Mirot and Déprez, 'Les ambassades anglaises', nos. ccxxvii–ccxxviii; J. J. N. Palmer and A. P. Wells, 'Ecclesiastical reform and the politics of the Hundred Years War during the pontificate of Urban V', in *War, Literature and Politics in the Late Middle Ages*, ed. C. T. Allmand (Liverpool, 1976), 175.

[84] *Rot. Parl.*, II, 275.

[85] Palmer and Wells, 'Ecclesiastical reform', 175.

were Englishmen, they were nonetheless disrupting the normal exercise of local patronage.

Urban seemed likely further to increase the number of benefices at his disposal when he introduced measures to restrict pluralism even where sinecures were involved. In his bull *Horribilis* of 1 February 1363, he tried to limit the number of benefices and their value in accordance with the academic standing of the ecclesiastic,[86] but its terms were very general, and both it and the order on 24 September 1364 that clerks should declare their benefices held in plurality[87] seem to have been largely a dead letter in England. Urban's decree *Consueta* of May 1366, however, expressly included all sinecures and even expectative graces; there were special regulations for England which involved deprivation and excommunication for those not co-operating in declaring their benefices, and a maximum of two compatible benefices was to be retained.[88] Although it was only in the wake of *Consueta* that a concerted attempt was made to force pluralists to declare their interests, the pope's intentions were clear as early as 1363. The danger of a further increase in the number of provisors, and the manifest threat to royal clerks posed by the anti-pluralism measures, combined to create a situation in which parliament and government could unite in opposition to Urban's plans.

In the parliament which met on 20 January 1365 complaints were made about citations to the pope of persons of the realm in cases cognisable in the royal courts, provisions to benefices in lay patronage, and provisions to churches appropriated to religious houses or corporations.[89] The last abuse was a relatively new phenomenon; there had been a sudden increase in the early 1360s of provisions to appropriated benefices on the grounds that they had been vacant for so long that collation to them had lapsed to the Holy See. In the northern province there were at least sixteen of these during Urban's pontificate, thirteen of them in 1363 and 1364, but only two in his predecessor's time.[90]

86 Thompson, 'Pluralism', intro., 69. For the text see *Annales Monastici*, III, 413–14.

87 *CPL*, IV, 12.

88 Thompson, 'Pluralism', intro., 71–2; C. J. Godfrey, 'Pluralists in the province of Canterbury in 1366', *JEH*, 11 (1960), 24. For the text see *Reg. Langham*, 1–5.

89 *Rot. Parl.*, II, 283–4.

90 The figures are based on cases where the provision is known to have failed because the church was appropriated. Only three Scottish provisions during the period can be said with a degree of certainty to have been fruitless for this specific reason, in 1345, 1365 and 1366, but evidence for the 1360s is very patchy. Especially in Scotland, petitions for benefices on the basis of technical lapse due to earlier canonical irregularity were quite numerous.

These provisions disturbed monasteries, some of which had held the churches for many years, and undermined processes drawn up by bishops, confirmed by cathedral chapters and sanctioned by royal licence. The delays inherent in the appropriation procedure, most notably the need to wait for the church to fall vacant before the annexation could take effect, could easily create an element of doubt which might encourage a clerk to try his luck with a provision. But the number of provisions to appropriated churches was certainly greatly increased in the early 1360s, and parliament was quite justified in drawing attention to the fact.[91]

A new statute was drawn up, which emphasised the link between the legislation against provisions and the process of praemunire. It legislated for the first time specifically about benefices in lay patronage, and it upheld the rights of the royal courts both generally and on the particular question of provisions to appropriated churches.[92] It confirmed the statutes of 1351 and 1353, and was clearly an extension to that legislation rather than its reiteration or replacement.

The 1365 statute was in part a procedural adjustment to the processes used against those who infringed the statutes of the early 1350s, laying down that the penalties decreed in 1351 – fine, compensation, renunciation of the bull and the need to find sureties – were to take effect if the offender was arrested, but that the 1353 legislation was to be used if he was not. The 1351 statute ordained for those who could not be arrested outlawry and writs for arrest, and the seizure by the king of the profits of their benefices unless these were attached to a collegiate or conventual community. The act of 1353 tightened the procedure, not only by decreeing that a writ of arrest should be issued against those not appearing within two months, but also by ordering confiscation of lands and possessions, with outlawry to follow if the offender could not be found. The seizure of the profits of benefices was an empty gesture if the offender – who might be merely an agent of the provisor – had no benefice to seize; the 1353 clause covered all possessions and was thus a tougher sanction, as well as laying down a more effective procedure in cases of default.[93]

The 1365 statute also contains a clause forbidding provisions which might disturb English incumbents who hold their benefices

91 Barrell, 'Papal involvement in appropriations', esp. 32–6.

92 *Statutes of the Realm*, I, 385–7; *Rot. Parl.*, II, 284–5.

93 Graves, 'Legal significance', *passim*.

by reasonable title, unless the papal grant has already been fully effective; this is to apply also to the future if prejudice is thereby done to the king, his subjects, or the laws and customs of the realm. This vague wording may have been intended to have wide application, but it has been suggested that it referred in particular to the attempts being made by Urban V to deprive pluralists, many of whom were royal servants, of their excess benefices.[94] This danger must surely have been in the minds of many of those who were responsible for drawing up the legislation; as in the case of provisions to appropriated churches, the statute was a reaction to a contemporary feature of papal policy.

The significance of the 1365 statute is a matter for scholarly debate.[95] Firstly, there is the question of where the initiative for fresh legislation originated, a matter which involves consideration of political factors as well as of provisions and anti-pluralism measures. Secondly, there is the level of enforcement, and the extent to which papal exactions were resisted under the terms of the 1365 act as opposed to under pre-existing procedures.

It has been argued that Anglo-Papal relations were severely damaged following Urban V's refusal to grant a dispensation to allow Edward III's son, Edmund of Langley, to marry the rich heiress Margaret of Flanders. This led to an attack by the government on Urban's reforms. When in the winter of 1364–5 the pope made his refusal manifest, the king, to whom the rejection was not totally unexpected, took action and prevented the publication of Urban's mandate of September 1364 that all pluralists should certify their benefices.[96] In such circumstances, the government had a vested interest in the promulgation and enforcement of the statute which followed early in 1365. This argument is entirely plausible in view of the fact that the new legislation mentioned specifically appeals in cognisable cases (always a concern of the crown) and provisions to appropriated benefices (which impugned royal licences to monasteries), and probably dealt too with the threat to deprive pluralists.

[94] Palmer and Wells, 'Ecclesiastical reform', 178.

[95] The discussion which follows draws on arguments put forward by Palmer and Wells, 'Ecclesiastical reform'; J. J. N. Palmer, 'England, France, the Papacy and the Flemish succession, 1361–9', *Journal of Medieval History*, 2 (1976), 339–64; and Lunt, *Financial Relations ... 1327–1534*, 348–51. Readers are referred to these works for alternative interpretations of Anglo-Papal relations in the 1360s.

[96] Palmer and Wells, 'Ecclesiastical reform', 177–8.

If the initiative for the legislation of 1365 came from the government, was its enforcement also a matter for governmental action? Palmer and Wells contrast the 1365 statute with that of 1353 by arguing that private individuals were now allowed to institute proceedings against provisors. 'Anyone deprived of their benefice by papal legislation would therefore have a right of action in the royal court against the provisor who succeeded him. The papal provisor was thereby placed at the mercy of the English pluralist, and the fate of Urban's reforms in the hands of those who had a vested interest in their failure.'[97] It is not clear that under earlier legislation the initiative necessarily had to come from the crown, but it may well have been the case that a rather greater number of private actions, albeit largely by royal servants, was envisaged in 1365, which would explain the significance of an otherwise rather superfluous passage in the statute urging all classes of society to co-operate in enforcing the law.

Certainly there was opposition to papal exactions in the mid-1360s, and the government played its part in it. Urban's untimely demand for arrears of the tribute was rejected;[98] there may have been some discussion of the possible withdrawal of Peter's Pence – the only other papal tax which fell directly on the laity – in the parliament of 1365;[99] the funds of the papal collector were temporarily impounded.[100] Action was taken at around the same time against William de Dalton, who was trying to have the new tax in the north annulled at the curia in favour of the 1291 assessment,[101] with the danger that the pope would export even more treasure from the realm. On 12 May 1365 the justices of the Bench were told to abide by the form of legislation against appeals abroad in all pleas then or thereafter before them, any earlier royal command notwithstanding; it was added that parliament had ordered the appearance within two months of anyone bringing about a citation abroad in a case cognisable in the king's court or suing in an alien court against a judgement, under pain of being put out of the king's protection.[102] This is clearly a reference to the recent statute, and implies that the king intended – or wished to be seen to intend – to enforce it more stringently than earlier legislation.

[97] Ibid., 178–9. [98] *Rot. Parl.*, II, 290.
[99] *Chron. Reading*, 163–4. See above, p. 19.
[100] Lunt, *Financial Relations ... 1327–1534*, 10–11; Lunt, *Accounts*, 225.
[101] Reg. Hatfield, fols. 45v–46; Reg. Appleby, pp. 161–2; cf. *CCR 1364–68*, 205.
[102] *Foedera*, III, 764; *CCR 1364–68*, 106–7.

Evidence for the use of the 1365 statute as such is, however, hard to find. Throughout the 1360s and into the 1370s orders to seize certain bulls and arrest their bearers were very common. The phrase 'prejudicial to the king and his people' or variations of the same were always used, and the ban was normally on export as well as import so that the king could protect his right to hear advowson cases. These mandates were very similar to those of the 1340s, in the wake of the 1343 ordinance. They defended long-standing royal prerogatives; and while their use in such numbers in the 1360s demonstrates that there was some tension between England and the Holy See, they are not directly connected with the 1365 statute.[103]

The king also ordered the seizure of the temporalities of certain vacant benefices, including the deanery of York and prebend of Strensall, vacant by the death of Talleyrand de Périgord.[104] This has been seen as a means of applying pressure on the pope, or even as evidence of a policy of seizing the benefices of alien provisors.[105] In fact, it was concerned only with ensuring that the revenues of such benefices were not wasted during their vacancies, and in the event the papal collector levied intercalary fruits from both the deanery and Strensall, even though this was unusual in England.[106] Although the intention was expressed that future holders of these benefices should be suitable, meaning natives, this was not the case: Angelicus Grimaud was provided to the deanery in September 1366[107] and admitted on 11 November,[108] while Elias de St Irieux received Strensall.[109] If the seizure was part of an assault on alien provisors, then it was remarkably unsuccessful.

Indeed, the anger of 1365 did not persist for very long. Although there was no change of heart on the tribute, any proposal to withdraw Peter's Pence was not pursued, and the arrest on papal monies was lifted. John de Cabrespino and his agents were able to export money in the late 1360s, even if only by letters of exchange. Nor should it be thought that Cabrespino's absence from England was caused by royal opposition; he seems to have been one of those collectors who preferred to reside at the curia and carry on the work of collection through deputies.

103 Barrell, 'Ordinance of Provisors', 276.
104 *CPR 1364–67*, 61–2.
105 E.g. Palmer, 'England, France, the Papacy and the Flemish succession', 353.
106 See above, pp. 55–7.
107 *CPP*, I, 535; *Urbain V: lettres communes*, V, no. 16460.
108 YML, H1/3, fol. 81.
109 *Urbain V: lettres communes*, IV, no. 15272; cf. Reg. Thoresby, fol. 57v.

Deprivations of pluralists were almost always fruitless. Among many hopeful provisors whose graces failed were John Cheyne, whose provision to the prebend of Oxton in Southwell was intended to supplant the redoubtable Henry de Ingelby,[110] and Simon Lamborn, who tried to remove Hugh de Wymondeswold from the church of Leake.[111] Whether or not these provisions led to litigation, they threatened the vested interests of men high in church and state, and would probably have been hard to bring to effect in any case. One need only compare the difficulties experienced by those trying to remove Scottish incumbents who had not been ordained to realise that possession was nine-tenths of the law. The incumbents often had title from the king or another powerful layman; that alone might deter most provisors.[112] But although Urban may not have received the additional patronage he hoped for from the enforcement of his measures against pluralism, the crisis of the mid-1360s did not lead to a reduction in the number of provisions generally. In the province of York, 1368 and 1369 were years of many provisions, and most of them were successful.

If the crisis was caused by Urban's refusal to grant the marriage dispensation, then it must be concluded that the king gained little from his angry reaction. In 1366 the pope acceded to a royal request that a panel of cardinals should be set up to examine cases before any personal citations to the curia were issued,[113] but in so doing he gave way on no point of principle. The deprivations envisaged by *Consueta* were largely ineffectual, but the king did allow the bull to be executed and the declarations by pluralists to be made. A new statute was issued, but used very little if at all. On the important matters of provisions and papal taxation the outbursts of the mid-1360s had no effect, other than to confirm that payment of the tribute would not be resumed. In temporal matters, Edward kept up the pressure on the pope, with a marriage alliance with the Visconti of Milan, opposition to Urban's schemes in Italy, and the reactivation of Lancastrian claims in Provence.[114] But the king's annoyance in the winter of 1364–5 did not cause him to continue to harass Urban in the ecclesiastical sphere beyond the summer of 1366.

110 Lunt, *Accounts*, 388; cf. *CPP*, I, 536; *Urbain V: lettres communes*, V, no. 18168.

111 Lunt, *Accounts*, 391; cf. 350.

112 Help given by lords to clerks with several benefices was said by a chronicler also to be the reason for the failure of *Horribilis* in 1363: *Polychronicon*, VIII, 413.

113 *CPP*, I, 534–5.

114 Palmer, 'England, France, the Papacy and the Flemish succession', 356–9.

The resumption of the war with France in 1369 resuscitated parliamentary fear of papal intentions, and bitter hostility to the Holy See and its agents was a regular feature of the parliaments of the last few years of Edward III's reign. The sense of crisis was heightened by the military failures which marked the 1370s, and by the political problems which attended the king's decline into senility.

Parliamentary attacks on aliens were prominent in the 1370s, as they had been in the 1340s. But, unlike the period 1343–8, the criticism ranged widely and was not confined to pointing out the shortcomings of alien provisors. Native Englishmen who lived abroad and took the revenues of their benefices out of the country were also criticised. So were appeals abroad to the prejudice of the crown, and the activities of the papal collector Arnald Garnerii. Especially in the Good Parliament of 1376,[115] the Commons alleged that there was extensive brokering and purchase of benefices in Avignon; simony was alleged, and the covetousness of the church was said to rub off on lay patrons who were prepared to sell churches to people who would destroy them. Most of the accusations had a basis in truth, but parliament was guilty of considerable exaggeration. The outbursts of the 1370s reflect the fear and distrust which some elements among the laity had felt for the whole period of the Avignon Papacy.

The reason for this was largely financial. The French king, Charles V, adopted the tactics of avoiding pitched battles, which had proved so calamitous at Crécy and Poitiers; rather, he allowed the English armies to indulge in fruitless and very expensive raids. Since parliament had to authorise the taxes which funded these expeditions, it was natural that it should both expect greater military success and object to any drain of money from the realm. Papal taxes, especially annates, and other payments made in order to procure provisions were obvious targets for parliament's wrath.

Gregory XI pursued no markedly new policy with regard to provisions, although he did order the levy of annates from successful expectative graces, which hitherto had been exempt, and he resorted to two unpopular practices. Unlike his immediate predecessors, he provided cardinals to parish churches: the rich rectory of Bishop Wearmouth was claimed not only by the English

[115] See *Rot. Parl.*, II, 333, 336–43 for anti-papal and anti-alien activity in this parliament.

cardinal Simon Langham but also by the alien Robert of Geneva,[116] while the valuable church of Houghton-le-Spring was given to Peter Flandrini.[117] In addition, cardinals again received faculties to accept a range of benefices up to a certain value.[118] Such measures recalled the tactless grants of Clement VI, and, in conjunction with the number of cardinals provided by Urban V who were still in possession of English benefices, provided ammunition to those who were only too ready to complain about the abuse of giving English benefices to foreign ecclesiastics.

The government's usual response, for instance in 1377,[119] was that existing measures were adequate to remedy the situation. The resumption of hostilities had led to a fresh seizure of alien priories,[120] and orders were sent to the bishops in both 1370 and 1374 to report on which benefices were held by foreigners.[121] Action against alleged spies was taken in October 1373, when the king wrote to the Dominican house in Oxford, stated that some enemy aliens who claimed to belong to the order had entered the house and were posing as students, and demanded the removal of all foreigners unless and until royal licence to the contrary was given.[122] In 1372, when parliament suggested that the export of money to beneficed clerks living abroad should be forbidden, the king claimed that such a step had already been taken.[123] Mandates were issued in the autumn of 1371 for the arrest and imprisonment of the agents of alien provisors.[124] The usual wartime restrictions on the import and export of prejudicial bulls and on travel were reimposed.

Evidence of specific action against papal authority is very elusive, at least in the province of York. The king did no more than uphold his powers of patronage and defend his courts' right to hear certain types of business. On papal taxation, steps were taken to discourage Arnald Garnerii from zealously levying more than was customary, but the normal work of collection appears to have been largely unaffected. It was only the subsidy of 1372 which aroused considerable royal opposition, and even that turned out to be negotiable. The king's readiness to come to an agreement with

116 Lunt, *Accounts*, 409, 473, 516; cf. *Rot. Parl.*, II, 339.

117 Lunt, *Accounts*, 427; cf. *Foedera*, III, 1037.

118 *CPL*, IV, 103.

119 *Rot. Parl.*, II, 367, 372–3.

120 Ibid., 302.

121 For 1370 see Reg. Appleby, p. 216; for 1374 see *Foedera*, III, 999; LAO, Reg. IXC, p. 29. Similar steps were taken in Clement VI's pontificate: e.g. *CCR 1343–46*, 224 (1343); *Foedera*, III, 90 (1346).

122 *Foedera*, III, 991; *CCR 1369–74*, 517.

123 *Rot. Parl.*, II, 312.

124 *CPR 1370–74*, 179.

Gregory XI over a number of contentious issues – on terms which suited him rather than parliament – was one of the principal causes of the unusually hostile attitude of the 1376 Good Parliament. The diplomacy is significant also because it demonstrates the areas in which king and pope were prepared to co-operate or at least to compromise.

Several historians have examined Anglo-Papal relations during the pontificate of Gregory XI.[125] Although little consensus has emerged, at least in the interpretation of the postures adopted by the two sides, it has been pointed out that the government miscalculated the level of opposition to the Papacy at home; the outburst of 1376 was the direct result of the policy of compromise. It has been argued that the pope conceded no point of principle, and that his conciliatory gestures were largely meaningless. The account which follows aims to examine royal policy in the light of events earlier in the reign, and to assess whether it was consistent with previous actions to uphold the king's rights and to work with rather than against the pope whenever possible.

A royal embassy to the pope in late 1373 discussed provisions and the novel exaction of annates from expectative graces. The pope was asked to respect the royal right to patronage in churches, especially during the vacancies of sees and religious houses, and to cease trying cases involving rights of advowson, since the royal courts had cognisance of such matters. He was also asked to cancel reservations, to stop citing Englishmen to the curia because of the perils of travel during wartime, and to postpone the subsidy until the end of the war.[126] To this combination of old claims and new grievances Gregory XI gave a conciliatory answer.[127] He said that he could not honestly revoke provisions already made, but promised to use his powers more moderately in the future, and to provide suitable persons to elective dignities and monasteries. He declined to abandon provisions to bishoprics, as had been demanded by the 1373 parliament,[128] but was willing to wait for

125 See G. Holmes, *The Good Parliament* (Oxford, 1975), esp. 7–20, 46–9; R. G. Davies, 'The Anglo-Papal concordat of Bruges, 1375: a reconsideration', *AHP*, 19 (1981), 97–146; Perroy, *L'Angleterre et le Grand Schisme*, chap. 1; Lunt, *Financial Relations . . . 1327–1534*, 351–5.

126 *Grégoire XI: lettres secrètes et curiales (non-Fr)*, no. 2374; cf. *CPL*, IV, 127.

127 *Foedera*, III, 1072. For the date see Perroy, *L'Angleterre et le Grand Schisme*, 45.

128 *Rot. Parl.*, II, 320. The desire for free elections is stressed in *Polychronicon*, VIII, 379–80; cf. 423; Walsingham, *Hist. Angl.*, I, 316; *Ypodigma Neustriae*, 319; *The Brut, or the Chronicles of England*, ed. F. W. D. Brie (2 vols., English Early Text Soc., 1906–8), II, 327.

long enough for an election to be notified to him and would provide the elect if suitable and please the king if possible. As will be shown,[129] in the Avignon period it was the provision which was the essential factor in the appointment of bishops, and it was far more suitable from the king's point of view to come to such an arrangement – albeit informally – with the pope than to bow to parliament's demands and thereby risk the vagaries of capitular election. On the vexed question of alien provisors, the pope said that he had provided none except cardinals and a Roman who lived in England; there is no evidence from the province of York that this statement was false, and Gregory agreed to moderate the use of provisions to aliens if he could. He also undertook to stop the exaction of annates from expectative graces, but pointed out that other taxes were needed because of the Papacy's heavy expenditure on the war in Italy. The pope also reminded the envoys that many provisions and expectancies were granted at the petition of universities and English lords.

It has been argued that these were merely the papal proposals and that they were unacceptable to the crown,[130] but there is no reason why the government should have viewed them with displeasure. Unprovocative use of the system of provision had always been acceptable to Edward III, and from the crown's point of view it offered a useful addition to royal patronage. Some interim agreement was, moreover, seemingly reached. Benefice cases involving regalian right were suspended both at the curia and in the royal courts; provisors were allowed to have unmolested possession; cases at the curia which did not affect regalian right could be conducted by proctors or, if the parties wished to appear in person, could be held elsewhere; collection of the subsidy was postponed.[131]

This agreement allowed time for fuller negotiations at Bruges in 1374 and 1375,[132] as a result of which many outstanding problems between king and pope were resolved. On 1 September 1375 Gregory issued a number of bulls which formed the basis of this composition.[133] The pope accepted that many English clerks owed their benefices to the king and confirmed their position, offering to

[129] Below, pp. 191–200. [130] Davies, 'Anglo-Papal concordat', 116.

[131] Ibid., 108–9; *Grégoire XI: lettres secrètes et curiales (non-Fr)*, no. 2930; *CPL*, IV, 201–2.

[132] Davies, 'Anglo-Papal concordat', 133; Perroy, *L'Angleterre et le Grand Schisme*, 35–8; cf. *Polychronicon*, VIII, 380–1, 424; Walsingham, *Hist. Angl.*, I, 317; *Ypodigma Neustriae*, 320.

[133] *Foedera*, III, 1037–9. The concordat was probably arranged by 15 July 1375: Holmes, *Good Parliament*, 46.

issue individual provisions on request. Ten disputes between royal clerks and provisors were settled in favour of the former; among the beneficiaries were John de Sleford, who had disputed a prebend of Ripon with Hugh de Arlam, and Thomas de Orgrave, the latest in a line of opponents for John de Provane in the prebend of Skelton in Howden. The cardinal Peter Flandrini's claims to the York prebend of Knaresborough and the church of Houghton-le-Spring were overridden, and the royal clerks who had opposed him emerged victorious. Gregory offered individual provisions for all the king's clerks affected by these decisions, if they so desired. This type of compromise was not new in itself, but it was unusual to dismiss the claims of provisors before their death or resignation or to issue judgements in so many cases simultaneously. Although the pope could claim to have controlled the procedure, he nonetheless tacitly recognised the justice of some of the royal clerks' claims, and thereby acknowledged the validity of the royal authority which had been behind them. The fact that so many suits were decided simultaneously and for political motives undermined the reputation of canon law for impartiality. Gregory also revoked the papal reservation on the benefices of pluralists and imposed silence on those who had brought suits against those who had not reported their benefices in 1366; he thereby accepted the failure of Urban V's decree against pluralism. Because of the dangers of travelling to Avignon in wartime, a special papal court was set up at Bruges, and for three years no Englishman was to be compelled to appear personally at the curia. Bishops were licensed to summon the proctors of cardinals and force them to repair church buildings on benefices held by members of the Sacred College. The pope declared that he would not levy annates or fruits wrongfully received from those newly provided or confirmed in accordance with this concordat. In return, he was to receive a reduced subsidy.

This agreement did not prevent the parliamentary outburst of 1376. There was no reason why it should have done, because its chief beneficiaries were the king and his servants, and the price was the concession over the subsidy. It offered no safeguards against the future abuse of provisions, but merely resolved a number of current disputes in favour of royal clerks. The pope's grant of a court at Bruges and his permission to enable steps to be taken to maintain cardinals' benefices were not major concessions, but they were not entirely trivial. The Bruges court certainly saved Englishmen from the dangerous journey to Avignon; and although it was criticised in parliament in 1377,[134] it nonetheless met one of the demands of the royal embassy of 1373. Damage caused by neglectful cardinals had long been a bone of contention and been seen as one of the abuses of provisions to aliens; although the pope was unwilling to end such provisions, he had at least shown that he appreciated the problem. The events of 1376 may indicate that the crown made a political miscalculation in coming to terms with Gregory XI, but that is not to say that many of the personnel of the court did not benefit from the agreements made both over individual benefices and in ending attempts to deprive pluralists.

The 1376 parliament, like many of its predecessors, accused the pope of levying taxes in England for his wars in Italy and to pay the ransoms of his French friends who had been taken prisoner by the English. What evidence is there for the perpetration of such alleged abuses, or for the popes showing undue partiality to France?

That some of the money raised in England was destined for military expenditure in Italy is beyond doubt. The papal wars in Italy, an essential preliminary to the return of the Holy See to Rome, were often openly given as the reasons for particular taxes, especially the subsidies of 1361–2 and the 1370s. On 1 May 1377 the collector Arnald Garnerii was told to pay 7000 florins to an English knight who was fighting for the Papacy in Italy.[135] The importance of the Italian war may not have been immediately obvious to the English parliament, but its sponsorship by papal taxation was not underhand. The charge of helping the French against England was more serious and often hard to substantiate, but there is evidence for it. The arrangements made for the subsidy of 1361–2 effectively meant that the pope was taxing the English clergy as a means of assisting with John II's ransom payments, and John also received sums of money from papal revenues collected in England by Hugh Pelegrini.[136] Gregory XI campaigned vigorously for the release of his brother Roger de Beaufort, who had been captured at the sack of Limoges in 1370; as well as diplomatic pressure, some of the money collected by Arnald Garnerii was assigned to Roger.[137] Whatever private arrangements may have been made for the reimbursement of the Camera, English money was still the means through which the pope helped some captive Frenchmen.

134 *Rot. Parl.*, II, 367. 135 *CPL*, IV, 159.

136 Ibid., III, 624, 625, 632; Lunt, *Accounts*, 92, 140. A total of £1176 13s 4d was paid.

137 Lunt, *Accounts*, 541. The total assigned is said to have been £1272 12s 8d.

A further indication of pro-French bias was the creation of a college of cardinals which was predominantly French, with a lesser number of Italians. Not all were necessarily hostile to English interests, but it was overwhelmingly French and Italian cardinals who benefited both from provisions and from the procurations paid to envoys negotiating for peace. On 12 April 1347 the king prohibited the payment of procurations to Anibaldus Gaetani and Stephen Aubert while they were working outside England, on the grounds that the bulls demanding them were prejudicial,[138] although in August 1348 and September 1350 the collection of procurations was permitted.[139] Also in 1350, the king asked that a cardinalate be conferred on an English clerk, pointing out that there had been no English cardinal for a long time despite the excellent churchmen produced by the two universities; he also reminded Clement VI that rich benefices in England were used to support members of the College. But the pope rejected Edward's nominees and created no English cardinal to offset the eleven Frenchmen promoted, allegedly on the recommendation of John II.[140] Although the archbishop of Canterbury, Simon Langham, was given a cardinal's hat in 1368, this did very little to alter the French predominance in the College. With the cardinals acting as the pope's advisers, such a situation was likely to lead only to the reinforcement of existing sentiments in favour of France. An English witness of the election of Urban VI in 1378 summed up his countrymen's feelings when he declared, 'All the temporal lords of England regarded the past French popes and cardinals as more potent adversaries of the said kingdom than the king of France was, and consider that, but for their instigation, a most firm peace would have been made between the kings.'[141] In essence, that was the chief reason for suspicion of the Papacy during Edward III's reign.

It will be apparent that there was a reasonably constant undercurrent of anti-papal feeling in the political life of fourteenth-century England. There is, however, virtually no comparable development in Scotland. In part, this may be a trick of the sources, for much of the evidence for opposition to the Papacy in England is to be found in parliamentary petitions, to which there is no comparable

[138] *Foedera*, III, 117. [139] Ibid., 167, 204. [140] *Chron. Baker*, 111–12.
[141] L. Macfarlane, 'An English account of the election of Urban VI, 1378', *BIHR*, 26 (1953), 84.

Scottish material. There is little indication in papal sources relating to Scotland that there was trouble on the scale experienced in England, but it should be noted that only four controversies relating to England are attested in the records of the Vatican. Two of these, the seizure of aliens' benefices and the refusal to pay the tribute, dealt with circumstances which were not applicable to Scotland. Resistance to the subsidy of the 1370s was probably strong in Scotland as well as in England, if the number of repeated mandates regarding its collection is anything to go by. The 1343 ordinance, which is the only piece of English legislation to be hinted at in papal sources during the Avignon period, aroused concern only because it was enforced. Most anti-papal activity in England could not be detected without the rolls of parliament.

On balance, however, it is unlikely that there was a high level of opposition to the Papacy in fourteenth-century Scotland. The Scots were much less suspicious than were the English of the French popes and their intentions, and few aliens were provided to Scottish benefices. After the Wars of Independence, Englishmen were generally not claimants to churches north of the border; although some clerics had pro-English sympathies, especially in the border areas which were periodically under English control, or supported the claims of Edward Balliol against David II, these men were not necessarily provisors. The Scots had fewer financial commitments in the war – probably proportionately fewer than the English – and did not share the English fear that papal revenues were being used to support the enemy. The ransom of David II was undoubtedly a heavy burden, but the pope helped the laity by imposing a tenth on the clergy to help with its payment. The papal collector was not a foreigner as he was in England, and he had less to collect than his English counterpart. There were fewer provisions, and a high proportion of them benefited university graduates; it was not easy to press the charge that the pope was promoting unsuitable persons to Scottish benefices. The Scots were not involved with the payment of procurations to papal nuncios who were trying to negotiate peace, and neither tribute nor Peter's Pence was paid in Scotland. Papal taxation was, therefore, politically less controversial than in England, and did not directly affect the laity.

It would be misleading and simplistic to say either that parliament and government in Scotland were too weak to resist papal authority, or that the 'special daughter' relationship between the

Scottish sees and the Papacy led to an identity of interest between the Holy See and Scotland. The apparent absence of opposition to papal exactions in Scotland should be regarded as a reflection on political attitudes and on the relatively small scale of papal intervention north of the border. Where an abuse was perceived, there was discernible opposition.

The resistance to Gregory XI's subsidy is one indication of this, but it was only in the fifteenth century that concern about the financial consequences of provisions led to legislation in Scotland. James I was concerned both about the use of provision to obtain benefices in contravention of the crown's wishes, and about the export of bullion to purchase churches and pensions at the papal court; in March 1428 an act of parliament ordained that any cleric who wished to leave the realm should approach his bishop or the chancellor, explain the reason for his journey, and promise to do no barratry, or in other words not to buy pensions out of the revenues of benefices. In part, this was symptomatic of the increased confidence of secular powers after the Great Schism, and of the confusion and opportunities presented by the conflict between the popes and General Councils. But there appear to have been more provisions to Scottish benefices in the fifteenth century than in the period before the Schism; and the absence of a fixed tax assessment meant that it was possible for petitioners to bid for vacant benefices as though at an auction. Inevitably, this was seen as an abuse, against which action had to be taken – or at least be seen to be taken. In reality, the legislation seems to have had relatively little effect, and for the same reasons as similar laws in fourteenth-century England. It was easier for the king to work with the Papacy, if necessary using the legislation as a bargaining counter, than to face the risks involved in confronting the spiritual head of Christendom.[142]

Two issues led to diplomatic tension between the Papacy and the Scottish crown in the decade before the outbreak of the Great Schism. The first related to the divorce in 1369 by David II of Queen Margaret Logie, who appealed to the Holy See against the actions of her former husband. The Papacy thereby became involved in the machinations of fourteenth-century Scottish politics, and embraced Margaret's cause with some enthusiasm. Royal envoys had to be sent to the curia, and the case was heard at

[142] See generally R. Nicholson, *Scotland: The Later Middle Ages* (2nd imp., Edinburgh, 1978), 293–4; Grant, *Independence and Nationhood*, 90–3.

length by auditors and cardinals; an interdict might have resulted had Margaret not died in 1375.[143] Gregory XI made a number of special gifts to the queen,[144] he sent letters to Scotland in defence of her rights,[145] and he paid for her funeral at Marseilles;[146] after her death alms were given to one of her former servants.[147]

The second issue concerned the rights of the Scottish crown during episcopal vacancies. The ancient custom whereby the movables of deceased prelates were applied to the king's uses and could not be disposed of by will had been abolished by David II, who allowed bishops to make a testament regarding their movable property.[148] In January 1372 the pope confirmed this arrangement and commissioned three bishops to ensure that it was observed,[149] but in March 1375 he had cause to complain that Robert II had reneged on his predecessor's promise; he ordered the restoration to Walter, bishop of Glasgow, of goods received by the crown when a false rumour circulated about his death, and threatened excommunication against those royal officials who seized the property of dead bishops in the king's name.[150]

Neither of these controversies was of major international importance. Indeed, Scotland figures but rarely in papal diplomatic correspondence in the years between the Wars of Independence and the Great Schism. The country is mentioned occasionally in the context of Anglo-French peace negotiations, and the popes offered some moral support to the captive David II. But in papal eyes England was of much greater importance, and inevitably so. However, that very importance created the circumstances for Anglo-Papal tension. Military, political, fiscal and (especially in the aftermath of the Black Death) social issues combined to make certain elements in England very suspicious of papal intentions. Opposition in parliament, reinforced by the occasional piece of legislation, was the means of expressing these suspicions. But in the final analysis the success of such opposition depended on the

143 *Chron. Bower* (Goodall), II, 379–80.

144 *Vat. Quel.*, VI, 358, 380; Burns, 'Sources', no. 251.

145 *CPL*, IV, 94, 99, 120; Tihon, *Lettres de Grégoire XI*, no. 914.

146 *Vat. Quel.*, VI, 577; Cal. IE 343, fol. 183v; Burns, 'Sources', no. 279.

147 IE 345, fols. 73v, 130v.

148 *Chron. Bower* (Goodall), II, 390–1.

149 *CPL*, IV, 167, 176.

150 Ibid., 145, 206; *Chron. Bower* (Goodall), II, 389. On royal rights in episcopal vacancies generally see G. Donaldson, 'The rights of the Scottish crown in episcopal vacancies', *SHR*, 45 (1966), 27–35.

attitude of the king, and he was prepared to act only when his own interests so dictated. He used the 1343 ordinance and other measures which protected his rights of patronage and defended his courts' cognisance in advowson cases. The seizure of the revenues of benefices held by non-resident aliens in 1346, forced upon the king for financial reasons, strained his relations with Clement VI almost to breaking point. But Edward III had nothing to gain from conflict with the Papacy: his chances of obtaining a favourable settlement for his French dominions depended on papal diplomacy; and it was much easier to use the system of provision for his own ends than to oppose it and thereby both antagonise the Papacy and run the risk of cathedral chapters making elections displeasing to him. The success or otherwise of papal provisions depended on many factors, but only rarely was anti-papal legislation one of them.

Chapter 4

JUDICIAL ASPECTS OF THE PAPACY

As has been seen, the well-established position of the papal curia as a court of law, especially for ecclesiastics, was but little affected by the existence in England of the Statute of Praemunire and other legislation designed to ensure that no one took abroad cases which were cognisable in the king's courts. Cases which were affected by the often intermittent enforcement of these royal laws were relatively few beside those which were taken to the curia and settled either there or by the appointment of judges-delegate or commissioners to check the accuracy of the statements of the aggrieved party and make a judgement locally. In the fourteenth century some individuals and institutions were given the privilege of having conservators, to whom they could address problems without having to involve themselves in the expense of travelling to Avignon and prosecuting a case there. Unfortunately, precise details of procedure and the legal arguments employed by the parties very rarely survive, although it is clear that the Papacy was involved in a wide range of legal controversies, affecting all parts of the church from great monastic orders down to obscure local clerks.

From the standpoint of the aggrieved party, recourse to papal justice offered, at least in theory, an opportunity to avoid some of the interminable delays inherent in most medieval judicial processes. Commissions to judges-delegate or conservators usually overrode certain delaying tactics which were commonly invoked: the right to appeal was postponed or removed; ecclesiastical censures could be used to compel the defendant and witnesses to appear; certain indults which might give the opponent the chance to prevaricate were declared null and void; and in addition restrictions imposed by Boniface VIII prohibiting judges from acting outside a particular diocese were often set aside.[1] But none

[1] For an example of this see YML, L2/2a, fol. 122–122v.

of this was intended to deny justice to any other party, and subsequent counter-appeals to the higher authority of the pope were permissible and frequent.

JUDGES-DELEGATE

In the thirteenth century a commission to a panel of judges-delegate had been a common way of settling a dispute.[2] Some religious bodies were frequently involved in such a procedure: the cartulary of Bridlington Priory records a number of early thirteenth-century cases which were referred to papal judges, most of them disputes over tithes.[3] Tithes were also at issue in the case between the prior and convent of Nostell and the abbot and convent of Meaux, which was delegated to the prior of Holy Trinity, York, and the chancellor and subdean of York by Nicholas III on 27 December 1278,[4] and the Meaux chronicle gives some details of how the case proceeded. Nostell initiated the dispute over the tithes of Wharram, claiming that the original agreement was greatly to the harm of that monastery. The church of Wharram belonged to the cathedral church of York as part of the prebend of Bramham, which the prior of Nostell held *ex officio*. Meaux agreed to renounce a composition of 30s and to submit to the judges, allegedly to save money and for the sake of peace. The judges decided that the disputed tithes should be taken by Meaux in return for an annual payment of 50s to the prior and convent of Nostell, who, in the event of default, could take all that belonged by common law to their church of Wharram.[5] A very similar result ensued in a case over tithes between the abbey of Salley and the rector of Gargrave, which was settled by a composition arranged by a cardinal in 1313, whereby the abbey agreed to make an annual payment of eight marks to the rector.[6]

In 1329 Archbishop Melton of York clashed with the bishop of Durham, Lewis de Beaumont, alleging that Beaumont had prevented him by force from making a lawful visitation of the

[2] See generally P. C. Ferguson, 'Medieval papal representatives in Scotland: legates, nuncios and judges-delegate, 1125–1286', Ph.D thesis, Columbia University (1987), esp. chap. 4; J. E. Sayers, *Papal Judges Delegate in the Province of Canterbury, 1198–1254* (Oxford, 1971).

[3] *Bridlington Cartulary*, 270, 298–9, 355, 363, 364, 416–17, 419, 421, 426–7.

[4] *Original Papal Documents in the Lambeth Palace Library*, ed. J. E. Sayers (*BIHR* Special Supp. VI, 1967), p. 27, no. 71.

[5] *Chron. Melsa*, II, 174–5.

[6] *Salley Cartulary*, I, 45–6.

churches of Allerton and Allertonshire, an area in the northern part of the diocese of York where archidiaconal rights were enjoyed by the church of Durham. Melton proceeded against his suffragan both locally and at the curia. On 20 May he appealed to John XXII,[7] while on 17 July he cited Beaumont to appear in York Minster on 2 October or the first law-day thereafter to answer for his part in the violent opposition to the visitation.[8] At the end of September Melton entrusted the case to three local churchmen, and on 2 October, when Beaumont had failed to appear, the auditor-general of the court of York announced his suspension from office; seven days later Beaumont had been excommunicated.[9] In the meantime, the pope had appointed as judges-delegate the abbot of Holm Cultram, the archdeacon of Carlisle and the prior of the Dominican house at Carlisle, but they were unhappy with their commission and on 19 October asked to be excused, ostensibly on the grounds of the lack of skilled legal help in Carlisle diocese, the distances which would be involved in carrying out their duties, and what was termed the fury of the people;[10] in truth, they were probably unwilling to put themselves in a position where they would have to decide upon a tricky question of jurisdiction and privilege concerning the two most powerful ecclesiastics in northern England. In May 1330 John XXII ordered three canons of Lichfield to absolve the bishop, prior and chapter of Durham from the canonical censures laid on them by the archbishop of York and his subordinates, and to make a full report to the pope about the dispute over jurisdiction and the actions of Melton and his official, which had allegedly contravened the rights of the church of Durham and interfered with Beaumont's appeals to the pope. After the failure of the commission to the judges-delegate, the pope now required the parties to send proctors to Avignon.[11] How the case subsequently proceeded is unclear, but in 1331 the parties came to a compromise over the disputed visitation rights.[12]

All these cases thus ended in compromise, and such was probably the normal outcome where the parties both had some legal basis for their standpoint, a basis which was usually easy to find amid the tangle of rights and exemptions which so complicated the administration of the late medieval church. Recourse to judges-delegate

[7] *Reg. Melton*, I, 140–2. [8] Ibid., 146–8. [9] Ibid., 148–9.
[10] Ibid., 93; *Northern Registers*, 359–60. [11] *CPL*, II, 320.
[12] *Reg. Melton*, I, 150–4.

was sometimes no more than a manoeuvre in the attempt to secure a favourable settlement, and although the judges did on occasion reach a decision, as in the case between Nostell and Meaux, the final settlement was probably often similar to one which could have been made by the parties out of court. The papal commissioners were usually local churchmen who understood local conditions, and few would have been willing to rock the boat by judging decisively for one disputant at the expense of the other. Their usual role was, therefore, little more than that of an arbitration service.

In the middle of the fourteenth century judges-delegate, either individuals or a panel, continued to be appointed, although deficiencies in monastic cartularies and other sources make their actions hard to determine, and usually only the commission survives. However, it is likely that the role of judges-delegate changed little, although they may have been appointed less frequently, especially under Clement VI and Innocent VI. There was a fresh increase in commissions under Urban V. On 16 June 1363 the prior of St Andrew's, York was told to summon the parties concerned and decide a dispute which had arisen between John de Crakanthorp, rector of St Wilfrid's in the city, and the executors of his predecessor, over whether the local custom of applying the personal goods of the late rector to the repair of church buildings should be upheld, the executors having allegedly refused to make the great repairs which the neglect of the last incumbent had rendered necessary.[13] A complex case of jurisdiction was committed on 25 October 1364 to the abbot of Alnwick and the prior and archdeacon of Durham. Following a petition by Robert de Auckland, vicar of Hartburn, they were to summon interested parties and make a decision concerning the jurisdiction of the archbishop of York, to whom two Durham priests had appealed after suffering at the hands of the official of Durham. In the course of hearing this appeal, John Heriz, commissary-general of the official of York, had ordered Auckland, who was then rural dean of Newcastle, to cite two witnesses, and on his failure to do so had cited him to appear himself, excommunicating him later for non-appearance, whereupon Auckland had appealed to the Holy See.[14] Auckland also appealed against some laymen who had allegedly intruded chaplains and priests into chapels within his

[13] *Urbain V: lettres communes*, II, no. 5785; *CPL*, IV, 35. For a similar case at the next vacancy in 1388 see *Court of York*, 58.

[14] *Urbain V: lettres communes*, III, no. 11156; *CPL*, IV, 45.

parish, thus depriving him of the tithes and burial dues to which he was entitled, and the bishop of London was told to summon certain named individuals.[15]

As in the thirteenth century, many of the disputes in the 1360s and 1370s which led to the appointment of judges-delegate concerned finance. On 13 September 1364, on the appeal of William Donke, vicar of All Saints, Pontefract, the bishop of Lincoln was appointed to judge whether restitution should be made to William of revenues which were said to have belonged to the vicar until Adam de Scargill agreed, in return for an enormous pension, to surrender these rights to the Cluniac priory in the town.[16] Scargill had been vicar for just a few days in November 1361, during which time a new ordination for the vicarage had been agreed,[17] and it is likely that he was presented by the prior and convent[18] on the confident assumption that he would be amenable to the change. Also in 1364, the archbishop of York was told to investigate whether Bishop Ralph Ireton of Carlisle had indeed been guilty of simony and illegal dealings in giving most of the revenues of the church of Torpenhow to the prioress and convent of Rosedale without the consent of the chapter of Carlisle and to the great prejudice of the current vicar, Stephen de Brouthon.[19] He was also mandated to investigate whether a pension should continue to be paid to the bishop of Durham from the church of Stamfordham, annexed to the priory of Hexham, now that the revenue of the church had fallen,[20] and whether a pension to the late bishop of Lincoln's chantry from the church of Northorpe should cease.[21] In December 1368 the archdeacon of Man was commissioned to decide the matter of a vicar's portion on the Isle of Man which the abbey of Rushen would not increase despite an expansion of population and a fall in the real value of his stipend; the vicar had been forced to appeal to the pope when the bishop of Sodor refused to act.[22] Sometimes, however, the complaint was

15 *Urbain V: lettres communes*, IV, no. 14727; *CPL*, IV, 51.

16 *Urbain V: lettres communes*, III, no. 11820, where the vicar is called William Dorili.

17 Reg. Thoresby, fols. 108v, 109; YML, M2/5, fols. 57v–59. The new vicar, Richard Donke, was admitted to the newly instituted vicarage, and William Donke succeeded him in April 1364: Reg. Thoresby, fol. 123v.

18 On 28 September 1359 the priory was permitted by the king to present to the vicarage: *CPR 1358–61*, 271. Because Pontefract was a Cluniac house, it was classed as an alien priory and so the king held the temporalities during the war with France.

19 *Urbain V: lettres communes*, III, no. 11868.

20 Ibid., no. 11775.

21 Ibid., no. 11687; *CPL*, IV, 90; cf. *Court of York*, 35.

22 *Vet. Mon.*, 332; *Urbain V: lettres communes*, VIII, no. 24454.

against the vicar: on 20 March 1371 the dean of Brechin was ordered to enquire into a complaint that the vicar of the prebend of Cromdale and Advie in Moray had not made an obligatory payment for several years;[23] and on 27 June the same clerk was told to investigate a complaint by the abbot and convent of Arbroath that the vicar of Inverness owed them money.[24]

Leading local ecclesiastics were sometimes appointed to investigate matters merely as agents in determining the facts of a case and in proceeding accordingly. In July 1364 Urban V ordered three Scottish bishops to look into the alleged overcharging by Dunfermline Abbey of clergy using Queensferry and stop the charges if the allegation proved to be correct.[25] Even when a case was heard at the curia, it was still necessary on occasion to conduct a local investigation. The dispute over a pension and tithes between St Mary's Abbey, York and the vicar of Middleton was entrusted to a papal auditor, but in November 1390 Boniface IX ordered the dean of Chester-le-Street to procure the examination of witnesses, send to the pope their depositions and details of the articles and interrogations of the parties, and tell him how much credence should be given to the instruments and letters presented on the part of the abbey.[26] The actual hearing was at the papal court, the dean being appointed only to gather evidence. This was almost certainly common practice earlier, although little evidence of such enquiries survives. Local commissioners were also sometimes appointed to execute sentences already made. In November 1363 the prior of Durham and others were told to put William de Norwich, rector of Stanhope, in the position which Thomas de Bridkirk had held before his death; Bridkirk had obtained three decisions in his favour against the bishop on the question of the tithes of calves and colts from certain named places within his parish.[27] On 5 January 1368 the abbot of Newminster was ordered to ensure that restitution was made to the priory of Durham of revenues belonging to it,[28] while on 14 May 1369 the archdeacon of Northumberland received a similar mandate in respect of the possessions of the chapel of Gateshead.[29]

[23] Reg. Av. 173, fol. 328–328v. [24] Reg. Av. 174, fol. 547.
[25] *Vet. Mon.*, 326; cf. *CPP*, I, 443 (dated 1363).
[26] Zutshi, 'Original papal letters', no. 408, citing Durham, Dean and Chapter Muniments 3.2.Pap.16.
[27] *Urbain V: lettres communes*, III, no. 11102; *CPL*, IV, 46.
[28] Zutshi, 'Original papal letters', no. 305, citing Durham, Dean and Chapter Muniments, 1.2.Pap.15. [29] *PRO List*, 301.

Even though in some cases the commissioner was not himself deciding the issue in favour of one or other party, he remained an integral part of a judicial process. Many supplications to the pope expressed a grievance which could be dealt with adequately only if someone with detailed local knowledge, supported by the necessary coercive power, became involved as judge or at least as investigator. Such an arrangement, by often sparing parties and witnesses the necessity of travelling to the curia and undertaking an expensive and lengthy sojourn there, was more convenient for all concerned.

CONSERVATORS

In the fourteenth century the practice of appointing judges-delegate was to some extent superseded by the issue of letters conservatory. These allowed an individual or institution to appeal to a panel of named ecclesiastics in the event of difficulty, thereby saving the cost and trouble of an appeal direct to the Holy See. Conservators could be granted to individuals, usually cardinals or papal officials, religious houses or entire orders, and this form of papal justice became popular after the Council of Vienne, when Clement V swept aside earlier restrictions on the activities and jurisdiction of those appointed.[30] Bodies exempt from episcopal jurisdiction, such as the Hospitallers and Cistercians, were particularly enthusiastic, a mark perhaps of their long history of close connections with the Papacy, but letters conservatory had wide application, and while sometimes they were granted for a fixed number of years there are also instances where no time limit was imposed. Only a few chance survivals in registers, cartularies and chronicles indicate how letters conservatory were used, but it is clear that the conservators performed a similar function to judges-delegate and were not under any obligation to side unfairly with the individual or corporation that had secured their appointment.

On 13 April 1344 Clement VI nominated conservators for the Cluniacs, the Scottish houses being entrusted to the abbots of Dunfermline, Coupar and Newbattle.[31] The bull had no time limit, and the scribe of the Paisley register commented that it was the best bull of its type.[32] Its use in our period is recorded in two cases affecting Paisley.

[30] McDonald, 'Relations', 242.

[31] *CPL*, III, 136.

[32] 'Littera conservatoria optima': *Paisley Registrum*, 314.

On 27 November 1351 the abbots of Dunfermline and Newbattle wrote to John Penny, subdean of Glasgow, and three canons of that church, citing the bull of 1344 and detailing an allegation by Paisley that Martin, bishop of Argyll, had occupied and seized the fruits of three churches in his diocese held by the abbey, to the detriment of Cluniac interests; as it was difficult to call a bishop so far to a case, and since the conservators wished to ensure that both sides incurred equal trouble and expense, the case was subdelegated to one or more of the addressees.[33] The case proceeded slowly. On 30 May 1362 Penny and William de Curry, canon of Glasgow, wrote to the clergy of Argyll and Sodor dioceses, informing them of the non-appearance on that day of Bishop Martin, despite the fact that he had been in Glasgow, and ordering them under pain of excommunication to announce his suspension.[34] The bishop was cited to appear in Glasgow Cathedral on 14 June, but five days before then he came to terms with the abbey.[35]

On 20 August 1367 the abbots of Dunfermline and Newbattle wrote to Robert, abbot of Kilwinning, and William, prior of Lesmahagow, citing the bull of Clement VI and appointing them to hear a case between Paisley and William More. The abbey had approached the conservators for redress, alleging a variety of intrusions, attacks and other enormities at the hands of More.[36] On 3 September Robert and William wrote to all the clergy in the dioceses of St Andrews, Glasgow and Dunblane, ordering them to cite More, his brother Gilchrist and a burgess of Linlithgow named John to appear in Glasgow on 1 October to answer to Paisley for the injuries said to have been inflicted on the monastery.[37] The dispute in fact concerned the sum of forty merks per annum, originally owed by Paisley to the order of Sempringham, but transferred by the latter to Reginald More in 1333[38] and now claimed by William.[39] In due course More too sought papal assistance, and on 17 April 1371 Gregory XI responded by commissioning the archdeacon of Dunkeld to investigate More's complaint that Paisley had seized his land and possessions as well as withholding the rent.[40] In the end, Paisley agreed to be bound to pay the rent and the arrears,[41] hardly a satisfactory outcome for the abbey, but testimony to the fact that having conservators did not

33 Ibid., 140–4. 34 Ibid., 144–5. 35 Ibid., 145–7. 36 Ibid., 33–7.
37 Ibid., 37–42. 38 Ibid., 31–2. 39 Ibid., 42–3.
40 Reg. Av. 173, fol. 334. 41 *Paisley Registrum*, 43–6.

allow an institution to transgress with impunity against earlier agreements.

The orders of friars also sometimes received letters conservatory. John XXII appointed conservators for the Carmelite order,[42] and his letter to the archbishop of York and the bishops of Norwich and Carlisle was copied into Zouche's register around the end of 1342.[43] Probably in February 1350 Zouche wrote to the bishop of St Asaph, pointing out that the latter had exceeded his authority by excommunicating Hugh, Carmelite prior of Denbigh. This had shown scant respect for the order's exemption from episcopal control, and the bishop had also disregarded the prior's petition for removal of the sentence, whereupon Hugh had appealed to Zouche as conservator. This incident appears to have been settled peacefully in the summer of 1350.[44] In December of that year the archbishop again exerted his authority in a similar connection: he ordered the prior of Hexham and the custodian of the spiritualities of York's peculiar jurisdiction in Hexhamshire to cite, find or excommunicate two Carmelites of Newcastle who had run away to Hexhamshire with property stolen from their house; the aiders and abettors of the apostate friars were also to be excommunicated in the event of their not appearing, and the archbishop was to be kept informed of events as they developed.[45]

In the case of individuals who received letters conservatory, the element of protection was probably often paramount. Thomas de Hatfield, bishop of Durham, was granted them in 1348 along with an indult exempting him from much of the metropolitan jurisdiction of the archbishop of York,[46] while the grant to Michael de Monymusk, bishop-elect of Dunkeld, in November 1370[47] may not be unconnected with the fact that one of his rivals for the see was royal chancellor. Cardinals might find the existence of a panel of judges useful anywhere in Christendom, although Aymar Robert needed all the help he could get in England after his provocative and wide-ranging expectative grace.[48] There is very

42 *CPL*, II, 190. 43 Reg. Zouche, fol. 255.

44 A. H. Thompson, 'Some letters from the register of William Zouche, archbishop of York', in *Historical Essays in Honour of James Tait*, ed. J. G. Edwards, V. H. Galbraith and E. F. Jacob (Manchester, 1933), 333–4, 342–3, but for the date of the settlement see Reg. Zouche, fol. 270. For a similar case in Lincoln, with which Melton became involved in 1332, see *Reg. Melton*, III, 115.

45 *Priory of Hexham*, I, app., pp. lxxviii–lxxx; Reg. Zouche, fol. 262v.

46 *CPP*, I, 138. 47 *Urbain V: lettres communes*, IX, no. 27833.

48 *CPL*, III, 74. He was granted conservators in 1342 (ibid., 85), 1345 (ibid., 212) and 1351 (ibid., 367).

little evidence of individuals calling conservators into action, although Archbishop Melton responded on at least two occasions in the 1320s to appeals from Napoleon Orsini, prebendary of Lincoln.[49] In many cases the letters may have been seen as little more than insurance, providing an immediately accessible tribunal in the event of the churchman's worst fears being realised.

BENEFICE CASES

The wide use of papal provisions led to a large number of disputes over benefices. The claim of the English crown that advowson cases were cognisable in the royal courts, and the involvement in some of the disputes of clerks presented by the king, meant that there was a potential clash of jurisdictions. The Statute of Praemunire provided clarification of the royal position, but at no time did the government attempt to prohibit appeals to the pope on benefice matters if no infringement of royal rights was likely.

Benefice suits were rarely heard locally, although the pope sometimes ordered a local investigation into factual matters. In June 1364 Urban V told the chancellor of York to investigate the case of John de Metham, who had received a canonry and prebend of Howden but was being deprived of the fruits by the chapter and could not gain admission.[50] In Scotland, the prior of Lesmahagow was told on 3 April 1371 to enquire into a claim to the church of Buittle,[51] while on 17 May 1376 the abbot of Saddell was ordered to investigate a petition by Andrew Macraciane, rector of Kilcoman in the Isles, who was being disturbed by William Macleod, who had received a provision on the grounds that the church had devolved to the Holy See;[52] Macraciane had been summoned to Elgin by the succentor of Moray in his capacity of executor of the provision.[53] Such commissions of enquiry are rarely encountered in surviving evidence, although some factual information must often have been needed when the case was heard by judges unfamiliar with detailed local conditions.

49 *Reg. Melton*, III, 47–9, 74.

50 *Urbain V: lettres communes*, III, no. 11652. Metham was not a provisor: he had been instituted locally in November 1347 (Reg. Zouche, fol. 274v) even though he was well below the canonical age (see *CPL*, III, 392). By 1372 he had apparently lost a case in the royal courts (Reg. Thoresby, fol. 76–76v) and thereafter may have been dispossessed (cf. *CPL*, IV, 201).

51 Reg. Av. 173, fol. 336.

52 Reg. Vat. 289, fol. 689–689v. For the provision to Macleod (18 February 1375) see Reg. Av. 196, fols. 60–61.

53 Watt, *Dictionary*, 367.

On 2 July 1373 Archbishop Thoresby passed on to the priors of Lenton and Thurgarton and the archdeacon of Stowe a mandate sent to him as papal judge-delegate in connection with Richard de Tyso's claim to a canonry and prebend of Lichfield. The local bishop had ordered Tyso to demonstrate the reasons behind his claim, but Tyso had appealed to the court of Canterbury, as a result of which the bishop of Coventry and Lichfield had approached the pope for redress. In order to pursue his investigation Thoresby had to order Tyso's citation,[54] but it seems that the question was not speedily resolved. By 1375 Tyso had been arrested as a contumacious excommunicate, although the king ordered his release as he in turn had appealed to the Holy See and for protection of the court of Canterbury in a legally acceptable manner and had found bail.[55] Thoresby apparently had had power to judge this case, but it revolved around the extent of the bishop's jurisdiction rather than being a simple dispute over a benefice.

Half a century earlier, Archbishop Melton was involved in a number of benefice cases which were heard in England, and gave his subordinates power both to act and to make a decision.[56] He was also appointed as papal judge-delegate along with the abbot of Fountains and the dean of York to determine between rival claims to a prebend in Ripon, and his mandate to the official of the York court in August 1325 certainly implies that the apostolic letters had given the judges full authority to conclude the suit.[57] However, in a dispute over the church of Ratcliffe-on-Soar in 1320, Melton and his fellow judges did no more than order the citation of the incumbent before the pope to answer a charge made by a cardinal who had been provided to the rectory that the English clerk had been intruded into the benefice with the help of lay power. The prior of Lenton was also to be cited because he had refused to accept the cardinal's proctor who had come to claim the church on the provisor's behalf.[58] Although the work of judges-delegate was frequently interrupted by fresh appeals to the Holy See, in this case John XXII had himself required that the rector and prior be sent to him. This was not a decision to be left to Melton and his colleagues.

54 Reg. Thoresby, fol. 78–78v.

55 *CCR 1374–77*, 200.

56 *Reg. Melton*, I, 127–8, 128, 128–9, 139; II, 19, 79, 106, 138.

57 *Memorials of Ripon*, II, 93–4.

58 *Reg. Melton*, III, 29–32; cf. *CPL*, II, 194. For the provision see *CPL*, II, 183. In November 1323 John XXII sent Melton and others a further mandate to cite the prior of Lenton, who had not accepted the provision to the cardinal despite excommunication: *CPL*, II, 234.

Disputants may well have preferred hearings at the curia where a disputed benefice was at issue, even though the York court was often asked to preserve the status quo while the suit at the curia was pending.[59] It is unclear in what circumstances by the middle of the fourteenth century local judges could indeed issue definitive judgements in benefice cases in which the Papacy had become involved, although there was no firm papal monopoly in benefice suits: two auditors in turn heard a case over the border vicarage of Norham, in which both parties had received provision, but it was still said that the nature of the case meant that it would not normally have devolved to the Holy See.[60] Nonetheless, local hearings seem to have been rare, maybe because in benefice cases there had to be a winner and a loser. Although some compensation might be given to the unlucky candidate, there was no possibility of the sort of face-saving compromise which judges-delegate could help to arrange in tithe cases or clashes over details of jurisdiction, and so benefice disputes were usually heard by the highly qualified and experienced auditors of the papal palace or Rota.

The activities of these auditors were defined by John XXII in 1331 in his constitution *Ratio juris*,[61] which governed the procedure of this court for over a century and a half. The auditors, who acted alone, naturally in accordance with universal canon law,[62] were prohibited from receiving considerations or talking about the case while it was in progress, but the hearing could be delayed if one of the parties raised an objection to the judge or to the place where it was being conducted. At the end of the case the winner had to arrange for the lifting of the sequestration which had been imposed on the disputed benefice by the bishop, or failing that the pope, when an initial sentence was pronounced against the possessor. A letter of justice to make the judgement executory was also required, and the decision was publicly announced so as to allow

59 *Court of York*, e.g. 12–13, 23, 27–8, 32–3, 37, 39.

60 *Urbain V: lettres communes*, IX, no. 25684. For the provisions see ibid., V, nos. 16131, 16527; cf. no. 17298.

61 *Dictionnaire de droit canonique* (7 vols., Paris, 1935–65), VII, col. 745.

62 On the procedure before church courts generally see J. J. Robertson, 'Canon law as a source', in *Stair Tercentenary Studies*, ed. D. M. Walker (Stair Soc., 1981), 119–20; O. J. Reichel, *A Complete Manual of Canon Law* (2 vols., London, 1896), II, 262–334; D. Owen, 'Ecclesiastical jurisdiction in England, 1300–1550: the records and their interpretation', *Studies in Church History*, 11, ed. D. Baker (Oxford, 1975), 209. On the Rota specifically see N. Hilling, *Procedure at the Roman Curia* (New York, 1907), 135–6; Mollat, *Popes*, 299–302; J. J. Robertson, 'Scottish legal research in the Vatican archives: a preliminary report', *Renaissance Studies*, 2 (1988), 340–4.

objections to be made, a practice which at least on occasions led to a fresh appeal which was then entrusted to another auditor.[63] The auditors dealt with cases from all over Europe: Robert de Stratton, canon of Lincoln, was involved as a judge in at least five in 1373–5 affecting benefices in the Low Countries.[64] But the details of their exercise of jurisdiction are rarely known, and information on the development of benefice suits has to be culled from a variety of sources, unless by chance a collection of documents relating to a particular case survives. The best known such collection concerns a dispute over the church of Mitton, appropriated to the abbey of Cockersand but granted by Urban V on 7 December 1367 to Thomas Sotheron,[65] but there survive also a few battered folios relating to the hearing before William de Gunello, auditor of the papal palace, of the case over the deanery of Aberdeen between Adam de Tyningham and Michael de Monymusk.[66]

Monymusk was provided to the deanery in 1361 following the consecration of Walter de Coventre as bishop of Dunblane,[67] and by 10 February 1363 he was considered locally to be in possession.[68] By this time, however, he had a rival in Tyningham, who had been given Monymusk's deanery of Dunblane on the latter's promotion to Aberdeen,[69] but now claimed the richer benefice on the grounds that Coventre had held it and the parish church of Inverarity for several years without the necessary dispensation; he was provided on 20 March 1362.[70] In February 1364 the case was still in progress,[71] but Tyningham's proctor was more attentive than his opponent's in negotiating the potential pitfalls in the protracted and complex legal manoeuvres before the auditor, and so Tyningham emerged victorious.[72] Monymusk was ejected from the benefice and perhaps retired to the deanery of Dunblane to lick his wounds.[73] To add injury to insult the defeated claimant was still held liable for the annates due from his original provision, because he had peacefully held the deanery for several years, and on 4 August 1366 he obliged himself to pay the arrears.[74] Tyningham

63 Mollat, 'La collation', 57–62; Mollat, *Popes*, 299.

64 Tihon, *Lettres de Grégoire XI*, nos. 1962, 2069, 2372, 2911, 3131. For the names of some other English auditors at this time see W. Ullmann, *The Papacy and Political Ideas in the Middle Ages* (London, 1976), no. IX, 466–7.

65 McNulty, *Thomas Sotheron*.

66 Coll. 474, fols. 62–66.

67 *CPP*, I, 375; Reg. Av. 147, fol. 263–263v.

68 *Aberdeen Registrum*, I, 93.

69 *CPP*, I, 379.

70 Reg. Av. 148, fols. 168v–169; Coll. 14, fol. 167v.

71 *CPP*, I, 480.

72 Coll. 474, fol. 66; cf. *CPP*, I, 506.

73 Watt, *Fasti*, 80–1.

74 Instr. Misc. 2453.

retained the deanery without apparent opposition until his promotion to the see of Aberdeen in 1380.[75]

A very common practice in the case of disputed benefices was surrogation, whereby a clerk received the right to a benefice formerly enjoyed by another who had died or tired of the struggle. On 19 November 1343 James de Multon was surrogated into the right to a prebend of Howden claimed by John de Caldeu, whose provision had been opposed by the archbishop of York and Robert de Askeby and had been referred to the papal auditor Oliver de Zerzeto.[76] Multon prevailed when a rival with royal title resigned his claim.[77] Not all surrogations were as successful. In July 1363 and again in December 1367 Urban V surrogated Robert de Pothow into the claim of Hugh de Bolton to the church of Aughton; there had been a dispute between Hugh and Ellerton Priory over whether the church was appropriated, and the case, heard by the auditor John Robinelli, was still not concluded when Hugh resigned,[78] although in the event the priory ultimately won the suit and the church remained annexed to it.[79] On 18 January 1368 Peter Galon was surrogated into the right of John de Nesbit to the deanery of Lanchester. Both Nesbit and John de Hesille had claimed canonical possession on the death of John de Newbiggin, and each had said that he had legally received the dignity. The case had been heard by several auditors after its referral to the curia, Nesbit asserting that he had been deprived of the deanery by Hesille.[80] Galon achieved collation on 12 June 1370,[81] but this appears to have been arranged locally by means of exchange and his predecessor was John de Derby, a royal nominee,[82] so the papal grant may have availed him little.

Lawsuits could be prolonged almost indefinitely by means of surrogation, but sometimes the practice was used actually to solve a dispute. On 27 July 1357 Thomas Mount de Wykham was granted his petition for surrogation into the right of John de Denton to one of the Norwell prebends in Southwell; there had been a suit in the papal palace between Denton and John de Thoresby, later archbishop of York, in which Denton had obtained a decision in his favour only to be despoiled of the benefice by William de

[75] Watt, *Fasti*, 7. [76] *CPP*, I, 30; *CPL*, III, 96. [77] *CPR 1345–48*, 227.
[78] *Urbain V: lettres communes*, I, no. 2498; VII, no. 20906; cf. *CPP*, I, 440.
[79] Lunt, *Accounts*, 213, 376, 392. [80] *Urbain V: lettres communes*, VII, no. 20962.
[81] Reg. Hatfield, fol. 67v.
[82] *CPR 1367–70*, 218; for his institution see Reg. Hatfield, fol. 66v.

Northwell.[83] Thoresby and Denton had both claimed the stall by expectative graces[84] on the death of Elias de Counton in 1329,[85] while William de Northwell and his successor John de Northwell received royal grants.[86] On 22 March 1344 William received the stall back from John in an exchange,[87] even though in October 1342 the pope had ordered his citation after he had violated the sequestration imposed after Denton had won three sentences in the curia.[88] It was into this dispute that Mount was projected, and his position was confirmed by Urban V under date of 8 November 1362.[89] The suit was settled on 25 February 1364 when Mount received a fresh surrogation, this time into the right of William de Northwell, on the petition of a cardinal to whom he was a chaplain and servant.[90] Mount was soon threatened by William de Ardene, who accepted the prebend as a result of expectative graces[91] and was claiming it in 1366,[92] but he held on to the benefice until he resigned it in exchange with another Southwell prebend in May 1370.[93]

A rather similar case is furnished by the prebend of Bole in York. On the death of Thomas de Neville at the curia in 1361, a provision was made to the cardinal Androin de la Roche,[94] while Alexander de Neville obtained local collation and a subsequent royal grant on the grounds that the king had recently had possession of the temporalities of the see.[95] Despite Neville's apparently powerful position, it was Androin who made his claim good and paid annates on the provision,[96] and it was only after the cardinal's death in October 1369 that the suit was neatly settled by the provision of Neville,[97] who was admitted by the chapter in June 1370[98] and held the prebend until his consecration as archbishop of York in 1374.

83 *CPP*, I, 300. 84 *CPL*, II, 257, 240.

85 J. Le Neve, *Fasti Ecclesiae Anglicanae*, ed. T. D. Hardy (3 vols., Oxford, 1854), III, 437.

86 *CPR 1330–34*, 478; *CPR 1338–40*, 463. 87 Reg. Zouche, fol. 220; cf. fol. 4–4v.

88 *CPL*, III, 86. 89 *Urbain V: lettres communes*, II, no. 5845.

90 Ibid., III, no. 9332. By 1360 the provisor had fallen foul of the Statute of Praemunire and had to seek a pardon from outlawry in 1366: Graves, 'Legal significance', 76. He is there called Thomas de Ikham, but it is almost certain that Mount is referred to. See also above, p. 130. 91 *CPP*, I, 385, 462; *Urbain V: lettres communes*, I, no. 3504.

92 *Court of York*, 37; cf. Godfrey, 'Pluralists', 32. 93 Reg. Thoresby, fol. 68.

94 *CPP*, I, 321, 376. Philip de Beauchamp also made a supplication for this prebend (ibid., 374), but without success. 95 Reg. Thoresby, fol. 49; *CPR 1361–64*, 93.

96 YML, L1/7, p. 870; R. G. Davies, 'Alexander Neville, Archbishop of York, 1374–1388', *YAJ*, 47 (1975), 89; Lunt, *Accounts*, 414.

97 *Urbain V: lettres communes*, IX, no. 27499.

98 YML, H1/3, fol. 94; cf. Reg. Thoresby, fol. 68v.

The existence of a clerk with an expectative grace could be very troublesome for an incumbent. Hugh de Arlam was collated to the deanery of Chester-le-Street on 18 March 1365,[99] but was disturbed by Ralph Scull de Setrington, who claimed to have accepted the benefice by virtue of an expectancy, even though this was limited to benefices worth thirty marks with cure and twenty without and the deanery was valued at fifty marks.[100] The long lawsuit which ensued was still continuing in 1370 because Ralph persistently raised fresh points. Hugh, who then had no other benefice, complained that he had spent all he had on the suit without receiving the fruits of the deanery, and although his position was confirmed by Urban V,[101] there is no evidence that the suit was swiftly terminated, and in any event Arlam had to pay annates on his confirmation[102] to add to what he had already spent on the litigation.

Arlam had even less luck in his quest for the prebend of Studley in Ripon, to which he was provided on 4 March 1372.[103] His rival John de Sleford had received a royal grant on 21 December 1371 on the basis of a past vacancy of the see of York,[104] and after the royal right to present had been established in the king's courts he was collated to the benefice on 10 June 1372[105] and had his tenure ratified by Edward III on 11 November.[106] As part of a diplomatic agreement between the king and Gregory XI, Sleford received provision on 1 September 1375 as a means of solving his dispute with Arlam.[107] Even then, the suit may have dragged on. Arlam's appeal to the Holy See had led to the prebend being sequestrated by the archbishop, and it was not until May 1378 that an order was sent to lift this seizure.[108]

Another benefice case which was resolved by the same diplomatic agreement was that concerning the prebend of Skelton in Howden, which had been held until 28 September 1346 by Adam de Haselbeche, who on that day exchanged it with Ralph Tervill for the chapel of Norton.[109] Following the death of Tervill in May 1348[110] the prebend was disputed between John de Helwell and

99 Reg. Hatfield, fol. 61.

100 This was the figure in 1291, and it was also given in the bull in Arlam's favour in 1370 and in the collectors' accounts, but the revised assessment was £14: *Taxatio*, 315, 330; *RPD*, III, 91, 104; cf. *Urbain V: lettres communes*, IX, no. 27071; Lunt, *Accounts*, 407, 522.

101 *Urbain V: lettres communes*, IX, no. 27071.

102 Lunt, *Accounts*, 407, 522.

103 Ibid., 462.

104 *CPR 1370–74*, 166.

105 Reg. Thoresby, fol. 75v; cf. fols. 74–75.

106 *CPR 1370–74*, 210.

107 *Foedera*, III, 1037–8.

108 Reg. A. Neville, I, fols. 6v–7; *Memorials of Ripon*, II, 137–8.

109 Reg. Zouche, fol. 223v; cf. fol. 11v.

110 Ibid., fol. 329.

Henry de Rosse. Helwell claimed to have held it for fourteen months by virtue of Archbishop Zouche utilising a papal indult to make presentations to prebends, when on 21 June 1349 the pope ordered that so long as no one else had a right to it the chancellor of Rouen, papal chaplain and auditor of the papal palace, who was hearing the suit, should award it to him.[111] Rosse had an expectative grace dated 6 July 1343[112] and had acquired the Howden prebend of Barnby by 1351 when he resigned it for the purpose of exchange.[113] Helwell's confirmation, however, failed in the face of two provisions to a clerk from Piedmont, John de Provane, who was given the prebend on 23 June 1347 on the death of Haselbeche[114] and again on 14 June 1349 because it had been reserved to papal collation in the lifetime of Haselbeche before he exchanged benefices with Tervill.[115] Provane paid annates and appears to have had possession,[116] but after his death was mistakenly reported he had to face a challenge from Alexander de Neville, who was instituted on 8 November 1362[117] and professed to believe that the man claiming to be Provane was an impostor.[118] The latter, however, won three sentences against Neville, and the fruits of the benefice were sequestrated by both ordinary and papal authority.[119] By December 1369 Neville was doubting that he could win,[120] and he presumably resigned soon afterwards, for on 26 October 1371 the king presented Thomas de Orgrave after winning the right to present against Provane in the royal courts.[121] Orgrave was instituted by Archbishop Thoresby the following spring[122] and provided at Provane's expense in September 1375.[123] The man from Piedmont was, therefore, ousted. He was perhaps unlucky to be reported dead, especially with someone as determined and as powerful as a Neville waiting in the wings; but his sad example shows how precarious the tenure of some provisors could be, even if the papal justices were prepared to confirm their position.

Lawsuits could be complicated and involve a number of claims and counter-claims, as in the case of the prebend of St Peter's in

[111] *CPP*, I, 168; *CPL*, III, 342. [112] *CPP*, I, 64; *CPL*, III, 134.
[113] Reg. Zouche, fol. 276–276v. [114] *CPP*, I, 125; *CPL*, III, 240. [115] *CPL*, III, 343.
[116] Lunt, *Accounts*, 80; cf. 116. [117] Reg. Thoresby, fol. 282. [118] *CPP*, I, 504.
[119] Reg. Thoresby, fols. 219v, 327; cf. fol. 284v.
[120] *Urbain V: lettres communes*, IX, no. 26283.
[121] *CPR 1370–74*, 144; Reg. Thoresby, fol. 75–75v. [122] Reg. Thoresby, fol. 75–75v.
[123] *Foedera*, III, 1038.

Beverley. The incumbent, Andrew de Offord, was threatened in 1357 by a rival who proved to be very determined: John de Blebury, a clerk of the bishop of Winchester, was provided on 14 January and 16 April 1357,[124] and again on 8 November 1362.[125] It appears that he had his case against Offord committed to a papal auditor, but Offord managed to have his rival's letters of provision impounded in the papal chancery and was thus able to triumph. Blebury again appealed to the pope, and the case was heard by another auditor, the pluralism of Offord being stressed. On 6 September 1358, in response to a petition, Innocent VI declared that the vice-chancellor should see that justice was done.[126] In fact, Offord died late in 1358[127] and was succeeded in his claim to the prebend by Richard de Drax, who was provided on 2 December.[128] Litigation followed between Drax and Blebury,[129] and although the curial clerk Drax won at the papal court,[130] Blebury was now stronger locally and received a royal grant in March 1360 after the king had recovered the right to make a presentation to the prebend.[131] On 5 January 1362 Richard Suglworth was surrogated into Drax's right against Blebury[132] in a case which was now being heard by the auditors John Habert, treasurer of Rennes, and Aymeric, bishop of Lodève, and this grant was confirmed by Urban V under date of 8 November 1362,[133] the same day as his rival's last provision, although in fact by this time Blebury had been collated to the prebend and Suglworth had received compensation in the form of a portion of some tithes in Winchester diocese.[134] This seems to have ended the suit, although in November 1366 Blebury was threatened again, this time by Roger de Freton.[135] He was perhaps wise to exchange his benefice in 1368 for a prebend in the collegiate church of Wilton.[136]

The persistence of Blebury led ultimately to his triumph despite the papal sentences against him, although there is also a hint of compromise in the compensation offered, it would seem at

124 *CPP*, I, 290, 333.

125 *Urbain V: lettres communes*, I, no. 1661; Dubrulle, *Registres d'Urbain V*, no. 466.

126 *CPP*, I, 333.

127 Ibid., 309. His confirmation in his benefices on 4 January 1359 (*CPL*, III, 604–5) was somewhat late in the day.

128 *CPP*, I, 310.

129 Ibid., 343, 353.

130 Lunt, *Accounts*, 131.

131 *CPR 1358–61*, 341; Reg. Thoresby, fol. 44v.

132 Lunt, *Accounts*, 131.

133 *Urbain V: lettres communes*, II, no. 5811.

134 Reg. Thoresby, fol. 52.

135 Lunt, *Accounts*, 297. This was unsuccessful: ibid., 388.

136 Reg. Thoresby, fol. 66.

Blebury's expense, to Suglworth in 1362. There is no evidence that the royal grant was in any way decisive, although it must also be said that the papal judgements were of little use to Drax and Suglworth.

In these cases and in many others like them in Scotland and northern England the arguments presented to the auditors remain largely elusive. Benefice litigation was usually linked to the practice of papal provision, and the question at issue was often whether a particular grant was legitimate, especially whether the pope had a reason to provide at that particular vacancy. If there were two rival provisors, then the question of precedence was important. Who had the earlier grace? Was one clerk better qualified than the other? Did one provision contain a clause which would give its recipient a prior or stronger claim? Much must have hinged on the accuracy or otherwise of the supplications from which provisions sprang, and even minor discrepancies or errors of form could be exploited by a rival. For in the final analysis the auditors were lawyers. Their job was not primarily to show pity to an impoverished claimant, but to judge impartially in accordance with canon law on the basis of the evidence and arguments presented to them. If a disputant or his representative were careless, victory might well pass to another.

It is very difficult to quantify the use of papal justice in northern Britain in the period just before the Great Schism. Although a few commissions to judges-delegate survive, there is little to show how they acted in individual cases. Nothing remains to indicate how some of the letters conservatory were utilised, if at all, although those which had no time limit could clearly be used with effect for many years. Even where benefices were concerned, the story has to be pieced together from scattered and sometimes contradictory evidence. But it is clear that despite the Statute of Praemunire, many disputes were settled under the auspices of the pope, through his auditors and judges-delegate. There is no reason to suppose that the Papacy displayed bias in its judgements, nor that it wantonly prolonged cases for its own profit. Medieval litigation was notoriously slow, and no institution, especially the Holy See, could afford to be seen to abdicate any rights, but judges-delegate and conservators could help parties to arrive at a satisfactory compromise, and a benefice suit could be concluded by surrogating the same clerk into both claims. At the end of the day, the Papacy must have had some reputation for fairness, for if it had not, many fewer litigants than was the case would have been prepared to exert themselves and spend money in appealing to it.

Chapter 5

THE PAPACY AND THE BISHOPS

The local ecclesiastical hierarchy was headed by the bishops. To them fell the ultimate responsibility for the administration of their diocese and for the control of their flock, and upon them was also laid a considerable burden of secular business. For bishops were great temporal lords as well as leaders of the church; many had already been deeply involved in royal and local administration, and most could expect to be employed by the crown as counsellors or commissioners and even in matters of local defence. They could also expect to receive instructions from the papal curia on both routine and particular matters; and by the fourteenth century the great majority of sees throughout Europe were being filled by the practice of provision. The importance of bishops in the administrative arrangements of crown and Papacy meant that both powers had a more than passing interest in their appointment and in their subsequent careers.

The Scottish bishops had had unusually close links with the Papacy even at a time when the authority of the Holy See was much less keenly felt in England. The old theory pressed by York, backed by papal pronouncements and injunctions until the 1160s, was that the archbishop of York was metropolitan of the Scottish sees as well as those of Durham and Carlisle. This claim never advanced far beyond theory except in the case of Galloway, where local traditions of independence and a geographical link with England across the Solway caused the bishops of Whithorn to look towards York rather than Scotland; and by the end of the twelfth century the other Scottish sees had become 'special daughters' of the Papacy in accordance with the terms of the bull *Cum universi*,[1] after which even the theoretical claim of York lapsed for some time. Scotland did not have an archbishop of its own until 1472,

1 *Gesta Regis Henrici Secundi Benedicti Abbatis*, ed. W. Stubbs (2 vols., Rolls Series, 1867), II, 234–5; *Chronica Rogeri de Houedene*, ed. W. Stubbs (4 vols., Rolls Series, 1868–71), II, 360–1; III, 173–4.

and since the pope effectively acted as metropolitan of Scotland the bishops were bound to have relatively close links with the Papacy. The pope commissioned panels of prelates to examine and confirm bishops-elect, and generally acted in a supervisory capacity, although his authority must often have seemed very distant compared with that of a local archbishop.

YORK'S METROPOLITAN JURISDICTION

Even in England, the authority of the archbishop of York was limited by tradition and circumstance. There were only two northern English suffragan sees at this period: Durham and Carlisle. After 1216 the bishops of Carlisle were almost always loyal to the archbishop, but the wealth of Durham, its sizable palatinate, its strategic position on what came to be the East March, and the king's desire to have as bishops of Durham men whom he considered suitable servants,[2] meant that disputes between York and Durham over jurisdiction, especially visitation rights, were very common. These were in turn further complicated by the powerful position of the Benedictine priory of Durham and its frequent conflicts with the bishop and the archbishop. Even within the diocese of York, the largest in England, the archbishop's jurisdiction was limited: the archdeaconry of Richmond was administered virtually as a separate see except in those areas where episcopal orders were canonically necessary; the church of Durham had archidiaconal jurisdiction in Howdenshire and Allertonshire, and the parish of Crayke was an integral part of Durham diocese;[3] the chapters of York itself and of the great collegiate minsters of Beverley, Ripon and Southwell all had their peculiars. On the other hand, the archbishop exercised some jurisdiction in Galloway and had contacts with the bishops of Sodor.

Despite *Cum universi*, the bishops of Whithorn continued to look to York for leadership. In the fluid political situation and relative peace of the period before the Scottish Wars of Independence, this link could readily be maintained. Indeed, it continued into the fourteenth century, only to be effectively ended by the advent of the age of papal provisions to all bishoprics, even those as poor as Whithorn, where the bishop had little patronage or

[2] Donaldson, 'Patronage and the church', I, 391.

[3] F. Barlow, *Durham Jurisdictional Peculiars* (London, 1950), 53–115. See also K. Emsley, 'The Yorkshire enclaves of the bishops of Durham', *YAJ*, 47 (1975), 103–8.

revenue, and where the diocese was, according to contemporary sources, much affected by war and other economic dislocation.

The loyalty of the bishop of Whithorn was not unquestioned. In April 1323 Archbishop Melton appointed a proctor to go to the papal curia to prevent the confirmation or consecration there of the bishop-elect Simon de Wedale. Melton also wrote to John XXII and several cardinals, protesting that Wedale owed obedience to him as metropolitan.[4] It seems that the bishop-elect, perhaps taking advantage of the aftermath of Robert Bruce's victory over Edward II, made an attempt to equate his position with that of the other Scottish bishops and seek confirmation of his election direct from the Holy See. In the event he was unsuccessful. Following confirmation by Melton and consecration at Westminster, Wedale made the customary profession of obedience to York in February 1327,[5] and thereafter Galloway continued to be treated as an integral part of the northern province. Melton attempted to make a collation to the vicarage of Glenluce in 1329 on account of an unacceptably long vacancy,[6] and after the archbishop's death the chapter summoned Wedale to a convocation. He declined to come, although this was ostensibly because of the shortage of time and the dangerous state of the marches rather than an expression of overt disobedience;[7] certainly he made a profession to Archbishop Zouche on 27 August 1344,[8] and among documents of ecclesiastical importance he was even apparently sent a letter concerning a clerical subsidy to Edward III.[9] His successor was Michael de Malconhalgh, who was confirmed by York on 26 June 1355 and consecrated on 12 July at Southwark.[10] As bishop-elect he was given a safe-conduct to come to England,[11] and in a later safe-conduct, issued in January 1358, he was said to be a suffragan of York needing to see the archbishop on certain matters concerning himself and his see.[12]

Malconhalgh is the last bishop of Galloway known to have

4 *Reg. Melton*, I, 78–9. 5 Watt, *Fasti*, 130; cf. *Reg. Melton*, I, 87–8.

6 *Reg. Melton*, I, 92–3.

7 Reg. 5A, fol. 116. Wedale refers to himself as a suffragan of York. Bishop Bury made a formal protestation that the chapter of York had no power to summon him to this convocation when the see of York was vacant, and the chapter conceded the point: *RPD*, III, 483–9. 8 Reg. Zouche, fols. 281v–282. 9 Ibid., fol. 281.

10 *Councils and Ecclesiastical Documents Relating to Great Britain and Ireland*, ed. A. W. Haddan and W. Stubbs (3 vols. in 4 parts, Oxford, 1869–73), vol. II, pt. I, 63; Stubbs, *Registrum Sacrum Anglicanum*, 56. For Malconhalgh's profession on 26 June see Smith, 'Vicars-general register', no. 136. 11 *CPR 1354–58*, 240.

12 *Foedera*, III, 387; *Rot. Scot.*, I, 818.

considered himself a suffragan of York. His death in 1359 was followed by the election of Thomas Macdowell, who was supplanted by a provisor, also called Thomas.[13] Although a papal source states that the diocese was in the province of York,[14] there is no evidence that the second Thomas made a profession of obedience to Archbishop Thoresby. This set a precedent for his successor Adam de Lanark, whose election was confirmed or quashed by the pope, who proceeded to provide him to the see.[15] Lanark had been confessor to the Scottish king David II[16] and may, therefore, have been able to count on royal support in his refusal to submit to York. As there is no strong reason to suppose that Macdowell would not have seen himself as a suffragan of the archbishop, it must be concluded that it was the use of papal provision, especially a direct appointment by Innocent VI in face of a local election, which ended Whithorn's link with York. It is strange that York made no attempt to maintain its jurisdiction across the Solway, although Thoresby, always a pragmatist, probably accepted that the metropolitan authority of his see in part of Scotland could not continue indefinitely. The Great Schism, when the governments of England and Scotland supported different lines of popes, consolidated the breach and made it irreparable; but it was the provisions which removed the necessity to profess to York as a prerequisite for enjoying episcopal authority in Galloway, and which set a precedent which later bishops were only too ready to follow.

The position of the see of Sodor or the Isles was rather different. It seems to have been part of the province of York until 1153, and some bishops continued to seek confirmation from York, or occasionally Dublin, as late as the early thirteenth century, although by that time the diocese formed part of the province of Trondheim. When the Hebrides were ceded to Scotland by the Treaty of Perth in 1266, patronage of the see was transferred to the Scottish crown, and thereafter the bishops were usually Scots or Manxmen,[17] although the see continued to be in Trondheim province. When the election of William Russell was confirmed by Clement VI on 27 April 1349, the pope sent the customary letter to the metropolitan,[18] although a few weeks later he permitted Russell to make his profession to Trondheim by proxy,[19] a

[13] *CPP*, I, 351; *Vet. Mon.*, 314–15. [14] Cal. OS 22, fol. 247.
[15] Watt, *Fasti*, 130; *Urbain V: lettres communes*, III, no. 12480. [16] Watt, *Dictionary*, 325.
[17] Watt, *Fasti*, 197. [18] *CPL*, III, 279. [19] *CPP*, I, 168.

concession which further weakened the already rather anachronistic link between the Norwegian metropolitan and the bishop of Sodor. However, when the next bishop, John Donkan, was provided in November 1374 the archbishop was still informed,[20] and it was only after the Schism divided the medieval church that two distinct lines of bishops appeared, based on the Isle of Man and the Hebrides respectively.

The question of the status of the bishop of Sodor in practice is rather less straightforward. A commission of Archbishop Thoresby in 1354, ordering the bishops of Carlisle and Sodor to confer benediction on the abbot of Cockersand, states that both are suffragans of York,[21] although this may be an error, since a letter of October 1353 to the bishop of the Isles alone contains an erasure where the scribe may erroneously have written words declaring Bishop Russell to be a suffragan.[22] The latter commission relates to work in Furness, a deanery which was very distant from York and the archbishop's favoured manors but close to the Isle of Man, where the bishop of Sodor usually resided. It was sensible to seek help from a brother-bishop in such circumstances, and indeed Archbishop Zouche had asked the bishop of Sodor to perform ordinations on 17 December 1351, when there was also a ceremony in the Augustinian friary in York.[23] But did Russell act as a suffragan of York, in the manner of an assistant with a titular or impoverished see, or on an informal basis when his help was required? The argument for the first rests on a chance remark in the salutation of one of Thoresby's commissions, which was also addressed to the bishop of Carlisle, who was certainly a suffragan; and perhaps no great attention need be paid to it. And although the archbishops of York frequently made use of assistants with Irish sees or titular sees in the eastern Mediterranean, the bishop of Sodor does not fall into such a category. His diocese was accessible, secure and, moreover, not poor: the common services were set at 660 florins, more than Ross, Brechin or Dunkeld, and nearly twenty times the original figure for Whithorn.[24] So we are left with the option that the bishop of the Isles occasionally helped the archbishop of York, perhaps for a fee but not on the basis of compulsion; such a conclusion is reinforced by a letter in March 1372 from Bishop Appleby of Carlisle to Bishop Russell, request-

20 Reg. Vat. 273, fols. 96v–97. 21 Reg. Thoresby, fol. 31. 22 Ibid., fol. 12.
23 Reg. Zouche, fols. 288v–289; Ord. Reg. Zouche, fols. 53v–54. No details of the Furness ordination survive. 24 Hoberg, *Taxae*, 112; cf. 103, 23, 48, 28.

ing his help during Appleby's illness in consecrating oil and making chrism in the church of Dalston.[25]

Although the papal chancery was aware that Sodor and Whithorn were juridically connected to ecclesiastical provinces outside Scotland, bulls of general application which were sent to Scotland were usually despatched to the bishop of Whithorn along with the rest of the Scottish episcopate, although up to 1360 the see was sometimes listed also along with the other suffragans of York.[26] In 1355 the see of Sodor appeared with Orkney and other suffragans of Trondheim,[27] but the bishop was among those Scottish prelates to whom the papal collector William de Grenlaw was recommended in May 1373.[28] As far as the Camera was concerned, Whithorn appears among dioceses *in Scotia* in the *Liber Censuum*,[29] which was originally composed around 1193, and Galloway was taxed along with the rest of the Scottish church in the 1270s and 1290s, even though at that time its bishop was certainly a suffragan of York. Grenlaw's account includes references to Whithorn, and it is clear that from the thirteenth century it was considered part of Scotland for taxation purposes. This need occasion no surprise, since it was sensible for the collectorates to be demarcated by political rather than ecclesiastical divisions when secular support was so desirable. Sodor too was taxed with the Scottish sees in 1291, but it is not clear how it fitted into the network of papal collectorates. The account of Grenlaw, rendered in 1362, makes no mention of the diocese or any benefice within it, and the bishop was not among the Scottish prelates notified of the papal tenth on 1 July 1372.[30] On 8 December 1374 the new bishop of Sodor, John Donkan, formerly papal collector in Ireland, was appointed collector in his diocese.[31]

In 1345 Bishop Hatfield of Durham swore to be faithful and obedient to the archbishop of York,[32] but on 22 September 1348

[25] Reg. Appleby, p. 247.

[26] *Innocent VI: lettres secrètes et curiales*, no. 1700; *CPL*, III, 631. Along with other prelates of England and Wales, the bishop of Whithorn was sent a letter in February 1418 on the subject of heresy (*CPL*, VII, 22). This should be seen as a reflection of the chaos of the Schism, and possibly of Scotland's reluctance to accept Martin V, rather than of Galloway's return to the jurisdiction of the archbishop of York. In 1422 Whithorn is said to be immediately subject to the Holy See (*CPL*, VII, 287).

[27] *Innocent VI: lettres secrètes et curiales*, no. 1700.

[28] *Grégoire XI: lettres secrètes et curiales (non-Fr)*, no. 1779.

[29] *Liber censuum*, I, 232.

[30] *Grégoire XI: lettres secrètes et curiales (non-Fr)*, no. 843.

[31] Ibid., no. 3018. For the Irish commissions see *CPL*, IV, 68; *Grégoire XI: lettres secrètes et curiales (non-Fr)*, no. 1191.

[32] Reg. Zouche, fol. 284.

Clement VI released him from his oath of fealty to the extent that he, his vicar-general, official, chancellor, treasurer and crucifer could not be excommunicated, suspended or subjected to interdict by the archbishop.[33] It may be surmised that this was a frequent source of friction between Hatfield and his metropolitan. Archbishop Thoresby's register continually refers to Hatfield as a suffragan of York, and for his part the bishop of Durham made several formal protestations of his exemption in convocations, his proctors announcing that Thomas was exempt from obedience and subjection to the archbishop and his church, and that he agreed to what was said and done in convocation only insofar as the exemption was not prejudiced.[34] In 1363 Thoresby retaliated by pointing out to Urban V that Hatfield was undisciplined, unlearned, rich and dissolute, and he petitioned for the revocation of the exemption. Urban responded that the archbishop of Canterbury should investigate and revoke the indult if the facts were as Thoresby stated.[35] It is not known what became of this crisis, but in 1375, when Gregory XI allowed Archbishop Neville to make a visitation of Durham before visiting his own city and diocese, Hatfield is described in unflattering terms and is said to have used his exemption to perpetrate things which required correction.[36]

There were other reasons for friction between York and Durham besides the indult and traditional antipathies. Zouche probably blamed Hatfield for inspiring an outrage by two Durham clerks in York Minster on 6 February 1349.[37] In 1358 Hatfield had to obtain a formal acquittance from the king to counteract his alleged connivance in an attack at Kexby on Thomas de Salkeld, titular bishop of Chrysopolis and assistant to the archbishop.[38] In July 1376 the king forbade Neville to make his visitation of Durham, even though it was to have been by papal authority, and to extort procurations there, on the grounds that this would threaten the bishop's status as count palatine and was likely to cause a disturbance in a strategically sensitive area.[39] The old antagonisms between York and Durham were by no means dead, and although exemptions similar to Hatfield's were obtained by some

33 *CPP*, I, 137–8; *CPL*, III, 283.

34 *Northern Convocation*, 86–9 (1351), 91–4, 100 (1360), 101–3, 104–5 (1376), 109–12 (1380).

35 *CPP*, I, 472. 36 *CPL*, IV, 212.

37 Reg. Zouche, fol. 29; *Northern Registers*, 397–9; R. B. Dobson, 'The later Middle Ages, 1215–1500', in *A History of York Minster*, ed. G. E. Aylmer and R. Cant (Oxford, 1977), 44. 38 *Foedera*, III, 389.

39 *Historians of the Church of York*, III, 284–6; *Scriptores Tres*, App. CXXVI, pp. cxliii–cxliv.

bishops in the province of Canterbury, the archbishop of York had very few suffragans and may, therefore, have felt Durham's independence all the more keenly.

THE APPOINTMENT OF BISHOPS

By the middle of the fourteenth century the practice of having bishops elected by their cathedral chapters was beginning to be seriously affected by the extensive use of the papal right to provide. This exercise of authority by the Holy See was much more marked in the case of bishoprics than any other ecclesiastical benefice or office, a situation which is perhaps unsurprising in view of the exalted position of the medieval diocesan in both church and state. Elections, although they continued, came to be significant only when they suggested to the pope whom he might appoint, and even then they were usually quashed rather than being merely confirmed, the pope proceeding to levy service taxes in return for the ensuing bull of provision. Some elections, moreover, were the result of royal pressure, especially in the more important sees; in other cases the choice of the chapter was disregarded and another clerk provided.

Although sometimes the sources imply that there was a distinction between a confirmation and a case where the election was quashed and the elect provided, in practice it must have been a very fine one. John XXII allowed John de Kirkby to regard his election and consecration as bishop of Carlisle in 1332 as valid despite the fact that the see had been reserved for provision,[40] and no payment of service taxes is recorded.[41] But in all other cases of confirmation services were demanded, although William Rae of Glasgow, who was confirmed in 1339, was released by Benedict XII from his obligation to pay for his predecessor as well as for himself.[42] If all cases where service taxes were due are considered to be provisions, then the only bishops in our period who did not owe their position to papal favour were Wedale and Malconhalgh of Whithorn and probably the bishops of Orkney. Provision was the normal method of appointment for a bishop in mainland Britain, and all those who hoped to influence the choice had to proceed within the well-defined framework of the system.

40 *CPL*, II, 403.
41 Lunt, *Financial Relations ... 1327–1534*, 758–9; cf. Hoberg, *Taxae*, 65.
42 *Vet. Mon.*, 274; *Vat. Quel.*, V, 55. For earlier payments see *Vat. Quel.*, IV, 81, 93.

Some bishops were provided directly without election, although this was rare, and usually controversial since the provisor was often opposed by a local candidate chosen in the traditional manner. William de Landallis was provided to St Andrews on 18 February 1342 on the recommendation of David II, Philip VI of France and the cathedral chapter, who could not make a canonical election until after the resignation of the claimant William Bell, who had been elected a decade earlier.[43] This was an unusual case. Alexander Bur, provided to Moray on 23 December 1362,[44] may not have been elected locally, although the chronicler Bower implies that he was.[45] Alexander Stewart seems to have been provided directly to Ross in November 1350; his predecessor resigned to a cardinal, and Stewart appears to have resided at Avignon.[46] There is no record in this instance of a capitular election in favour of Stewart or anyone else.

Stewart was a clerk whose career had apparently linked him closely with the Papacy. He was appointed a papal chaplain on 6 August 1346,[47] a title which had also been held by Thomas de Rossy before his provision to the see of Sodor in 1331.[48] Alexander de Kininmund I had relied much on papal favour earlier in his career and was a papal chaplain and auditor of the papal palace when he was provided to Aberdeen in 1329.[49] Another bishop who was closely connected with the curia before his promotion was Thomas de Appleby. Although he was a canon of the cathedral priory of Carlisle and appears to have been locally elected, the chapter may have chosen him because he was well known at Avignon and was acting as an Augustinian penitentiary there.[50] The prior of Carlisle, John de Horncastle, who had been abortively elected by the canons at the previous vacancy, was still alive, but the chapter may have considered that it would be safer to select a candidate with a history of service to the Holy See.[51]

Another curial clerk may have been the Thomas whose provision to the see of Whithorn on 31 December 1359 overrode the

43 Watt, *Fasti*, 294; *Chron. Bower* (Goodall), I, 363.

44 *Vet. Mon.*, 321; *Urbain V: lettres communes*, II, no. 8072.

45 *Chron. Bower* (Goodall), II, 366.

46 *Vet. Mon.*, 294.

47 Coll. 456, fol. 3v.

48 *CPL*, II, 341.

49 Watt, *Dictionary*, 299–300; *Vet. Mon.*, 245–6.

50 *CPP*, I, 396. For the provision see *Urbain V: lettres communes*, II, no. 8035 (n.d.); Dubrulle, *Registres d'Urbain V*, no. 199 (7 June 1363); Eubel, *Hierarchia*, I, 289 (12 June).

51 Cf. J. R. L. Highfield, 'The English hierarchy in the reign of Edward III', *TRHS* 5th series, 6 (1956), 122.

election of Thomas Macdowell and ushered in the age of papal provisions to that bishopric. This Thomas is not given a surname in the sources, but there are strong reasons for thinking that he was the Thomas de Wedale who was rehabilitated in October 1344 after holding a benefice uncanonically for several years.[52] Thomas de Wedale is not attested under that name after 1354, but he would have been only around forty years of age in 1359 and was closely involved with the papal curia and probably resident there for long periods.[53] Despite his holding a church in Scotland, he would not have been well known to cathedral chapters there, but his position at the curia and his services to the Holy See would have made him just the type of man who might petition the pope for a bishopric as a reward for his labours, and what more appropriate than a see in an area in which he was beneficed and which had been held by his kinsman Simon de Wedale until less than five years earlier.

Clerks who were not resident at the curia and did not receive a claim through local election could approach the pope for favour in the same manner as a supplication for a lesser benefice. On the death of Bishop Kirkby, the canons of Carlisle elected their prior, John de Horncastle. The king gave his assent to the choice on 10 January 1353,[54] and the archbishop of York asked his vicar-general to confirm the election, which had been done by 12 February.[55] The king ordered the release to Horncastle of the temporalities of the see on 22 February.[56] The prior's joy was, however, short-lived. Gilbert de Welton, an important secular clerk with a number of benefices in the northern province, had been provided on 13 February[57] and was consecrated at Avignon on 21 April.[58] Despite the fact that there had been considerable opposition in parliament to the system of provisions, and sentiments in favour of free elections had been expressed in the Statute of Provisors just two years before, Welton seems to have prevailed over the prior of Carlisle without much trouble. The temporalities were released to him on 26 June,[59] and in July the new bishop, who had had to

52 The provisor held the church of 'Kyrteum' (*Vet. Mon.*, 314), while Wedale was parson of 'Kircome' or 'Kritome' (Reg. Supp. 7, fol. 45v; Coll. 14, fol. 158v). The identity of the church is in doubt, but it was probably in Whithorn diocese and in the patronage of the bishop. Simon de Wedale was bishop at the time at which Thomas received the parsonage. Cf. above, chap. 1, n. 251.

53 Watt, *Dictionary*, 579–80.

54 *CPR 1350–54*, 384.

55 Smith, 'Vicars-general register', nos. 5–6; cf. Reg. Thoresby, fol. 2v.

56 *CPR 1350–54*, 408–9.

57 *CPL*, III, 482; *PRO List*, 296.

58 Reg. Welton, p. 1.

59 *CPR 1350–54*, 470.

obtain a safe-conduct from Guy de Boulogne, bishop of Porto, to pass through France,[60] ordered John de Welton to take possession of the temporalities and appointed a proctor to present and publish on his behalf his bulls of provision to the see of Carlisle and other papal letters.[61]

The role of Edward III in these events is not clear. It has been suggested that the king assented to the election of Horncastle and then secured his own candidate's appointment at the curia, but there is no reason why he should have seen the need to play so devious a game.[62] In particular, it would have been unnecessary and undesirable to release the temporalities to Horncastle if he was actively supporting Welton at Avignon, and there is in any case no evidence that Welton was the king's candidate. He was not a royal servant; rather, his career had been centred in diocesan affairs in York, where he had acted as official to Archbishop Zouche.[63] His promotion may well be connected with a visit he made to Avignon around the time in question to receive the pallium on behalf of Archbishop-elect Thoresby;[64] in any event, his own initiative and record of service as an ecclesiastical administrator probably counted for more with Innocent VI than any royal backing.

The support of Edward III was of greater significance in the more important sees, or at least it was necessary for the king to employ the correct tactics, as is seen at two successive vacancies at Durham.

On the death of Lewis de Beaumont in 1333, the chapter elected one of its number, Robert de Graystanes, on 15 October and asked for the royal assent. This was apparently not granted, because the king had sent his faithful servant Richard de Bury to the papal curia to recommend himself for provision to the see,[65] a task which Bury undertook unwillingly, if his biographer is to be believed.[66] Whatever his personal misgivings, Bury was provided on 14 October[67] and duly consecrated in December,[68] although by this time Graystanes had also been consecrated following his confirmation by his metropolitan, Archbishop Melton.[69] Not surprisingly,

[60] *Innocent VI: lettres secrètes et curiales*, no. 256; *CPL*, III, 610.
[61] Reg. Welton, p. 105.
[62] The suggestion is made in Davies, 'Anglo-Papal concordat', 124–5.
[63] Reg. Zouche, fol. 248v. [64] *CPL*, III, 469, 487; cf. Highfield, 'Relations', 99.
[65] Le Neve, *Fasti*, VI, 107.
[66] *Scriptores Tres*, 127–8. [67] *Reg. Bury*, 3–6; *CPL*, II, 405.
[68] *Scriptores Tres*, 128; Murimuth, *Continuatio Chronicarum*, 71; *Chron. Ed. I and Ed. II*, I, 359–60. [69] *Reg. Melton*, I, 98–100, 103; *Chron. Ed. I and Ed. II*, II, 118.

it was to Bury that Edward III released the temporalities of the see,[70] and Melton was compelled to order the clergy of Durham to obey the provisor despite the election and consecration of Graystanes.[71] The unlucky monk returned to the cloister, and it was said that Bury owed his success to the supplications of nobles and his own ambition.[72]

Bury was well known at Avignon. He was a papal chaplain,[73] and had acted as Edward III's envoy in 1330.[74] Although his mission appears an exercise in arrogance, other clerks suggested themselves for bishoprics, often with notable success, as we have seen, and it was in fact little different from a supplication, backed by the king, for a lesser benefice. But if it is true that Edward refused to accept the election of Graystanes, how did he come to be consecrated? Was there a serious breakdown in communications, or did Melton support the chapter's choice in full knowledge of Bury's mission and the king's intentions? Bury apparently did not make a profession of obedience to Melton as his metropolitan until 1337.[75] Was the delay coincidence, or did Bury feel that Melton had aimed to thwart him in 1333?

Whatever the answers to these questions, it is clear that at this point papal involvement was not seen as inevitable. The election of Graystanes by the monks of Durham Priory appears to have been seen there as the first stage in a purely local procedure whereby the bishop-elect would in due course be confirmed by the archbishop of York and consecrated. The chapter approached Melton, not the pope, and the archbishop felt able to proceed in accordance with traditional practice without waiting for instructions from Avignon and possibly even in defiance of the king. For his part, the king achieved his objective, but not without some local opposition occasioned by the capitular election of another. In a strategically sensitive area in wartime, this was undesirable from the government's standpoint, and it was not allowed to happen at the next vacancy.

On 12 April 1345, just two days before Bishop Bury died,

70 *CPR 1330–34*, 487; *RPD*, IV, 179–80.

71 *Reg. Melton*, I, 103–4.

72 Murimuth, *Continuatio Chronicarum*, 171.

73 *CPL*, II, 343.

74 N. Denholm-Young, 'Richard de Bury (1287–1345)', *TRHS* 4th series, 20 (1937), 147; Emden, *BRUO*, 325.

75 Reg. Melton, fol. 605; cf. *Reg. Melton*, I, 109–10. Melton had demanded his obedience in April 1334 and probably February 1335: *Reg. Melton*, I, 104, 107.

Edward III recommended Thomas de Hatfield to the pope.[76] No reason was given, but it was without doubt connected with the impending vacancy at Durham, where the king was determined to promote a loyal servant. This time the king also acted at home. The *congé d'élire* was granted on 23 April,[77] and Hatfield was elected on 8 May,[78] almost certainly under royal pressure as there is no reason why the bishop-elect would have been well known in any other capacity to the monks of Durham. The pope received Edward's letter, and when it was pointed out by the cardinals in consistory that Hatfield was unlettered and unsuitable, Clement VI is said to have made the flippant remark that on this occasion he would have made an ass a bishop if the king of England had asked him to do so.[79] This story may be apocryphal, a reflection by the monks of St Albans on the allegedly unsuitable character of the new bishop, but it may contain a grain of truth when set in a precise diplomatic context. The parliamentary ordinance of 1343, which set out to limit certain types of provision, led to very strained relations between Clement and Edward, but a visit to England by the papal nuncios Nicholas, archbishop of Ravenna, and Peter, bishop of Astorga, in the early part of 1345 appears to have clarified the limited nature of the king's opposition to provisions and done much to reassure the pope about the English government's intentions.[80] The nuncios were licensed to leave England on 22 February 1345,[81] and so it is likely that their favourable report reached Avignon in good time for the king's suggestion that Hatfield be provided to Durham to be well received there. This sudden improvement in relations between king and pope was perhaps instrumental in Hatfield receiving provision to Durham on 9 June.[82]

One of the most notable features of the appointment of bishops at this time is how easily a provisor overcame the claim of a clerk who had been elected locally. Graystanes, Horncastle and Macdowell all seem to have been unable or unwilling to make a fight of it, even though the provision which ousted Macdowell was a

[76] *Foedera*, III, 35. For Bury's death see *RPD*, IV, 363; *Scriptores Tres*, 130. Murimuth, *Continuatio Chronicarum*, 171, erroneously gives the date as 14 May.

[77] *CPR 1343–45*, 455.

[78] *Scriptores Tres*, 137. His election was confirmed by Archbishop Zouche on 1 June: Smith, *Episcopal Appointments and Patronage*, 119–20.

[79] *Ypodigma Neustriae*, 284; *Chron. Angliae*, 20.

[80] Barrell, 'Ordinance of Provisors', 275; Murimuth, *Continuatio Chronicarum*, 161–2.

[81] *Foedera*, III, 31. [82] *Reg. Bury*, 221–4; cf. *CPL*, III, 202 (8 June).

novelty in Whithorn, Horncastle had received the temporalities of Carlisle and Graystanes had been consecrated. This submission to papal authority can be sharply contrasted with the active opposition to many provisors who had been granted lesser benefices, but it seems that where bishoprics were at issue resistance was extremely limited and the papal right to provide accepted, however reluctantly, as an authority superior to capitular election.

The most bitter disputes therefore occurred where the election itself was a subject of controversy. This could happen where the constitution of the electoral body was insufficiently clear, as in the case of the bishopric of Argyll in the early 1340s. Following the death of Bishop Andrew, Martin claimed election by the chapter and Angus by the city and diocese. A lawsuit ensued, which was ended by the convenient death of Angus, whereupon Martin resigned his right by election and was provided.[83] Although ostensibly the dispute was over the election rights of various groups within the diocese, there was also a political dimension. Angus was the clerk of David II,[84] whereas Martin was supported by Edward Balliol and Edward III,[85] and on 20 March 1342 Edward III even wrote to a cardinal on Balliol's behalf, recommending Martin and asking for support for him at the curia.[86] Similar considerations came into play at Dunkeld at around the same time. By Januarv 1338 both Richard de Pilmor and Malcolm de Innerpeffray had been elected, and in due course Edward III wrote to a cardinal in support of the latter.[87] By 25 April 1342 Innerpeffray was dead, and Duncan de Strathern, whose political affiliations are unknown, had been elected. Pilmor won the suit and was provided on 5 July 1344,[88] but Strathern was not forgotten. He was given three of his rival's former benefices,[89] and at the next vacancy, in 1347, he in turn was provided,[90] the election of Robert de Den, allegedly made in ignorance of the papal reservation of the see, being set aside.[91] These cases and all others like them were heard at the papal court, and although papal involvement in these circumstances was not new, any lack of unanimity on the part of the electors gave the pope an added opportunity for intervention at a time when the Papacy's control of episcopal appointments was becoming ever tighter.

[83] *Vet. Mon.*, 283–4; Watt, *Fasti*, 26–7. [84] *CPL*, III, 82.
[85] Watt, *Dictionary*, 181. [86] *Foedera*, II, 1189.
[87] Watt, *Fasti*, 96; Watt, *Dictionary*, 278; *Foedera*, II, 1189. [88] *Vet. Mon.*, 280–1.
[89] *CPL*, III, 150, 182, 183; Coll. 281, fol. 115. [90] *Vet. Mon.*, 288–9.
[91] *CPL*, III, 245.

In England, the political situation was more stable than in Scotland, and the convention of capitular election much more firmly established. There could still be a dispute, however, as at York on the death of William de Melton. The *congé d'élire* was granted on 13 April 1340,[92] and on 2 May twelve of the seventeen canons present chose their dean, William de la Zouche, and the remainder the king's nominee William de Kildesby.[93] As a result of the division in the chapter, both parties appealed to Avignon, and pressure was applied to prevent Zouche from going: on 13 August Benedict XII had to tell the archbishop of Canterbury to use the threat of excommunication to compel those hindering Zouche's journey to desist from such action.[94] When he was able to travel, the unlucky dean was attacked near Geneva and blackmailed into swearing an oath which the pope had to relax.[95] On 18 January 1341 the king issued a commission against Zouche, stating that he had not obtained royal assent of his election but rather had chosen to prosecute his claim at the curia, and accusing him of embezzlement of royal treasure, betrayal of the realm and the king's council, and murder.[96] On 14 March Edward III wrote to Benedict XII on much the same lines, referring to Kildesby as archbishop-elect of York.[97] Benedict came to no decision on the matter,[98] but on the accession of the new pope Clement VI Zouche was wise enough to resign and accept provision, the election of Kildesby having been annulled by a cardinal.[99] The king was no doubt disappointed, but he issued safe-conducts to Zouche[100] and on 19 September 1342 the temporalities were restored to him.[101]

Despite the pressure which he applied on both Zouche and the pope, Edward III had failed to secure the appointment of Kildesby. Zouche had indubitably received more votes than his rival, but medieval theory stressed the authority of 'the weightier part' (*valentior pars*), which was not always equivalent to a numerical majority. Although his involvement in negotiating the Anglo-Imperial alliance in the late 1330s made him the object of suspicion at the Holy See,[102] Kildesby's case was not hopeless, but in the end

[92] *CPR 1338–40*, 462.
[93] Cf. *Historians of the Church of York*, II, 417–18.
[94] *CPL*, II, 549.
[95] Ibid., 547–8, 578; cf. 550.
[96] *CPR 1340–43*, 109–10.
[97] *Foedera*, II, 1118, dated 1340, which must be incorrect since Archbishop Melton did not die until 5 April 1340: *Historians of the Church of York*, II, 417.
[98] Murimuth, *Continuatio Chronicarum*, 121.
[99] *CPL*, III, 52.
[100] *CPR 1340–43*, 502; *CCR 1341–43*, 645; *Foedera*, II, 1210.
[101] *CPR 1340–43*, 514.
[102] Déprez, *Les préliminaires de la Guerre de Cent Ans*, 363.

royal support was not enough. It seems that Zouche abandoned his strong claim by election and threw himself on the mercy of Clement VI. This tactic succeeded, and once again the provision appears to have been the final act in the drama. Neither the king nor Kildesby seems to have been eager to resist the pope's decision.

The Scottish king too was unsuccessful after the see of Dunkeld fell vacant on the death of John Luce. Initially the chapter elected John Rede, but he had resigned his right by 13 November 1370.[103] John de Carrick, royal chancellor from 1370 to 1377,[104] also came to be elected, probably as a royal candidate for the bishopric rather than a free choice on the part of the chapter. In the exchequer year of 1370–1 he was given a grant from government funds to go to the curia in pursuit of his claim,[105] but the investment was wasted because Urban V had provided Michael de Monymusk.[106] The precise chronology is uncertain, but Rede's position was probably similar to that of Macdowell in Whithorn a decade earlier. In return for his willingness to submit to the provisor, he was granted the deanery of Ross by Gregory XI in 1371, Urban V having approved of this course of action before his death,[107] just as Macdowell successfully petitioned for a canonry of Glasgow, with reservation of a prebend, after resigning his claim.[108] Carrick proved a tougher nut to crack, and the strong support of the king encouraged him to press on, but it availed him little.

From these examples it is obvious that in the appointment of a bishop papal provision was the trump card. A promotion-conscious clerk who happened to be in the right place at the right time could seek preferment from the pope with some confidence that he would prevail over the choice of the chapter. Although royal support was useful, the king's wishes were not always adhered to. Bury's provision defeated the claim of Graystanes, but minority support among the canons of York and determined royal pressure on his behalf could not give Kildesby victory over Zouche. It was desirable for the king to suggest a name to the pope while simultaneously prevailing upon the chapter also to elect his candidate, as was the case with Hatfield.

The net result of the extension of the system of provision was to

[103] Watt, *Dictionary*, 467; *Handbook of British Chronology*, 308.
[104] *Handbook of British Chronology*, 181–2.
[105] *Exch. Rolls*, II, 356.
[106] *Urbain V: lettres communes*, IX, no. 27887. He too may have been elected: Watt, *Fasti*, 97.
[107] Watt, *Dictionary*, 467; cf. Reg. Av. 176, fols. 55v–56.
[108] *CPP*, I, 351.

remove all vestiges of untrammelled choice from many cathedral chapters. In Scotland, the chapter could still suggest a clerk whom the pope might be prepared to favour in the absence of another and more persuasive suggestion, but in the generally wealthier and politically important sees of northern England the stakes were higher. The Avignon popes tightened their grip on promotions to the episcopate. John XXII allowed Kirkby's election to stand, and the monks of Durham and Archbishop Melton apparently considered Graystanes' election to be valid; there was no inevitability of a provision. Even in 1340 the chapter of York could hold an election which ultimately resulted in provision possibly only because the canons were unable to agree. But moves for Hatfield's provision went ahead simultaneously with, and even in advance of, his election by the chapter, and Welton easily overcame Horncastle, an experience which encouraged the canons of Carlisle to select at the next vacancy a candidate likely to receive papal approval. This is not to say that chapters freely abdicated their privileges, but in secular cathedrals many of the canons themselves owed their status to papal provision, and all cathedral communities must have realised the extent of the jurisdiction of the Avignon popes. In such circumstances both self-interest and realism militated against defiance of the papal right to provide.

By whatever means men came to be bishops they had to be examined for their suitability if this was not already clear, and then consecrated. Records of examinations are rare, and only three have come to light, for Alan de Moray and Thomas de Fingask, bishops-elect of Caithness, and William Rae of Glasgow. All were examined at the curia by a panel of three cardinals, and in view of the 'special daughter' relationship between the Scottish sees and the Papacy this was probably common practice where examinations were required, although in an earlier period the usual method had been for the pope to delegate the examination to three Scottish bishops, who also had authority to confirm the election.[109] It may be that there were fewer investigations into the quality of bishops-elect in the fourteenth century than formerly, since most were now graduates and well known to the pope from earlier supplications and other contacts, but examinations continued to be held if there were doubts about the clerk's suitability, as in the case of the bishop-elect of Lincoln in 1362, when Urban V commissioned

[109] J. Dowden, 'The appointment of bishops in Scotland during the medieval period', *SHR*, 7 (1909–10), 9–10.

three abbots to enquire.[110] All the Scottish bishops of the period, at least where the celebrant is named, were consecrated at the curia, usually by a cardinal, except those bishops of Galloway who did not receive provision. Earlier, this procedure too had been conducted locally, and the apparent necessity in the fourteenth century for Scottish bishops to go to the curia for consecration is a further feature of the increased centralisation imposed by the Avignon popes. In English sees the position was rather different. Zouche, Welton and Appleby were consecrated at the papal court,[111] but Bishops Bury and Hatfield both received episcopal orders from John Stratford of Canterbury,[112] having received papal licences to be consecrated by any catholic bishop[113] in an attempt to distance themselves from the irksome link with their metropolitan in York. The archbishop of York was entitled to the pallium, which could be conferred at the curia or elsewhere. Zouche was granted a faculty to wear it on 12 July 1342,[114] when he was probably still at Avignon, but Thoresby, who was translated to York from Worcester, sent an envoy to collect it. Its despatch was delayed by the untimely death of Clement VI, and it was eventually conferred on 6 April 1353, Innocent VI having told the bishops of Winchester and London to assign it to Thoresby and send his oath of fealty to the pope.[115]

Some mandates survive ordering bishops to go to their dioceses, such as those to William de Landallis of St Andrews on 18 March 1342,[116] Patrick de Locrys of Brechin on 11 December 1351,[117] and John Luce of Dunkeld on 29 June 1355.[118] Such orders may have been more common than the sources suggest, as the fourteenth-century popes took a dim view of new prelates tarrying at the papal court.

Being provided to a see was an expensive business, especially if a long lawsuit had to be paid for in addition to service taxes and all the other costs of obtaining a bull of provision. Some prelates were permitted to contract loans to defray their heavy expenditure, for

[110] Fierens and Tihon, *Lettres d'Urbain V*, no. 480. See generally A. K. McHardy, 'The promotion of John Buckingham to the see of Lincoln', *JEH*, 26 (1975), 127–35.

[111] *Historians of the Church of York*, II, 418; Reg. Welton, p. 1; Reg. Appleby, p. 141. The consecration was not necessarily carried out by the pope himself, however, despite indications to the contrary: see *CPL*, III, 85; Reg. Appleby, p. 160.

[112] Murimuth, *Continuatio Chronicarum*, 71, 172; *Scriptores Tres*, 128; cf. Stubbs, *Registrum Sacrum Anglicanum*, 53.

[113] *Reg. Bury*, 8–9; *CPL*, III, 214.

[114] *CPL*, III, 70.

[115] Reg. Thoresby, interleaved before fol. 6; *CPL*, III, 487–8.

[116] *CPL*, II, 557.

[117] Ibid., III, 431; *Brechin Registrum*, II, 394.

[118] *Vet. Mon.*, 308–9.

instance Richard de Pilmor, who was allowed in July 1344 to contract a loan of 3000 florins on the movable and immovable property of his see for four years because of the expenses he had incurred in obtaining the bishopric of Dunkeld,[119] or his rival and successor Duncan de Strathern, who was granted leave in November 1347 to borrow 2000 florins to meet his expenses at the curia.[120] Some bishops who did not face litigation were also permitted to contract loans, such as William Russell of the Isles in 1349[121] and Alexander Stewart of Ross in 1351.[122] Others raised charitable subsidies from the clergy of their diocese, by papal authority if necessary.[123] William de la Zouche was allowed to hold the York prebend of Laughton after his consecration,[124] and on 4 May 1344 he was permitted to hold benefices to an annual value of £100 in order to help defray expenditure incurred during his appointment.[125] As a result of this, the rectory of Brompton was temporarily united to his mensal income.[126]

Papal help to bishops who found themselves short of cash at the start of their episcopates was not a new phenomenon under Clement VI. John XXII had appropriated the church of Bolton Percy to the income of Archbishop Melton, and the latter had appointed a vicar to fulfil his pastoral responsibilities in the parish.[127] But faculties to contract loans disappear from the sources after Clement VI's death, and there is much less evidence of papal assistance to bishops in financial difficulty, even though the initial outbreak of the Black Death had caused considerable economic dislocation, which probably had an adverse effect on the collection of episcopal revenues. It may be that the papal chancery changed its policy of registration; if there was indeed a reluctance to allow new bishops to borrow money, then many of the delays in paying service taxes would be explained.

Attempts have been made to categorise bishops into royal servants, regular clergy, graduates, papal officials and so forth, but this is a minefield of definition and some men fall into several categories.[128] Most of the bishops of the middle of the fourteenth

[119] *CPL*, III, 9, 173; *Clément VI: lettres closes (Fr)*, no. 956; *Vet. Mon.*, 281.

[120] *CPL*, III, 264. [121] Ibid., 305. [122] *Vet. Mon.*, 296.

[123] E.g. Bishop Hatfield of Durham (*CPP*, I, 100; *CPL*, III, 188, 216); Bishop Rae of Glasgow (*Glasgow Registrum*, I, 251–2). [124] *CPP*, I, 11; *CPL*, III, 52.

[125] *CPP*, I, 53; *CPL*, III, 116.

[126] Lunt, *Accounts*, 118; *CPL*, III, 470; Reg. Zouche, fol. 270v.

[127] *CPL*, II, 235; YML, L1/8, fol. 276. [128] Highfield, 'English hierarchy', *passim*.

century were, however, university graduates, Hatfield being a notable exception, and most were secular clerks who had held a number of benefices, especially prebends in cathedral or collegiate churches, before their consecration, often using royal and papal favour to further their collection. Regular bishops appear in only a few sees, and these were normally fairly poor. John de Kirkby, John de Horncastle and Thomas de Appleby were all canons of the cathedral priory of Carlisle, but Appleby was a papal penitentiary and Horncastle's election was set aside by Innocent VI. In Scotland, two regular bishops were in office in 1342: Maurice, formerly abbot of Inchaffray, in Dunblane, and Simon de Wedale, once abbot of Holyrood, in Whithorn. Wedale's successor, Michael de Malconhalgh, had been prior of Whithorn. Two Dominican friars became bishops of the poorest Scottish sees: Martin de Ergadia in Argyll and Adam de Lanark in Whithorn. The pope also provided William de Deyn, abbot of Kilwinning, to Aberdeen in 1344, William Russell, abbot of Rushen, to Sodor in 1349, and Patrick de Locrys, canon-regular of St Andrews, to Brechin in 1351.[129] But the Papacy apparently did not believe at this time that regulars were likely to make more suitable bishops than seculars. Wedale and Malconhalgh were promoted without any papal involvement, and all the others were elected locally.

The careers of the secular clerks who were promoted to the episcopate were varied, although most had been successful accumulators of livings. Gilbert de Welton of Carlisle had held six churches, three prebends and a hospital;[130] and Philip Wilde, bishop of Brechin, was dean of the church and had been its chancellor, and he also held prebends in Glasgow and Dunkeld and expectation of one in St Marcel near Paris.[131] These careers were by no means exceptional. Even after election or provision clerks continued to pay close attention to their material needs. On 20 April 1353 Welton was granted a request to be able to retain his benefices in the province of York for a time after his consecration, on the grounds that until Archbishop Thoresby had received the pallium Welton's prebends in York and Southwell would fall to the king under regalian right if they were to be vacated.[132] Angus

[129] Locrys was rector of Tannadice and sometime claimant to the parsonage of Tyninghame, but he appears nonetheless to have been a member of the Augustinian cathedral priory rather than of the collegiate church of St Mary on the Rock: Coll. 14, fol. 159v. [130] Emden, *BRUO*, 2012–13.

[131] Watt, *Dictionary*, 582; *CPP*, I, 199, 201; *CPL*, III, 413. [132] *CPP*, I, 241.

de Ergadia, already parson of Dunoon, was provided to the church of Liston and the hospital of Rathven during the period when he was litigating over the see of Argyll, receiving assurances that his claim would not thereby be prejudiced.[133] The rivals over Dunkeld in the early 1340s, Richard de Pilmor and Duncan de Strathern, both became papal chaplains[134] and received allowances of victuals.[135]

The fourteenth-century episcopate drew its members from a variety of backgrounds. In neither northern England nor Scotland was promotion to a bishopric an exclusive prerogative of the nobility; indeed, aristocratic bishops were probably rarer in the fourteenth century than the fifteenth. But in the years just before the Great Schism, the bishops all owed their position to papal favour. Some relied exclusively on it; others put their faith in royal pressure or in their election by a local chapter. But none could do entirely without it. For better or worse, the Papacy now enjoyed effective control over all episcopal appointments in the whole of mainland Britain.

CONTACTS BETWEEN THE PAPACY AND THE BISHOPS

Their status in the church meant that bishops were in a good position to make supplications to the pope on behalf of themselves, their clerks, relatives and other connections. Most were requests for provisions, but sometimes the bishop asked for a dispensation or indult for himself or someone else, or for ratification of a donation such as that by the Scottish kings to the church of Aberdeen of tenths between the rivers Dee and Spey.[136] Some bishops made more petitions than others, especially early in their episcopates when their personal presence at the curia made this especially opportune. In June 1349 Clement VI granted eleven requests made by William Russell of Sodor, including a faculty to unite to his see goods, lands and property given to it by temporal lords, power to grant some dispensations, and provisions to canonries in Brechin, Beverley and St David's.[137] Groups of petitions were also granted in favour of Thomas de Appleby of Carlisle in June 1363[138] and

[133] *CPL*, III, 82; Coll. 281, fol. 106. [134] *CPL*, III, 126; Reg. Vat. 217, fol. 349.

[135] *Vat. Quel.*, VI, 692, 699. Supplies were, however, sometimes granted to others in different circumstances, e.g. to Thomas, bishop of Sodor, in 1344: ibid., 699.

[136] *CPP*, I, 409–10; cf. *CPL*, IV, 33–4; *Urbain V: lettres communes*, II, no. 5293; Coll. 14, fol. 169. [137] *CPP*, I, 168–9. [138] Ibid., 437–8.

Thomas de Hatfield of Durham in July 1345.[139] The three greatest practitioners of the art of supplicating the pope were, however, the two archbishops of York and John de Pilmor, bishop of Moray. Pilmor's many petitions to Clement VI for himself and his connections[140] doubtless betray a close personal link. As well as being a papal chaplain,[141] he had, as bishop, been vicar in spirituals to Clement VI when the latter was archbishop of Rouen in the 1330s,[142] when Pilmor was almost certainly accompanying the young David II, who lodged for several years at Château Gaillard on the Seine. A link of this sort meant that an approach to the pontiff on behalf of Moray clerks or for such matters as the confirmation of the annexation of the churches of Altyre, Birnie and Alvie to the chaplains of Elgin Cathedral or authorisation for the sentence of excommunication against those occupying the houses of canons was likely to be viewed favourably at the curia. The archbishops, with their vast diocese and large staffs, needed to make more petitions than their brethren in lesser sees, but even so Thoresby made a huge number of supplications, and he had also been a frequent petitioner when he was bishop of St David's and Worcester.

Bishops were also in an excellent position to receive favours from the Papacy, or the right to issue dispensations in cases where papal authority was normally required. Several received the common indult to choose a confessor who could grant plenary remission at the hour of death; these included John de Kirkby of Carlisle in 1350[143] and Alexander de Kininmund II of Aberdeen in 1371.[144] In June 1349 William Russell of Sodor received a plenary indulgence for himself and others.[145] The English prelates received various other indults. Thoresby and Welton were allowed to celebrate mass before dawn and in places subject to an interdict,[146] and the former was permitted to have a portable altar.[147] Thoresbv was also allowed to have polluted churches and cemeteries reconciled by a mere priest when this seemed opportune,[148] and a similar indult was granted to Bishop Wardlaw of Glasgow in September 1376.[149] On 10 July 1365 Thomas de Appleby was given authority by the papal *camerarius* to visit his diocese by deputy.[150]

139 Ibid., 100. 140 Ibid., 76, 109, 110, 157, 200–1, 250. 141 Ibid., 200.
142 Ibid., 76. 143 *CPL*, III, 403. 144 Reg. Av. 180, fol. 388.
145 *CPP*, I, 169. 146 Ibid., 244–5, 242. 147 *CPL*, III, 491.
148 *Urbain V: lettres communes*, VII, no. 22185; Reg. Thoresby, fol. 148; cf. *CPP*, I, 342.
149 Reg. Vat. 288, fol. 313. 150 Reg. Appleby, p. 159.

Following the arrival of the Black Death in the province of York, Archbishop Zouche saw the need to obtain a licence to carry out ordinations at other than the canonically prescribed times.[151] These special ordinations took place on 30 January, 24 April and 26 June 1350,[152] and were all conducted by Zouche's assistant, the titular archbishop of Damascus, who was given a commission on 17 January 1350 in respect of the first of these ceremonies.[153] The archbishop had evidently feared that the plague would lead to a shortage of duly ordained priests, and the extra opportunities for promotion were necessary because the orders of subdeacon, deacon and priest could only be conferred one at a time. However, the numbers presenting themselves were not unusually large, and even those with benefices were often in no greater hurry than normal, although the extra ceremonies did allow those such as Robert Scott, rector of Nunnington, to receive all three orders in the space of ten weeks in the spring of 1350.[154]

The large number of provisions to benefices in bishops' gift meant that they sometimes had to obtain faculties from the pope to enjoy limited exercise of their own patronage. In 1362–3 William Rae, bishop of Glasgow, supplicated on behalf of a clerk for expectation of a prebend in the cathedral,[155] while his successor, Walter de Wardlaw, received a number of faculties from Gregory XI to confer canonries and other benefices.[156] Bishop Bury of Durham complained that his patronage was being seriously impaired by provisions,[157] and in 1342 he was granted leave to reserve six benefices in his gift for persons of his choice.[158] On 11 December 1362 Thoresby was allowed to collate to three benefices in the face of papal grants,[159] although those favoured apparently had to be doctors or licentiates of law or theology like John de Waltham, who received the prebend of South Newbald on 22 October 1368,[160] or the archbishop's relative and namesake John de Thoresby, who obtained the prebend of Grindale on 7 December 1367.[161] It was typical of Urban V's belief in the importance of academic achievement that he limited the arch-

151 *CPP*, I, 178; *CPL*, III, 332.

152 Ord. Reg. Zouche, fols. 38v–41, 45–46, 48–48v.

153 Reg. Zouche, fol. 287v.

154 Ord. Reg. Zouche, fols. 44, 45v, 48. He had been instituted on 31 January: Reg. Zouche, fol. 167.

155 *CPP*, I, 400; *Urbain V: lettres communes*, II, no. 7581.

156 Reg. Av. 173, fols. 510v, 535v–536; Reg. Av. 197, fol. 207–207v; Reg. Vat. 288, fol. 148–148v.

157 *RPD*, III, 503–7; *Northern Registers*, 380–3.

158 *CPL*, III, 54.

159 *CPP*, I, 387; *Urbain V: lettres communes*, I, nos. 1179, 4644.

160 Reg. Thoresby, fol. 67.

161 Ibid., fol. 66; cf. *CPP*, I, 482.

bishop's choice in this way, but even if the pope imposed no restrictions on the bishop's right to choose, the need for such faculties emphasises the serious effect on episcopal patronage which provisions caused, and demonstrates why so many supplications from bishops asked for benefices to be conferred on clerks or friends who in the thirteenth century would have been promoted by the prelate himself.

Some bishops were granted letters conservatory for a period fixed by the Papacy. On the day of his exemption from York's jurisdiction, Thomas de Hatfield was given conservators for five years.[162] Michael de Monymusk, one of the claimants to Dunkeld in 1370, was, as bishop-elect, given letters conservatory for three years.[163] Thomas de Fingask, bishop of Caithness, was granted similar protection on 12 April 1363.[164] Bishops were also involved in executing these and other letters conservatory. The bishops of Brechin, Caithness and Ross were named in a mandate attached to those granted to Gilbert Fleming, dean of Aberdeen, in April 1346,[165] while Archbishop Zouche was named as executor of letters on behalf of the abbot of St Edmunds in 1345[166] and the abbot of Chester in 1346 and 1348,[167] as well as acting as conservator of the Carmelite order.[168]

Bishops were in fact troubled by a large number of mandates from Avignon. The most numerous group comprised letters executory attending papal provisions, both direct grants and expectative graces. In addition to those registered at Avignon, a large number of mandates of this type were sent to bishops in connection with graces *in forma pauperum*. These were usually subdelegated to prominent local clergy, and it is likely that subexecutors were normally appointed in other cases as well. Nonetheless, even if the bishop did not personally have to induct the provisor, he still had the nuisance of dealing with the mandate and was ultimately responsible for its execution.

It is hard to ascertain whether mandates to provide were issued to churchmen *ex officio* or by the selection of individuals, although as some executors were actually named and some bishops were troubled far more than others it is likely that the papal chancery's choice was not wholly arbitrary. Archbishop Thoresby, for instance, was appointed much more regularly than his predecessor

162 *CPP*, I, 138. 163 *Urbain V: lettres communes*, IX, no. 27833.
164 Ibid., I, no. 4454. 165 *CPL*, III, 213. 166 Ibid., 164.
167 Ibid., 187, 300; Reg. Zouche, fol. 243. 168 See above, p. 172.

Zouche, and while Bishop Bury was employed six times between 1342 and 1345, Thomas de Hatfield received only seven such mandates before 1370. Gilbert de Welton's presence at the curia in April and May 1353 caused him to be appointed as executor of six provisions at this time. The Scottish bishops were in general more extensively involved in executing provisions than their northern English counterparts, with Clement VI making particularly heavy use of two successive bishops of Brechin, Adam de Moray and Philip Wilde. Moray was given thirty-one mandates to provide between 1342 and 1349, while Wilde received nine such commissions during his short episcopate in 1350–1. It is unclear why these bishops of the small and rather poor diocese of Brechin were singled out, although possibly some sort of payment was involved. By contrast, some Scottish bishops such as Alexander Bur of Moray received few mandates of this sort, and the contemporary bishops of Galloway apparently none at all.

Bishops were sometimes asked to see to it that a provision was effective even though they had not been among the original executors. On 5 May 1354 William Rae and the chapter of Glasgow were told to execute the provision to Henry de Smalham of the archdeaconry of Teviotdale.[169] The original bulls of March 1354 had named the abbot of Kelso, the dean of Glasgow and a foreign ecclesiastic as executors.[170] But even bishops were sometimes accused of not having carried out a papal command. Hatfield failed to ensure that the much-disputed church of Bishop Wearmouth was given to William de Ardene;[171] and Thoresby was alleged not to have properly investigated and carried out the annexation of a moiety of Bubwith to Byland Abbey,[172] although this inaction was probably a result of the fact that no vacancy in the benefice had thus far occurred. Many provisions and appropriations bore no fruit, but this was often for reasons beyond the executors' control: two provisions could be made at the same vacancy; royal grants and prohibitions could impede papal graces; vacancies could be wrongly reported; or men with expectancies could gain better preferments before their expectation was realised.

The dispensing power of the Papacy also affected the bishops. Although dispensations from impediments and irregularity were usually issued at the curia by the pope or his team of penitentiaries,

169 Burns, 'Sources', no. 158.

170 *CPL*, III, 516.

171 Ibid., IV, 65; *Urbain V: lettres communes*, VI, no. 20032.

172 *CPL*, IV, 32; cf. III, 572.

it was normally the task of the ordinary to put them into effect locally. Bishops with large or populous dioceses, therefore, often received a good deal of business of this nature from the Holy See, although local conditions could influence the number of mandates to execute dispensations. In Scotland, the practice of attempting to damp down feuds by a well-judged marriage often involved the Papacy, because the parties were often closely related, and the Scottish bishops were thus involved in a good deal of matrimonial business. This was rarer in England, but where evidence exists it suggests that bishops carried out the orders to grant marriage dispensations only after a few months had elapsed. Hatfield was sent a mandate on 7 March 1368 which he effected on 4 November of that year,[173] while an order sent by Urban V to the archbishop of York on 26 June 1366 was delegated to the chancellor of York and a canon of Llandaff just under a year later.[174]

Much more numerous, at least in England, were dispensations from defect of birth, granted either directly by penitentiaries or by bishops under faculties to bestow a certain number on local clerks. In York's massive archiepiscopal registers there are notes of many dispensations issued to individuals by papal authority,[175] and a few also appear in Carlisle and Durham records.[176] Bishops were also involved in granting dispensations for clerks to be ordained under age and in bringing to effect other mandates from the Penitentiary. In 1366 William, cardinal-priest of St Laurence in Lucina, ordered Thoresby to release William Morehous from the irregularity he had incurred by celebrating mass when suspended.[177] Bishops also had a role to play in the creation of notaries public, although they were rarely allowed by the pope to nominate as many as they desired: in 1353 Thoresby petitioned to be able to create twelve, but had to be content with a faculty for five.[178] The papal monopoly on licensing notaries in England, where imperial rights of nomination were not recognised, was closely guarded, although it was sensible to commit the choice, or at least the examination, of candidates to local prelates.

173 Ibid., IV, 74; *Urbain V: lettres communes*, VII, no. 22255; Reg. Hatfield, fol. 48.

174 *Urbain V: lettres communes*, V, no. 17787; Reg. Thoresby, fol. 293.

175 Reg. Zouche, fols. 3, 5, 28v, 31v, 45v–46, 47v, 52v, 53v, 55, 57v, 60, 60v, 65, 67, 68v, 74v, 79, 89, 106, 123v, 143v, 155, 156, 159, 173v, 175, 175v, 177, 178, 208, 208v, 213, 276, 292v, interleaved before 295; Reg. Thoresby, fols. 29v, 90v–91, 97v–98, 122, 138, 138–138v, 171v, 176–176v, 193, 213v, 247v, 253, 282v, 291v.

176 Reg. Kirkby, fols. 221v, 228v–229; Reg. Welton, pp. 5, 14, 42, 43, 53, 55, 58, 64, 76, 79, 117; Reg. Appleby, pp. 154, 167, 231; Reg. Hatfield, fols. 49, 50.

177 Reg. Thoresby, fols. 140v–141.

178 *CPP*, I, 245.

The high rank enjoyed by bishops in the church hierarchy naturally meant that they were involved in the collection of papal taxation, and were canvassed when the pope wished to raise extraordinary levies such as the subsidy of the 1370s. They were also involved as judges-delegate and in business relating to the religious orders. In England in particular, leading bishops with close ties of service to Edward III were often instructed to intercede with the royal government, either to encourage the king to listen to the pope's exhortations to make peace with the Valois kings of France, or to persuade him to revoke anti-papal legislation such as the ordinance of 1343 or to reverse such policies as the seizure of benefices held by non-resident aliens, a step forced on Edward in 1346 by the heavy cost of the Crécy campaign. Thoresby was sent several letters asking him to persuade the king to liberate Charles de Blois, the French-backed claimant to the duchy of Brittany, who had been imprisoned by the English,[179] and he and Bishops Welton and Hatfield were asked to further a mission by a papal legation to draw attention to the threat posed to the Holy See in Italy by the Visconti of Milan.[180] Hatfield apparently planned to fight for the pope in Italy in the early 1370s. Gregory XI wrote to him in November 1371 encouraging him in this enterprise and offering a safe-conduct,[181] but the expedition did not take place because Edward III required the bishop's presence on the Scottish border.[182] A warlike expedition to Italy might have suited Hatfield well: he had been on the 1346 campaign, had fought at Crécy and had celebrated the funeral of the king of Bohemia who had fallen there;[183] and he was frequently involved in border conflicts. Although all northern English bishops had to be aware of political and military realities, we may surmise that the secular-minded Thomas de Hatfield was more valuable to the pope in a political capacity than a purely ecclesiastical one.

Although the Franco-Scottish alliance was an important feature of the Hundred Years War, the Avignon popes paid little attention to Scotland in their protracted and ultimately fruitless attempts to negotiate a general peace in western Europe which would clear the way for a crusade. Largely as a result of this, the Scottish bishops

179 *CPL*, III, 609, 617, 621; *Innocent VI: lettres secrètes et curiales*, no. 940. Thoresby was royal chancellor from 1349 to 1356.

180 *CPL*, III, 631.

181 *Grégoire XI: lettres secrètes et curiales (Fr)*, no. 484; *CPL*, IV, 98; cf. *Grégoire XI: lettres secrètes et curiales (non-Fr)*, no. 420.

182 *Foedera*, III, 936.

183 Murimuth, *Continuatio Chronicarum*, 199; *Chron. Baker*, 79, 85–6.

were rarely asked by the pope to take a particular political stance. In 1372 Gregory XI instructed the bishops of Aberdeen, Glasgow and St Andrews to ensure that the new king Robert II kept his predecessor's promise not to continue the old practice whereby a dead bishop's movables were applied to the king's use and could not be disposed of by will.[184] Bishop Landallis of St Andrews was further asked to intercede with Robert for the restoration to Queen Margaret of certain privileges which had been withdrawn,[185] and in the previous year the bishops of Aberdeen, Dunblane and Tournai had been told to demand restitution of Margaret's goods.[186] But these were isolated mandates, seemingly connected with the change of dynasty in 1371 and Margaret's requests for help from the Holy See. The peripheral position of Scotland in European politics made its bishops much less significant than those of northern England in terms of papal diplomacy and political activity.

Diocesan bishops thus received a wide variety of papal mandates on routine matters and a few connected with politics or special circumstances such as the proclamation in 1349 of the Jubilee indulgence[187] or the appearance in continental Europe of groups of Flagellants after the Black Death.[188] Archbishop Thoresby of York in particular received a number of bulls issued as a result of individual supplications to the pope. But the mandates appear often to have been passed on to subordinates or dealt with slowly with no sense of urgency. Much episcopal administration was routine and was conducted by officers who constituted a local bureaucracy, and papal mandates which were of a standard form were almost certainly accorded no special treatment. Moreover, the labour involved in executing papal orders was minimal in comparison to the number and range of royal mandates and items of normal diocesan administration. The bulky episcopal registers of northern England indicate that there were large numbers of institutions to benefices and absence licences which were dealt with in accordance with an established pattern which can have been little disturbed by the relatively small volume of papal business which came to the average bishop of Scotland and northern England.

184 *Aberdeen Registrum*, II, 122–4; cf. Donaldson, 'Rights of the Scottish crown', 29.
185 *Grégoire XI: lettres secrètes et curiales (non-Fr)*, no. 530.
186 Cal. Reg. Av. 173, fol. 290; Tihon, *Lettres de Grégoire XI*, no. 914.
187 *Clément VI: lettres closes (non-Fr)*, no. 2047; cf. *CPL*, III, 311.
188 *CPL*, III, 311; *Clément VI: lettres closes (non-Fr)*, no. 2091.

The main point of contact between the bishops and the Holy See was, therefore, their appointment. Without papal backing, or at least papal acquiescence, no churchman of the middle of the fourteenth century could expect to rise to a bishopric. But once that original hurdle had been overcome and service taxes and other dues paid, few bishops were closely involved with papal affairs, even though most made supplications to the pope and received a few mandates in return. Papal provisions seriously limited the patronage of almost all leading ecclesiastics, and in that respect bishops were aware – uncomfortably aware, perhaps – of the increased centralisation achieved by the Avignon Papacy. Influence at the curia was valuable, and for Thomas of Whithorn and Appleby of Carlisle it was probably essential for their promotion, but no English or Scottish prelate of the fourteenth century was able to use such influence to play a major role on the European stage, as Cardinal Beaufort was to do in the fifteenth century and Cardinal Wolsey in the sixteenth. The bishops were unable to avoid links with the papal court, but how close those links were depended largely on how much they needed the pope and how much the pope needed them.

Chapter 6

THE PAPACY AND THE REGULARS

By the fourteenth century a number of religious orders had been established for many years in both Scotland and England. Their houses were very much part of the local scene, and their activities, both internally and where they touched the secular world, were well known. Bishops visited monasteries which were not exempt from their jurisdiction, and confirmed or at least received professions of canonical obedience from newly elected abbots and priors. The fourteenth century was not one of great change for religious communities, and in consequence contacts between the Papacy and the regulars were fewer and arguably much less significant than in the great period of foundation and expansion in the twelfth and thirteenth centuries.

Such contacts as there were bear considerable similarity to those involving the secular clergy, but with one important distinction. Those who were professed in a religious order lived under regimes which dictated that much of their contact with the Papacy was via the head of their convent, and this in turn meant that the Holy See tended to deal with institutions rather than individuals and received relatively few supplications asking for favours to be granted to single monks, canons or friars. The religious orders were, moreover, international bodies; and especially in the case of the friars and the younger reformed orders, in which an elaborate system of visitation and control had been employed from the outset, they transcended political boundaries in a way which was becoming increasingly uncommon among the secular clergy.

This internationalism should not, however, be overstressed, especially in the case of remote Scotland. Even south of the border the onset of a period dominated by war between Plantagenet and Valois severely undermined the relationship between continental mother-houses and their dependencies and cells in England. Most of the houses affected, the so-called alien priories, were small, although the group included the Cluniac establishments, which were technically offshoots of the great Burgundian abbey of Cluny but sometimes rivalled in wealth and prestige the largest establishments of their area. The majority of the mother-houses were on French soil, the link being a legacy of the Norman Conquest and Angevin Empire, and the alien priories were sometimes staffed by monks supplied directly from the larger house in France; parliament frequently complained about the activities of alleged spies and enemy agents within them.

From the king's point of view, the principal danger from alien priories was that at least some of their revenues were taken abroad. The profits and advowsons of these houses were, therefore, regularly seized by the crown in time of war, until in 1414 they severed their continental links or were suppressed. The same financial considerations dictated legislation to prevent Cistercians, Premonstratensians and others from sending annual payments abroad to their mother-houses or to the central organs of their order.[1] This was backed up by royal orders such as that to Furness Abbey in 1343 not to send any money overseas or allow regulars to go abroad without licence.[2] The government took legal action in connection with the decree in the same year that the heads of Premonstratensian and Cistercian monasteries should pay to the king any sums normally due to a foreign mother-house. The abbots of Kirkstall and Meaux both denied that any such payments were customary, and they were vindicated at inquisition.[3] Occasionally the king in fact allowed some payments to be made. In 1345 the abbot of Cluny received papal backing against certain English priors who had refused to pay him a subsidy, and in this instance Edward III allowed a levy, but apparently only on condition that he received a third of the proceeds himself.[4] He also allowed the Premonstratensians to levy sums for the expenses of proctors at the papal court who were working to uphold the order's privileges, provided that no other tribute was paid.[5] But it was now virtually impossible for foreign monasteries to collect revenues granted to them in England in earlier and very different days. By 1368, for example, the abbey of Clairvaux had despaired of obtaining regularly its rent of £20 from the monastery of

[1] *Statutes of the Realm*, I, 150–2 (Statute of Carlisle, 1307).

[2] *Furness Coucher*, I, 218–19.

[3] *Kirkstall Coucher*, 312–15; *Chron. Melsa*, III, 29–30. See also *Collectanea Anglo-Premonstratensia*, ed. F. A. Gasquet (3 vols., Camden Soc., 1904–6), I, 60–1.

[4] *CPL*, III, 19; *CPR 1345–48*, 63; *CCR 1346–49*, 28; *CPR 1354–58*, 221.

[5] *CPR 1350–54*, 214, 305; *CPR 1354–58*, 32; *CPR 1358–61*, 542; *CPR 1361–64*, 177–8.

Rufford, and received permission to exchange the source of revenue for something more easily collected.[6]

By the fourteenth century the laymen whose ancestors had lavished gifts and lands on monastic establishments had largely turned their attention to chantries and secular colleges. This was an international phenomenon, and several reasons can be advanced for it. The expansion of town life in many parts of Europe gave merchants and craftsmen wider opportunities for showing generosity to the church than they had enjoyed in the past, and it was dictated by civic pride that they should direct their benefactions towards local chantries and collegiate institutions, or towards rebuilding or enlarging the parish church. Economic difficulties caused by war and plague may also have had an adverse effect on lay grants, but the chief reason seems to have been a fear of increasing laxity in traditional monasteries. Although it is impossible to assess how far individual houses had deviated from the ascetic zeal of their founders, it is generally accepted that monastic life had become more comfortable by the fourteenth century. Indeed, when Benedict XII attempted to regulate the Benedictines in 1336 and the Augustinian canons in 1339, some reforms such as meat-eating were tacitly accepted and subjected to control rather than prohibition, and the greatest achievement was probably the establishment of a regular cycle of provincial chapters for houses which in the past had often been largely autonomous. The reform of 1339 had the effect of blending together the previously separate Augustinian chapters of the provinces of Canterbury and York, although the north continued to use its own series of statutes, drawn up at Healaugh in the thirteenth century, rather than accept the Canterbury rules.[7] Reforms based on administrative changes rather than on enforcement of earlier ideals were typical of the bureaucratic and centralising attitude of the Avignon Papacy, and they reflect a state of affairs where emphasis on organisational matters had largely supplanted enthusiasm for a return to asceticism. Even the new regulations apparently proved irksome: on 1

[6] *CPL*, IV, p. xix. This is probably connected with Rufford's farm of a moiety of the church of Rotherham: see *CPR 1340–43*, 474; *Foedera*, III, 875; *CFR 1368–77*, 75.

[7] For the Benedictine reforms see D. M. Knowles, *The Religious Orders in England* (3 vols., Cambridge, 1948–59), II, 3–4. For the text of Benedict XII's constitutions of 1339 see *Chapters of the Augustinian Canons*, ed. H. E. Salter (Oxford Historical Soc., 1920), 214–67; on the Healaugh statutes see ibid., xx; and cf. J. C. Dickinson, *The Origins of the Austin Canons and Their Introduction into England* (London, 1950), 174, where their universal acceptance is questioned.

June 1342 Clement VI suspended sentences which had been imposed under the new rules and absolved those affected.[8] Throughout monastic history patrons appear to have had the notion that prayer and intercession were more valuable if offered by brethren living under strict and austere discipline, and when such a life was seen to have ceased to be the norm donations to monasteries dwindled.

The only enclosed order still with a reputation for austerity was the Carthusian, and it alone received substantial support from benefactors in the later Middle Ages. A Charterhouse was established with royal blessing at Beauvale in Nottinghamshire in 1343, and in 1352 Clement VI granted the house an indult to enjoy all the privileges of the order.[9] These favours and papal confirmation of special liberties granted to Beauvale on its foundation were carefully inscribed in the cartulary of the house.[10] In 1379 Urban VI agreed to the petition of Michael de la Pole to found a Charterhouse in Hull in lieu of the nunnery of the order of St Clare projected by his father, a bull of Gregory XI to the same effect having been rendered invalid by the death of that pope.[11] In obtaining and jealously guarding privileges granted to them by the Holy See, the Carthusians resembled other orders, but Charterhouses were never as numerous or as popular as Cistercian abbeys in their heyday, nor did they provide a home for more than a very few monks. The level of contemplation and opportunity for private prayer enjoyed by Carthusian monks in their individual cells appealed to the religious ideals of the late medieval laity, but few donors were sufficiently wealthy or sufficiently committed to enclosed monasticism to be able or willing to sponsor the establishment of houses.

The situation was rather different in the case of the friars. A number of houses were founded in northern England, but some quickly failed such as the house of the friars of the Holy Cross at Farndale, planned by Thomas Wake of Liddell in 1347,[12] and

8 *Chron. Hemingburgh*, II, 394–7. The rubric states that the breach of the rules concerned failure to send monks to university, but this is not clear from the text. For Clement's relaxation of Benedict's constitutions see also the remarks of an anonymous chronicler quoted in *Chron. Reading*, 81.

9 Dugdale, *Monasticon*, VI, 13; *CPL*, III, 434.

10 VCH, *A History of Nottinghamshire*, ed. W. Page (2 vols., London, 1906–10), II, 106.

11 Reg. A. Neville, I, fols. 47–49, 62v; cf. *CPL*, IV, 91; *Urbain V: lettres communes*, IV, no. 14925.

12 See, however, D. M. Smith, 'The house of Crutched Friars at Farndale', *Borthwick Institute Bulletin*, 4 (1987), 16–17. He points out that Robert de Wilberfosse, member of

others are so obscure that their date of establishment is in serious doubt. But the friars had few houses in Scotland before 1300 and were able to expand there to a limited extent in the fourteenth century. In line with instructions of Gregory X and Boniface VIII papal approval was required before friars could accept a new site for an oratory. The Dominicans in 1348[13] and the Austin friars in 1360[14] were both licensed to set up houses in Scotland, and in November 1346 Clement VI allowed the Franciscans to accept sites given by Robert I and David II in Lanark and possibly Inverkeithing because they were present in only three Scottish dioceses and had suffered from the effects of war.[15] The granting of permission does not, however, imply that the friars actually managed to expand on the scale envisaged, nor that the establishment of oratories was immediate: the English Austins took over a quarter of a century to set up four houses allowed under a faculty of 1364.[16] Various factors could occasion delay: the Franciscans at Bemaken on the Isle of Man discovered that the bishop of Sodor was too distant to execute the papal mandate ordering him to set up the oratory, and in 1373 Gregory XI allowed the bishop of Llandaff or another catholic bishop to consecrate it instead.[17]

The friars and other centralised orders received a number of general bulls confirming their rights and privileges. This was in keeping with their tradition of close connections with the Papacy, and the acquisition of such documents reflects little more than continued fear among the religious orders that bishops, kings or other laymen would find ways to threaten their exemptions, privileged status or revenues. The bulls were insurance against loss of worldly position in an age when popular esteem for the religious had declined, but little more than this; it is fruitless to attempt to correlate individual papal confirmations with particular political or social developments.

domus Sancte Crucis in Farnedale, was ordained in 1347–8 (Ord. Reg. Zouche, fols. 19, 21v, 25), which strongly suggests that there was an initial attempt to settle Wake's land. The onset of the plague and the death of the childless Wake probably combined towards the failure of the house. For earlier attempts by this order to establish houses in the province of York see H. F. Chettle, 'The Friars of the Holy Cross in England', *History*, 34 (1949), 215–16.

13 *CPP*, I, 144; *CPL*, III, 304.

14 Reg. Av. 144, fol. 383–383v.

15 W. M. Bryce, *The Scottish Grey Friars* (2 vols., Edinburgh and London, 1909), II, 149; cf. *CPP*, I, 121; I. B. Cowan and D. E. Easson, *Medieval Religious Houses: Scotland. With an Appendix on the Houses in the Isle of Man* (2nd edn, London, 1976), 126–7.

16 Roth, *English Austin Friars*, I, 240, 305, 326, 343.

17 *CPL*, IV, 186; Cowan and Easson, *Medieval Religious Houses*, 238.

Much the same is true of bulls issued to individual monasteries ratifying grants of lands or privileges. In the twelfth and thirteenth centuries most houses had received a number of these, and often they detail all the rights and possessions enjoyed by the monastery. This type of bull was probably much less common in the period under review. Although this may partly be a result of the fact that many cartularies were compiled before 1300 and include later material only on an occasional basis, it is reasonable to suppose that fewer bulls were needed as fewer new donations to monasteries were made. Also, general confirmations of privileges and immunities, such as those granted to the monks of Holm Cultram in 1306[18] or to Rufford Abbey in 1360,[19] tended to be replaced by bulls ratifying particular agreements.[20] But the Papacy's recognition of an order or monastery's rights and its blessing of arrangements newly entered into was clearly still seen as desirable. When Archbishop Zouche visited the abbey of St Mary's in York in 1344 several bulls were produced to bolster the convent's claims to certain tithes, portions and pensions;[21] and in the same year the proctor of Furness Abbey produced a bull of Boniface VIII in York Minster and had it certified by the archbishop's court.[22] In January 1369 Paisley Abbey showed the bishop of Glasgow bulls detailing Cluniac privileges such as the exemption from ordinary jurisdiction.[23] However, to receive a papal bull was not always considered an urgent priority: the agreement over teinds made between the bishop of Dunblane and Dunfermline Abbey in 1354 was not ratified by the Papacy for nineteen years;[24] and nearly seventeen years elapsed before papal confirmation was obtained for an arrangement in 1356 whereby the abbey of Scone exchanged the church of Carrington for the more accessible church of Blairgowrie and agreed to pay an annual pension to Cambuskenneth.[25]

18 Dugdale, *Monasticon*, v, 603; cf. *The Register and Records of Holm Cultram*, ed. F. Grainger and W. G. Collingwood (Cumberland and Westmorland Antiquarian and Archaeological Soc. Record Series, 1929), 102.

19 Zutshi, 'Original papal letters', no. 256; Bell, 'List of original papal bulls', no. 179.

20 For some examples see A. D. M. Barrell, 'The Papacy and the regular clergy in Scotland in the fourteenth century', *RSCHS*, 24 (1991), 107.

21 Dugdale, *Monasticon*, III, 530.

22 *Furness Coucher*, II, 793–4; for the bull see ibid., I, 550–1.

23 *Paisley Registrum*, 328–30.

24 Reg. Av. 191, fols. 166v–168v.

25 Ibid., fols. 106v–107v. In 1391 an exchange between the abbeys of Saddell and Crossraguel was confirmed thirty years after it had been successfully brought to effect: *Highland Papers*, IV, 142–4.

In these and other matters, the Avignon popes did little more than confirm and clarify legal rights enjoyed by religious orders and individual houses within them. For all Benedict XII's efforts, the Papacy was unable or unwilling to change or reform the practices of the regular life in a way which was likely to stimulate religious renewal. In a period marked neither by monastic fervour nor yet by widespread condemnation this was, perhaps, inevitable.

The wide-ranging papal taxation system touched the regulars as it did secular clerks. Abbots and priors who were provided by the pope had to pay service taxes or annates, and after 1344 monasteries had to pay annates on benefices appropriated by papal authority. Carlisle Priory had to pay a mark each year in census, and 15d per annum was owed by the church of Scarborough, which was held by Cîteaux. Monies were also extracted from some monasteries visited in the 1350s by the papal collectors.[26] But none of these taxes fell on all monasteries. Some orders had escaped even tenths during the time in which income taxes had been the Papacy's principal source of revenue from the British Isles; their almost total demise after the 1330s meant that religious houses and the churches appropriated to them faced few demands from papal collectors. Most monasteries in the middle of the fourteenth century were much more heavily oppressed by royal exactions than papal.[27]

The absence of major developments in the religious orders in the fourteenth century meant that the regulars were rarely the subject of diplomatic correspondence between the pope and national governments. An exception is, however, provided by the Knights Hospitaller. A certain amount of confusion in the affairs of the order in Scotland generally, and in the 1370s the conflicting claims of Rhodes and the English prior, with involvement by Edward III, led to a large number of papal mandates and instructions being issued.[28] Plans for an expedition to the Holy Land also involved the English government, as was inevitable in time of war. In 1365 John de Paveley, prior of the Hospitallers in England, and four preceptors were told to attend the assembly of the order at Carpentras, convened to discuss defence against the Turks,[29] and by 1375 a

[26] See above, pp. 19–21, 63. For the payment of annates for appropriated benefices see Barrell, 'Papal involvement in appropriations', 28–31.

[27] Cf. McDonald, 'Relations', 23.

[28] For an account of the Hospitallers in Scotland between 1312 and 1418 see *The Knights of St John of Jerusalem in Scotland*, ed. I. B. Cowan, P. H. R. Mackay and A. Macquarrie (Scottish History Soc., 1983), xxx–xl.

[29] *CPL*, IV, 15, 51; *Urbain V: lettres communes*, IV, no. 14786.

general passage of 500 knights and the same number of esquires had been decreed, England and Ireland being asked to contribute thirty-eight brothers and thirty-eight esquires.[30] The priors of England and Ireland were told to assign to named persons the money collected for the expedition,[31] but it is unclear whether the English government allowed any of it to be exported. Here, as so often, secular powers became involved only because there were juridical or financial implications which extended outside the ecclesiastical sphere.

There were similar implications when the head of a religious house was provided by the pope. Anti-papal elements in the English parliament found it very easy to criticise a state of affairs in which religious houses were entrusted to provisors who would not adequately rule them. The 1348 parliament claimed that the pope had given abbeys and priories to aliens, cardinals and other unsuitable persons, and had thereby destroyed the religious life as well as damaging the patronage of the king and other lords.[32] Four years later a statute was promulgated which put those who had purchased abbeys and priories outside the king's protection.[33] In fact, provisions to religious houses in Scotland and northern England were very rare in the fourteenth century, and some of the grants which were made proved unsuccessful. There is a marked contrast between the situation in the British Isles and that in France, where John XXII alone made over 200 provisions to abbeys and over 730 to conventual priories.[34] When this statistic is set against the fact that, of 206 houses of Augustinian canons existing in England and Wales in 1395, only three had hitherto been the target of provision,[35] it can be appreciated that the level of the supposed abuse of provisions to monasteries was considerably overstated by contemporaries.

Furthermore, many of the provisions to religious houses in

[30] *Grégoire XI: lettres secrètes et curiales (non-Fr)*, no. 3634; *CPL*, IV, 111, 141–2; *Foedera*, III, 1044–5.

[31] *Grégoire XI: lettres secrètes et curiales (non-Fr)*, no. 3655; *CPL*, IV, 141, 142.

[32] *Rot. Parl.*, II, 171.

[33] Ibid., 243; *Statutes of the Realm*, I, 323–4.

[34] McDonald, 'Relations', 306–7. The corresponding figure for John XXII in England is ten; Clement V made six provisions, Benedict XII none, and Clement VI eleven: ibid., 284.

[35] R. L. Storey, 'Papal provisions to English monasteries', *Nottingham Medieval Studies*, 35 (1991), 79.

Scotland and northern England came about because an elected abbot or prior discovered that his house was in fact subject to a papal reservation, sought confirmation from the pope, and was provided on the formal quashing of his election.[36] Examples include Thomas Biseth, prior of St Andrews, in 1354,[37] Richard de Kelet, prior of Cartmel, in 1369,[38] and John, abbot of Holyrood, in 1373.[39] The procedure was very similar to that which prevailed in many Scottish episcopal sees, and often no opponent emerged and disruption to the life of the convent was presumably minimal.

However, the reservation of a monastery did offer an opportunity to an ambitious clerk to supplicate for a provision which would rival and possibly overcome the claim of the locally elected candidate. On 22 June 1351 a student at Paris, John de Stramiglot, was given provision to the abbey of Dunfermline despite the local election of John Black, who had been confirmed by the diocesan in apparent ignorance of the papal reservation which fell on the benefices of those dying while making the Jubilee pilgrimage to Rome.[40] The provisor prevailed, and Black had to be content with a pension and later appointment to the dependent priory of Urquhart.[41] Stramiglot's presence at Paris may have been the result of Benedict XII's reforms, which encouraged university attendance by Benedictines, but whatever his reason for being there his residence outside the monastery probably influenced his decision to petition for provision. The university of Paris regularly supported supplications by its members, and so both the theory and the practice of the system of provision would have been well known to Stramiglot. Although the abbey was unquestionably in the pope's gift on account of the circumstances of the vacancy, a petition by the convent for Black to be confirmed as abbot would almost certainly have been approved had Stramiglot not intervened on his own behalf.

As in this example and in the case of bishops, the claim of the provisor seems usually to have been accepted even by the locally elected rival. It was very different when the papal right to provide ran against another jealously guarded jurisdiction, as happened in the priory of Tynemouth following the promotion of Thomas de

[36] Cf. ibid., 78. [37] Reg. Supp. 27, fol. 299; *CPL*, III, 530.

[38] *Urbain V: lettres communes*, VIII, no. 24545. He had to resign the priory, but seems to have been reinvested with it.

[39] Reg. Av. 191, fol. 414–414v.

[40] *Vet. Mon.*, 297–8. [41] *Chron. Bower* (Goodall), II, 349.

la Mare to the great abbey of St Albans in 1349. Tynemouth was a cell of St Albans, despite occasional local objections and counter-claims by the crown,[42] and this subjection was confirmed by papal judges-delegate in 1247 by means of a compromise whereby St Albans appointed the prior and could remove him at will, but he had to be instituted by the bishop of Durham and swear canonical obedience to him.[43] An indignant St Albans chronicler saw an evil conspiracy at the curia in 1349 to deprive the abbey of its rights. The papal collector Hugh Pelegrini demanded annates from the new prior, Clement de Whathamstede, on the grounds that Thomas de la Mare had been blessed at the curia and that therefore his former priory was liable to provision; the cardinals and others at the papal court waited eagerly for provision to be made, until Thomas – at great expense – procured a bull which allowed him to bestow Tynemouth on one of his monks.[44] The king also intervened to prevent the levy of annates. He told Pelegrini that the priory was not vacant at the curia and that it was an important border fortress, the revenues of which were needed for the defence of the realm, and the collector was forced to admit defeat.[45]

The Papacy also became involved in the internal affairs of monasteries when a dispute between rival local claimants led to an appeal to the Holy See. One example is the long-running feud at Meaux between William de Dringhow and John de Rysley. Dringhow had been elected abbot in 1349, but in 1353 he was deprived after a visitation by the abbots of Fountains and Louth Park, an event instigated – allegedly with bribery – by Rysley. Rysley persuaded the visitors to set aside the election of Thomas de Sherborne on the grounds that he was blind in one eye and appoint himself instead.[46] Rysley made his profession of obedience to Archbishop Thoresby on 29 August 1353,[47] and proceeded to persecute Dringhow by trying to deprive him of the allowance he had been granted on his deprivation. Dringhow left the monastery and appealed to the pope, who reappointed him and cited Rysley and the abbot of Fountains to appear before him. On 4 July 1356

[42] See generally *History of Northumberland*, ed. E. Bateson, A. B. Hinds, J. C. Hodgson, H. H. E. Craster, K. H. Vickers and M. H. Dodds (15 vols., Newcastle, 1893–1940), VIII, 34–123.

[43] Dugdale, *Monasticon*, III, 315.

[44] *Gesta Abbatum Monasterii Sancti Albani*, ed. H. T. Riley (3 vols., Rolls Series, 1867–9), II, 390–2; cf. *CPP*, I, 172; *CPL*, III, 314.

[45] *Gesta Abbatum*, II, 393–4; Lunt, *Accounts*, 131, 156. It appears from the collector's account that the royal letter was addressed to Hugh's brother, Raymond Pelegrini.

[46] *Chron. Melsa*, III, 83–7, 93–4.

[47] Reg. Thoresby, fol. 22.

Rysley resigned, hoping for the election of his friend John de Hull. He was to be disappointed; Robert de Beverley was chosen, and Beverley persuaded Dringhow to abandon his suit in return for increased allowances.[48] Rysley retired to Roche Abbey, but at the next vacancy in 1367 he was again prepared to cause trouble. On the death of Beverley on 27 November, the convent was divided between supporters of Hull and backers of the prior, John de Newton. The abbot of Kirkstall tried to engineer a move to Meaux, and in the face of this the convent came to a compromise and on 6 December restored Dringhow to the abbacy. Rysley, who was at the curia, commenced proceedings against his old rival on the grounds that the monks of Meaux had never been released from their obligations of obedience to Rysley. Ultimately Meaux had to come to terms with him in order to persuade him to abandon his claim.[49]

A rather similar dispute occurred at the priory of Newbrough. John de Thresk, who had become prior in 1332,[50] held the monastery until shortly before 4 June 1351, when a corrody which had been granted to him was approved by Archbishop Zouche.[51] He was succeeded by Thomas de Hustewaite, but the priory was occupied – allegedly unlawfully and simoniacally – by John de Kylington; Hustewaite appealed to the pope, who in 1359 ordered the bishop of Lincoln to visit the monastery and correct faults found there.[52] The bishop reappointed Thresk,[53] but by 1366 Archbishop Thoresby had heard rumours of the indiscreet rule of the prior and the carelessness of his officials; bankruptcy was threatened, and so he proposed to conduct a visitation himself.[54] Thresk, however, continued as prior until his death in 1369, when Hustewaite was again elected and confirmed by the archbishop.[55] As the bishop of Lincoln had acted under a papal commission, annates were said to be owed, but the house was stated to be in lay patronage and nothing was collected.[56]

Not all papal interventions succeeded in fulfilling their objective. In 1359 the bishop of Dunkeld was told to remove the abbot of Iona and bestow the monastery on some suitable person,

48 *Chron. Melsa*, III, 107–11, 113–16; cf. Reg. Thoresby, fol. 194v.

49 *Chron. Melsa*, III, 163, 165–6. His successor, William de Scardburgh, was also chosen as a compromise candidate against the conflicting claims of Hull and Newton: ibid., 171–2.

50 Dugdale, *Monasticon*, VI, 317; *Reg. Melton*, II, 147.

51 Reg. Zouche, fol. 171v.

52 *CPL*, III, 607.

53 Lunt, *Accounts*, 514.

54 Reg. Thoresby, fol. 184.

55 Ibid., fols. 188v–189; Dugdale, *Monasticon*, VI, 317. Cf. Baildon, *Monastic Notes*, I, 148, for references to John de Thresk in 1368–9.

56 Lunt, *Accounts*, 514.

receiving his oath to the Holy See. The incumbent, however, continued to act as abbot until at least 1405, despite immoral conduct, his election finally being confirmed by Benedict XIII in 1397.[57] It should be noted that this involvement, and that at Meaux and Newbrough, was not a manifestation of the right to provide. It was a response to local requests for papal intervention, either to remedy alleged failings or to resolve personal conflicts within regular communities. Although the Holy See was given a role in determining who should rule the monastery, the initiative did not stem from Avignon, and the investigations – and indeed the actions – were also undertaken largely at the local level.

Even though abbots and priors were rarely appointed by the pope, the system of provision still greatly affected them because in varying degrees it limited their patronage. Direct provisions to the parochial benefices which were in monasteries' gift were uncommon compared with grants of prebends in cathedrals and collegiate churches, but expectative graces certainly did affect the availability of the livings upon which the regulars relied to reward servants and benefactors and oblige influential laymen. Of 133 expectancies *in forma pauperum* found in the register of Archbishop Zouche, dating from Clement VI's pontificate, no fewer than 96 promised benefices in the patronage of the religious orders. Other clerks received graces *in forma speciali* which were registered in Avignon. In June 1365 Walter Trayl and John de Drumbreck both received reservations of benefices in the gift of Arbroath Abbey, and in due course they accepted the vicarages of Monifieth and Kinnernie respectively.[58] But despite the inconvenience caused, especially to houses like Arbroath which were the object of many expectative graces, it is unlikely that monastic patronage was ever totally subverted by provisions; certainly in England monasteries continued to be able to present men without papal title to benefices in their gift, even houses like St Mary's, York, whose extensive collection of advowsons attracted large numbers of hopeful provisors. But the large number of papal grants affecting monastic patronage, especially under Clement VI and Urban V, may well have led to considerable disenchantment with the system among

[57] *Highland Papers*, IV, 135–6, 149–51, 156–8. On this and Iona in the fifteenth century see A. I. Dunlop, 'Notes on the church in the dioceses of Sodor and Argyll', *RSCHS*, 16 (1966–8), 179–84.

[58] For Trayl see *CPP*, I, 505; *Urbain V: lettres communes*, IV, no. 13756; Watt, *Dictionary*, 540. For Drumbreck see *Urbain V: lettres communes*, IV, no. 13145; Watt, *Dictionary*, 158.

heads of houses even if they themselves rarely had to fight off rivals with papal provisions.

In the fourteenth century regulars below the level of head of house had communication with the Papacy only relatively rarely. A few received provision in their own right; these were overwhelmingly regular canons, who were frequently presented to vicarages in churches appropriated to their house in line with the permission enjoyed by the Premonstratensians and frequently granted to Augustinian houses enabling members to hold benefices.[59] During the Schism and thereafter such permission was granted to regulars of all orders,[60] but the relaxation of the rules was not prevalent in Scotland and England before 1378. As a result, few regulars – at least below the rank of head of house – directly benefited from the system of provision.

In 1305 papal privileges to individual regulars were almost unknown in England, but their number increased under the Avignon popes, especially from the time of Clement VI.[61] Such licences and dispensations, many of them very similar to those bestowed on the secular clergy, were probably much less controversial than provisions or papal taxes, although they could weaken the bonds of discipline which underpinned the religious life. Regulars of all grades in the hierarchy received indults to choose a confessor and have him grant plenary remission of sins at the hour of death, a favour which appears to have caught the imagination of pious Christians in the fourteenth century, especially after the arrival of the Black Death. Few were as concerned as the abbot of Melrose, William of St Andrews, who saw fit to receive the indult from at least three different popes,[62] but many were prepared to pay for one plenary indulgence. The pope could also release clerks from requirements of canon law or from the rules of their order. In particular, regulars could be given leave to eat flesh-meat under certain conditions even where this contravened their rule. In 1351 the abbot of Holm Cultram was granted permission to have his confessor license him to eat meat in view of his infirmity,[63] and in

[59] H. M. Colvin, *The White Canons in England* (Oxford, 1951), 24.

[60] A. H. Sweet, 'Papal privileges granted to individual religious', *Speculum*, 31 (1956), 602–8; Roth, *English Austin Friars*, II, 284, 318, 320, 327–8, 332, 334, 348, 351, 369.

[61] McDonald, 'Relations', iii.

[62] Cal. Reg. Av. 135, fol. 350v; *Urbain V: lettres communes*, VI, no. 18445; Cal. Reg. Av. 187, fol. 61v. Cf. an abbot William of Melrose who was given a similar indult in 1350: *CPL*, III, 400.

[63] *CPP*, I, 215; *CPL*, III, 461.

1364 Adam de Lanark, bishop of Whithorn and himself a Dominican friar, was allowed to license the eating of meat by regulars at his table provided that they had not come in with the specific intention of partaking in such a feast.[64] Some illegitimates were dispensed from restrictions imposed by their defect of birth so as to be able to be promoted within their orders, in very similar fashion to the way in which illegitimate secular clerks were allowed to hold benefices with cure of souls and exchange them.[65]

Sometimes a religious house or individual was accorded a particular honour. In 1335 the abbot of Paisley was given the right to use a mitre and ring and other pontifical insignia and to bestow solemn benediction,[66] while during the Schism, when such favours were more freely bestowed than in the past, similar grants of *pontificalia* were made to the abbots of Holyrood[67] and Scone.[68] Another privilege, and one which sometimes carried with it exemption from the rules and jurisdiction of religious orders, was that of appointment as a papal chaplain of honour, a status bestowed by Gregory XI on John de Ballothyn, canon of Holyrood, Thomas de la Fingloy, canon of Guisborough, and John de Frichi, monk of Rievaulx.[69] These favours were again more frequent in the financially more straitened and correspondingly slacker times of the Schism than the period immediately before it.

The regular life, which many entered at an early age, did not always suit those professed in it. Some ran away. If they later reconsidered their decision and wanted to return to their house, the Holy See could be asked to assist in the process of reconciliation. Much of this work may have passed through the Penitentiary, the records of which do not survive from the fourteenth century, but the popes ordered some reconciliations directly, especially after Benedict XII's constitution *Pastor Bonus* of 1335, naming three executors.[70] Among those who benefited were Joan Blankefrontis, nun of Moxby, in 1345,[71] Thomas de Craven, monk of Easby, in 1356,[72] the Carmelite friar Roger de Gisboure in 1363,[73] and John

[64] *CPP*, I, 476. [65] For dispensations generally see below, chap. 7.

[66] *Paisley Registrum*, 429. [67] *Liber censuum*, I, 231.

[68] *Scone Liber*, 152–3; *CPL Ben. XIII*, 47–8.

[69] PRO, Roman Transcripts, 31/9/59, pp. 360, 361, 362. For Ballothyn cf. Coll. 358, fol. 167; Cal. Reg. Av. 185, fol. 215–215v.

[70] See generally C. Harper-Bill, 'Monastic apostasy in late medieval England', *JEH*, 32 (1981), 1–18. [71] *CPL*, III, 188. [72] Reg. Av. 133, fol. 291.

[73] *CPL*, IV, 35; *Urbain V: lettres communes*, II, no. 5782.

de Urwell, monk of Melrose, in 1371.[74] A number of such reconciliations were required in the aftermath of the Jubilee of 1350, when some regulars who made the pilgrimage fell foul of their superiors. Monks who had gone to the papal curia without leave also had to be reconciled to their houses, as were Simon de Leverton of Rufford and John de Monte of Holm Cultram in 1355.[75] Not all apostates, however, repented. Richard de Fores, formerly of Kinloss, intruded himself into the border vicarage of Norham around 1363 and was still in possession in 1366.[76] It is impossible to say how many regulars abandoned the life to which they had pledged themselves, or what proportion of these had second thoughts. Nor is it possible to assess how often the heads of houses exerted themselves to recover members who had apostatised; many of those whose exploits are recorded were restless spirits and probably troublesome within the confines of a community. The nature of the reception of those who received papal help to return to their monasteries can of course only be guessed at.

Only occasionally was the first entrance of someone into a religious community a matter of wider than local concern. The pope was involved in certain cases, such as when Innocent VI ordered that an acolyte be received into Iona Abbey in 1353,[77] but this involvement was more frequent on the continent than in the British Isles.[78] The same is true of transfers from one order to a less strict one,[79] although a few examples of this are found, especially in northern England. In 1347 papal sanction was granted to a Carmelite from York diocese who decided to become a Benedictine in Sicily,[80] and in 1351 another Carmelite was allowed to enter St Mary's Abbey in York on account of physical weakness.[81] The ordinary could sometimes permit a clerk to transfer to another order, as in the case of William de Irton, vicar of Sutton-on-the-Forest and Augustinian canon of Marton, who in 1368 joined the Benedictine monastery at Durham.[82] However, although Irton's successor was instituted by the archbishop,[83] an unnamed vicar paid £12 in annates to the collector, which implies that he may have needed papal confirmation of possession;[84] and when John

[74] Cal. Reg. Av. 174, fol. 527–527v. [75] *CPL*, III, 572–3. [76] *CPP*, I, 511, 512.
[77] *CPL*, III, 490. [78] McDonald, 'Relations', 312. [79] Ibid., 313.
[80] *CPP*, I, 109. [81] *CPL*, III, 429. [82] Reg. Thoresby, fol. 187; cf. fol. 187v.
[83] Ibid., fol. 187v. [84] Lunt, *Accounts*, 528.

Rollock joined a Bethlehemite community in 1372, his former vicarage of Lintrathen was filled by provision.[85]

The heads of religious houses were often named as executors of papal bulls, especially provisions, but most received only a handful of such mandates and Cistercian abbots were involved only rarely. In the period from 1342 to 1378 the most frequently named regulars in Scotland were the prior of St Andrews and the abbot of Holyrood with eight each, the abbot of Arbroath with nine, and the abbot of Dunfermline with fourteen.[86] In northern England, the prior of Durham was sent eight by Urban V,[87] and the abbot of St Mary's, York received no fewer than twenty-nine between 1342 and 1370 concerning provisions in the northern province, as well as being the executor of a grant to a cardinal of a canonry and prebend in any cathedral or collegiate church in England.[88] Some regulars were appointed as executors of licences to be absent, such as the abbot of Paisley for the archdeacon of Glasgow in 1342[89] or the abbot of St Mary's and the prior of St Andrew's, York for the vicar of Sutton-on-the-Forest in 1363.[90] Some acted as conservators or as judges with *ad hoc* commissions; others were ordered to help religious from other monasteries to be reconciled to their orders or to arrange for individuals to be received into particular houses.

None of these duties was sufficiently frequently imposed to be unduly onerous, but contacts between the Papacy and the regulars were more numerous and more diverse than might at first be thought. The great majority of monks, nuns, canons and friars had little personal contact with the Holy See unless they suffered from a birth defect, desired an indulgence or licence, or had left their house without leave. A few were involved with the system of provision, although this was more likely to affect abbots and priors. The head of the house, whether provided or not, could expect to be involved in sending petitions to the Holy See on behalf of himself or his monastery or in executing papal mandates. None of this impinged

[85] Reg. Av. 183, fol. 437–437v. On Rollock see J. P. B. Bulloch, 'The Crutched Friars', *RSCHS*, 10 (1950), 162–3. But note that the house in question, St Germains, was never one of Crutched Friars: A. Macquarrie, 'The Bethlehemite Hospital of St Germains, East Lothian', *Transactions of the East Lothian Antiquarian and Field Naturalists Society*, 17 (1982), 5.

[86] For details see Barrell, 'The Papacy and the regular clergy', 120 nn. 94–7.

[87] *Urbain V: lettres communes*, I, nos. 974, 1457, 2264, 3944, 4659; II, no. 7813; III, no. 9491; VII, no. 21258.

[88] Ibid., VII, no. 21500.

[89] *CPL*, III, 64.

[90] *Urbain V: lettres communes*, II, no. 4994.

too heavily on monastic life. The exemptions, privileges and rights to revenues enjoyed by monasteries were, however, seen as essential to the continuation of that life, and it is here that contacts with the Papacy remained important. Popes confirmed the position of orders and houses and ratified new arrangements, and could be relied on to oppose lay encroachments. The popes, of course, also tried occasionally to regulate the affairs of monasteries, and more often interfered with the exercise of monastic patronage. So, although the regulars were, to a greater or lesser extent, cut off from the outside world, they remained very much part of the universal church; as such they both required and encouraged contact with the Papacy.

Chapter 7

PAPAL LICENCES, DISPENSATIONS AND FAVOURS

Despite frequent crises in the diplomatic relations between the Holy See and temporal governments in the later Middle Ages, the authority of the Papacy as the dispenser of grace and spiritual licences remained almost totally unchallenged. It took many decades for the reservations of those such as Wyclif to obtain sufficiently wide currency to upset the established order, and the manifest excesses of the Renaissance Papacy probably had greater influence than any academic or theological objections to the papal dispensing power. Certainly in the period before the Great Schism such objectors were kept on the sidelines, and the popes were approached by numerous individual clerics and laymen seeking dispensations and indults which only the Papacy could grant. These were essentially of three types: release from some provision of canon law to allow the recipient to take some action in the future; pardons for past transgressions so that they would no longer prove disadvantageous in this world or the next; and favours so as to permit pious Christians to enjoy a fuller spiritual life. Some clerics needed to be dispensed from certain requirements of canon law to enable them to hold benefices and be promoted in the church, especially if they were tainted with illegitimate birth; laymen required papal absolution for attacks on clerks, the burning of churches, participation with excommunicates in religious services or criminal acts, forging papal bulls, and more commonly if they had married within the prohibited degrees of kindred or affinity or intended to do so.[1]

It is dangerous to attempt to quantify the use of different types of favour. Although almost all papal graces were issued as the result of a supplication by the interested party or a sponsor, very few petitions for favours and dispensations survive in the extant

[1] On the issues raised in this chapter see generally J. A. F. Thomson, '"The Well of Grace": Englishmen and Rome in the fifteenth century', in *The Church, Politics and Patronage in the Fifteenth Century*, ed. R. B. Dobson (Gloucester, 1984), 99–114.

registers; this is especially true in the case of the commoner licences and indults. This drives historians to the papal registers of bulls issued, with all the problems which that entails.[2] Furthermore, only a proportion – perhaps a small proportion – of favours and dispensations received registration at all, either because the papal chancery saw it as unnecessarily time-consuming or because the beneficiaries did not think it worthwhile to pay to have their bull registered. For England further information about papal graces can be gleaned from the episcopal registers, which include many mandates from papal penitentiaries[3] to the bishops, especially in cases of illegitimacy. But it must still be concluded that only some papal licences and dispensations are known to us; and so it is fruitless to present a study of them in numerical terms.

INDULGENCES

Whatever the deficiencies of the sources, however, it is certain that very many men and women received the indult to choose a confessor who could give them, provided that they were penitent, plenary remission from sins at the hour of death. Literally hundreds of these can be found in the period under review, the recipients being of all classes, both clerics and lay people. Many grants were to married couples and some to families; sometimes clerks and laymen in the same family received the licence at the same time. On other occasions a local notable was given the right to nominate a certain number of persons for this papal grace: the bishop of Whithorn was allowed to name eight in 1360,[4] while in the previous year indults to choose confessors and receive plenary absolution at the hour of death had been granted to two Scottish envoys along with their wives and twelve others of the realm with their wives.[5] Usually it is impossible to say who ultimately benefited from these block grants, but occasionally it is possible to speculate by noting from the papal registers the names of those who received the indult on the day when the petition was granted. Henry de Walton, archdeacon of Richmond, was allowed on 21 February 1352 to nominate four, and he may well have chosen Richard de Scrope and his wife Blanche, and the rectors of Foston

[2] See above, pp. 80–2.

[3] The records of the Penitentiary were kept separate from those of the Chancery, and are lost for this period. On the Penitentiary generally see Mollat, *Popes*, 303–5; Robertson, 'Scottish legal research', 344–6. [4] *CPP*, I, 350. [5] Ibid., 346.

and Barwick.[6] The austere Urban V sometimes attached a condition to grants he made, requiring the recipient to wear long garments at least to knee length, presumably as a token that this spiritual favour had been bestowed; and Gregory XI occasionally limited the duration of the indult to one year.[7] It is not clear why these conditions were attached on certain occasions, nor whether they were innovations by the popes in question or merely begin to appear in the sources then.

Any analysis of the relative frequency of these indults from year to year must pay due consideration to the deficiencies of the sources, but it is clear that the English were much more enthusiastic than the Scots. The advent of the Black Death led to an increased number of them in both Scotland and northern England, doubtless as the transience of earthly things became even more apparent than usual. Indeed, on 23 March 1349 Clement VI granted a general licence of plenary remission to the archbishop, clergy and people of the province of York;[8] it was to last until Midsummer, although since the plague ravaged the northern province in the late summer and autumn of 1349 its usefulness will have been less than might have been hoped. In England demand for these licences remained high into the pontificate of Innocent VI, but in Scotland the desire for them seems to have tailed off for a few years, before a rush of them in the years 1359–62.[9] Very few clerks or laymen in the province of York received this indult from Urban V after 1364, although many had availed themselves of the opportunity in the previous two years; the arrival of the second pestilence in 1361–2 may have had some effect here. In Europe as a whole Urban continued to grant these licences throughout his pontificate, although the proportion of British (including Irish) entries in his registers declines notably from 38 per cent in his first year and over half in his second to around 10 per cent by the later 1360s. For the pontificate as a whole there are 639 English entries, but only twelve Scottish and thirteen Irish. The overall picture is clear, but it is rather less apparent both why demand for the indult dwindled in

[6] Ibid., 225; *CPL*, III, 453.

[7] E.g. Cal. Reg. Av. 193, fol. 625v and Cal. Reg. Av. 202, fol. 485, for two Scottish examples.

[8] *CPL*, III, 289; cf. Reg. Zouche, fols. 248–248v, 285v; *Chron. Melsa*, III, 69. A similar remission was granted to those dying in the 1375 plague: Walsingham, *Hist. Angl.*, I, 319, 369.

[9] The great majority of these are found only in the Avignon Registers, which illustrates the problem of using the Vatican Registers calendared in *CPL* for these years.

England in 1364 and why its popularity in Scotland revived in the 1370s, when at least thirty-nine were granted. The pattern cannot readily be explained in terms of plague, politics, or even the vagaries of the sources; and to some extent local fashion may have had some effect on the numbers sought.

Overall, the reason for the popularity of the indult to choose a confessor able to grant a penitent sinner plenary absolution at the hour of death lies in the spirituality of fourteenth-century Christians. Much stress was placed on the pains of hell and purgatory, and the dangers of sin were brought home to the illiterate by wall-paintings and stained glass such as that still to be seen in the York church of All Saints, North Street. In such circumstances it was understandable that pious men and women should see the need to receive papal licences to be forgiven their trespasses at the time when they were destined to be judged by their Maker. It would be too cynical to say that the Papacy fostered the doctrine of purgatory so as to be able to sell indulgences and remissions which to a more sceptical age might have had limited worth in the sight of God, although it would be fair to conjecture that the Holy See, particularly in the immediately pre-Reformation period, was not blind to the financial advantages to be had by playing on fears of punishment in the world to come. But if people had seen no necessity for licences to receive plenary remission it is inconceivable that they would have been sought in such numbers. It must, therefore, be concluded that these indults were viewed with a certain reverence, and that many considered them well worth acquiring.

Christians who were unable to acquire papal indults to choose a confessor able to grant plenary absolution could reduce their time in purgatory by visiting named churches on given days and lending appropriate assistance to the fabric of the church or the poor. The period under review also saw a Jubilee indulgence granted to those who visited the basilicas of St Peter and St Paul and the church of St John Lateran in 1350 or were lawfully hindered from doing so or died during their stay in Rome.[10] How many Scots and English went to Rome it is impossible to say, but some regulars left their monasteries without permission in order to enjoy the spiritual advantages of the Jubilee, including Richard de Fishwyk, monk of Salley.[11] Fishwyk was obviously very concerned about his well-

[10] *CPL*, III, 311. Edward III initially prevented his subjects from making the pilgrimage: *Chron. Knighton*, II, 65–6. [11] *CPL*, III, 382.

being in the next world, because in January 1351 he obtained a licence to choose a confessor and receive plenary absolution at death.[12]

Papal indulgences for the fabric of churches were strictly limited, in this period often to a year and forty days to those penitents who visited and helped to build or restore the church on given days, usually the major feasts of the year and the feast day of the saint to whom the church was dedicated.[13] Those visiting the hospital of Killingwoldgraves on St Mary Magdalene's day would, however, receive only a hundred days' remission of enjoined penance,[14] and those going to North Burton church only a year, or a hundred days for the octaves of certain feasts.[15] Petitioners sometimes hoped for more generous remissions, but they were usually disappointed; moreover, Urban V limited the duration of the indulgence to ten years in each case.[16] These indulgences were generally uncommon in northern England and even rarer in Scotland, although several are attested in the period between 1363 and 1365. While this may be a trick of the sources, it is possible that visiting churches in return for small reductions of time in purgatory enjoyed something of a vogue in the more peaceful years after the Treaty of Brétigny. A further factor was probably the reduction under Urban V in indulgences granted by a number of bishops resident at Avignon, who collectively granted longer periods of indulgence than the pope was prepared to concede.[17] Although the spiritual benefits were on the face of it small, these indulgences doubtless had a function in the fourteenth-century church in that they encouraged support for projects to build and repair edifices dedicated to the worship of God by promising helpers a shorter time in purgatory.

PERSONAL INDULTS

As we have seen, indults to choose a confessor and receive from him plenary absolution at the point of death were common.

[12] Ibid., 407.

[13] Episcopal indulgences, of which there were several in this period, were usually shorter, e.g. forty days. [14] *CPP*, I, 231; *CPL*, III, 467. [15] *CPL*, III, 470.

[16] *Die päpstlichen Kanzleiregeln*, 17.

[17] C. R. Cheney, 'Illustrated collective indulgences from Avignon', in *The Papacy and England, 12th–14th Centuries* (London, 1982), no. XVI, 361; cf. 356. On the bishops' indulgences generally see E. M. Donkin, 'A collective letter of indulgence for an English beneficiary', *Scriptorium*, 17 (1963), 316–23.

Sometimes, however, notables were given leave to choose a confessor for some other purpose: bishops and kings could be granted the right to have confessors with wider powers than normal;[18] and Thomas de Allerton was allowed to have a confessor while on crusade.[19] Bishops and prominent laymen were also sometimes given indults to have a portable altar and to celebrate or hear mass before dawn or in a place subject to interdict. These faculties were on occasion granted together, although often only the right to a portable altar was conceded. The orders of friars found portable altars useful, if not essential, for their pastoral work, and these needs were recognised by the Papacy. Innocent VI permitted the Austin friars to set up a portable altar outside their oratories and celebrate on it in the presence of prelates and lords, and this was confirmed by Urban V.[20] Urban also confirmed his predecessor's grant to the Carmelite order which allowed its members to celebrate in places subject to an interdict.[21]

Various other indults could be granted. Certain Scottish ecclesiastics were permitted by papal licence to make a will to dispose of their personal goods, including Alexander Stewart, papal chaplain and archdeacon of Ross, in 1347,[22] the collector Grenlaw in 1370,[23] and the queen's clerk John de Mar in 1346.[24] David de Wollore, whose many benefices included the church of Hornsea, a prebend in York and a claim to the rich rectory of Bishop Wearmouth, was allowed to have an assistant to be named by himself if he was ever infirm.[25] In 1363 Urban V permitted Margery de Mere of York diocese, who was allergic to fish, to have milk, cheese and eggs during Lent if this was necessary for her health.[26] The variety of personal favours sought shows both the concerns of individuals and the sort of restrictions placed upon them by the church.

MARRIAGE DISPENSATIONS

Most dispensations sought by laymen concerned impediments to a marriage already entered into or planned. Papal sanction was

18 E.g. *CPP*, I, 100, 242, 244–5, 365.

19 *Urbain V: lettres communes*, III, no. 11489. In 1364 Urban V granted a licence to choose a confessor to all Christians fighting the Turks, and plenary remission of sins for all crusaders: Fierens and Tihon, *Lettres d'Urbain V*, nos. 1266, 1195.

20 *Urbain V: lettres communes*, II, no. 6552; III, no. 11527.

21 Ibid., III, no. 10800.

22 *CPP*, I, 127; *CPL*, III, 252.

23 *CPL*, IV, 83; *Urbain V: lettres communes*, IX, no. 26633.

24 *CPP*, I, 116.

25 *Urbain V: lettres communes*, III, no. 11209.

26 Ibid., II, no. 5675; *CPL*, IV, 31; *CPP*, I, 456.

theoretically necessary if the parties were related within the fourth degree of kindred or affinity, in other words if they had a common great-great-grandparent or if either of them had licitly or illicitly been joined in one flesh to the kindred of the other; a man could not lawfully marry a woman if he had fornicated with her sister or her first, second or third cousin. A tie could also be established between godparents and godchildren at baptism or confirmation.[27] The regulations were so complicated and so wide that many marriages within village communities must have been inside the prohibited degrees, but passed – or were allowed to pass – without objection. Those of higher social class probably saw it as expedient to seek regularisation of an unlawful marriage either before it was contracted or when the impediment was discovered, so that any children would not be illegitimate.

In the fourteenth century far more marriage dispensations relate to Scotland than to England. This implies either that the Scots were more scrupulous about the regulations or that there was a greater need for such dispensations in Scotland than south of the border. The latter seems more probable, as the idea that a well-timed marriage might damp down a feud seems to have been widely prevalent. The dispensation granted to the future Robert II and Euphemia, countess of Moray, in 1355 was said to be necessary both to settle a dispute between Robert and Euphemia's brother, the earl of Ross, and because Robert could not find a wife of equal birth outside the prohibited degrees.[28] In 1366 the bishop of Glasgow was told to dispense John de Maxwell so that he could marry Isabella Lindsay, to whom he was related in the fourth degree of affinity, in order to cement peace.[29] John and Mariota Campbell needed a dispensation in the same year because there was such a dearth of nobles in the Highlands.[30] William de Brechton and Margaret Preston, who were related in the fourth degree of affinity, were permitted to contract marriage in 1364 because plague and war had allegedly removed other suitable partners.[31] Such factors were less often cited in northern England, where the governing class was rather larger.

When a dispensation was sought before the marriage was contracted no penance was normally imposed, although in 1361

[27] Thomson, '"Well of Grace"', 104.

[28] *CPP*, I, 287; *Vet. Mon.*, 307. This was validated in 1375: Cal. Reg. Av. 197, fol. 172.

[29] *Urbain V: lettres communes*, V, no. 17574.

[30] Ibid., no. 17012; *CPL*, IV, 56.

[31] *Urbain V: lettres communes*, III, no. 11674.

the son of Robert the Steward offered to endow a chapel with twelve merks per annum within a year if he was allowed to marry Margaret, countess of Menteith.[32] It was rather different when a marriage had already been entered into, and in such cases it seems that penances were often imposed if the parties had united in full awareness of their impediment but not if they had joined together in ignorance of it.[33] The offspring of illicit marriages were usually declared legitimate.

A study of those cases where a penance was imposed shows that instances where a couple openly and deliberately defied canon law and later had qualms were not very frequent; most sought a dispensation in advance, as soon as the impediment came to light or not at all. In 1351 the abbot of Welbeck was ordered to dispense a couple who had married without banns and fully aware that they were related in the fourth degree of kindred on both sides, enjoining a salutary penance.[34] John de Douglas had to donate ten merks to each of two chaplaincies to be founded within two years in order to continue in his marriage to Agnes Graham, with whose niece by marriage Douglas had lived.[35] In 1360 the bishop of Dunblane was told to dispense John de Drummond and Margaret, countess of Menteith, who had married in order to end a feud knowing that they were related in the fourth degree of kindred, to release them from excommunication, and to declare their offspring legitimate, but in return the parties were to be separated for a time to be determined by the bishop and to found or choose an altar in Dunblane Cathedral and give to it goods worth ten merks per annum; they also had to provide dowries of five merks each to two poor girls.[36] But penances are not always recorded even when the parties knowingly broke canon law. In 1367 the bishop of Sodor was told to absolve Lachlan son of John Maclean and Mary of the Isles from the excommunication they had incurred by marrying without banns and to dispense them to remain in their marriage, declaring their children legitimate.[37] But even where no penance was imposed it was still necessary to bear the costs of obtaining the bull of dispensation; such expenditure was beyond the capabilities

32 *Vet. Mon.*, 317–18; Reg. Supp. 35, fol. 191v; cf. *CPP*, I, 376. For Margaret's four marriages, all within the prohibited degrees, see J. H. Cockburn, 'Miscellanea Dunblanensia', *Book of the Society of Friends of Dunblane Cathedral*, 7 (1957), 129–30.

33 Cf. Thomson, '"Well of Grace"', 105.

34 *CPL*, III, 456.

35 Ibid., 165; *Vet. Mon.*, 282–3; Reg. Supp. 7, fol. 29v; cf. *CPP*, I, 79.

36 *Vet. Mon.*, 315–16.

37 *CPL*, IV, 63; *Urbain V: lettres communes*, VI, no. 19787.

of most villagers, and doubtless acted as a disincentive even to the wealthy. Only consideration of the perils of their children's bastardy can have carried weight in some cases.

Complications sometimes arose where a child marriage was concerned. In 1345 the bishop of St Andrews was told to nullify the marriage between Hugh Giffard and Elizabeth More, since they had married while under age, had not consummated the union and had renounced it when they reached puberty.[38] Cristin Maccrath forced one Margery to contract marriage with his six-year-old son against her consent, and on his son's death married her himself. In 1354 the pope declared that the marriage with the son was to be no impediment to the union of Cristin and Margery.[39] A complicated case was entrusted in May 1364 to the bishop of Lichfield. When she was aged nine, Isabella de Scaresbrok of York diocese had been espoused to Henry Molineux, but was abducted and forced into marriage by John de Yorke. Isabella's relations succeeded in rescuing her from John's clutches, and when she reached marriageable age she fulfilled her contract with Henry. The angry John brought an action before the official of York, and so terrified her and her supporters that they feared to defend the case before the archbishop.[40] However, it was more normal for prelates to be told merely to investigate whether the facts were as stated and then grant a dispensation by papal authority than to be mandated to look into the background to as complicated a case as this.

It is impossible to say how many couples married ignorantly or knowingly within the prohibited degrees and failed to seek dispensation. It is also impossible to assess what proportion of supplications for marriage dispensations encountered papal refusal, as only in special circumstances would these be recorded. Perhaps the most significant rejection during our period was Urban V's denial of Edward III's plea for his son Edmund to be allowed to marry the heiress to much of the Low Countries,[41] but here politics undoubtedly played a major part. In the main, the Papacy was probably willing to grant dispensations to couples related within the prohibited degrees, either to allow them to marry or to permit them to remain in a marriage already contracted, at least if some cogent reason was adduced or suitable remorse shown for having entered into unlawful wedlock.

38 *CPL*, III, 187; *Vet. Mon.*, 284; Reg. Vat. 218, fol. 51.

39 *CPL*, III, 524.

40 Ibid., IV, 44; *Urbain V: lettres communes*, III, no. 11134.

41 See above, p. 149.

DISPENSATIONS FROM ILLEGITIMACY

Among the clergy one of the commonest dispensations required was from illegitimate birth. In the fifteenth century at least a man of illegitimate birth whose parents were both lay could be ordained to holy orders only with a papal dispensation, unless he entered religion, because an episcopal dispensation sufficed only for minor orders.[42] Defect of birth was a major handicap, for it usually had to be mentioned in all future supplications to the pope for whatever purpose, and it meant that a clerk needed a further dispensation if he wanted to exchange benefices or accept more.

Dispensations from illegitimacy were usually granted by the pope or one of his penitentiaries, with the bishop being responsible for execution. Sometimes, however, a prelate was authorised to grant a certain number of clerks a dispensation from defect of birth so that they could be promoted to holy orders and hold a benefice with cure of souls. Archbishop Zouche of York was allowed to dispense ten in 1342,[43] and seven years later, on account of the plague, he was permitted to dispense forty clerks who were under age and illegitimate.[44] A similar faculty granted in July 1345 to Bishop Hatfield of Durham[45] was clearly useful for many years. The licence was limited to poor scholars and clerks unable to go to the curia, and could be employed for twelve sons of unmarried parents, six illegitimate sons of married persons, and six sons of priests. Although Hatfield's register is incomplete, he was still able to grant eight dispensations under this faculty in the period 1366–8, all to sons of unmarried persons except that to the son of the priest George de Clifton on 16 March 1368.[46]

The normal practice, however, was for the illegitimate clerk to petition the Holy See for release from his impediment. Few of these petitions have survived, and it is impossible to guess at their number or know how many were rejected. Most appear to have been straightforward supplications for promotion to orders and an ordinary benefice to be allowed, but William de Rimington, monk of Salley, who was learned in philosophy and theology, petitioned

42 Thomson, '"Well of Grace"', 102; I have not been able to ascertain whether this was the case in the fourteenth century.

43 *CPP*, I, 5; *CPL*, III, 87.

44 *CPP*, I, 178.

45 Ibid., 100; *CPL*, III, 215.

46 Reg. Hatfield, fols. 46v–48.

in 1358 for a dispensation to be promoted to any dignity, even the abbatial.[47]

Mandates to bishops to grant dispensations from illegitimacy are rather commoner than supplications, although the papal registers clearly contain only a fraction of the total number issued; only a limited number can be traced from incidental references in future petitions. In July 1342 the archbishop of York was told to grant eleven dispensations from defect of birth, mostly involving sons of priests and the adulterous issue of married men,[48] and it would be reasonable to suppose that he and other ordinaries were sent many more such mandates throughout the period. Many dispensations can be found in the English episcopal registers, especially those for the large diocese of York; most were granted on the authority of penitentiaries, although some are said to be by papal authority, including one granted in 1349 on the basis of a letter of John XXII.[49] There is no knowing how full the bishops' registers are in this regard, but it is clear that many clerks did require papal help to remedy their birth defects and that the pope delegated much of the routine work to cardinal-penitentiaries, who then informed the bishops of their decisions.

No bishops' registers survive for Scotland, and references elsewhere to dispensations from illegitimacy are far too incomplete to allow any comparison to be drawn with England. Most of those which appear in the papal registers are slightly unusual cases involving a wider dispensation than normal. In January 1343 a clerk of St Andrews diocese was dispensed from defect of birth so as to hold one benefice with cure and one without.[50] In May 1345 Adam de Montacute, monk of Paisley, was dispensed as the illegitimate son of a married man to be able to be promoted to any dignity;[51] and in 1364 Adam de Wedale, canon of Jedburgh, was dispensed from illegitimate birth so as to be eligible for election to any benefice or dignity of his order.[52] It must be assumed that there were many routine dispensations in Scotland of which no trace now remains.

Complications could arise even where no attempt had been made by the clerk to conceal his defect. In November 1369 John de Saunford, canon of London, was rehabilitated on the petition of

47 *CPP*, I, 332; *Salley Cartulary*, II, 183. See Reg. Av. 191, fols. 114v–115 for a similar dispensation to a monk of Dunfermline in 1373.

48 *CPL*, III, 65–7, 90–2.

49 Reg. Zouche, fol. 28v.

50 *CPL*, III, 87.

51 Ibid., 177.

52 *Urbain V: lettres communes*, III, no. 11663.

Queen Philippa after a doubt had arisen about the validity of his illegitimacy dispensation and his provisions to canonries of Wells and Beverley. He had been dispensed as the son of an unmarried man and an unmarried woman, but when he was born his mother had in fact been married to another man, her union with whom was later declared invalid.[53]

Rather commoner were extensions of dispensations to cover pluralism or the right to enjoy further promotion. In 1343 William de Tikhill was allowed to hold two sinecure benefices in addition to the church of Stanhope despite his illegitimate birth.[54] In 1360 Bartholomew of the Isles, already dispensed as the son of a priest, was permitted to hold a canonry and prebend.[55] Sometimes a dispensation was extended to cover particular benefices; on other occasions a clerk petitioned that his birth defect need not be mentioned in future graces.

Being of illegitimate birth was certainly a nuisance to clerks who could not be blamed for their parents' indiscretion, as it was necessary to seek a further dispensation in order to hold two or more compatible benefices or to exchange livings, both of them common practice at this time. But there is no evidence to suggest that a natal defect was usually a permanent bar to advancement in the church. Some such as William de Dingthon[56] and John de Hervethorp[57] held a string of benefices, and Adam de Moray even became bishop of Brechin.[58] Although it was necessary to abide by the rules, it is true to say that men born out of wedlock could become fully involved in the life of the church; the only difference between them and their colleagues of legitimate birth was the closer monitoring of illegitimates' careers.

LICENCES FOR PLURALISM

Even for those clerks who were legitimate papal dispensations were sometimes needed to sanction pluralism. Two forms of pluralism must, however, be distinguished: holding two or more benefices deemed to involve the cure of souls on the one hand, and having one with cure and any number without on the other. John XXII had realised the abuse of several benefices with responsibility for the souls of the faithful being in the hands of one clerk who had to

53 Ibid., VIII, no. 23849; *CPL*, IV, 78; cf. XX.
54 *CPP*, I, 13–14; *CPL*, III, 68.
55 *CPP*, I, 350.
56 *Urbain V: lettres communes*, VI, no. 19885; *CPL*, IV, 63.
57 *Urbain V: lettres communes*, VIII, no. 24537.
58 *CPL*, II, 283.

be absent from one or more of his churches; and his constitution *Execrabilis* of 1317 had been intended to curb this practice. It apparently had some success, since by the middle of the century few ecclesiastics had more than one benefice with cure, although many held a number of sinecure prebends as they were entitled to do. Urban V tried to limit the holding of sinecures as well, first by equating the number of benefices which could be held with the clerk's academic qualifications and then by limiting all clerks, in England at least, to two compatible benefices only. These measures were largely ineffectual,[59] and the situation over the period remained basically constant: a clerk could hold several benefices and expectancies so long as they were compatible and provided that any defect of birth had been adequately overcome; if he wanted to hold more than one benefice with cure he needed a special dispensation.

It has been argued that licences to hold incompatible benefices were perhaps the most frequent dispensations in the fifteenth century.[60] In the middle of the fourteenth they seem to have been relatively rare, and only a few clerks, often prominent ones, were permitted to hold two benefices which technically carried the cure of souls. Not surprisingly, these licences became even harder to obtain under the strict regime of Urban V, and after his anti-pluralism measure of 1366 some clerks were driven to seek dispensation to hold more than two benefices even if these were compatible under the old rules.

One of the features of Urban's bull *Consueta* of 1366 was that all pluralists, even if they held compatible benefices or a single benefice and an expectative grace, had to declare their interests within six months.[61] Those who did not were excommunicated and had to seek absolution. This was granted to Ralph de Nottingham, who had a church and expectation of a prebend of Southwell,[62] and to John de Clisseby, who held the church of Simonburn and awaited a prebend in Lincoln.[63] In January 1368 the Scottish collector William de Grenlaw was rehabilitated so as to hold the archdeaconry of St Andrews, which he had held along with the deanery of Glasgow without stating that both benefices were with cure, but he had already resigned the deanery for a

[59] See above, p. 152.

[60] Thomson, '"Well of Grace"', 102.

[61] *Reg. Langham*, 1–5.

[62] *Urbain V: lettres communes*, VI, no. 20329.

[63] Ibid., no. 20330.

simple prebend, and he had to resign the archdeaconry and be provided to it anew.[64]

It is undeniable that Urban V was stricter in his attempts to curb pluralism than his two immediate predecessors had been. He gave a brusque answer to the ill-judged petition of behalf of Thomas Harkars for the removal of a clause in a bull of Innocent VI ordering him to resign a benefice.[65] Hugh de Wymondeswold, precentor of York, rector of Leake, and holder of other benefices, was told in November 1362 that he must leave university and reside on one of his cures;[66] and later there were unsuccessful attempts to deprive him of the precentorship[67] and Leake.[68] But Urban should not be seen as a lone voice crying in the wilderness, for Clement VI and Innocent VI had not allowed unfettered pluralism. Although several licences to hold two incompatible benefices were issued, it remained a mark of special favour; and the very fact that it was necessary to seek such a dispensation to hold just two benefices with cure shows that the spirit of *Execrabilis* was still very much alive.

LICENCES FOR NON-RESIDENCE

One of the most castigated evils of the medieval church has been absenteeism from benefices with cure, although in fact this was carefully regulated and there are several examples in the northern bishops' registers of clerks being brought to book for non-residence. Under Boniface VIII's constitution *Cum ex eo* ordinaries were permitted to dispense scholarly clerks to attend university for up to seven years, and much use was made of this; sometimes also a clerk was allowed to be absent in the service of some lord or of the bishop, and royal clerks seem to have been automatically exempted from residence. On occasions the absentee was permitted to put the fruits of his benefice to farm, and generally he was exempted from personal attendance at diocesan synods, but he was normally expected to provide a suitable substitute to serve the parish, and thus the cure of souls may have been less seriously impaired than has sometimes been asserted. It should be noted also that in England

[64] Ibid., VII, nos. 21524, 22188; *CPL*, IV, 71–2; Coll. 14, fol. 174v; Burns, 'Sources', no. 224.

[65] *CPP*, I, 476. For the grant of Innocent VI see ibid., 255; Reg. Supp. 26, fol. 153. It is not clear which benefice he had to resign.

[66] *CPP*, I, 386.

[67] Lunt, *Accounts*, 386; *Reg. Langham*, 57; Reg. Thoresby, fols. 68, 73v.

[68] Lunt, *Accounts*, 391.

at least the terms of *Cum ex eo* applied only to rectors and not to vicars, who were bound to residence by the statutes formulated by the papal legates Otto and Ottobuono in the thirteenth century; this point was almost invariably stressed in the institutions of vicars.[69] Licences from the archbishop of York sanctioning non-residence by vicars are extremely rare. Marmaduke, vicar of Kirkbymoorside, was allowed on 22 January 1369 to be absent at Cambridge University, but this was by papal indult[70] and was most unusual. Bishop Hatfield of Durham was more liberal in granting vicars licence to be absent; Robert Barker, vicar of Hartburn, was allowed to go to the Holy See to appeal against a sentence of excommunication imposed by the commissary of the official of York,[71] and the vicars of Kelloe[72] and Pittington[73] were also licensed to go to the curia; the vicars of Whittingham in 1362[74] and of Warkworth in 1368[75] were both allowed to be absent at a university. In 1363 Bishop Appleby of Carlisle was permitted to dispense ten vicars to study canon law for seven years,[76] but there is no evidence that this was ever used.

Some clerks saw the need to seek papal licences for non-residence, although it is rarely clear why episcopal favour would not suffice. Perhaps in some instances the ordinary had refused to grant a licence, but it is more likely that papal help was solicited in order to ensure that an ecclesiastic would not be deprived of the fruits of his benefice while absent, or when the seven years' study of *Cum ex eo* had elapsed, or where *Cum ex eo* and the legatine constitutions did not cover the proposed non-residence. Stephen Maleon, canon of York, was concerned in 1345 that he should receive the revenues of all his benefices so long as he resided on one of them; and Guy Kieretti did not want the war to impair his enjoyment of revenues from his archdeaconry of Glasgow.[77] In 1345 Thomas de Dalton, rector of Brigham, received a licence to

[69] On *Cum ex eo* see generally L. E. Boyle, 'The constitution "Cum ex eo" of Boniface VIII: education of parochial clergy', *Mediaeval Studies*, 24 (1962), 263–302. See also C. J. Godfrey, 'Non-residence of parochial clergy in the fourteenth century', *Church Quarterly Review*, 162 (1961), 433–46.

[70] Reg. Thoresby, fol. 187v. The only other example I have noted is the licence granted to Thomas de Saxindale, vicar of a moiety of Gedling in Nottinghamshire, who in July 1363 was allowed to go to the papal curia in connection with matters on his conscience: ibid., fol. 254v.

[71] Reg. Hatfield, fols. 44v, 60v.

[72] Ibid., fol. 63.

[73] Ibid., fol. 67v.

[74] Ibid., fol. 56v.

[75] Ibid., fol. 65.

[76] *CPP*, I, 437; *Urbain V: lettres communes*, II, no. 6371.

[77] *CPL*, III, 187, 64. For similar indults see ibid., 225; *CPP*, I, 123.

study civil law for three years in order to complete his doctorate and to be ordained priest only at the end of that time;[78] the study of civil law required a papal dispensation. The higher faculties of theology and canon law, so beloved of Urban V, attracted the Augustinian William de Irton, vicar of Sutton-on-the-Forest, and William de Walton, vicar of Clapham, and they were dispensed to be absent by that pope.[79] But, even though non-residence was widespread in the fourteenth century, sinecure benefices were normally involved and there is little evidence for wanton licensing of absenteeism by either popes or bishops.

Connected with the licences to be absent were faculties to archdeacons and others to conduct visitations by deputy and still receive procurations. Cardinals such as Peter de Prés, archdeacon of York,[80] and Anibaldus Gaetani, archdeacon of Nottingham,[81] were the usual beneficiaries. The controversial Aymar Robert, who had accepted the archdeaconry of the East Riding as part of his grant of benefices in the northern province of up to a thousand marks in value, was allowed to visit it by deputy for five years in 1349;[82] and the equally mistrusted Talleyrand de Périgord was allowed to visit the contested deanery of York by proxy.[83] Innocent VI and Urban V both permitted Archbishop Thoresby to have churches and cemeteries reconciled by a suitable priest when necessary,[84] and the bishop of Glasgow was given a similar faculty in 1376.[85]

As has been stated, an incumbent allowed to be non-resident was usually required to provide a suitable substitute, generally a stipendiary priest removable at will. In the case of prebends in cathedral and collegiate churches, however, vicars were normally appointed on a permanent basis both in the cathedral or college and, if the prebend was based on a parish church, in that church as well. On 9 April 1350 Robert de Thresk was allowed to appoint a perpetual vicar in the prebend of Thorpe in Howden, where the other portions were already served by vicars, and this was confirmed in 1354.[86] Residence as a canon usually conferred a right to share in the daily distributions of the church, but when the York prebend of Bilton had been founded it had been laid down that

[78] *CPL*, III, 214. [79] *Urbain V: lettres communes*, II, no. 4994; III, no. 10561.
[80] *CPL*, III, 146, 338. [81] Ibid., 73, 147. [82] Ibid., 289. [83] Ibid., 255.
[84] *CPP*, I, 342; *Urbain V: lettres communes*, VII, no. 22185; Reg. Thoresby, fol. 148.
[85] Reg. Vat. 288, fol. 313. [86] *CPL*, III, 356, 537.

canons holding it, even if they resided, had to pay £20 yearly for the privilege of sharing in the distributions; in 1346 William de Ferriby was specially exempted from this payment.[87] In a petition made around 1364 it was pointed out that canons of York and some other cathedrals who wished to reside had to provide sumptuous entertainment during a probationary year, with the danger that there would be a complaint at the end about miserliness and the exercise would have to be repeated. The pope asked the cardinal-bishop of Tusculum to investigate this clear disincentive to residence,[88] but it is not known what came of this.

DISPENSATIONS TO BE PROMOTED UNDER AGE

A papal dispensation was needed to hold benefices or be ordained priest below the canonical age of twenty-four, although, as with dispensations for defect of birth, the Papacy sometimes licensed a bishop or religious house to relax the requirements in a stated number of cases. It was usually alleged that plague had caused a shortage of priests in a particular locality. Archbishop Zouche was not only permitted to ordain persons who were under age and illegitimate in the aftermath of the Black Death;[89] he was also allowed to celebrate extra ordinations to meet the demand for speedy promotion of clerks to holy orders.[90] But it was the second outbreak of the pestilence in 1361–2 which caused the more serious shortage of priests in northern England. Urban V granted several faculties to ordain clerks under age,[91] and in view of his reluctance to set aside the requirements of canon law except when absolutely necessary it must be assumed that complaints about the dearth of priests had some basis in reality. It is probable that the effect of the first outbreak of plague had been merely to remove the surplus of ordained clerks; the potential for spiritual damage was greater in the second pestilence.[92]

Although ordination lists survive from northern England they are not sufficiently detailed to allow analysis of how these faculties were used. Bishop Appleby of Carlisle certainly did not use up his

[87] Ibid., 190. [88] *CPP*, I, 475. [89] Ibid., 178.

[90] Ibid.; *CPL*, III, 332. For the extra ordinations see Ord. Reg. Zouche, fols. 38v–41, 45–46, 48–48v.

[91] *CPP*, I, 437, 445, 464, 476, 480; *Urbain V: lettres communes*, II, no. 5554; III, no. 10772.

[92] The plague of 1361–2 was especially virulent among the young: see e.g. *Chron. Melsa*, III, 159, 162; *Chron. Knighton*, II, 116.

entire quota immediately, for his register records dispensations to be ordained under age in favour of John de Askeby on 1 August 1366 and William de Dalton on 1 February 1367.[93] Nor, before the plague, was Archbishop Zouche hasty in utilising his faculty of March 1344 to dispense six persons aged twenty to hold benefices with cure:[94] this bull was employed to allow the institution of John de Staunton to the church of Staunton as late as February 1347.[95]

Similar dispensations could also be granted to individuals, usually prominent ones with influential sponsors. Thomas de Percy, canon of Chester-le-Street, was dispensed in 1351 to hold a benefice with cure in his nineteenth year; his petition was backed by the king, Queen Isabella, the earls of Lancaster and Arundel, and Henry de Percy.[96] Alexander and Thomas de Neville, members of another famous northern family, were dispensed to hold a benefice with cure each when only fourteen, and at eighteen they were holding the rectories of Aysgarth and Brantingham respectively.[97] Even Urban V permitted the holding of benefices under age if the church was not thereby deprived of divine services and the cure of souls was not neglected. Not all dispensations to be ordained under age are, however, recorded as such in the registers, and the number of them can be augmented considerably by noting incidental mentions of defects of age in petitions for provisions. Philip de Beauchamp was only five when he was given reservation of a prebend in Southwell in May 1345,[98] and in 1361, when he was still under age, he asked – fruitlessly – for the prebend of Bole in York and the rich church of Brantingham, having already accumulated prebends in Lincoln and Crediton and the chapel of Tickhill.[99] But in many respects these cases come to notice because they were unusual. Even taking into account the few clerks who are known to have received holy orders or benefices under age without the requisite dispensation, and the unknown number whose indiscretions have not been recorded for posterity, it is unlikely that many under the canonical age, still less young children, held benefices with cure in northern Britain in the years before the Great Schism.

93 Reg. Appleby, pp. 151, 173. For his faculty see *CPP*, I, 437.
94 *CPP*, I, 46, 51; *CPL*, III, 116.
95 Reg. Zouche, fol. 117v.
96 *CPP*, I, 210; *CPL*, III, 431.
97 *CPL*, III, 262, 431; Smith, 'Vicars-general register', no. 114.
98 *CPL*, III, 176, 151. 99 *CPP*, I, 374.

OTHER DISPENSATIONS

Many clerks and some laymen tried to avoid other requirements of canon law or church practice. Some petitioned for remission of the examination normally required before a provisor could receive a benefice, but these supplications were usually rejected.[100] So was the petition of Robert de Erskin to be released from a vow to fight against the Saracens in the Holy Land and visit Sinai, although it was suspended for a year if it had been made for a fixed time.[101] Some received papal licences to visit the Holy Land, a journey which, at least sometimes, seems to have required papal permission. The knight John de la Pole was allowed in 1343 to visit the Holy Sepulchre with sixteen companions,[102] and Urban V granted an indult to a Hospitaller to do so with twelve companions despite apostolic prohibitions.[103]

Some, however, offended first and whether for career reasons or remorse sought pardon and dispensation from irregularity later. John de Akum had been bailiff of York, and by his authority and that of his colleagues criminals had been condemned to death; he had later been ordained and accepted a prebend in the chapel of St Mary and the Holy Angels in York. In being rehabilitated after his participation in bloodshed he had to pay annates for his stall.[104] A number of clerks were pardoned their transgression in being improperly ordained or celebrating services while under suspension. In 1366, on the authority of a cardinal, Bishop Hatfield dispensed Thomas Eyr, who had hit a Carmelite friar in the face and drawn blood.[105] Not all petitions were, however, granted. John Bateman de Couton of York diocese was allowed to become a public notary but was refused permission to minister in the orders he had received before bigamy or to enjoy the privilege of clergy.[106]

A few individuals went beyond the pale. Alan de Otheley allegedly fornicated with several local women, revealed the confessions of his parishioners, and although perjured and excommunicated continued to minister the sacraments until the parishioners petitioned the pope to be rid of him.[107] Some lapsed into heresy, although this was a lesser problem in the British Isles than in parts of

[100] Ibid., 238, 249. [101] Ibid., 346. [102] Ibid., 31.

[103] *Urbain V: lettres communes*, III, no. 10855.

[104] *CPP*, I, 237; *CPL*, III, 471; Lunt, *Accounts*, 138. [105] Reg. Hatfield, fol. 46.

[106] *CPP*, I, 90. [107] *Urbain V: lettres communes*, III, no. 11236.

Europe, especially before the arrival of Wycliffite heterodoxies in England during the Schism. On 20 October 1349 Clement VI issued a general mandate against the Flagellants, who were active in parts of Europe but only on a very limited scale in England.[108] There do seem to have been heretics in York diocese, however, for on 18 August 1355 Innocent VI wrote to Archbishop Thoresby with a mandate to proceed against those in his diocese who claimed that it was impossible to merit eternal life by good works and that original sin was no fault.[109] Nothing further is recorded about these heretics or their fate, but it is an interesting indication of heterodoxy in northern England before the onset of Lollardy. Many individuals, of course, will have erred and strayed both morally and theologically, for such is human nature, but it must be assumed that if these cases reached the Holy See they were dealt with by the papal penitentiaries under the seal of the confessional. Their tongues were less loose than that of Alan de Otheley.

THE CREATION OF NOTARIES AND PAPAL CHAPLAINS

A frequent point of contact between the Papacy and individuals in the locality was provided by the creation of notaries public.[110] Notaries could be appointed directly by the pope, usually in response to a petition, or they might be created as the result of a faculty granted to a leading ecclesiastic to examine and confer the office on a certain number of men. Sometimes the petitioner was given less than he had asked for: Bishop Welton of Carlisle was allowed to create four in 1353, two of whom could be in holy orders, but he had asked for eight.[111] Occasionally an ecclesiastic was allowed to nominate a number of notaries but someone else was deputed to examine them: Thomas de Bridkirk, canon of Auckland, was permitted in July 1351 to name two, but the examination was committed to the prior of Durham.[112] Many of those appointed directly were examined at the curia, such as the many found fit in the 1360s by the papal vice-chancellor Peter,

108 *CPL*, III, 311. Over 120 came to London from Zeeland and Holland: Avesbury, *De Gestis*, 407–8; cf. *Chron. Reading*, 112; *Chron. Angliae*, 29; Walsingham, *Hist. Angl.*, I, 275.

109 *CPL*, III, 565; *Innocent VI: lettres secrètes et curiales*, no. 1693.

110 See generally C. R. Cheney, *Notaries Public in England in the Thirteenth and Fourteenth Centuries* (Oxford, 1972), esp. chap. 6 for the appointment of notaries.

111 *CPP*, I, 242; *CPL*, III, 502.

112 *CPP*, I, 215; *CPL*, III, 435.

cardinal of St Anastasia's.[113] Urban V in particular frequently stressed that the notary was not to be married or in holy orders, but on 11 May 1369 the bishop of Durham was allowed to create as notary a priest and a married clerk.[114] Archbishop Thoresby was given a faculty on 6 October 1363 to create four notaries if they were unmarried and not in holy orders, and he used it to nominate John del Grene in 1363, William de Stillyngton in 1365 and Richard Warthill in 1368.[115]

It is hazardous to calculate the number of notaries created, but there were certainly several dozen at least in northern England during the period. In Scotland, the normal method was for a bishop to be licensed to create a certain number, although William de Grenlaw was permitted to do likewise for three clerks in 1353, four more in 1358, and a further six in 1372, two of whom could be in orders and two married.[116] John Leche of Sodor diocese in 1369 and Hugh de Dalmehoy of St Andrews diocese in 1371 were appointed directly by the Holy See,[117] but this was an unusual method of creation in Scotland at this time. The diocese of Sodor was short of notaries, and Bishop Russell was allowed to create six in 1349 and three more in 1363,[118] but fewer faculties were granted to the other Scottish bishops, and in some dioceses there may already have been an adequate supply.[119]

Notaries could expect to be kept busy writing and authenticating documents. A more honorific and less burdensome appointment was that of papal chaplain. Appointment conferred exemption from ordinary jurisdiction and from that of a religious superior, and this may explain why so many beneficiaries were members of religious orders such as William de Kirketon, canon of Newbrough.[120] Gregory XI was the most generous of the Avignon popes when it came to appointing chaplains of honour, but

113 E.g. *Urbain V: lettres communes*, II, nos. 6751, 6769, 6778, 6781, 6809, 6813; III, nos. 12002, 12005, 12034, 12037, 12087, 12100; V, no. 17994; VII, nos. 22548, 22555, 22561, 22567; VIII, no. 24902; IX, no. 27465. The vice-chancellor was usually the examiner of candidates for the office of notary: Mollat, *Popes*, 289.

114 *Urbain V: lettres communes*, VIII, nos. 24920, 24923.

115 Reg. Thoresby, fols. 133, 313–313v, 148v.

116 *CPL*, III, 503; Reg. Av. 138, fol. 45; Reg. Av. 184, fol. 618.

117 *Urbain V: lettres communes*, VIII, no. 24897; Cal. Reg. Av. 180, fol. 631.

118 *CPP*, I, 168, 394.

119 On notaries in Scotland see J. Durkan, 'The early Scottish notary', in *The Renaissance and Reformation in Scotland*, ed. I. B. Cowan and D. Shaw (Edinburgh, 1983), 22–40. Notaries are attested in Scotland from 1287 (Cheney, *Notaries Public*, 33–4), but few are named in fourteenth-century sources.

120 *CPL*, III, 461.

most of the recipients of the title were French, relatively few being Scottish or English.[121]

A great miscellany of business – grumbles, petitions for rehabilitation, requests for favours – came before the pope, and in some respects it is these affairs which defy neat definition which show most clearly the breadth of papal involvement in local life. For instance, Innocent VI received in 1360 a petition from William de Sutton, vicar of the chapels of Thornton and Allerthorpe within the parish of Pocklington, pointing out that he and other vicars ministered the sacraments and received fees and tithes, but burials were in the parish church, several miles away. Sutton asked for and was granted the right to bury the dead in the chapels and cemeteries of the outlying parts of the parish, though without prejudice to the rector of the parish church.[122] On 15 June 1369 Urban V wrote to the abbot of Alnwick, saying that in a recent Scottish church council it had been decided that all those who intruded into benefices should be excommunicated; proceedings had been initiated – although in vain – against John Fullour of Durham diocese, who had used lay power to seize the church of Yetholm in the diocese of Glasgow. The abbot was ordered to see to the execution of the sentence, with use of the secular arm if necessary.[123] In 1364 the pope granted David II's supplication for the confirmation of the foundation of a chantry in Roxburgh,[124] and in 1369 he granted the petition of John de Brereton, chaplain of a chantry in the York church of St Michael, Spurriergate, and confirmed the foundation of and grants to the chantry, which had been set up in 1336.[125] But it should be remembered that not all petitions were granted, even if they were made by prominent men: Innocent VI would not allow the annexation of the church of Slaidburn to the duke of Lancaster's proposed chapel at the place where his uncle, Earl Thomas, had died.[126]

Such rejections serve as a reminder that the Avignon popes before the Schism did not blindly accede to every request put before them. They undoubtedly did use their dispensing power to

[121] See generally B. Guillemain, 'Les chapelains d'honneur des papes d'Avignon', *Mélanges d'archéologie et d'histoire*, 64 (1952), 217–38. [122] *CPP*, I, 354.

[123] *Urbain V: lettres communes*, VIII, no. 24681.

[124] *CPP*, I, 476. For the foundation of this chantry see *Kelso Liber*, II, 385–99; *Glasgow Registrum*, I, 244–7, 257–61.

[125] *Urbain V: lettres communes*, VIII, no. 24481; YML, L1/8, fol. 101v.

[126] *CPP*, I, 271–2.

release many from the constraints of canon law and conventional practice, but only in particular and closely controlled circumstances. Ecclesiastics of all grades in the hierarchy and laymen of all social classes sought papal sanction for things which they wanted to do and things which they had illicitly done. They sought it in order to satisfy their needs temporal and spiritual, and neither church government nor church life could have functioned without the papal prerogative to dispense. In the fourteenth century this was not employed with unrestrained wantonness, but rather to satisfy the reasonable needs and desires of the men and women of Christian Europe. But during the Schism and afterwards, the Papacy's financial problems encouraged rather more liberal use of the Holy See's dispensing power, and to some extent this led to increasing emphasis on the doctrine that the pope was able to relieve sinners of the consequences in the next world of their actions in this one. The overriding motive became financial rather than spiritual, and so the wide acceptance of the validity of the pope's dispensing power which was apparent in the middle of the fourteenth century developed into the criticism of indulgences and wide-ranging favours which was to be such a feature of the Reformation.

CONCLUSION

Writing in 1935, Barraclough observed, 'Like all bureaucracies, the centralized Church of the fourteenth century was built up on rules and regulations; its strength as well as its weakness was system; its life-breath was order and method.'[1] The historian who seeks to examine the impact of papal policies in particular localities comes to realise the implications of the powerful force exercised by the curial bureaucracy. Under the Avignon popes, at least at levels below those of political ambition and high diplomacy, it was the system itself which held sway. Those who wished to avail themselves of its opportunities had to play by its rules; those who abided by the rules could expect at least a fair hearing and a fair chance of success.

In its broad outline, the system was universal. But its application was not. What the Papacy could do was partly influenced by political considerations, for the executive actions of the curia and its agents could be performed only with the consent of the secular authorities. The power of the English crown was sufficient to deter the popes from levying regular tenths, as too great a proportion of the proceeds went to the king as the price for the levy. In 1366 Edward III was strong enough to reject, once and for all, the demand for the arrears of the tribute. Intercalary fruits were collected only rarely in England after 1342. The levy of annates, the tax to which the Holy See turned after the effective demise of tenths, could be impeded by royal writs of prohibition. The English king may have used the anti-papal legislation at his disposal only sparingly, but its very existence, and the opposition in parliament which had largely inspired it, showed that there were limits to the exercise of papal plenitude of power.

What the Papacy actually did was determined by how much its powers of bestowal, judgement or dispensation were needed by the

[1] Barraclough, *Papal Provisions*, 103.

people of Christian Europe. This is perhaps most clearly seen in the vexed matter of provisions, the vast majority of which were inspired by a supplication from a hopeful cleric. Some of these were curialists; some were from overseas; most were not. The number of provisions was directly related to the demand for them: from clerks who felt that they offered a more lucrative or more effective means of promotion than local advancement, and from kings, lords temporal and spiritual, and other patrons who saw them as a useful addition to their own ability to reward servants and friends. It is on the matter of provisions where we see one of the most important differences between Scotland and northern England. North of the border, provisions usually benefited graduates; in England they did not. There were fewer provisions in Scotland, and they were not regarded as an abuse of the papal prerogative in the way that Clement VI's expectative graces to Aymar Robert and Gerald Domar were in England. Local patronage in Scotland was less heavily disturbed than in England; this in turn meant that there was less to impel churchmen there into the system of papal provision. It also partly explains the apparent lack of opposition to provisions in David II's Scotland.

This relative paucity of provisions in fourteenth-century Scotland did not continue into the fifteenth, nor perhaps did the widespread acquiescence in the system. Under the Avignon popes, Scotland did not have a different outlook compared with England, but arguably its church – and its society – were at a slightly different stage of development. The evidence for unordained clerks points to that. So, in a rather less obvious way, does the large number of dispensations to marry. What is significant is that these irregularities were frequently being brought to the pope's attention, which shows that Scotland formed part of the universal church and was involved in its conventions.

Compared with even the northern part of England, Scotland was a poor country, and its church was correspondingly impoverished. But more widespread political and economic factors also affected the church. Both lowland Scotland and the border counties of England had suffered grievous damage during the Wars of Independence, as the fluctuating fortunes of the protagonists were reflected in the destruction of economic activity in areas exposed to plundering raids. The bitter and ultimately insoluble clash of jurisdiction between Plantagenet and Valois in Aquitaine caused a series of conflicts which greatly increased the burden of taxation on both clergy and laity. The Black Death cut a swathe through the ecclesiastical establishment and disrupted the rural economy from which the church derived much of its revenue. The fourteenth century was indeed a period in which the spectres of famine, pestilence and war were never far below the surface of everyday life.

The effect of these economic factors on the church is, however, difficult to gauge. We must not take at face value tales of poverty told by those who wanted the pope or the king to be generous to them. Undoubtedly areas near the Anglo-Scottish border had suffered, and still suffered, from campaigns and the endemic skirmishing; parts of north-east Scotland were also regularly described as being impoverished by war. Poverty offered an excuse for failure to pay taxes, and this applied to papal levies as much as to royal demands. The revised assessment for the tenth in northern England caused papal collectors some difficulties, especially when they tried to collect in accordance with the superseded 1291 taxation. The value of some Scottish benefices was not known to papal agents, and the assessment of others varied widely over a relatively short period of time. Plague had a number of consequences. The level of mortality increased the number of vacancies and thereby the number of opportunities to seek provisions; this led to more demands for annates and a detectable rise in the level of papal involvement both in the matter of appointments and in the financial sphere. The shortage of priests, most serious after the 1361–2 outbreak, caused even Urban V to grant dispensations for ordinations below the canonical age; some of those who took orders after the Black Death may had been illiterate or morally unsuitable, as some contemporary chroniclers claimed, but it would be unwise to treat this as proved, and unfair to blame the Papacy for it. The suddenness of the arrival of the pestilence created a psychological reaction which was partly manifested by those who could afford it seeking personal indulgences in increased numbers. But the system could cope with the consequences of plague; it was the Hundred Years War which caused the difficulty, because of its political aspects. In England the Avignon popes were viewed with deep suspicion. Their taxes and provisions were regarded as sinister, almost as part of a pro-French plot. The competition between king and pope for the clergy's wealth became keener; the exigencies of war led to the crown's seizure of the revenues of aliens' benefices in 1346, which precipitated the greatest crisis in Anglo-Papal relations in the long reign of Edward III.

The sympathies of the Avignon popes were undoubtedly towards the Valois monarchy rather than towards the king of England. But the strength of the bureaucracy over which they presided largely nullified their personal aspirations as far as the church's routine business was concerned. Clement VI's provocative promotion of aliens in England and his outstandingly generous use of provisions aroused a considerable political storm but did not greatly affect the Papacy's role in the life of the church. Nor did Urban V's more laudable attempts to limit pluralism and to base preferment on academic ability. The system was too centralised and too rigid; it was based on law and legal processes, and in some respects had lost its capacity either to reform or to be reformed. Even the spiritual dimension of the fourteenth-century Papacy had become largely formalised, for favours were now subjected to the rigours of a bureaucratic process. This does not mean that the church was ripe for a major upheaval such as that of the sixteenth century; indeed, abuses such as pluralism, non-residence and scandalous promotions were probably less prevalent in our period than they had been in the second half of the thirteenth century. But the system could be abused, and the financially straitened circumstances of the Schism and beyond led to an increased willingness to sell favours, a practice which ultimately brought the medieval church into disrepute. The level of opposition in the English parliament in the fourteenth century should have served as a warning that the authority of the Holy See would be effective only for as long as its exercise was seen to be within acceptable bounds.

A study of a small corner of western Christendom over a period of some thirty-six years cannot hope to present findings which are applicable to the late medieval church as a whole. But it is only by examining the impact of the Papacy at the local level that we can assess the extent to which the theories of plenitude of power were realised in practical terms. In both northern England and Scotland the Avignon Papacy was involved in a range of activities. The popes sanctioned the appointment of bishops and used provisions to promote many lesser clerks. They had contact with religious houses and with those of all ranks and both sexes who needed dispensations or sought spiritual favours. They judged cases or appointed others to do so. They levied taxes. The involvement was considerable, but it must not be taken out of context. As the great episcopal registers of northern England demonstrate, the administration of the church at the diocesan, archidiaconal and ruri-decanal levels was carried out largely independently of papal intervention. The Papacy retained a role as overseer and as arbiter, but the scale and breadth of its involvement should be seen as a consequence of historical development rather than as a manifestation of deliberate policy on its part. Clerics and laymen had come to see the Papacy as a source of favour, and even though it had to be paid for, that favour was worth acquiring, as it sprang from the supreme authority in the church. The broad powers of the Holy See were widely, indeed almost universally, accepted in the fourteenth century; and although this was partly due to the innate conservatism of the medieval mind and a reluctance to break a mould which helped bind society together, there is evidence that the Papacy continued to be regarded with a mixture of respect and awe. Most individual clerics and laymen in northern Britain experienced the impact of papal policies only indirectly and infrequently, but those policies nonetheless formed part of the medieval system of government under which all were destined to live.

BIBLIOGRAPHY

MANUSCRIPT SOURCES

Carlisle, Cumbria County Record Office

DRC/1/1 Composite register including acts of Bishop John de Kirkby
DRC/1/2 Composite register including acts of Bishops Gilbert de Welton and Thomas de Appleby
(in microfilm edn)

Durham, Prior's Kitchen

Register of Bishop Thomas de Hatfield
(in microfilm edn)

Glasgow University, Department of Scottish History

Ross Fund collection of microfilms of material in the Vatican archives relating to Scotland
Collectorie
Instrumenta Miscellanea
Introitus et Exitus
Registra Avinionensia
Registra Supplicationum
Registra Vaticana
Collection of microfilms of transcripts from the Vatican archives relating to Scotland
Public Record Office, Roman Transcripts
Manuscript calendars of material in the Vatican archives relating to Scotland
Introitus et Exitus
Obligationes et Solutiones
Registra Avinionensia

Haddington, earl of

Unnumbered MS in possession of the earl of Haddington entitled 'Minute of the rollis of schireffis, Burrowes and Kirklandis anent King Davidis Ranson'
(from a photostat)

Bibliography

Lincoln, Lincolnshire Archives Office

Episcopal Registers VIII, IXC, X
(in microfilm edn)

York, Borthwick Institute of Historical Research

Reg. 5A	Register *sede vacante*
Reg. 9	Register of Archbishop William de Melton
Reg. 10	Register of Archbishop William de la Zouche
Reg. 10A	Ordination Register of Archbishop William de la Zouche
Reg. 11	Register of Archbishop John de Thoresby
Reg. 12	Register of Archbishop Alexander de Neville

(in microfilm edn)

York, Minster Library

H1/1, H1/3	Chapter Act Books
L1/7, L1/8	Torre MSS
L2/1	Magnum Registrum Album
L2/2a	Domesday Book
M2/1f	Register of *comperta* in the Court of Audience of the Dean and Chapter, with chapter act material, 1357–1485
M2/5	Miscellaneous Register, c. 1340–1507

WORKS OF REFERENCE

Cowan, I. B., *The Parishes of Medieval Scotland* (Scottish Record Society, xciii, 1967)

Cowan, I. B. and Easson, D. E., *Medieval Religious Houses: Scotland. With an Appendix on the Houses in the Isle of Man*, with foreword by D. Knowles and maps by R. N. Hadcock (2nd edn, London, 1976)

Dictionnaire de droit canonique (7 vols., Paris, 1935–65)

Emden, A. B., *A Biographical Register of the University of Oxford to AD 1500* (3 vols., Oxford, 1957–9)

Fasti Dunelmenses: A Record of the Beneficed Clergy of the Diocese of Durham down to the Dissolution of the Monastic and Collegiate Churches, ed. D. S. Boutflower (Surtees Society, cxxxix, 1926)

Fasti Parochiales, ed. A. H. Thompson, C. T. Clay and others (5 vols. to date, Yorkshire Archaeological Society Record Series, lxxxv, cvii, cxxix, cxxxiii, cxliii, 1933–85)

Handbook of British Chronology (3rd edn, ed. E. B. Fryde, D. E. Greenway, S. Porter and I. Roy, Royal Historical Society, 1986)

Hierarchia Catholica Medii et Recentioris Aevi, ed. C. Eubel and others (8 vols., Münster, 1913–79)

Hoberg, H., *Taxae pro Communibus Servitiis* (Studi e Testi, cxliv, Vatican City, 1949)

Le Neve, J., *Fasti Ecclesiae Anglicanae*, ed. T. D. Hardy (3 vols., Oxford, 1854)
Fasti Ecclesiae Anglicanae, 1300–1541 (new edn, compiled by H. P. F. King, J. M. Horn and B. Jones, 12 vols., London, 1962-5)
Spufford, P., *Handbook of Medieval Exchange* (Royal Historical Society, 1986)
Stubbs, W., *Registrum Sacrum Anglicanum. An attempt to exhibit the course of episcopal succession in England from the records and chronicles of the church* (Oxford, 1858)
Watt, D. E. R., ed., *Fasti Ecclesiae Scoticanae Medii Aevi ad Annum 1638* (2nd draft, Scottish Record Society new series, i, 1969)
A Biographical Dictionary of Scottish Graduates to AD 1410 (Oxford, 1977)

PRINTED PRIMARY SOURCES

Abstracts of the Charters and Other Documents Contained in the Chartulary of the Priory of Bridlington, ed. W. T. Lancaster (Leeds, 1912)
Accounts Rendered by Papal Collectors in England, 1317–1378, ed. W. E. Lunt, with additions and corrections by E. B. Graves (Philadelphia, 1968)
Acts of David II, King of Scots, 1329–1371, The, ed. B. Webster (*Regesta Regum Scottorum*, 6, Edinburgh, 1982)
Acts of the Parliaments of Scotland, The, ed. T. Thomson and C. Innes (12 vols., Edinburgh, 1814–75)
'Ambassades anglaises pendant la guerre de cent ans, Les', ed. L. Mirot and E. Déprez, *Bibliothèque de l'Ecole des Chartes*, 59 (1898), 550–77; 60 (1899), 177–214; 61 (1900), 20–58
Annales Monastici, ed. H. R. Luard (5 vols., Rolls Series, 1864–9)
Apostolic Camera and Scottish Benefices, 1418–88, The, ed. A. I. Cameron (Oxford, 1934)
Ausgaben der Apostolischen Kammer unter den Päpsten Urban V und Gregor XI (1362–78), Die, ed. K. H. Schäfer (*Vatikanische Quellen*, VI, Paderborn, 1937)
Avesbury, Robert of, *De Gestis Mirabilibus Regis Edwardi Tertii*, ed. E. M. Thompson (Rolls Series, 1889)
'Bagimond's Roll for the archdeaconry of Teviotdale, from a thirteenth-century transcript in the Vatican archives', ed. A. I. Cameron, *Scottish History Society Miscellany*, 5 (1933), 79–106
'Bagimond's Roll for the diocese of Moray', ed. C. Burns, *Scottish History Society Miscellany*, 10 (1965), 3–9
'Bagimond's Roll: statement of the tenths of the kingdom of Scotland', ed. A. I. Dunlop, *Scottish History Society Miscellany*, 6 (1939), 3–77
Brut, or the Chronicles of England, The, ed. F. W. D. Brie (2 vols., English Early Text Society, cxxxi, cxxxvi, 1906–8)
Calendar of Entries in the Papal Registers Relating to Great Britain and Ireland: Papal Letters, ed. W. H. Bliss, C. Johnson, J. A. Twemlow and others (London, 1893–)
Calendar of Entries in the Papal Registers Relating to Great Britain and Ireland: Petitions to the Pope, ed. W. H. Bliss (London, 1896)
Calendar of Papal Letters to Scotland of Benedict XIII of Avignon, 1394–1419, ed. F. McGurk (Scottish History Society 4th series, xiii, 1976)

Calendar of Papal Letters to Scotland of Clement VII of Avignon, 1378–94, ed. C. Burns (Scottish History Society 4th series, xii, 1976)
Calendar of Scottish Supplications to Rome, 1418–1422, ed. E. R. Lindsay and A. I. Cameron (Scottish History Society 3rd series, xxiii, 1934)
Calendar of Scottish Supplications to Rome, 1423–1428, ed. A. I. Dunlop (Scottish History Society 3rd series, xlviii, 1956)
Calendar of the Close Rolls Preserved in the Public Record Office (London, 1892–1963)
Calendar of the Fine Rolls Preserved in the Public Record Office (London, 1911–)
Calendar of the Patent Rolls Preserved in the Public Record Office (London, 1901–)
Chapters of the Augustinian Canons, ed. H. E. Salter (Oxford Historical Society, lxxiv, 1920)
Chartulary of the Cistercian Abbey of St Mary of Sallay in Craven, The, ed. J. McNulty (2 vols., Yorkshire Archaeological Society Record Series, lxxxvii, xc, 1933–4)
Chronica Johannis de Reading et Anonymi Cantuariensis, 1346–1367, ed. J. Tait (Manchester, 1914)
Chronica Monasterii de Melsa, ed. E. A. Bond (3 vols., Rolls Series, 1866–8)
Chronica Rogeri de Houedene, ed. W. Stubbs (4 vols., Rolls Series, 1868–71)
Chronicles of Edward I and Edward II, ed. W. Stubbs (2 vols., Rolls Series, 1882–3)
Chronicon Angliae, 1328–1388, ed. E. M. Thompson (Rolls Series, 1874)
Chronicon Domini Walteri de Hemingburgh, ed. H. C. Hamilton (2 vols., English Historical Society, 1848–9)
Chronicon Galfridi le Baker de Swynebroke, ed. E. M. Thompson (Oxford, 1889)
Chronicon Henrici Knighton, ed. J. R. Lumby (2 vols., Rolls Series, 1889–95)
Clément VI: lettres closes, patentes et curiales intéressant les pays autres que la France, ed. E. Déprez and G. Mollat (Paris, 1960–1)
Clément VI: lettres closes, patentes et curiales se rapportant à la France, ed. E. Déprez, J. Glénisson and G. Mollat (Paris, 1901–61)
Collectanea Anglo–Premonstratensia, ed. F. A. Gasquet (3 vols., Camden Society 3rd series, vi, x, xii, 1904–6)
Correspondence, Inventories, Account Rolls and Law Proceedings of the Priory of Coldingham, The, ed. J. Raine (Surtees Society, xii, 1841)
Coucher Book of Furness Abbey, The, ed. J. C. Atkinson and J. Brownbill (2 vols. in 6 parts, Chetham Society new series, ix, xi, xiv, lxxiv, lxxvi, lxxviii, 1886–1919)
Coucher Book of the Cistercian Abbey of Kirkstall, The, ed. W. T. Lancaster and W. P. Baildon (Thoresby Society, viii, 1904)
Coucher Book or Chartulary of Whalley Abbey, The, ed. W. A. Hulton (4 vols., Chetham Society old series, x, xi, xvi, xx, 1847–9)
Councils and Ecclesiastical Documents Relating to Great Britain and Ireland, ed. A. W. Haddan and W. Stubbs (3 vols. in 4 parts, Oxford, 1869–73)
Ecclesiastical Cause Papers at York: The Court of York, 1301–1399, ed. D. M. Smith (Borthwick Texts and Calendars, xiv, 1988)
Einnahmen der Apostolischen Kammer unter Benedikt XII, Die, ed. E. Göller (*Vatikanische Quellen*, IV, Paderborn, 1920)
Einnahmen der Apostolischen Kammer unter Innozenz VI, Die, ed. H. Hoberg (2 vols., *Vatikanische Quellen*, VII, VIII, Paderborn, 1955–72)

Einnahmen der Apostolischen Kammer unter Johann XXII, Die, ed. E. Göller (*Vatikanische Quellen*, I, Paderborn, 1910)

Einnahmen der Apostolischen Kammer unter Klemens VI, Die, ed. L. Mohler (*Vatikanische Quellen*, v, Paderborn, 1931)

Eulogium Historiarum sive Temporis, ed. F. S. Haydon (3 vols., Rolls Series, 1858–63)

Exchequer Rolls of Scotland, The, ed. J. Stuart and others (Edinburgh, 1878–1908)

Foedera, Conventiones, Literae et Cuiuscunque Generis Acta Publica, ed. T. Rymer (Record Commission edn, 4 vols. in 7 parts, London, 1816–69)

Formelbuch des Heinrich Bucglant, Das, ed. J. Schwalm (Hamburg, 1910)

Gesta Abbatum Monasterii Sancti Albani, ed. H. T. Riley (3 vols., Rolls Series, 1867–9)

Gesta Regis Henrici Secundi Benedicti Abbatis, ed. W. Stubbs (2 vols., Rolls Series, 1867)

Giraldus Cambrensis, *Opera*, ed. J. S. Brewer, J. F. Dimock and G. F. Warner (8 vols., Rolls Series, 1861–91)

Highland Papers, ed. J. R. N. MacPhail (4 vols., Scottish History Society 2nd series, v, xii, xx, 3rd series, xxii, 1914–34)

Historiae Dunelmensis Scriptores Tres: Gaufridus de Coldingham, Robertus de Graystanes et Willielmus de Chambre, ed. J. Raine (Surtees Society, ix, 1839)

Historians of the Church of York and Its Archbishops, The, ed. J. Raine (3 vols., Rolls Series, 1879–94)

Historical Papers and Letters from the Northern Registers, ed. J. Raine (Rolls Series, 1873)

Innocent VI: lettres secrètes et curiales, ed. P. Gasnault and M.-H. Laurent (Paris and Rome, 1959–)

Joannis de Fordun Scotichronicon, cum Supplementis et Continuatione Walteri Boweri Insulae Sancti Columbae Abbatis, ed. W. Goodall (2 vols., Edinburgh, 1759)

Knights of St John of Jerusalem in Scotland, The, ed. I. B. Cowan, P. H. R. Mackay and A. Macquarrie (Scottish History Society 4th series, xix, 1983)

Lettres de Grégoire XI (1371–1378), ed. C. Tihon (4 vols., Analecta Vaticano-Belgica, xi, xx, xxv, xxviii, Brussels and Rome, 1958–75)

Lettres d'Urbain V (1362–1370), ed. A. Fierens and C. Tihon (2 vols., Analecta Vaticano-Belgica, ix, xv, Brussels, 1928–32)

Lettres secrètes et curiales du pape Grégoire XI (1370–78) intéressant les pays autres que la France, ed. G. Mollat (Paris, 1962–5)

Lettres secrètes et curiales du pape Grégoire XI relatives à la France, ed. L. Mirot, H. Jassemin, J. Vielliard and G. Mollat (Paris, 1935–57)

Lettres secrètes et curiales du pape Urbain V se rapportant à la France, ed. P. Lecacheux and G. Mollat (Paris, 1902–55)

Liber Cartarum Prioratus Sancti Andree in Scotia, ed. T. Thomson (Bannatyne Club, 1841)

Liber censuum de l'Eglise romaine, Le, ed. P. Fabre and L. Duchesne (3 vols., Paris, 1889–1952)

Liber Ecclesie de Scon (Bannatyne Club, 1843)

Liber S. Marie de Calchou, ed. C. Innes (2 vols., Bannatyne Club, 1846)

Liber Sancte Marie de Melros, ed. C. Innes (2 vols., Bannatyne Club, 1837)

Liber S. Thome de Aberbrothoc, ed. C. Innes and P. Chalmers (2 vols., Bannatyne Club, 1848–56)

List of Diplomatic Documents, Scottish Documents and Papal Bulls Preserved in the Public Record Office (PRO Lists and Indexes, xlix, 1923)

'List of original papal bulls and briefs in the Department of Manuscripts, British Museum, A', ed. H. I. Bell, *EHR*, 36 (1921), 393–419, 556–83

Memorials of Beverley Minster: The Chapter Act Book of the Collegiate Church of S. John of Beverley, AD 1286–1347, ed. A. F. Leach (2 vols., Surtees Society, xcviii, cviii, 1898–1903)

Memorials of Ripon, ed. J. T. Fowler (4 vols., Surtees Society, lxxiv, lxxviii, lxxxi, cxv, 1882–1908)

Monasticon Anglicanum, ed. W. Dugdale (new edn, ed. J. Caley, H. Ellis and B. Bandinel, 6 vols. in 8 parts, London, 1846)

Murimuth, Adam, *Continuatio Chronicarum*, ed. E. M. Thompson (Rolls Series, 1889)

Notes on the Religious and Secular Houses of Yorkshire, ed. W. P. Baildon and J. W. Walker (2 vols., Yorkshire Archaeological Society Record Series, xvii, lxxxi, 1895–1931)

Original Papal Documents in the Lambeth Palace Library, ed. J. E. Sayers (*BIHR* Special Supplement VI, 1967)

Päpstlichen Kanzleiregeln von Johannes XXII bis Nicolaus V, Die, ed. E. von Ottenthal (Innsbruck, 1888)

Polychronicon Ranulphi Higden Monachi Cestrensis, ed. C. Babington and J. R. Lumby (9 vols., Rolls Series, 1865–86)

Priory of Hexham, Its Chroniclers, Endowments and Annals, The, ed. J. Raine (2 vols., Surtees Society, xliv, xlvi, 1864–5)

'Reconstruction of the lost register of the vicars-general of Archbishop Thoresby of York, A', ed. D. M. Smith, *Borthwick Institute Bulletin*, 3 (1983-4), 29–61, 102–13

Records of the Northern Convocation, The, ed. G. W. Kitchin (Surtees Society, cxiii, 1907)

Register and Records of Holm Cultram, The, ed. F. Grainger and W. G. Collingwood (Cumberland and Westmorland Antiquarian and Archaeological Society Record Series, vii, 1929)

Register of John de Halton, Bishop of Carlisle, AD 1292–1324, The, ed. W. N. Thompson, with introduction by T. F. Tout (2 vols., Canterbury and York Society, 1913)

Register of the Priory of St Bees, The, ed. J. Wilson (Surtees Society, cxxvi, 1915)

Register of William Melton, Archbishop of York, 1317–1340, The, ed. R. M. T. Hill and D. Robinson (3 vols. to date, Canterbury and York Society, 1977–88)

'Registers of the archdeaconry of Richmond, The', ed. A. H. Thompson, *YAJ*, 25 (1920), 129–268

Registres d'Urbain V (1362–1363), Les. Receuil des bulles de ce pape, ed. M. Dubrulle (Paris, 1926)

Registrum de Dunfermelyn, ed. C. Innes (Bannatyne Club, 1842)

Registrum Episcopatus Aberdonensis, ed. C. Innes (2 vols., Spalding and Maitland Clubs, 1845)

Registrum Episcopatus Brechinensis, ed. C. Innes (2 vols., Bannatyne Club, 1856)
Registrum Episcopatus Glasguensis, ed. C. Innes (2 vols., Maitland Club, 1843)
Registrum Episcopatus Moraviensis, ed. C. Innes (Bannatyne Club, 1837)
Registrum Johannis de Trillek, Episcopi Herefordensis, AD MCCCXLIV–MCCCLXI, ed. J. H. Parry (Canterbury and York Society, 1912)
Registrum Monasterii de Passelet, 1163–1529, ed. C. Innes (Maitland Club, 1832)
Registrum Palatinum Dunelmense, ed. T. D. Hardy (4 vols., Rolls Series, 1873–8)
Registrum S. Marie de Neubotle, ed. C. Innes (Bannatyne Club, 1849)
Registrum Simonis de Sudbiria Diocesis Londoniensis AD 1362–1375, ed. R. C. Fowler, with introduction to vol. II by C. Jenkins (2 vols., Canterbury and York Society, 1927–38)
Registrum Simonis Langham Cantuariensis Archiepiscopi, ed. A. C. Wood (Canterbury and York Society, 1956)
Richard d'Aungerville of Bury: Fragments of His Register and Other Documents, ed. G. W. Kitchin (Surtees Society, cxix, 1910)
Rotuli Parliamentorum (6 vols. and index, London, 1783–1832)
Rotuli Scotiae in Turri Londinensi et in Domo Capitulari Westmonasteriensi asservati (2 vols., London, 1814–19)
'Sources of British and Irish history in the Instrumenta Miscellanea of the Vatican archives', ed. C. Burns, *AHP*, 9 (1971), 7–141
Statutes of the Realm (11 vols., London, 1810–28)
Statutes of the Scottish Church, 1225–1559, ed. D. Patrick (Scottish History Society, liv, 1907)
Suppliques d'Urbain V (1362–1370), ed. A. Fierens (Rome, Brussels and Paris, 1914)
Taxatio Ecclesiastica Angliae et Walliae Auctoritate P. Nicholai IV circa AD 1291 (London, 1802)
Testamenta Eboracensia, ed. J. Raine and others (6 vols., Surtees Society, iv, xxx, xlv, liii, lxxix, cvi, 1836–1902)
Thomas Sotheron v. Cockersand Abbey: A Suit as to the Advowson of Mitton Church, 1369–70, ed. J. McNulty (Chetham Society new series, c, 1939)
Urbain V: lettres communes, ed. M.-H. Laurent, P. Gasnault, M. Hayez and members of the French School at Rome (11 vols., Paris and Rome, 1954–86)
Vetera Monumenta Hibernorum et Scotorum Historiam Illustrantia, ed. A. Theiner (Rome, 1864)
Walsingham, Thomas, *Historia Anglicana*, ed. H. T. Riley (2 vols., Rolls Series, 1863–4)
Ypodigma Neustriae, ed. H. T. Riley (Rolls Series, 1876)

SECONDARY WORKS

Barlow, F., *Durham Jurisdictional Peculiars* (London, 1950)
Barraclough, G., *Papal Provisions* (Oxford, 1935)
Barrell, A. D. M., 'Papal involvement in appropriations in Scotland and northern England, 1342–1378', *Northern History*, 24 (1988), 18–37
'Papal relations with Scotland and northern England, 1342–70', Ph.D thesis, University of St Andrews (1989)

'William de Grenlaw, papal collector in Scotland, and his account', *Innes Review*, 42 (1991), 3–18

'The Ordinance of Provisors of 1343', *Historical Research*, 64 (1991), 264–77

'The Papacy and the regular clergy in Scotland in the fourteenth century', *RSCHS*, 24 (1991), 103–21

'The effect of papal provisions on Yorkshire parishes, 1342–1370', *Northern History*, 28 (1992), 92–109

Bock, F., 'Some new documents illustrating the early years of the Hundred Years War (1353–1356)', *Bulletin of the John Rylands Library*, 15 (1931), 60–99

Boyle, L. E., 'The constitution "Cum ex eo" of Boniface VIII: education of parochial clergy', *Mediaeval Studies*, 24 (1962), 263–302

Bryce, W. M., *The Scottish Grey Friars* (2 vols., Edinburgh and London, 1909)

Bulloch, J. P. B., 'The Crutched Friars', *RSCHS*, 10 (1950), 89–106, 154–70

Carstens, C., 'The enforcement of the Statute of Provisors', Ph.D thesis, Harvard University (1937)

Catto, J. I., 'An alleged Great Council of 1374', *EHR*, 82 (1967), 764–71

Cheney, C. R., *Notaries Public in England in the Thirteenth and Fourteenth Centuries* (Oxford, 1972)

The Papacy and England, 12th–14th Centuries (London, 1982)

Chettle, H. F., 'The Friars of the Holy Cross in England', *History*, 34 (1949), 204–20

Cockburn, J. H., 'Papal collections and collectors in Scotland in the Middle Ages', *RSCHS*, 1 (1926), 173–99

'Miscellanea Dunblanensia', *Book of the Society of Friends of Dunblane Cathedral*, 7 (1957), 120–30; 8 (1958–9), 18–27, 69–78

Colvin, H. M., *The White Canons in England* (Oxford, 1951)

Cooper, T. N., 'The Papacy and the diocese of Coventry and Lichfield, 1360–1385', *AHP*, 25 (1987), 73–103

Crawford, B. E., 'Peter's Pence in Scotland', in *The Scottish Tradition*, ed. G. W. S. Barrow (Edinburgh, 1974), 14–22

Davies, C., 'The Statute of Provisors of 1351', *History*, 38 (1953), 116–33

Davies, R. G., 'Alexander Neville, Archbishop of York, 1374–1388', *YAJ*, 47 (1975), 87–101

'The Anglo-Papal concordat of Bruges, 1375: a reconsideration', *AHP*, 19 (1981), 97–146

Deeley, A., 'Papal provision and royal rights of patronage in the early 14th century', *EHR*, 43 (1928), 497–527

Denholm-Young, N., 'Richard de Bury (1287–1345)', *TRHS* 4th series, 20 (1937), 135–68

Déprez, E., *Les préliminaires de la Guerre de Cent Ans: la Papauté, la France et l'Angleterre* (Paris, 1902)

'La conférence d'Avignon (1344): l'arbitrage pontifical entre la France et l'Angleterre', in *Essays in Medieval History Presented to Thomas Frederick Tout*, ed. A. G. Little and F. M. Powicke (Manchester, 1925), 301–20

Dickinson, J. C., *The Origins of the Austin Canons and Their Introduction into England* (London, 1950)

Dobson, R. B., 'The later Middle Ages, 1215–1500', in *A History of York Minster*,

ed. G. E. Aylmer and R. Cant (Oxford, 1977), 44–109
Donaldson, G., 'The rights of the Scottish crown in episcopal vacancies', *SHR*, 45 (1966), 27–35
Donaldson, R., 'Patronage and the church. A study in the social structure of the secular clergy in the diocese of Durham (1311–1540)', Ph.D thesis, University of Edinburgh (1955)
Donkin, E. M., 'A collective letter of indulgence for an English beneficiary', *Scriptorium*, 17 (1963), 316–23
Dowden, J., 'The appointment of bishops in Scotland during the medieval period', *SHR*, 7 (1909–10), 1–20
The Medieval Church in Scotland (Glasgow, 1910)
Driver, J. T., 'The Papacy and the diocese of Hereford, 1307–1377', *Church Quarterly Review*, 145 (1947), 31–47
Dunlop, A. I., 'Notes on the church in the dioceses of Sodor and Argyll', *RSCHS*, 16 (1966–8), 179–84
Durkan, J., 'The early Scottish notary', in *The Renaissance and Reformation in Scotland*, ed. I. B. Cowan and D. Shaw (Edinburgh, 1983), 22–40
Emden, A. B., Review of Le Neve, *Fasti*, I and II, *Medium Aevum*, 32 (1963), 93–7
Emsley, K., 'The Yorkshire enclaves of the bishops of Durham', *YAJ*, 47 (1975), 103–8
Ferguson, P. C., 'Medieval papal representatives in Scotland: legates, nuncios and judges-delegate, 1125–1286', Ph.D thesis, Columbia University (1987)
Flanagan, U., 'Papal provisions in Ireland, 1305–78', *Historical Studies*, 3 (Cork, 1961), 92–103
Fowler, K., *The King's Lieutenant. Henry of Grosmont, First Duke of Lancaster, 1310–1361* (London, 1969)
Godfrey, C. J., 'Pluralists in the province of Canterbury in 1366', *JEH*, 11 (1960), 23–40
'Non-residence of parochial clergy in the fourteenth century', *Church Quarterly Review*, 162 (1961), 433–46
Grant, A., *Independence and Nationhood: Scotland 1306–1469* (London, 1984)
Graves, E. B., 'The legal significance of the Statute of Praemunire of 1353', in *Anniversary Essays in Mediaeval History by Students of Charles Homer Haskins* (Boston and New York, 1929), 57–80
Greenway, W., 'The Papacy and the diocese of St David's, 1305–1417', *Church Quarterly Review*, 161 (1960), 436–48; 162 (1961), 33–49
Guillemain, B., 'Les chapelains d'honneur des papes d'Avignon', *Mélanges d'archéologie et d'histoire*, 64 (1952), 217–38
La cour pontificale d'Avignon (1309–1376): étude d'une société (Paris, 1962)
Haines, R. M., *The Administration of the Diocese of Worcester in the First Half of the Fourteenth Century* (London, 1965)
Harper-Bill, C., 'Monastic apostasy in late medieval England', *JEH*, 32 (1981), 1–18
Heath, P., *Church and Realm, 1272–1461* (London, 1988)
Highfield, J. R. L., 'The relations between the church and the English crown from the death of Archbishop Stratford to the opening of the Great Schism (1349–78)', DPhil. thesis, University of Oxford (1950–1)

'The English hierarchy in the reign of Edward III', *TRHS* 5th series, 6 (1956), 115–38
Hilling, N., *Procedure at the Roman Curia* (New York, 1907)
History of Northumberland, ed. E. Bateson, A. B. Hinds, J. C. Hodgson, H. H. E. Craster, K. H. Vickers and M. H. Dodds (15 vols., Newcastle, 1893–1940)
Holmes, G., *The Good Parliament* (Oxford, 1975)
Housley, N., *The Avignon Papacy and the Crusades, 1305–1378* (Oxford, 1986)
Jacob, E. F., 'Petitions for benefices from English universities during the Great Schism', *TRHS* 4th series, 27 (1945), 41–59
Knowles, D. M., *The Religious Orders in England* (3 vols., Cambridge, 1948–59)
Linehan, P. A., 'A fourteenth-century history of Anglo-Scottish relations in a Spanish manuscript', *BIHR*, 48 (1975), 106–22
Lunt, W. E., 'The first levy of papal annates', *AHR*, 18 (1912), 48–64
'William Testa and the parliament of Carlisle', *EHR*, 41 (1926), 332–57
Papal Revenues in the Middle Ages (2 vols., New York, 1934)
Financial Relations of the Papacy with England to 1327 (Cambridge, Mass., 1939)
Financial Relations of the Papacy with England, 1327–1534 (Cambridge, Mass., 1962)
Luttrell, A., 'The crusade in the fourteenth century', in *Europe in the Late Middle Ages*, ed. J. R. Hale, J. R. L. Highfield and B. Smalley (London, 1965), 122–54
McDonald, P., 'The relations between the Papacy and the religious orders in England, 1305–1352', DPhil. thesis, University of Oxford (1984)
Macfarlane, L., 'An English account of the election of Urban VI, 1378', *BIHR*, 26 (1953), 75–85
McHardy, A. K., 'The promotion of John Buckingham to the see of Lincoln', *JEH*, 26 (1975), 127–35
Macquarrie, A., 'The Bethlehemite Hospital of St Germains, East Lothian', *Transactions of the East Lothian Antiquarian and Field Naturalists Society*, 17 (1982), 1–10
Mollat, G., 'Innocent VI et les tentatives de paix entre la France et l'Angleterre', *Revue d'histoire ecclésiastique*, 10 (1909), 729–43
'La collation des bénéfices ecclésiastiques à l'époque des papes d'Avignon', introduction to *Jean XXII: lettres communes* (Paris, 1921)
'Le Saint-Siège et la France sous le pontificat de Clément VI (1342–1352)', *Revue d'histoire ecclésiastique*, 55 (1960), 5–24
The Popes at Avignon, 1305–1378, trans. J. Love (London, 1963)
Nicholson, R., *Scotland: The Later Middle Ages* (2nd imp., Edinburgh, 1978)
Owen, D., 'Ecclesiastical jurisdiction in England, 1300–1550: the records and their interpretation', *Studies in Church History*, 11, ed. D. Baker (Oxford, 1975), 199–221
Palmer, J. J. N., 'England, France, the Papacy and the Flemish succession, 1361–9', *Journal of Medieval History*, 2 (1976), 339–64
Palmer, J. J. N. and Wells, A. P., 'Ecclesiastical reform and the politics of the Hundred Years War during the pontificate of Urban V', in *War, Literature and Politics in the Late Middle Ages*, ed. C. T. Allmand (Liverpool, 1976), 169–89
Pantin, W. A., 'Grosseteste's relations with the Papacy and the crown', in *Robert*

Grosseteste, Scholar and Bishop, ed. D. A. Callus (Oxford, 1955), 178–215
Perroy, E., *L'Angleterre et le Grand Schisme d'Occident* (Paris, 1933)
Plucknett, T. F. T., 'The case of the miscreant cardinal', *AHR*, 30 (1924), 1–15
Ramsay, J. H., *Genesis of Lancaster, or the Three Reigns of Edward II, Edward III, and Richard II, 1307–1399* (2 vols., Oxford, 1913)
Reichel, O. J., *A Complete Manual of Canon Law* (2 vols., London, 1896)
Renouard, Y., *The Avignon Papacy, 1305–1403*, trans. D. Bethell (London, 1970)
Robertson, J. J., 'Canon law as a source', in *Stair Tercentenary Studies*, ed. D. M. Walker (Stair Society, xxxiii, 1981), 112–27
'Scottish legal research in the Vatican archives: a preliminary report', *Renaissance Studies*, 2 (1988), 339–46
Roth, F., *The English Austin Friars, 1249–1538* (2 vols., New York, 1961–6)
Samaran, C. and Mollat, G., *La fiscalité pontificale en France au xive siècle* (Paris, 1905)
Sayers, J. E., *Papal Judges Delegate in the Province of Canterbury, 1198–1254* (Oxford, 1971)
Smith, D. M., 'The house of Crutched Friars at Farndale', *Borthwick Institute Bulletin*, 4 (1987), 16–17
Smith, W. E. L., *Episcopal Appointments and Patronage in the Reign of Edward II. A Study in the Relations of Church and State* (Chicago, 1938)
Storey, R. L., 'Papal provisions to English monasteries', *Nottingham Medieval Studies*, 35 (1991), 77–91
Sweet, A. H., 'Papal privileges granted to individual religious', *Speculum*, 31 (1956), 602–10
Thibault, P. R., *Pope Gregory XI: The Failure of Tradition* (Lanham, 1986)
Thompson, A. H., 'Pluralism in the mediaeval church, with notes on pluralists in the diocese of Lincoln, 1366', *Associated Architectural Societies Reports and Papers*, 33 (1915), 35–73; 34 (1917), 1–26; 35 (1919–20), 87–108, 199–242; 36 (1921), 1–41
'Some letters from the register of William Zouche, archbishop of York', in *Historical Essays in Honour of James Tait*, ed. J. G. Edwards, V. H. Galbraith and E. F. Jacob (Manchester, 1933), 327–43
Thomson, J. A. F., '"The Well of Grace": Englishmen and Rome in the fifteenth century', in *The Church, Politics and Patronage in the Fifteenth Century*, ed. R. B. Dobson (Gloucester, 1984), 99–114
Tihon, C., 'Les expectatives *in forma pauperum*, particulièrement au xive siècle', *Bulletin de l'Institut historique belge de Rome*, 5 (1925), 51–118
Ullmann, W., *The Papacy and Political Ideas in the Middle Ages* (London, 1976)
Victoria County History, *A History of Nottinghamshire*, ed. W. Page (2 vols., London, 1906–10)
A History of Yorkshire East Riding, ed. K. J. Allison (6 vols. to date, London, 1969–)
Watt, D. E. R., 'Sources for Scottish history of the fourteenth century in the archives of the Vatican', *SHR*, 32 (1953), 101–22
'University clerks and rolls of petitions for benefices', *Speculum*, 34 (1959), 213–29

'University graduates in Scottish benefices before 1410', *RSCHS*, 15 (1966), 77–88
Wood, D., *Clement VI: The Pontificate and Ideas of an Avignon Pope* (Cambridge, 1989)
Wright, J. R., *The Church and the English Crown, 1305–1334* (Toronto, 1980)
Zutshi, P. N. R., 'Original papal letters in England, 1305–1417: a study and a calendar', Ph.D thesis, University of Cambridge (1981)

INDEX

It is impracticable to provide a full index of some of the most important themes of this book. In such cases, therefore, only the principal discussion has been indexed, these instances being indicated by bold type. Users of the index should also note that references to named prebends of cathedrals or collegiate churches are listed solely under the general heading for the church in question.

Abborthkoc, Matthew de, 42
Abbroyot, John de, 93
Aberdeen
  bishop of, 28, 65, 211; *see also* Deyn, William de; Kininmund, Alexander de (I); Kininmund, Alexander de (II); Rate, John de; Tyningham, Adam de
  canon of, 74n
  canonries and prebends of, 67, 90, 95, 117; Cruden, 112; Oyne, 54
  dean of, 62, 207
  deanery of, 41, 51n, 95, 176–7
  diocese of, taxation in, 24, 36, 74
  precentorship of, 93
  royal grant to church of, 39, 204
Abernyte (dioc. Dunkeld), 24
absenteeism, *see* non-residence
Abyrcromby, Alexander de, 43
Acaster Malbis (dioc. York), 90
Acciaiuoli of Florence, 76n
Ad Regimen, 91
Aigrefeuille, William de, cardinal, 43
Akum, John de, 97, 248
Albert, Stephen, cardinal, 43, 94, 118n
Albornoz, Peter Gomez de, cardinal, 94
Aldburgh (dioc. York), 107
Aldingham in Furness (dioc. York), 45–6
Alfred, king of England, 18
alien priories, 87, 126–7, 139, 154, 213–14
aliens
  provisions to, 91, 133, 134, 136–8, 145, 146, 151, 153–4, 156, 160, 220, 256; *see also under individual clerks*
  royal seizure of benefices of, 65, 94, 110, 114, 138–41, 144, 151, 160, 163, 210, 255–6
Aligod, John, 105
Allerthorpe (dioc. York), 251
Allerton, Ralph de, 105
Allerton, Thomas de, 235
Allerton, 166
Allertonshire, 17, 166, 185
Alnwick (dioc. Durham), abbot of, 167, 251
Altyre (dioc. Moray), 205
Alvie (dioc. Moray), 205
Ampleforth (dioc. York), vicarage of, 134
  see also York, canonries and prebends of
Anagni, 1
Andrew, bishop of Argyll, 197
Andrew, bishop-elect of Dunkeld, 62
Angus, William de, 97
annates, 15n, 33–55, 75, 76, 81, 145, 157, 178, 179, 180
  assessments for, 34–8, 40, 55
  early levies of, 23, 33, 69, 70
  excuses for non-payment of, 44–7, 50
  liability for, 33, 38–9, 59, 145, 176, 219; after death of provisor, 42–3
  link between provisions and, 12, 33, 133, 141–2, 255
  on expectative graces, 38, 40, 153, 155, 156
  on provisions to regulars, 31, 38, 219, 222, 223
  payments direct to Camera of, 39
  relative slowness of payment of, 29, 62, 64
  royal interference in collection of, 41–2, 44–5, 68, 222, 253
  subcollectors of, 70–1
  yield from, 47–9, 57

Index

Appleby, John de, 93
Appleby, Thomas de, bishop of Carlisle, 188–9, 203, 204
  appointment of, 192, 201, 212
  licences to, 205, 244, 246–7
  relations with papal collectors of, 20, 52–3
Appleby (dioc. Carlisle), church of St Laurence in, 111
appropriations
  interference by provisions with, 96, 119–20, 128–9, 147–8, 149, 177
  payment of annates on, 33, 38, 39, 219
Aquitaine, papal collectors from, 15, 68
Arbroath (dioc. St Andrews)
  abbey of, 104, 169, 224
  abbot of, 228
Ardelors, Ingram de, 96
Ardene, William de, 117–18, 178, 208
Argyll
  archdeacon of, 90
  bishop of, 73, 74; *see also* Andrew; Ergadia, Martin de
  claim to see of, 89, 204
  diocese of, 90, 171
Arlam, Hugh de, 157, 179
Armagh, archbishop of, 32
Armstrong, Gilbert, 96, 110
Arreton (dioc. Winchester), 66
Arundel, earl of, 247
Arundel, Edmund, 58
Arundel, Thomas, 112
Askeby, John de, 247
Askeby, Robert de, 113, 177
Askham, Thomas de, 134
Aslacby, William Couper de, 128
Asshebourn, John de, 113
Assier, Rigaud d', papal collector, 66
Asti, merchants of, 15
Aston-en-le-Morthen (dioc. York), 58
Astorga, bishop of, *see* Peter, bishop of Astorga
Atwick (dioc. York), 105
Aubert, Audoin, cardinal, 56
Aubert, Stephen, cardinal, *see* Innocent VI, pope
Auckland, Robert de, 167–8
Auckland, collegiate church of, 84
  canon of, 249
  prebends of: Byers Green, 46; Shildon, 101
audientia litterarum contradictarum, 11
auditors, papal, *see* Rota
Aughton (dioc. York), 177
Augustinian canons, 192, 215, 220, 225, 227, 245
Avignon
  chaplaincy in, 66
  clerk from, 120
  reasons for Papacy's exile in, 1–2
Avignon Registers, 80–2, 232n
Axminster (dioc. Exeter), 110
Aymeric, bishop of Lodève, 181
Ayr (dioc. Glasgow), 40
Aysgarth (dioc. York), 247

Balcaska, Thomas de, 97
Balliol, Edward, 160, 197
Ballothyn, John de, 226
Bannockburn, battle of, 24–5
Barker, Robert, 244
Barking (dioc. Norwich), 74
Barnard Castle, John of, 94
barratry, legislation against, 161
Barton, Henry de, 43
Barwick (dioc. York), 232
Bateman, John, *see* Couton, John Bateman de
Bath and Wells, expectative graces in diocese of, 107n
  see also Wells
Baumburgh, John de, 116
Beauchamp, Philip de, 178n, 247
Beaufort, Henry, cardinal, 212
Beaufort, Roger de, 76, 158
Beaumont, Lewis de, bishop of Durham, 165–6, 194
Beauvale (dioc. York), priory of, 216
Beck, John de, 44
Bedlington (dioc. Durham), 35, 134
Bekingham, Simon de, 100, 101n
Bell, Richard, 128
Bell, William, 192
Bellers, Hugh, *see* Middelton, Hugh Bellers de
Bemaken (dioc. Sodor), friary at, 217
Benedict XII, pope, 8, 60, 198
  provisions by, 79, 91, 133; to aliens, 138; to regulars, 220n
  relations with regulars of, 215–16, 219, 220n, 221, 226
  taxes levied by, 25, 55, 191
Benedict XIII, pope, 224
Benedictines, 215, 221, 227
benefices, lawsuits over, **173–82**
Bermondsey (dioc. Winchester), priory of, 14
Beverley, Robert de, 223
Beverley, William de, 101
Beverley, collegiate church of, 84, 185

Beverley (*cont.*)
canonries and prebends of, 49, 93, 121, 204, 241; St Katherine's Altar, 58; St Mary's Altar, 110; St Peter's Altar, 180–2
provostship of, 100
Birnie (dioc. Moray), 205
Biseth, Thomas, 221
bishops,
appointment of, **191–204**
contacts with Papacy of, **204–11**
examinations of, 200–1
mandates to travel to diocese to, 201
petitions to Papacy by, 88, 204–5
regular, 203
see also under individual bishops
Bishop Wearmouth (dioc. Durham), 95, 117–19, 137, 153–4, 208, 235
Black, John, 221
Black Death, 21, 28, 106, 115, 122, 141, 145, 162, 202, 206, 211, 215, 232, 233, 239, 246, 255
Blairgowrie (dioc. St Andrews), 218
Blakeborn, Henry de, 95
Blankefrontis, Joan, 226
Blebury, John de, 181–2
Blida, Adam de, 106
Blois, Charles de, 210
Bohemia, 14
king of, 210
Bokingham, John de, 92–3, 131
Bolton, Hugh de, 177
Bolton, Matthew de, 101–2
Bolton (dioc. Durham), 113
Bolton (dioc. York), priory of, 108
Bolton Percy (dioc. York), 202
Bonde, William, 41
Boner, Robert, *see* Synelington, Robert Boner de
Boniface VIII, pope, 1, 62n, 91, 164, 217, 218, 243
Boniface IX, pope, 169
Bononia, James de, 136
Bordon, John de, 60
Bosco, Andrew de, 90
Bothevil, John de, 58
Boulogne, Guy de, cardinal-bishop of Porto, 194
Boulton, John de, 119, 131
Bower, Walter, chronicler, 192
Bowet, Henry, 127
Bowness (dioc. Carlisle), 46, 48, 53
Boxley (dioc. Canterbury), 66
Boyle, William, 23, 111
Brantingham (dioc. York), 44, 137, 247
Braydeley, William de, 60
Brechin
archdeaconry of, 67
bishop of, 207; *see also* Locrys, Patrick de; Moray, Adam de; Wilde, Philip
bishopric of, taxation of, 188
canonry of, 204
chancellor of, 203
dean of, 169, 203
diocese of, taxation in, 36
Brechton, William de, 236
Brereton, John de, 251
Brétigny, treaty of, 24, 87, 234
Bridkirk, Thomas de, 131, 169, 249
Bridlington (dioc. York), priory of, 104, 105, 165
Brigham (dioc. York), 244
Brittany, duchy of, 210
Bromley, Roger de, 116
Brompton, Robert de, 54
Brompton (dioc. York), 93, 137, 145, 202
Brouthon, Stephen de, 168
Bruges, 26, 65, 77
concordat at, 26, 156–8, 179
papal court at, 26, 157–8
Brunnum, Adam de, 127
Bubwith (dioc. York), 208
Bucton, Thomas de, 60
Buggewille, Reginald de, 100–1
Buittle (dioc. Whithorn), 173
bulls, papal, control of import and export of, 136, 151, 154
Bulmer, Robert de, 101
Bur, Alexander, bishop of Moray, 30, 90, 192, 208
Bur, Thomas, 86, 111
Burstall (dioc. York), priory of, 107, 127
Burton, Nicholas de, 132
Bury, Richard de, bishop of Durham, 186n, 195, 206, 208
appointment of, 194–5, 199, 201
Bury St Edmunds (dioc. Norwich), abbot of, 207
Bydik, Richard, 101
Byland (dioc. York), abbey of, 208

Cabasolle, Philip de, cardinal, 94
Cabrespino, John de, papal collector, 15, 66, 151
accounts of, 48–9, 52, 70
benefices of, 67
collection of annates by, 35, 44, 48–50, 52, 53, 78
collection of census by, 20–1, 78
collection of intercalary fruits by, 56–7

collection of legacies to Holy Land by, 60
commissions to, 14
contacts with king of, 49–50, 65, 68–9
ineffectiveness of, 14, 20–1, 49–50, 53, 78
subcollectors of, 72; *see also* Caroloco, John de
Caithness
bishop of, 28, 207; *see also* Drumbreck, Malcolm de; Fingask, Thomas de; Moray, Alan de
chancellorship of, 90
earl of, *see* Maddadson, Harald
levy of Peter's Pence in, 18
Calabre, William de, 89
Calais, 115
Caldbeck (dioc. Carlisle), 47
Caldeu, John de, 177
Caldwell, John, 40
Cambridge, university of, 87, 244
Cambuskenneth (dioc. St Andrews), abbey of, 218
camerarius, papal, 10, 13, 205
Cammon, William de, 40
Campbell, John, 236
Campbell, Mariota, 236
Campeden, John de, 39, 93
Campeden, Walter de, 99
Canterbury
abbot of St Augustine's at, 31
archbishop of, 18, 25, 31, 32, 190, 198; *see also* Islip, Simon; Langham, Simon; Stratford, John
court of, 174
Capocci, Nicholas, cardinal, 145
Cardoill, William de, 127
Cariti, Bertrand, 18, 74n
Carleton, Thomas de, 136
Carlisle
archdeacon of, 53, 166
bishop of, 172, 185, 188; expectative grace to benefice in gift of, 101–2; *see also* Appleby, Thomas de; Halton, John de; Ireton, Ralph; Kirkby, John de; Welton, Gilbert de
chapter of, 168, 200
diocese of, 166; dispensations in, 209; papal provisions in, 105, 112; plague in, 21; taxation in, 17, 37, 47–9
parliament of (1307), 132, 134, 142
prior of, 25; *see also* Horncastle, John de
prior of Dominicans at, 166
priory of, 203; payment of census by, 19, 20–1, 78, 219
Caroloco, John de, papal subcollector, 14, 49, 51, 53, 56, 71–2
Caron, Alexander de, 96, 119
Carpentras, 219
Carrick, John de, 112, 199
Carrington (dioc. St Andrews), 218
Carrothurs, Adam de, 96
Carthusians, 216
Cartmel (dioc. York), prior of, 41, 221
Catton (dioc. York), 46
Cavers (dioc. Glasgow), 119–20
census, 19–21, 55, 64, 78, 219
Châlons, canonry of, 67
chaplains, papal, 67, 89, 95, 180, 192, 204
appointment of, 226, 250–1
Charles V, king of France, 87, 153
Château Gaillard, 205
Chester, Richard de, 98, 131
Chester (dioc. Coventry and Lichfield), abbot of, 207
Chester-le-Street, collegiate church of, 84
canon of, 247
dean of, 169
deanery of, 101, 179
prebend of: Pelton, 101
Chestrefeld, John de, 35, 93
Cheyne, John, 152
Chrysopolis, bishop of, *see* Salkeld, Thomas de
Cistercians, 5, 63, 170, 214, 216, 228
Cîteaux, abbey of, 19, 219
Clairvaux, abbey of, 214–15
Clapham (dioc. York), 245
Clave, Gerlac de, 145
Clement IV, pope, 91
Clement V, pope, 37, 70n, 91, 170, 220n
Clement VI, pope (Peter Roger), 2, 8–9, 88, 114, 190, 201, 205, 249
appointment of judges and conservators by, 167, 170, 171
attitude to pluralism of, 243
dispensations and licences of, 204, 232
provisions by, 8–9, 66, 91, 93n, 100n, 113, 121, 122, 133, 204, 208, 256; expectative graces, 89–90, 103, 104, 105, 106, 107, 136, 145, 146, 224, 254; to aliens, 110, 114, 133, 134–5, 136–8, 154, 254, 256; to bishops, 144, 187, 196, 198, 199; to regulars, 220n
relations with England of, 10, 65, 115, 133–44, 159, 163, 196
relations with France of, 9, 10, 133
relations with regulars of, 216, 217, 220n, 224

Clement VI (*cont.*)
revocation of expectative graces of, 95, 110, 111
taxes levied by, 32, 33, 56, 133
Clement VII, pope (Robert of Geneva), 61, 94
Clervaus, Thomas, 95, 118, 119
Cliffe (dioc. York), 40
Clifford, John Pole de, 104
Clifton, George de, 239
Clipston, Robert de, 135
Clisseby, John de, 242
Clitheroe (dioc. Coventry and Lichfield), 54n
Cluniacs, 126, 168, 170–2, 213–14
Cluny
abbey of, 214
abbot of, 65, 214
Cockersand (dioc. York)
abbey of, 128–9, 176
abbot of, 188
Codelyng, William, 218
Coldingham (dioc. St Andrews), prior of, 70
collectors, papal, **64–78**
accounts of, 6, 10, 16, 33, 75–7
see also Assier, Rigaud d'; Cabrespino, John de; Concoreto, Itier de; Deyn, William de; Donkan, John; Garnerii, Arnald; Grenlaw, William de; Peblis; John de; Pelegrini, Hugh; Pelegrini, Raymond; Sistre, Bernard de; Testa, William; Vicia, Baiamundus de
collegiate churches, expectative graces to, **100–1**
see also Auckland; Beverley; Chester-le-Street; Darlington; Howden; Lanchester; Norton; Ripon; Southwell
commends, 93, 202
Comminges, John Raymond de, cardinal, 140
Comyn, William, 95
Concoreto, Itier de, papal collector, 13n
conservators, 67, 170–3, 182, 207, 228
Consueta, 147, 152, 242
Conveth (dioc. St Andrews), 95
Cornwall, archdeaconry of, 90
Counton, Elias de, 178
Coupar (dioc. Dunkeld), abbot of, 170
Couper, William, *see* Aslacby, William Couper de
Coupland, rural deanery of, 17
Couton, John Bateman de, 248
Coventre, Walter de, bishop of Dunblane, 93, 95, 176
Coventre, William de, 58
Coventry and Lichfield
bishop of, 53n, 54n, 174, 238; *see also* Stretton, Robert
diocese of, papal provisions in, 108n
see also Lichfield
Crakanthorp, John de, 167
Craven, Thomas de, 226
Crayke (dioc. Durham), 185
Crécy, battle of, 115, 153, 210
Crediton, collegiate church of, prebend of, 247
Crichton (dioc. St Andrews), 59n
Croft (dioc. York), 127–8
Cromdole, John de, 45, 97, 109
Crondall (dioc. Winchester), 66
Crophill, Alan de, 120
Crossraguel (dioc. Glasgow), abbey of, 218n
Crosthwaite (dioc. Carlisle), 43, 48, 53, 127
Culdees, 5
Culter (dioc. Glasgow), 97
Cum ex eo, 243–4
Cum universi, 5, 18, 184, 185
Cumberland, 17, 25, 35
Cunerys, David de, 96
curia, papal, Frenchness of, 2
curiales, 88, 91, 123, 181, 192–3, 254
Curry, William de, 93, 171
Cusornio, Aymeric de, 97

Dale, Roger del, 107
Dalmehoy, Hugh de, 250
Dalston (dioc. Carlisle), 189
Dalton, Thomas de, 244–5
Dalton, William de, 150
Dalton, William de, 247
Damascus, archbishop of, 206
Dante, 1
Darlington, collegiate church of, 84
prebend of, 132
Daventre, Ralph, 42
David II, king of Scotland, 162, 187, 197, 205, 217
divorce of, 161
imprisonment and ransom of, 5, 23–4, 70, 73n, 87, 160, 162
petitions to pope of, 87, 192, 251
presentations to benefices by, 58, 116
Deer (dioc. Aberdeen), abbot of, 59
Den, Robert de, papal subcollector, 28, 73, 116, 197
Denbigh (dioc. St Asaph), Carmelite prior of, 172

Denton, John de, 177–8
Derby, John de, 177
Derby, Richard de, 39
Deuza, Gaucelin, cardinal, 140
Deyn, William de, bishop of Aberdeen, papal collector, 15, 59, 73, 203
Dingthon, William de, 241
dispensations, 38–9, 66, 204, 205, 251–2
  for non-residence, 243–6
  for pluralism, 117, 241–3
  from illegitimacy, 97, 209, 226, 230, 231, 239–41
  to be ordained under age, 97, 209, 239, 246–7, 255
  to marry, 10, 149, 152, 209, 230, 235–8, 254
Domar, Gerald, cardinal, 133, 134, 138, 254
Donkan, John, bishop of Sodor, papal collector, 188, 189
Donke, Richard, 168n
Donke, William, 168
Douglas, earl of, 119
Douglas, Hugh de, 116
Douglas, John de, 237
Douglas (dioc. Glasgow), 67
Dover, 69
Drax, Richard de, 54, 181, 182
Driffeld, William de, 92
Dringhow, William de, 222–3
Drumbreck, John de, 224
Drumbreck, Malcolm de, bishop of Caithness, 29
Drummond, John de, 237
Dryburgh (dioc. St Andrews), abbey of, 63
Dublin, 187
  prebend of, 66
Dugaldi, John, 90
Dunblane
  altar in cathedral of, 237
  archdeacon of, 59
  bishop of, 86, 211, 218, 237; chaplain of, 86; *see also* Coventre, Walter de; Maurice; William
  deanery of, 176
  diocese of, 171
Dundrennan (dioc. Whithorn), abbey of, 46
Dunfermline (dioc. St Andrews)
  abbey of, 103, 109, 169, 218, 221
  abbot of, 31, 170, 171, 228
  monk of, 240n
Dunkeld
  archdeacon of, 171
  bishop of, 223; expectative graces to benefices in gift of, 109; *see also* Andrew; Luce, John; Monymusk, Michael de; Peblis, John de; Pilmor, Richard de; Strathern, Duncan de
  bishopric of, taxation of, 188
  deanery of, 38n
  prebends of, 90, 203; Forgandenny, 109; Rattray, 97
  precentorship of, 40
Dunnottar (dioc. St Andrews), 93
Dunoon (dioc. Argyll), 204
Duns, Thomas de, 109
Durham
  archdeacon of, 167
  archdeaconry of, 90
  bishop of, 6, 17, 168, 222, 250; expectative graces to benefices in gift of, 101, 105; *see also* Beaumont, Lewis de; Bury, Richard de; Hatfield, Thomas de
  church of St Nicholas in, 101
  diocesan authorities of, 120
  diocese of: dispensations in, 209; papal provisions in, 105, 112; taxation in, 17, 47–9
  official of, 167
  prior of, 25, 167, 169, 228, 249
  priory of, 31n, 100, 166, 169, 185, 194–5, 196, 200, 227; expectative graces to benefices in gift of, 101, 134n, 136
  relationship with York of, 172, 185, 189–91
Dysart (dioc. St Andrews), 109

Easby (dioc. York), monk of, 226
Easington (dioc. York), 129
East Grinstead (dioc. Chichester), 66
East Retford (dioc. York), 107
East Riding, archdeaconry of, 110, 131, 138, 245
Eboraco (or Gizerbortz), John de, 60n
Edinburgh, college of St Giles in, 19
Edmund of Langley, son of Edward III, 149, 238
Edward I, king of England, 4, 6, 37, 132
Edward II, king of England, 4, 115, 186
Edward III, king of England, 14, 68, 72, 115, 126n, 141, 144–5, 152, 153, 156, 163, 179, 186, 210, 214, 219, 233n, 238
  actions against provisions by, 65, 110, 134

Edward III (*cont.*)
and appointment of bishops, 194, 195, 197, 198–9
and papal taxation, 21, 22–3, 24, 41–2, 64, 253
involvement in Scotland by, 116, 119, 197
petitions to pope of, 87
presentations to benefices by, 87, 114, 116, 119, 127, 134, 135–6
relations with France of, 24, 65, 115, 125
Edward, prince of Wales, son of Edward III, 24, 87, 145
Edzell (dioc. St Andrews), 67
Elgin (dioc. Moray), 173, 205
Ellerton (dioc. York), priory of, 177
Ellon (dioc. Aberdeen), 43, 74, 89, 96
Elon, Adam de, 96
Ely, bishop of, 25
Emeldon, William de, 116
Emery, William, 86
Empryngham, John de, 72
Ergadia, Angus de, 89, 96, 197, 203–4
Ergadia, Martin de, bishop of Argyll, 29, 171, 197, 203
Erskin, Robert de, 248
Eskiheved, Thomas de, 43
Essex, archdeaconry of, 71
Eston, John de, 117
Euphemia, countess of Moray, 236
Execrabilis, 91, 242, 243
Exeter, expectative graces in diocese of, 107n
expectative graces, **98–111**
in forma communi pauperum, 38, 79, 83, 84, 85, 102–8, 111, 134n; number of, 104–5, 145, 146, 224
payment of annates on, 38, 40, 153, 155, 156
success of, 98, 102, 106–8
Eyr, Thomas, 248

Falkirk (dioc. St Andrews), 54, 109
Fargiis, Raymond de, cardinal, 140
Farndale (dioc. York), friary at, 216
Fearn (dioc. Ross), abbey of, 63
Fercythe, Peter, 40
Ferriby, John de, 42
Ferriby, William de, 246
Fettercairn (dioc. St Andrews), 74n
Fetteresso (dioc. St Andrews), 96
Fewston (dioc. York), 106, 107
Fieschi, John de, 44
Fieschi, Luca, cardinal, 18
Fieschi, Nicholinus de, 139
Fieschi, William de, 139
Fingask, Thomas de, bishop of Caithness, 30, 200, 207
Fingloy, Thomas de la, 226
Fishlake (dioc. York), 137
Fishwyk, Richard de, 233–4
Flagellants, 211, 249
Flanders, clerk from, 59
Flandrini, Peter, cardinal, 154, 157
Fleming, Gilbert, 62, 95, 207
Fogow, Richard de, 110
Forde, William de, 99
Fores, Richard de, 227
Foston (dioc. York), 231
Fountains (dioc. York)
abbey of, 43, 53
abbot of, 174, 222
France
king of, payments by papal collectors to, 76, 158
provisions to monasteries in, 220
Freton, Roger de, 51, 112, 181
friars, 213, 216–17
Austin, 63n, 188, 217, 235
Carmelite, 172, 207, 227, 235, 248
Dominican, 154, 166, 203, 217, 226
Franciscan, 217
of Holy Cross, 216–17, 228n
Frichi, John de, 226
Fridaythorpe (dioc. York), vicar of, 52
fruits wrongfully received, 57–60, 75, 157
Fullour, John, 251
Furness (dioc. York)
abbey of, 214, 218
rural deanery of, 188

Gaetani, Anibaldus, cardinal-bishop of Tusculum, 42, 95, 140, 159, 245
Gaetani, John, *see* Orsini, John Gaetani de
Galloway, 59n, 184, 185, 186, 187
see also Whithorn
Galon, Peter, 118, 177
Gamrie (dioc. Aberdeen), 90, 111
Ganon (or Govan), John, 119, 120
Garforth (dioc. York), 101
Gargrave (dioc. York), 165
Garnerii, Arnald, papal collector, 15, 54n, 61, 65, 66, 71, 158
accounts of, 38, 49, 70, 76, 77
benefices of, 67
collection of annates by, 35, 38, 40, 41, 43, 45, 46–7, 49, 50, 53, 55, 69
collection of census by, 20
collection of subsidy by, 26, 76

commissions to, 14–15
contacts with king of, 68, 69
opposition to, 15, 50, 69, 153, 154
subcollectors and assistants of, 72; *see also* Nigris, Laurence de
Gateshead (dioc. Durham), 169
Gaucelin, cardinal, 18
Gedling (dioc. York), 244n
Gemelyng, John de, 128
Geneva, Robert of, cardinal, 118, 154
see also Clement VII, pope
Geneva, 198
Gerald of Wales, 18
Germany, 14
Ghent, abbot of St Bavon's in, 21
Giffard, Hugh, 238
Giffart, John, 93
Giles, cardinal-bishop of Tusculum, 117
Gilling (dioc. York), 44
Gisboure, Roger de, 226
Gizerbortz, John de, *see* Eboraco, John de
Glasgow, 171
archdeacon of, 228
archdeaconry of, 244
bishop of, 90, 211, 218, 236, 245; *see also* Rae, William; Wardlaw, Walter de
canonries and prebends of, 67, 90, 93, 108–9, 110, 116n, 199, 203, 206, 243; Cardross, 109; Durisdeer, 92; Old Roxburgh, 116–17; Renfrew, 109; Stobo, 39, 57, 67
canons of, 171
cathedral of, 171; payment of census by, 19, 20
chancellorship of, 95
chapter of, 208
dean of, 119, 208
deanery of, 67, 242
diocese of, 171
subdean of, 171
treasurership of, 67n
Glencairn (dioc. Glasgow), 67n, 90
Glendonwym, Matthew de, 119–20
Glenluce (dioc. Whithorn), 186
Godewyk, John, 101
Gomez, Peter, *see* Albornoz, Peter Gomez de
Good Parliament (1376), 15, 26, 153, 155, 158
Govan, John, *see* Ganon, John
Graham, Agnes, 237
Graunt, Thomas le, 93
Graystanes, Robert de, 194–5, 196–7, 199, 200
Greatham (dioc. Durham), 42n, 131
Gregory X, pope, 217
Gregory XI, pope (Peter Roger), 1, 2, 9, 87n, 190
appointment of collectors by, 14
appointment of judges by, 171
appointment of papal chaplains by, 226, 250–1
attitude to pluralism of, 157
career before election of, 66
dispensations and licences of, 206, 232
provisions by, 92, 118, 119, 155–6, 157, 199; expectative graces, 105; to aliens, 94, 153–4, 156
relations with England of, 9, 153–8, 179
relations with regulars of, 216, 217, 226, 250
relations with Scotland of, 161–2, 211
taxes levied by, 23, 26–7, 33n, 38, 56, 61, 153, 155–6, 161
Grene, John del, 250
Grenlaw, William de, 67n
Grenlaw, William de, papal collector, 38n, 39, 50, 74n, 86, 189, 235, 250
account of, 16, 20, 37, 47, 59, 73, 75, 77, 189
benefices of, 46, 57, 67, 242–3
collection of annates by, 37, 40, 47
collection of census by, 20
collection of fruits wrongfully received by, 59
collection of procurations by, 63
commissions to, 15, 54n, 61, 63, 65
subcollectors of, 72–4; *see also* Tyningham, Adam de
Grimaud, Angelicus, cardinal, 57, 113, 151
Grimaud, William, *see* Urban V, pope
Grosseteste, Robert, bishop of Lincoln, 79
Guînes, treaty of, 144–5
Guisborough (dioc. York), canon of, 226
Gunello, William de, 176
Gunfort, William, 42
Gynewell, John de, bishop of Lincoln, 98
Gysburn, Roger de, 108

Habert, John, 181
Haddington (dioc. St Andrews), priory of, 103
Haltemprice (dioc. York), prior of, 107
Halton, John de, bishop of Carlisle, 36, 37, 70n
Hamburg, church of, 104
Harkars, Thomas, 92, 110, 243
Harold, John, 90
Harrow (dioc. London), 66
Hartburn (dioc. Durham), 167, 244

Haselbeche, Adam de, 113, 179
Hatfield, Thomas de, bishop of Durham, 203, 205, 208, 209, 210, 244, 248
  appointment of, 195–6, 199, 200, 201
  licences to, 239
  relations with papal collectors of, 52
  relations with York of, 172, 189–91, 207
  subsidy levied by, 28
Haughton-le-Skerne (dioc. Durham), 42n, 135
Hawick (dioc. Glasgow), 90
Hayton, John de, 41
Healaugh (dioc. York), priory of, 215
Hebrides, 187, 188
Helwell, John de, 179–80
Hemingbrough (dioc. York), 47, 140
Hemyngburgh, John de, 107
Hemyngburgh, Richard de, 107
Henry, duke of Lancaster, 87, 88, 247, 251
Henry III, king of England, 21
Henry VIII, king of England, 125
Henry, vicar of Ellon, 42–3
Henry, John, 43, 53n
Heppe, Robert de, 94
Hereford, bishop of, *see* Trillek, John
heresy, 189n, 248–9
Heriz, John, 167
Hervethorp, John de, 241
Hesille, John de, 177
Heslerton (dioc. York), 106
Hethe, Nicholas de, 94, 135
Hewden, George Sicilie de, 117
Hexham (dioc. York)
  prior of, 172
  priory of, 168
Hexhamshire, 172
Holland, 249n
Holm Cultram (dioc. Carlisle)
  abbey of, 53, 63, 218, 227
  abbot of, 166, 225
Holy Land
  journeys to, 219–20, 248
  legacies to, 59, 60
Holyrood (dioc. St Andrews)
  abbey of, 19, 203, 221, 226, 228
  canons of, 54, 109, 226
Honorius III, pope, 20
Horncastle, John de, prior of Carlisle, 20–1, 192, 193–4, 196–7, 200, 203
Horncastle (dioc. Lincoln), 66
Hornsea (dioc. York), 137, 140, 235
Horribilis, 147, 152n
Hospitallers, 105, 107, 128, 170, 219–20, 248
Houghton-le-Spring (dioc. Durham), 137, 154, 157
Howden, collegiate church of, 84
  prebends of, 54, 100, 173, 177; Barnby, 180; Skelton, 157, 179–80; Thorpe, 245
Howdenshire, 17, 185
Hugh, Carmelite prior of Denbigh, 172
Hull, John de, 223
Hull (dioc. York), Charterhouse in, 216
Hundbit, Walter, 42, 86
Hungary, 14
Hunsingore (dioc. York), 107
Hustewaite, Thomas de, 223
Hutton Bushel (dioc. York), 44

Idvies (dioc. St Andrews), 93
Ikham, Thomas de, 130, 178n
  see also Wykham, Thomas Mount de
Ilkley (dioc. York), 46
Inchaffray (dioc. Dunblane), abbot of, 203
income taxes, 13n, 22–7, 55, 64, 69, 70, 219, 253
  assessments for, 22, 23, 24–5, 26
  for ransom of David II, 23–4, 70, 73n, 160
  see also subsidies
indulgences, 231–4
  see also indults to choose confessor
indults
  to celebrate mass before dawn and in interdict, 205, 235
  to choose confessor, 205, 225, 231–3, 234–5; *see also* indulgences
  to collate
  to benefices, 99, 180, 206–7
  to eat flesh-meat, 225–6
  to have churches and cemeteries reconciled by priest, 205, 245
  to have portable altar, 205, 235
  to visit by deputy, 205, 245
Ingelby, Henry de, 45, 100, 113, 135, 152
Innerpeffray, Malcolm de, 197
Innocent III, pope, 17, 18, 21, 22
Innocent VI, pope (Stephen Aubert), 9, 201, 249, 251
  appointment of collectors by, 14, 15
  appointment of judges by, 167, 181
  attitude to pluralism of, 243
  career before election of, 140, 159
  dispensations and licences of, 117n, 232, 245
  provisions by, 66, 83, 122, 243; expectative graces, 105, 110, 111n, 145, 146; to aliens, 145; to bishops, 187, 194, 203

relations with England of, 144–5
relations with France of, 144
relations with regulars of, 227, 235
revocation of expectative graces of Clement VI by, 95, 110, 111
taxes levied by, 21, 23–6, 56, 62
intercalary fruits, 55–7, 64, 71–2, 151, 253
Inverarity (dioc. St Andrews), 58, 93, 176
Inverkeithing (dioc. St Andrews), friary at, 217
Inverness (dioc. Moray), 169
Iona (dioc. Sodor)
abbey of, 223, 227
abbot of, 223–4
Ireland, papal taxation in, 13, 77, 189
Ireton, Ralph, bishop of Carlisle, 168
Irton, William de, 95, 227, 245
Isabella, queen of England, 247
Isle of Man, 31, 168, 188, 217
Isles, Bartholomew of the, 241
Isles, Mary of the, 237
Isles, diocese of, *see* Sodor
Islip, Simon, archbishop of Canterbury, 31n
Italy, wars in, 2, 13, 24, 26, 152, 156, 158, 210

James I, king of Scotland, 161
Jarum, Robert de, 94
Jedburgh (dioc. Glasgow), canon of, 240
Jervaulx (dioc. York), abbot of, 23
Jesmond (dioc. Durham), 45
Johannis, Hamo, 74n
John, abbot of Holyrood, 221
John, burgess of Linlithgow, 171
John, king of England, 21
John II, king of France, 24, 65, 87–8, 158, 159
John XXII, pope, 175, 186, 191, 200, 202
appointment of judges and conservators by, 166, 172, 174
attitude to pluralism of, 241–2
dispensations of, 240
provisions by, 79, 91; to aliens, 117, 137, 138; to regulars, 220
relations with regulars of, 220
taxes levied by, 17, 18, 21, 22, 23, 55, 64
John of Gaunt, earl of Richmond, son of Edward III, 65, 99
Jubilee, 91, 94, 211, 221, 227, 233
judges-delegate, 164, 165–70, 174, 175, 182, 210, 228

Karale, John de, 103–4
Kelet, Richard de, 221
Kelleby, Ralph de, 125
Kelloe (dioc. Durham), 244
Kelso (dioc. St Andrews)
abbey of, 63
abbot of, 31, 208
Ker, Brice, 90, 111
Kerrot, Robert, 53
Ketenis, John de, 62
Ketenis, Simon de, 74n
Kexby (dioc. York), 190
Keyingham (dioc. York), 54, 129
Kieretti, Guy, 244
Kilcoman (dioc. Sodor), 173
Kildesby, Robert de, 52, 94
Kildesby, William de, 100, 127, 128, 198–9
Kildwick (dioc. York), 97
Killingwoldgraves (dioc. York), 234
Kilmany (dioc. St Andrews), 96
Kilwinning (dioc. Glasgow), abbot of, 31, 171, 203
Kininmund, Alexander de (I), bishop of Aberdeen, 192
Kininmund, Alexander de (II), bishop of Aberdeen, 73–4, 86, 205
Kininmund, Thomas de, 95
Kinkell (dioc. Aberdeen), 58, 116
Kinloss (dioc. Moray), abbey of, 227
Kinnell (dioc. St Andrews), 96
Kinnernie (dioc. Aberdeen), 224
Kinnettles (dioc. St Andrews), 24, 42, 86
'Kircome' (or 'Kritome'), 59, 193n
Kirk Ella (dioc. York), 137
Kirkby, John de, bishop of Carlisle, 23, 193, 203, 205
appointment of, 191, 200
Kirkby, William de, 98
Kirkbymoorside (dioc. York), 244
Kirkchrist (dioc. Whithorn), 59n
Kirkcolm (dioc. Whithorn), 59n
Kirkcowan (dioc. Whithorn), 59n
Kirkden, *see* Idvies
Kirkennan, *see* Kirkcowan
Kirketon, William de, 250
Kirkham (dioc. York), 129
Kirkinner (dioc. Whithorn), 59n
Kirkland (dioc. Carlisle), 53
Kirkliston, *see* Liston
Kirkmabreck (dioc. Whithorn), 46
Kirknewton (dioc. Durham), 35, 94
Kirkstall (dioc. York), abbot of, 31n, 214, 223
'Kritome', *see* 'Kircome'
Kylington, John de, 223
Kylwos, Alexander de, 23, 73n, 93

Lacer, Robert, 108
Lamborn, Simon, 152
Lanark, Adam de, bishop of Whithorn, 30, 187, 203, 226
Lanark (dioc. Glasgow), friary at, 217
Lancaster, duke of, *see* Henry, duke of Lancaster
Lancaster, earl of, *see* Thomas, earl of Lancaster
Lancaster (dioc. York)
  prior of, 49
  priory of, 146
Lanchester, collegiate church of, 84
  deanery of, 177
  prebend of, 66
Landallis, William de, bishop of St Andrews, 192, 201, 211
Landoy, Richard de, 58
Lane, Richard atte, *see* Walton, Richard atte Lane de
Lang, Thomas, 96
Langeton, Peter de, 110
Langham, Simon, archbishop of Canterbury, cardinal, 94, 118, 119, 153–4, 159
Langholme, John de, 53
Langton (dioc. York), 145
Laurencekirk, *see* Conveth
Leake (dioc. York), 90, 135–6, 152, 243
Leche, John, notary, 250
Leche, John, rector of Hawick, 90
Lenevaunt, Walter, 95
Lenton (dioc. York), prior of, 174
Lesmahagow (dioc. Glasgow), prior of, 171, 173
Lethnot (dioc. Brechin), 96
letters conservatory, *see* conservators
Leverton, Simon de, 227
Leverton, William de, 100
Lewes (dioc. Chichester), prior of, 14
Lewis IV, emperor, 3
Lichfield
  canonry and prebend of, 174
  canons of, 166
  treasurer of, 66
  treasurership of, 66
  see also Coventry and Lichfield
Liddell (dioc. York), 216
Limoges, sack of, 158
Limousin, 2
Lincoln, 172n
  bishop of, 92n, 168, 200–1, 223; chantry of, 168; *see also* Grosseteste, Robert; Gynewell, John de
  canon of, 176
  canonries and prebends of, 66, 242, 247; Welton Beckhall, 74
  official of, 23
  prebendary of, 173
Lindsay, Isabella, 236
Linköping, 50
Linlithgow (dioc. St Andrews), 171
Lintrathen (dioc. St Andrews), 228
Liston (dioc. St Andrews), 89, 116, 204
Llandaff
  bishop of, 217
  canon of, 209
loans
  by papal collectors, 68, 69, 77
  contracted by bishops, 27, 28, 201–2
Locrys, Patrick de, bishop of Brechin, 30, 31, 201, 203
Lodève, bishop of, *see* Aymeric, bishop of Lodève
Logie, Margaret, *see* Margaret, queen of Scotland
London
  bishop of, 168, 201
  canon of, 240
  dwelling of papal collectors in, 13, 77
  inhabitants of, 44, 60n
  prebends of, 66, 74
Long Preston (dioc. York), 108
Lothian
  archdeacon of, 73n
  archdeaconry of, 36, 70
Louth Park (dioc. Lincoln), abbot of, 222
Low Countries, lawsuits over benefices in, 176
Lucare, Bernard de, 120
Luce, John, bishop of Dunkeld, 199, 201
Luco, Guy de, 58
Lund, John de, 113
Lunt, W. E., 7, 16
Lyons, 60n
Lythe (dioc. York), 131
Lytthon, William de, 109

Maccrath, Cristin, 238
Maccrath, Margery, 238
Macdowell, Thomas, 187, 192–3, 196–7, 199
Maclean, Lachlan son of John, 237
Macleod, William, 173
Macraciane, Andrew, 173
Maddadson, Harald, earl of Orkney and Caithness, 18
Maidstone (dioc. Canterbury), 66
Maillesec, Guy de, cardinal, 94

Malconhalgh, Michael de, bishop of Whithorn, 29, 186–7, 191, 203
Maleon of Flanders, Stephen, 59, 244
Man, archdeacon of, 168
see also Isle of Man
Manfield (dioc. York), 110
Mar, David de, 54, 90, 96
Mar, earl of, payment of census by, 19
Mar, John de, 235
Mare, Thomas de la, 221–2
Margaret, countess of Menteith, 237
Margaret, queen of Scotland, 161–2, 211
Margaret of Flanders, 149
Marmaduke, vicar of Kirkbymoorside, 244
Marnham (dioc. York), 105
Marseilles, 162
Marshall, John, 41, 45, 131
Martin, bishop of Argyll, *see* Ergadia, Martin de
Martin V, pope, 189n
Marton (dioc. York)
canon of, 227
prior of, 128
priory of, 128
Marton-in-Craven (dioc. York), 95
Maubert, John, 14n
Maurice, bishop of Dunblane, 203
Maxwell, John de, 236
Meaux, Richard de, 58
Meaux (dioc. York)
abbey of, 54, 129, 165, 167, 222–3, 224
abbot of, 214
Melbourne, John de, 140
Melrose (dioc. Glasgow)
abbey of, 119, 120
abbot of, 225
monk of, 227
Melton, William de, archbishop of York, 172n, 173, 174, 198, 202
payment of taxes by, 32
relations with Durham of, 165–6, 194–5, 200
relations with Whithorn of, 186
Menteith, countess of, 237
Mercer, Thomas, 97, 120
Mere, Margery de, 235
Metham, John de, 173
Methven (dioc. St Andrews), 97
Middelton, Hugh Bellers de, 106
Middelton, Richard de, 116
Middelton, Thomas de, 100
Middleton (dioc. York), 169
Milan, 152, 210
see also Visconti
Mitton (dioc. York), 121, 128–9, 176
Moffet, Walter de, 73n
Molineux, Henry, 238
Monifieth (dioc. St Andrews), 224
Montacute, Adam de, 240
Monte, John de, 227
Monte Florum, Paul de, 52, 132
Montrose (dioc. Brechin), 37n
Monymusk, Michael de, bishop of Dunkeld, 29–30, 41, 117, 172, 176, 199, 207
Monymusk (dioc. Aberdeen), 19
Monypeny, Robert, 96
Moray, Adam de, bishop of Brechin, 208, 241
Moray, Alan de, bishop of Caithness, 29, 200
Moray, 73
bishop of, 72–3; *see also* Bur, Alexander; Pilmor, John de
canonries and prebends of, 38, 46, 90, 110; Botary, 67; Cromdale and Advie, 169; Rhynie, 111
countess of, *see* Euphemia, countess of Moray
diocese of, taxation in, 37
precentor of, 23
precentorship of, 44, 111
succentor of, 173
treasurership of, 90
More, Elizabeth, 238
More, Gilchrist, 171
More, John, 117
More, Reginald, 171
More, William, 171
Morehous, William, 209
Morin, Walter, 113
Morpath, Thomas de, 134
Mount, Thomas, *see* Wykham, Thomas Mount de
Mouswald (dioc. Glasgow), 96
Moxby (dioc. York), nun of, 226
Multon, James de, 177
Murimuth, Adam, chronicler, 134, 139
Murviedro, archdeaconry of, 67
Musgrave (dioc. Carlisle), 53
Muskilburgh, John de, 61–2
Musselburgh (dioc. St Andrews), 109
Muston (dioc. York), 106

Narbonne, canonries of, 67
Nesbit, John de, 177
Neville, Alexander de, archbishop of York, 90, 100, 113, 178, 180, 190, 247
Neville, Thomas de, 178, 247

Neville's Cross, battle of, 5
Newbattle (dioc. St Andrews), abbot of, 170, 171
Newbi, Thomas de, 118
Newbiggin, John de, 177
Newbrough (dioc. York)
  canon of, 250
  priory of, 45, 223, 224
Newcastle (dioc. Durham)
  Carmelite friars of, 172
  church of St Nicholas in, 102
  rural dean of, 167
Newham, John de, 95
Newminster (dioc. Durham), abbot of, 169
Newport, William, 117–18, 119
Newton, John de, 223
Nicholas, archbishop of Ravenna, 21, 196
Nicholas III, pope, 165
Nicholas IV, pope, taxation of, 38
Nidaros, *see* Trondheim
Nigris, Laurence de, papal subcollector, 72, 74
non-residence, 84, 256
  episcopal licences for, 83, 106, 211, 243–4
  papal dispensations for, 244–5; executors of, 228
Norham (dioc. Durham), 175, 227
Normanton (dioc. York), 128
North Burton (dioc. York), 234
Northallerton (dioc. York), 41
Northorpe (dioc. Lincoln), 168
Northumberland, 25, 35
  archdeacon of, 169
Northwell, John de, 178
Northwell, William de, 130, 177–8
Norton, collegiate church of, 84
  prebends of, 48, 120
Norton (dioc. York), chapel of, 179
Norwich, bishop of, 172
Norwich, William de, 130–1, 169
Nostell (dioc. York)
  prior of, 131, 165
  priory of, 165, 167
notaries public, 66, 209, 248, 249–50
Nottingham, Ralph de, 242
Nottingham
  archdeacon of, 245
  archdeaconry of, 39, 136
  sheriff of, 130
Nunnington (dioc. York), 206

Ockham, William de, 3
Offord, Andrew de, 120, 181
Offord, John de, 114
Ogston, Reginald de, 95
Olby, Walter de, 132
Ordinance of Provisors (1343), 134–5, 136, 142, 143, 151, 160, 163, 196
ordinations
  during Black Death, 206, 246
  in Scotland, 58, 96–7, 152, 254
Orgrave, Thomas de, 157, 180
Orkney, 15, 189
  bishops of, 191
  earl of, *see* Maddadson, Harald
  levy of Peter's Pence in, 18
Orsini, John Gaetani de, cardinal, 117
Orsini, Napoleon, cardinal, 52, 173
Otheley, Alan de, 248, 249
Otley (dioc. York), 52
Otto, cardinal, 244
Ottobuono, cardinal, 244
Ox, Andrew, 93
Oxford
  Dominican house in, 154
  university of, 87

Paisley (dioc. Glasgow)
  abbey of, 40, 63, 170–2, 218
  abbot of, 40, 226, 228
  monk of, 240
pallium, 27, 194, 201, 203
papal palace, auditors of, *see* Rota
Papal States, 13
Paris, Matthew, chronicler, 61
Paris, university of, 86–7, 221
Parker, John, 44
Parton, *see* Kirkcowan
Pastor Bonus, 226
patronage, lay, papal involvement with benefices in, 45–6, 128, 143, 147, 148, 223
patronage, local, protection by king of, 128–9
Paull (dioc. York), 127
Paveley, John de, 219
Peblis, Adam de, 92
Peblis, John de, bishop of Dunkeld, papal collector, 15, 26, 61, 67
Pelegrini, Elias, 120
Pelegrini, Hugh, papal collector, 15, 51, 65–6, 158
  accounts of, 47–8, 70, 76
  benefices of, 66–7
  collection of annates by, 35, 39, 42, 47–8, 222
  collection of legacies to Holy Land by, 60

collection of procurations by, 63
commissions to, 14, 63
contacts with king of, 42, 65, 68, 69, 222
subcollectors and assistants of, 71, 72, 74
Pelegrini, Raymond, papal collector, 13n, 15, 32, 66
benefices of, 66
collection of annates by, 23, 42, 47, 51, 52, 222n
collection of tenths by, 23
commissions to, 14
contacts with king of, 65, 68, 69, 222n
opposition to, 15
penitentiaries, papal, 192, 203, 208, 231, 239, 240, 249
Penitentiary, papal, 11, 209, 226, 231n
Penny, John, 171
Penreth, Thomas de, 97
Percy, Henry de, 247
Percy, Richard de, 107
Percy, Thomas de, 247
Périgord, Talleyrand de, cardinal, 43, 56, 66, 114–15, 133, 138, 145, 151, 245
Perpignan, archdeacon of, 140
Perth (dioc. St Andrews), 24
treaty of, 187
Peter, bishop of Astorga, 21, 196
Peter, cardinal of St Anastasia's, 249–50
Peter's Pence, 17–19, 55, 64, 71, 150, 151, 160
Petrarch, 1
Philip VI, king of France, 139, 192
Philippa, queen of England, 241
Piedmont, clerk from, 180
Pilmor, John de, bishop of Moray, 88, 205
Pilmor, Richard de, bishop of Dunkeld, 197, 202, 204
Pilmor, Thomas de, 97
Pilmor, William de, 38
Pittington (dioc. Durham), 244
plague, *see* Black Death
pluralism, 48, 49, 58, 117–19, 123, 256
deprivations on grounds of, 95–6, 117, 152
dispensations for, 117, 241–3
measures against, 9, 10, 146, 147, 149–50, 157, 241–2, 256
Pocklington (dioc. York), 251
Poitiers, battle of, 24, 88, 145, 153
Poland, 14
Pole, John, *see* Clifford, John Pole de
Pole, John de la, 248
Pole, Michael de la, 216
Pontefract (dioc. York)
church of All Saints in, 168
priory of, 168
pontificalia, grants of, 19, 226
Porto, cardinal-bishop of; *see* Boulogne, Guy de
Pothow, Robert de, 177
poverty, claims of, 46, 89–90, 255
Praemunire, Statute of, *see* Statute of Praemunire
praemunire facias, writ of, 130
Pray, John, 111
Premonstratensians, 63, 214, 225
Prés, Peter de, cardinal, 94, 140, 245
Prestenwyc, John de, 103
Preston, Margaret, 236
Prignano, Bartholomew de, *see* Urban VI, pope
procurations, 62–3
for papal collector, 62, 65, 70, 72
for papal legates and nuncios, 62, 70, 159, 160
from exempt monasteries, 63, 219
prohibition, writs of, 127–8, 253
Provane, John de, 93, 157, 180
Provence, 65, 152
provisions, papal, **79–124**
direct, **111–20**; geographical distribution in Scotland of, 83; reasons for failure of, 112–13, 117, 119–20, 208
executors of, 66, 81, 82, 98, 102, 103, 104, 107, 121–2, 173, 207–8, 228
motu proprio, 86
number of, 83–4, 141, 146, 152
success of, 86, 111–12
supplications for, **86–91**
to aliens, 91, 133, 134, 136–8, 145, 146, 151, 153–4, 156, 160, 220, 256; *see also under individual clerks*
to benefices in lay patronage, 45–6, 128, 147
to bishops, **155–6, 191–200**; *see also* service taxes
to graduates, 85–6, 103, 160, 254
to regulars, 27, 31, 38, 146, 219, 220–2, 225, 228
types of, 79–80
see also annates; expectative graces
Provisors, Ordinance of, *see* Ordinance of Provisors
Provisors, Statute of, *see* Statute of Provisors
Pulhowe, William de, 107
Pullur, Adam, 109

Queensferry, 169
Quercu, Raymond de, 18
Quimper, clerk from diocese of, 74n

Rae, William, bishop of Glasgow, 28, 191, 200, 206, 208
Ramsay, Michael, 97
Ratcliffe-on-Soar (dioc. York), 95, 174
Rate, John de, bishop of Aberdeen, 29, 44
Rathven (dioc. Aberdeen), 83, 96, 204
Ratio juris, 175
Ravenna, archbishop of, *see* Nicholas, archbishop of Ravenna
Raymbaut, William, 146
Raymond, John, *see* Comminges, John Raymond de
Rede, John, 109, 199
regalian right, 87, 114, 115, 127, 134, 136, 156, 203
  in Scotland, 116n
religious houses
  confirmations to, 218, 229
  disputes in, 221, 222–4
  reconciliation of apostates to, 226–7, 228
  see also under individual houses
religious orders
  confirmations to, 217, 229
  reform of, 215–16, 219, 221
  see also Augustinian canons; Benedictines; Carthusians; Cistercians; Cluniacs; friars; Hospitallers; Premonstratensians; Sempringham, order of
Rennes, treasurer of, 181
Repton (dioc. Coventry and Lichfield), priory of, 136
Rerrick (dioc. Whithorn), 46
reservations of benefices, **91–8**
Retford, William de, 48
Rheims, 14
Rhodes, 219
Richard II, king of England, 144
Richmond
  archdeacon of, 17n, 48, 231
  archdeaconry of, 23, 39, 48, 98, 140, 185
  earl of, *see* John of Gaunt
Rienzo, Cola di, 1
Rievaulx (dioc. York), monk of, 226
Rimington, William de, 239–40
Rimini, bishop of, 76n
Ripon, collegiate church of, 82, 84, 185
  canonries and prebends of, 101, 157, 174; Monkton, 41; Nunwick, 101, 131; Sharow, 92; Studley, 132, 179; Thorpe, 117
Robelyn, Adam, 71
Robert, abbot of Kilwinning, 171
Robert I, king of Scotland, 116n, 186, 217
Robert II, king of Scotland, 162, 211, 236
  son of, 237
Robert, Aymar, cardinal, 109–10, 133, 134, 138, 145, 172, 245, 254
Robinelli, John, 177
Roche, Androin de la, cardinal, 178
Roche, Guy de la, 39
Roche (dioc. York), abbey of, 223
Rochester, 50
Roger, Hugh, cardinal, 2
Roger, Peter, cardinal, *see* Clement VI, pope
Roger, Peter, cardinal, *see* Gregory XI, pope
Rol, Walter de, 39
Rollock, John, 227–8
Romaldkirk (dioc. York), 46
Rome, 1, 2, 158, 221, 233
Roos (dioc. York), 85, 106
Rosedale (dioc. York), priory of, 168
Roselay, Thomas de, 39
Ross (Ireland), 50
Ross (Scotland), 50, 73
  archdeacon of, 235
  bishop of, 207; *see also* Stewart, Alexander
  bishopric of, taxation of, 188
  canonries and prebends of, 90; Cullicudden, 109; Nonakiln and Roskeen, 109
  chancellorship of, 93
  dean of, 23, 73n
  deanery of, 93, 199
  earl of, 236
Rosse, Henry de, 180
Rosse, James de, 93
Rossy, Thomas de, bishop of Sodor, 30, 93, 192, 204n
Rota, 11, 175–6, 177
  auditors of, 62, 95, 97, 175–6, 177, 180, 181, 182, 192
Rothbury (dioc. Durham), 35, 41, 45, 60, 131
Rotherham (dioc. York), 215n
Rouen
  archbishop of, 26, 88n, 205
  chancellor of, 180
Roxburgh (dioc. Glasgow), 251
Rufford (dioc. York), abbey of, 214–15, 218, 227
Rushen (dioc. Sodor)
  abbey of, 218n

abbot of, 31, 203
Russell, William, bishop of Sodor, 30, 187, 188–9, 202, 203, 204, 205, 250
Rysley, John de, 222–3

sacra, 27
Saddell (dioc. Argyll)
abbey of, 218n
abbot of, 173
St Albans (dioc. Lincoln), abbey of, 222
St Andrews, William of, 225
St Andrews
archdeaconry of, 67, 242–3
bishop of, 28, 211, 238; chaplain of, 86; expectative graces to benefices in gift of, 86, 103, 109; *see also* Landallis, William de
canon-regular of, 203
chapter of, 192
collegiate church of St Mary on the Rock in, 96, 203n
diocese of, 109, 171; clerks of, 240, 250; taxation in, 36
prior of, 40, 221, 228
priory of, 40, 203n
St Asaph, bishop of, 172
St David's,
archdeacon of, 71
bishop of, *see* Thoresby, John de
canonry of, 204
church in diocese of, 90
St Germains (dioc. St Andrews), 228n
St Irieux, Elias de, cardinal, 56, 151
St Marcel, expectation of prebend of, 203
St Martial, Hugh de, cardinal, 43
Salisbury, prebends of, 66
Salkeld, Thomas de, 101, 127
Salkeld, Thomas de, bishop of Chrysopolis, 190
Salley (dioc. York)
abbey of, 165
monk of, 233, 239
Salyng, Geoffrey, 71
Sampson, Thomas, 114
Saunford, John de, 240–1
Savinhaco, William de, 42
Saxindale, Thomas de, 244n
Scarborough (dioc. York), 19, 20, 219
Scardburgh, William de, 223n
Scaresbrok, Isabella de, 238
Scargill, Adam de, 168
Scoenweder, Conrad, 87
Scone (dioc. St Andrews)
abbey of, 218
abbot of, 226
Scotland
level of opposition to Papacy in, 15, 159–61, 254
presentations by king of England to benefices in, 116, 119
Scott, Robert, 206
Scrope, Blanche de, 231
Scrope, Richard de, 231
Scull, Ralph, *see* Setrington, Ralph Scull de
Sedgefield (dioc. Durham), 113
Séez, monk of St Martin at, 146
Sempringham, order of, 171
service taxes, 16n, 27–31, 191, 201, 212, 219
Setrington, Ralph Scull de, 101, 179
Settrington (dioc. York), 51
Shaftesbury, collegiate church of, prebend of, 66
Shap (dioc. Carlisle), abbey of, 63
Sherborne, Thomas de, 222
Sherburn (dioc. York), 106
Sheriff Hutton (dioc. York), 128
Sicilie, George, *see* Hewden, George Sicilie de
Sicily, 227
Sigston (dioc. York), 136
Simonburn (dioc. Durham), 242
Sinai, 248
Sistre, Bernard de, papal collector, 13n 76n
collection of census by, 20
collection of legacies to Holy Land by, 60
collection of tenths by, 23
commissions to, 14, 32
contacts with king of, 68
Skipsea (dioc. York), 129
Skirlaw, Walter de, 131
Skirling (dioc. Glasgow), 116
Skutebury, Roger de, 97
Slaidburn (dioc. York), 251
Sleford, John de, 132, 157, 179
Slingsby (dioc. York), 35, 39, 51, 90, 112n
Smalham, Henry de, 54, 208
Snokere, William, 43
Sodor
bishop of, 15, 168, 217, 237; *see also* Donkan, John; Rossy, Thomas de; Russell, William
diocese of, 15, 171, 189; clerk of, 250
relationship with York of, 185, 187–9
Sotheron, Thomas, 121, 128–9, 176
Soulseat (dioc. Whithorn), abbey of, 63

South Cave (dioc. York), vicar of, 52
see also York, canonries and prebends of
Southwark (dioc. Winchester), 71, 186
Southwell, collegiate church of, 84, 185
canonries and prebends of, 40, 45, 93, 101, 178, 203, 242, 247; Dunham, 39; North Leverton, 100, 101; Norwell, 42, 51n, 120, 130, 177–8; Oxton, 100, 135, 152; Rampton, 40, 48; Woodborough, 101
Spark, Simon, 104
Spofforth (dioc. York), 117
spoils, 55, 60–2, 64
Spyny, William de, 93, 103, 104n
Stallys, John de, 54, 109
Stamfordham (dioc. Durham), 168
Stanhope (dioc. Durham), 44, 45, 130–1, 169, 241
Statute of Praemunire (1353), 125, 129–31, 144, 148, 164, 173, 178n, 182
Statute of Provisors (1351), 8n, 125, 141–4, 148, 193
Statute of Provisors (1365), 148–51
Statute of Provisors (1390), 144
Staunton, John de, 247
Staunton (dioc. York), 247
Stephani, Martin, 96
Stewart, Alexander, bishop of Ross, 29, 112, 192, 202, 235
Stillyngton, William de, 250
Stoke, John de, 43, 51
Stokton, John de, 23
Stowe, archdeacon of, 174
Stramiglot, John de, 221
Stratford, John, archbishop of Canterbury, 201
Strathern, Duncan de, bishop of Dunkeld, 112, 197, 202, 204
Strathmiglo (dioc. Dunkeld), 109
Stratton, Robert de, 89, 176
Stravelyn, David de, 119
Strensall, John de, 72
Stretton, Robert, bishop of Coventry and Lichfield, 29n
Strivelin, Friskin de, 96
Strode, William, 44
Sturton-le-Steeple (dioc. York), 113
subcollectors, papal, 23, 70–5
see also Caroloco, John de; Den, Robert de; Nigris, Laurence de; Tyningham, Adam de
subdeacon, 27
subsidies,
for bishops, 28, 70, 202
of 1360s, 24–6, 70, 158
of 1370s, 22n, 26–7, 70, 76, 154, 155–6, 157, 160, 161, 210
Suglworth, Richard, 181, 182
Sutton, John de, 144
Sutton, William de, 251
Sutton-on-the-Forest (dioc. York), 95, 227, 228, 245
Sweetheart (dioc. Glasgow), abbey of, 59n
Swynhope, Richard de, 116
Synelington, Robert Boner de, 106

Tankard, John, 106, 107
Tannadice (dioc. St Andrews), 203n
Tarbolton (dioc. Glasgow), 39
taxation, papal, *see* annates; census; fruits wrongfully received; Holy Land, legacies to; income taxes; intercalary fruits; Peter's Pence; procurations; *sacra*; service taxes; spoils; subdeacon; subsidies; tribute; visitation tax
taxation, royal, 27, 64, 139, 186, 219, 255
assessments for, 22, 25
tenths
papal, *see* income taxes; subsidies
royal, *see* taxation, royal
Tervill, Ralph, 99, 100, 139, 179
Testa, William, papal collector, 61n
Teviotdale
archdeacon of, 54
archdeaconry of, 208
rural dean of, 119
Theddemersh, Edmund de, 107
Thomas, bishop of Whithorn, *see* Wedale, Thomas de
Thomas, earl of Lancaster, 251
Thoresby, John de, 99, 100, 206
Thoresby, John de, bishop of St David's, bishop of Worcester, archbishop of York, 94, 100, 105, 174, 177–8, 180, 207, 208, 209, 210, 211, 222, 223, 249
grant of pallium to, 194, 201, 203
licences to, 99, 205, 206, 209, 245, 250
payment of taxes by, 19, 32–3
petitions to pope by, 88
relations with Durham of, 190
relations with Sodor of, 188
relations with Whithorn of, 187
Thornton (dioc. York), chapel of, 251
Thornton (dioc. York), church of, 23
Thresk, John de, 45, 223
Thresk, Robert de, 245
Thurgarton (dioc. York), prior of, 174
Tickhill (dioc. York), 128, 247
Tikhill, William de, 241
Todd, Thomas, 116–17

Tongland (dioc. Whithorn), abbey of, 63
Torpenhow (dioc. Carlisle), 168
Torre, James, 114n
Torreth, Thomas de, 109
Tostys, William de, 119
Tournai, bishop of, 211
Trayl, Walter, 224
Treswell (dioc. York), 107
tribute, 21, 64, 150, 152, 160, 253
Trillek, John, bishop of Hereford, 139
Trondheim
archbishop of, 188
province of, 18, 187, 189
Turk, John, 101
Turre, Bernard de, cardinal, 145
Turriff (dioc. Aberdeen), 45, 97
Tusculum, cardinal-bishop of, 92, 136, 246
see also Gaetani, Anibaldus; Giles; William
Tynemouth (dioc. Durham), priory of, 221–2
Tyningham, Adam de, bishop of Aberdeen, papal subcollector, 39, 72–3, 93, 176–7
Tyninghame (dioc. St Andrews), 203n
Tyso, Richard de, 174

Ulseby, Henry de, 120
universities, 156, 159, 216n, 221
graduates of, 85–6, 86–7, 103, 104n, 123, 160, 202–3, 254
Upton, Richard, 53
Urban V, pope (William Grimaud), 1, 9, 39, 67, 73, 190, 200–1, 251
appointment of judges by, 167, 173
attitude to pluralism of, 9, 10, 96, 119, 123, 146, 147, 149–50, 152, 157, 242–3, 256
dispensations and licences of, 10, 117n, 149, 206–7, 209, 232, 235, 238, 245, 246, 247, 248, 250, 255
indulgences of, 234
provisions by, 9, 66, 85, 87, 90–1, 91–2, 113n, 121, 147–8, 176, 177, 178, 179, 181, 199; expectative graces, 84, 105, 122–3, 146–7, 224; to aliens, 91, 146; to bishops, 199; to regulars, 41
relations with England of, 10, 21, 146–52, 238
relations with regulars of, 38, 41, 146, 224, 235
revocation of expectative graces of Innocent VI by, 110
taxes levied by, 21, 38, 56, 61, 150
Urban VI, pope (Bartholomew Prignano), 2, 159, 216
Urquhart (dioc. Moray), priory of, 221
Urwell, John de, 226–7
Utrecht, clerk from diocese of, 105

Vale Royal (dioc. Coventry and Lichfield), abbey of, 129
Valencia, diocese of, 67
Vatican Registers, 80–2, 232n
Vavasour, William, 107
Vereriis, Pontius de, 71, 74
Vicia, Baiamundus de, papal collector, 36, 37
Vienne, council of, 170
Villeneuve by Avignon, 92
Visconti, 22n, 65, 152, 210
visitation tax, 31–3

Wake, Thomas, 216, 217n
Wales, Peter's Pence in, 17, 18
Walpole (dioc. Norwich), 74
Waltham, John de, 99, 206
Walton, Henry de, 39, 98–9, 231
Walton, Richard atte Lane de, 101
Walton, William de, 245
Warchopp, Robert de, 97
Ward, Simon, 112–13
Wardlaw, Henry de, 116
Wardlaw, Walter de, bishop of Glasgow, 20, 29, 108–9, 162, 205, 206
Warkworth (dioc. Durham), 244
Warthill, Richard, 250
Wartre, Nicholas de, 85, 106
Washington (dioc. Durham), 97, 137
Wasil, John, 90
Waynflet, William de, 107
Wedale, Adam de, 240
Wedale, Simon de, bishop of Whithorn, 186, 191, 193, 203
Wedale, Thomas de, bishop of Whithorn, 29, 59, 187, 192–3, 212
Welbeck (dioc. York), abbot of, 237
Welles, Richard de, 51
Wellesbourne, John, 58–9, 60
Wells, canonries and prebends of, 66, 89, 241
see also Bath and Wells
Welton, Gilbert de, bishop of Carlisle, 208, 210
appointment of, 193–4, 200, 201
benefices of, 97, 203
licences to, 205, 249
relations with papal collectors of, 63
subsidy levied by, 28

Welton, John de, 194
Wemes, John de, 96
Wendlyngburgh, John de, 72
Westbroke, Henry, 128
Westbury, collegiate church of, canonry of, 87
Westminster, 186
  Great Council at, 21n–22n
  parliament at (1343), 133–4
Weston, Philip de, 93, 114–15, 138
Wetwang (dioc. York), vicar of, 52
  see also York, canonries and prebends of
Whalley (dioc. Coventry and Lichfield)
  abbey of, 54n
  abbot of, 121
Wharram (dioc. York), 165
Whathamstede, Clement de, 222
Whitby (dioc. York), abbey of, 104
Whitechirche, John de, 113
Whithorn
  bishop of, 59n, 189n, 201, 208; *see also* Lanark, Adam de; Malconhalgh, Michael de; Wedale, Simon de; Wedale, Thomas de
  bishopric of, taxation of, 188
  claim to see of, 197, 199
  prior of, 203
  priory of, 63
  relationship with York of, 5, 184, 185–7, 189
Whitkirk (dioc. York), 107
Whittingham (dioc. Durham), 35, 244
Wigton (dioc. Carlisle), 53
Wilberfosse, Robert de, 216n
Wilde, Philip, bishop of Brechin, 29, 30, 203, 208
William, bishop of Dunblane, 30
William, cardinal-bishop of Tusculum, 63
William, cardinal-priest of St Laurence in Lucina, 209
William, prior of Lesmahagow, 171
Wilton, collegiate church of, prebend of, 181
Winchester
  bishop of, 92n, 201; clerk of, 181; *see also* Assier, Rigaud d'; Wykeham, William de
  diocese of, portion of tithes in, 181
Withington (dioc. Worcester), 66
Wodehouse, John de, 99
Woderoue, William, 98
Wolferton, William de, 107
Wollore, David de, 95, 118, 119, 140, 235
Wolsey, Thomas, cardinal, 212
Wootton (dioc. Winchester), 58
Worcester, 104n
  bishop of, 92n; *see also* Thoresby, John de
Wyclif, John, 87, 230
Wykeham, William de, bishop of Winchester, 93
Wykham, Thomas Mount de (or Ikham, Thomas de), 130, 177–8
Wylyngton, Richard de, 44, 45
Wymondeswold, Hugh de, 90, 135–6, 152, 243
Wymondeswold, Richard de, 90

Yetholm (dioc. Glasgow), 251
York
  abbey of St Mary's in, 101, 102n, 107, 127–8, 169, 218, 224, 227
  abbot of St Mary's in, 25, 121, 128, 228
  archbishop of, 6, 54, 106n, 119, 128, 166, 167, 168, 172, 177, 179, 193, 209, 227, 240, 244; expectative graces to benefices in gift of, 99, 101; payment of taxes by, 17, 18–19, 25, 26, 31–3; petitions to pope of, 205; *see also* Melton, William de; Neville, Alexander de; Thoresby, John de; Zouche, William de la
  archdeacon of, 17n, 245
  archdeaconry of, 43, 94–5, 140
  Augustinian friary in, 188
  bailiff of, 248
  canonries and prebends of, 40, 87, 98–100, 203, 235; Ampleforth, 51, 112; Bilton, 245–6; Bole, 178, 247; Botevant, 98–9; Bramham, 165; Driffield, 43, 47, 51; Givendale, 98; Grindale, 35, 93, 99, 110n, 206; Holme, 42, 114n; Husthwaite, 58–9, 60; Knaresborough, 157; Langtoft, 84, 115; Laughton, 49, 92–3, 131, 202; Masham, 43, 56, 57, 89; North Newbald, 99; Osbaldwick, 43, 97; South Cave, 42n, 52, 94, 113, 132, 135; South Newbald, 99, 120, 206; Strensall, 43, 56, 57n, 66, 139, 151; Ulleskelf, 98, 117; Warthill, 110, 138; Weighton, 60; Wetwang, 42, 52, 127, 140; Wilton, 140; Wistow, 43, 49, 140
  canons of, 244, 246
  chancellor of, 165, 173, 209
  chapel of St Mary and the Holy Angels at, 97, 100, 107, 248
  chapter of, 51, 57n, 107, 114, 178, 185, 186n, 199, 200

church of All Saints, North Street, in, 233
church of All Saints, Pavement, in, 112–13
church of St Michael, Spurriergate, in, 251
church of St Saviour in, 107
church of St Wilfrid in, 167
court of, 166, 175
dean of, 174
deanery of, 56–7, 113–15, 138, 139, 151, 245
diocese of: dispensations in, 209, 240; heresy in, 249; papal provisions in, 104n, 105, 112; taxation in, 17, 25, 47–9
metropolitan jurisdiction of, 184, 185–91; over Durham, 172, 185, 189–91, 201, 207; over Scotland, 5, 184; over Sodor, 185, 187–9; over Whithorn, 5, 184, 185–7, 189
Minster of, 166, 190, 218; benefices in, 82, 84, 85, 88, 137–8, 145, 146; *see also under individual benefices*
official of, 167, 174, 194, 238
precentor of, 243
precentorship of, 243
prior of Holy Trinity in, 165
prior of St Andrew's in, 167, 228
province of, plague in, 232
subdean of, 165
subdeanery of, 48
treasurership of, 95, 140
Yorke, John de, 238
Yorkshire, 25, 131

Zeeland, 249n
Zerzeto, Oliver de, 177
Zouche, William de la, archbishop of York, 100, 105, 106, 113–15, 144, 172, 194, 207, 208, 218, 223, 224
appointment of, 198–9, 201
benefices of, 93, 113–14, 202
grant of pallium to, 201
licences to, 99, 180, 206, 239, 246, 247
payment of taxes by, 32
relations with Durham of, 190, 196n
relations with Sodor of, 188
relations with Whithorn of, 186

Cambridge Studies in Medieval Life and Thought
Fourth series

Titles in the series

1 The Beaumont Twins: The Roots and Branches of Power in the Twelfth Century
D. B. CROUCH
2 The Thought of Gregory the Great*
G. R. EVANS
3 The Government of England under Henry I*
JUDITH A. GREEN
4 Charity and Community in Medieval Cambridge
MIRI RUBIN
5 Autonomy and Community: The Royal Manor of Havering, 1200–1500
MARJORIE KENISTON MCINTOSH
6 The Political Thought of Baldus de Ubaldis
JOSEPH CANNING
7 Land and Power in Late Medieval Ferrara: The Rule of the Este, 1350–1450
TREVOR DEAN
8 William of Tyre: Historian of the Latin East*
PETER W. EDBURY AND JOHN GORDON ROWE
9 The Royal Saints of Anglo-Saxon England: A Study of West Saxon and East Anglian Cults
SUSAN J. RIDYARD
10 John of Wales: A Study of the Works and Ideas of a Thirteenth-Century Friar
JENNY SWANSON
11 Richard III: A Study of Service*
ROSEMARY HORROX
12 A Marginal Economy? East Anglian Breckland in the Later Middle Ages
MARK BAILEY
13 Clement VI: The Pontificate and Ideas of an Avignon Pope
DIANA WOOD
14 Hagiography and the Cult of Saints: The Diocese of Orléans, 800–1200
THOMAS HEAD
15 Kings and Lords in Conquest England
ROBIN FLEMING
16 Council and Hierarchy: The Political Thought of William Durant the Younger
CONSTANTIN FASOLT
17 Warfare in the Latin East, 1192–1291*
CHRISTOPHER MARSHALL
18 Province and Empire: Brittany and the Carolingians
JULIA M. H. SMITH
19 A Gentry Community: Leicestershire in the Fifteenth Century, *c.* 1422–*c.* 1485
ERIC ACHESON

20 Baptism and Change in the Early Middle Ages, *c.* 200–1150
PETER CRAMER

21 Itinerant Kingship and Royal Monasteries in Early Medieval Germany, *c.* 936–1075
JOHN W. BERNHARDT

22 Caesarius of Arles: The Making of a Christian Community in Late Antique Gaul
WILLIAM E. KLINGSHIRN

23 Bishop and Chapter in Twelfth-Century England: A Study of the *Mensa Episcopalis*
EVERETT U. CROSBY

24 Trade and Traders in Muslim Spain: The Commercial Realignment of the Iberian Peninsula, 900–1500
OLIVIA REMIE CONSTABLE

25 Lithuania Ascending: A Pagan Empire within East-Central Europe, 1295–1345
S. C. ROWELL

26 Barcelona and its Rulers, 1100–1291
STEPHEN P. BENSCH

27 Conquest, Anarchy and Lordship: Yorkshire, 1066–1154
PAUL DALTON

28 Preaching the Crusades: Mendicant Friars and the Cross in the Thirteenth Century
CHRISTOPH T. MAIER

29 Family Power in Southern Italy: The Duchy of Gaeta and its Neighbours, 850–1139
PATRICIA SKINNER

30 The Papacy, Scotland and Northern England, 1342–1378
A. D. M. BARRELL

*Also published as a paperback